Boy Culture

Boy Culture

An Encyclopedia

Volume 2

Shirley R. Steinberg, Michael Kehler, and
Lindsay Cornish, Editors

GREENWOOD

AN IMPRINT OF ABC-CLIO, LLC
Santa Barbara, California • Denver, Colorado • Oxford, England

Library of Congress Cataloging-in-Publication Data

Boy culture : an encyclopedia / Shirley R. Steinberg, Michael Kehler, and Lindsay Cornish, editors.
    p. cm.
 Includes bibliographical references and index.
  ISBN 978-0-313-35080-1 (hard copy : alk. paper) — ISBN 978-0-313-35081-8 (e-book)
 1. Masculinity. 2. Stereotypes (Social psychology) I. Steinberg, Shirley R., 1952- II.
Kehler, Michael. III. Cornish, Lindsay, 1979-
  BF692.5.B69 2010
  305.23081—dc22   2010021148

ISBN: 978-0-313-35080-1
EISBN: 978-0-313-35081-8

14 13 12 11 10   1 2 3 4 5

This book is also available on the World Wide Web as an eBook.
Visit www.abc-clio.com for details.

Greenwood
An Imprint of ABC-CLIO, LLC

ABC-CLIO, LLC
130 Cremona Drive, P.O. Box 1911
Santa Barbara, California 93116-1911

This book is printed on acid-free paper ∞
Manufactured in the United States of America

Contents

PART III

Small Screen, Silver Screen, Text, and Tunes

SECTION 7

Boys on Screen

Bob the Builder

Bob the Builder is a TV show centering on contractor Bob and his team of work vehicles, who work together to construct and fix buildings. The franchise is marketed to boys and appeals to one of the most iconic boyhood activities: building.

The concept was developed by Keith Chapman, founder of Chapman Entertainment and former product developer at Jim Henson studios. Chapman sold his intellectual property rights to children's media company HIT Entertainment, Ltd., through deals with CEO Peter Orton. Kate Fawkes of HIT Entertainment led the series' development.

Bob the Builder, produced by HOT Animation as a stop-action animated television program, first aired in the United Kingdom on BBC in 1999 as a 10-minute short. In the first year, HIT's revenues increased 60 percent, largely due to the success of the series (HIT Entertainment, 2000). The following year, the program was exported to the United States and became wildly popular. The program currently airs in over 100 countries, with voice-overs in different languages. Global sales have reached over U.S. $4 billion (Jenkins, 2008).

The series' main character is Bob, a builder. He owns his own construction business in the town of Bobsville, and works together with a team of machines and human friends to fix problems and build new structures. Dressed in blue overalls, yellow and red shirt, a yellow hard hat, work boots, and a tool belt, Bob's trademark look is easily identifiable to young children. Bob is well known for his phrase, "Can we build it?" to which the machines reply emphatically, "Yes, we can!" The program's theme song (sung by Neil Morrissey, the original voice of Bob) repeats those phrases as a chorus, while introducing the characters and themes of the show: teamwork, a positive attitude, the satisfaction of hard work, follow-through, and a job well done. The company emphasizes having fun while getting the job done. The simple anthem is well liked by children and was a club hit in the UK.

Bob's "machine team" consists of a fleet of anthropomorphized vehicles, each of whom have distinct personalities, jobs, and catchphrases for which they are known. The original team consisted of five trucks. Scoop, a yellow digger, is the leader of the team. He confidently states, "No prob, Bob!" The shy blue crane Lofty's catchphrase is "Uh, yeah, I think so!" Muck, the red digger dumper, yells, "Muck to the rescue!" Dizzy, an orange cement mixer—and the youngest team member until the addition of Benny—says, "Brilliant!" Roley, the vivacious green steamroller, says "Rock and roll!" New characters include Benny (a fuchsia, small robo digger who says, "It's unreal, banana peel!"), Scrambler (a blue all-terrain vehicle, says, "Let's Scram!"), and Dodger (a milk truck with a winch, who says, "Dodger delivers!").

Farmer Pickles is a townsperson who appears in some episodes. Travis is Pickles' turquoise tractor, who bumbles, "OK, Farmer Pickles." Spud the scarecrow, who says, "Spud's on the job! Ha, ha ha ha!," and Scruffty the dog round out the crew. Other animals on the show include Bird, the best friend of Roley, and Pilchard the cat. The town also has a red delivery truck, Packer ("Pick up and deliver!" and "Pack me up and watch me go-go!" are the character's catchphrases). Other minor humans and vehicles appear on the program.

The most controversial member of Bob's team is Wendy—Bob's friend and co-worker (catchphrase: "Well, we'd better get started, team!"). Wendy is known for speaking quietly and rationally and organizing the team—traditionally coded female characteristics in a patriarchal work context. When the series first aired, Wendy was referred to as Bob's loyal assistant, a role with lesser power than Bob's ownership and leadership position. However, as of 2008, the company refers to her as Bob's "business partner." This shift signals a response to the critique that the series' representation of patriarchal gender roles diminished the value of women, which is especially problematic for the girls who watch the program. Now that Bob and Wendy are represented as business partners, the show has attempted to shift toward a more equal gender dynamic—if not in story line, at least in job title.

Gender representation on *Bob the Builder* continues to negotiate a traditional masculinity by simultaneously engaging in hypermasculine building activities, yet doing so in a gentle, cooperative, and humble manner. The show also serves to elevate working-class culture in a media landscape where upper-class representations reign. The emphasis on hard work, teamwork, and joy in manual labor makes the show favorable to parents as well.

In 2005, the series changed directions in a move called "Project Build It." In this version of the program, Bob, Wendy, and the machines are contracted to build a new, "eco-friendly" community in Sunflower Valley. Bob attempts to protect the town from overdevelopment through his conscious building plans. This theme capitalizes on the social concern for environmental protection and concerns over climate change, gentrification, and unsustainable development.

Besides the television show, the franchise engages in an aggressive level of cross-production, with feature films, DVDs, CDs, books, coloring books, educational games, and international Web sites. Additionally, a merchandising scheme that licenses characters includes toys, clothing, sheets, backpacks, lunchboxes, bikes, plates, and a live-action touring stage show. These consumer strategies help suture the brand into the popular consciousness.

Further Reading

Bob the Builder Official Web site and Shopping Store. www.bobthebuilder.com.

HIT Entertainment PLC. *2000 Annual Report.* Retrieved March 17, 2009, from LexisNexis Academic Database.

Jenkins, Bob. "Blueprint for Success." *License! Global* 11, no.8 (September 2008): 3–4.

Christine Quail

Boys in American Film

The boy has a long history in Hollywood film, going back to the very earliest days of the industry, but due to what many consider racism and neglect in the film industry's choice of movies produced, it is almost always the white boy who is featured. As a result, this entry will deal primarily with the history of white boys in film. The 1930s, in particular, were a fertile period for boys to be showcased in films in all their rambunctious, unruly, and untamed glory, but often shaped and reformed by the guiding hand of a paternal or avuncular white male. In particular, the films starring the so-called Dead End Kids/Bowery Boys were being cranked out as late as 1958, the first one having been released in 1937. So popular were films featuring young stars that child star Mickey Rooney emerged as the most popular star of 1939 in *Variety* magazine's annual poll, published January 1940. The 1940s were marked by adult concerns pushing films starring boys or featuring tales of boyhood somewhat to the background. The 1950s saw the emergence of films targeted specifically at the male teenager/young adults market, including the dated but seminal *Blackboard Jungle* (1955) featuring the rotund rock star Bill Haley singing "Rock Around the Clock" with his band as well as the immortal *Rebel without a Cause* (1955). At the same time, a number of films, for example *High School Confidential* (1958), expressed the anxiety of adults about boy culture as juvenile delinquency.

The 1960s were marked by change and turmoil in Hollywood. A frenzy of takeovers and mergers impacted the film studios, while the emergence of multiplexes signaled not just a radical change in the business of films but also in the very nature of films that would be produced in the decades to come. This was also the decade in which British films came to the forefront—on the one hand with the angry young man pictures such as *The Loneliness of the Long Distance Runner* (1962) and *The Leather Boys* (1963), and on the other hand with big-budget historicals or epics such as *Lawrence of Arabia* (1962), *Becket* (1964), and *The Lion in Winter* (1964). Hollywood, anxious at the trend of declining theatre audiences and the increasing threat of television, responded with low-budget horror films, cheesy special-effects pictures, and above all, a slew of films that were aimed at bringing entire families back to the cinema theatres. (Perhaps they succeeded, because the top three films in terms of box-office records in the 1960s were all family friendly films, such as *101 Dalmatians* (1961), *The Jungle Book* (1967), and *The Sound of Music* (1965). And that is where the story really begins. . . .

1965–1969: Boys Are Only a Part of the Family

Much as the film industry recognized that young audiences were critical to their success, and even as youth movements struck roots all over the continent, the industry seemed singularly unable to produce films that understood their audience. Their attention was focused on the feel-good family film, a far cry from the films featuring angst-ridden young boys of the 1950s. For a while, however, their formula seemed to be working. *The Sound of Music* released in 1965 quickly became one of the most beloved films of all time. Although the film is set in late 1930s Austria, the two boys among the seven siblings (Friedrich, played by Nicholas Hammond, and Kurt, played by Duane Chase) of the von Trapp family are as all-American as you can get. In their fascination for and felicity with pranks and tormenting their governess, as also their ultimately respectful attitude towards their elders, the boys are typical of the filmic North American boy of the 1960s.

Throughout most of this decade, even as British cinema continued to feature boys in starring roles in a number of unusual and thoughtful films, Hollywood paid scant attention to them. Unlike the *Dead End Kids* films of the 1930s or the youth pictures of the 1950s, Hollywood in the 1960s had few representations of boys that accurately reflected the joys and pleasures as well as the pains and anguish of growing up from boys to men. Exemplifying the blind eye that Hollywood turned towards boys was that perhaps the most well-known boy of 1960s film was just an animated character: Mowgli, in the Disney animated film *The Jungle Book* (1967). Once again, Mowgli is the idealized version of the boy: loyal, brave, and resourceful against all odds. So are the boys in a lesser-known effort from 1966, *The Lemon Grove Kids Meet the Monsters*, noteworthy chiefly in being an evident tribute to the Dead End Kids/Bowery Boys films.

The Lemon Grove Kids were soon forgotten, leaving almost no significant impact on either popular culture or the film business itself. It was left to two British imports to hint that boys were certainly not all sugar and spice and all things nice. The first was the multi-Oscar winning musical *Oliver!* (1968), based on Charles Dickens' *Oliver Twist*, and the second, Lindsay Anderson's controversial *If* (1968), which showcased a student rebellion at an English private school that ends in a bloody revolt against the adult world. It would be fair to say, though, that even though Hollywood films in the 1960s started to presage the complexities in plot and character that would become the hallmark of the great American films of the 1970s, films for boys or featuring them continued to remain simplistic at best and condescending or exploitative at worst (as in the 1968 films *Young Runaways* and *Wild In the Streets*, the latter being an unusual attempt to marry the mismatched genres of political satire and teen exploitation). More complicated depictions of boys, especially ones that even acknowledged the existence of a distinct boy culture, would have to wait till the next decade.

1970–1979: Boys Exist, and George Lucas Will Deliver Them to Us!

The early 1970s was the last period in which complex, ambitious, and artistic films also ruled the box office. But it was the same decade in which Hollywood discovered that not only would boys watch films that appealed to their boyhood, but even men who had just stepped out of boyhood loved revisiting their boyhood days. This realization contributed to the start of Hollywood's overt reliance on summer blockbusters—when boys and young men would drive films about spaceships or comic book heroes or aliens or about nothing at all—but full of light, sound, and occasionally fury—to hitherto unimaginable box office grosses.

But before summer blockbusters took over, there came a film about boys that resonated not just with boys themselves but audiences at large. Nostalgically looking back at 1962, focused on a group of teenagers out of high school facing up to adult life, *American Graffiti* (1973) marked the emergence of director George Lucas as a talent to reckon with. Sensitively observed and performed, the film humorously laid bare the inner turmoil of boys turning into men without moralizing or didacticism. Boy culture, it seemed, had found a place in Hollywood film. Future coming of age stories such as *Breaking Away* (1979) and *Diner* (1982) would owe a serious debt to *American Graffiti*.

George Lucas, however, was just getting started. He was about to change the very dynamics of the film making business with what he was calling a space opera, inspired by sources as diverse as the Akira Kurosawa film *Hidden Fortress* (1958), Joseph Campbell's book *Hero of a Thousand Faces,* and the Flash Gordon film serials of the 1930s, among others. The film was *Star Wars* (1977) and it quickly became the object of intense adoration for boys of all ages. It would be no exaggeration to say that if there was one film that comprehensively impacted boy culture, it was this. No self-respecting boy could henceforth be ignorant of the *Star Wars* universe and its various characters and aim to fit into his peer group. Cultural commentators have often said that the *Star Wars* series provided American boys for the first time with mythologies that were uniquely American and that this was largely responsible for the enduring appeal of the saga.

Be that as it may, *Star Wars* illustrated to the powers that be in Hollywood that teenage boys could make a bigger difference to the box-office fortunes of a film than practically any other demographic. Hollywood henceforth would concentrate most of its resources on what became known as the summer blockbusters or tentpole films: usually crammed with special effects, focused on actions and visual effects rather than character development or strong screenplays, and with enormous potential for tie-ins and merchandizing. Hollywood was now not only in the business of creating and distributing film, it was now also actively in the business of feeding and often creating elements of boy culture.

1980–1989: Boys Can Be Banked Upon: Franchises and Teen Comedies

The last year of the 1970s saw three films taking cold, hard looks at alienated boys, street gangs, and juvenile delinquency: *The Wanderers* (1979), *The Warriors* (1979), and *Over the Edge* (1979). With the advent of the Reagan era, popular culture took a cold, not so hard look at itself and decided that such dark investigation was out and greed was good (as the lead character in the Oliver Stone's 1987 drama *Wall Street* would declaim to loud applause). Hollywood responded by lunging forward with lumbering steps in creating what Janet Maslin of the *New York Times* called in her review of *Diner* (1982), the "age of sequels and extravaganzas." The light shown by George Lucas was blazing brightly. Teenage, adolescent, and young adult male audiences were what Hollywood sought. And Hollywood believed that the best way to attract these audiences was through either sex or action, and preferably through characters that these audiences already knew and rooted for. In such a scenario, *Diner* appeared almost as a revelation. Again, like *American Graffiti,* it harkened back to the past, in this case the 1950s, but it struck a chord with the early eighties audience of young males who aspired to the testosterone-fueled bravado of *Rocky* and *Rambo* but couldn't help but connect to the confused meanderings of the lead characters.

Another film, again set in the 1950s but of a very different nature than *Diner,* also connected with boys. That film was *Porky's* (1981), and though it was hardly a secret, it told America that, yes, teenage boys did obsess an awful lot about sex. Produced in Canada with a cast of unknowns, *Porky's* went on to become a box-office sensation and an enduring film for and featuring boys. Two sequels followed in two year intervals, leaving critics, parents, and finally even their target audience less and less impressed with every outing. Equally influential, if more among filmmakers of teen films than among boys themselves, was John Hughes' *Breakfast Club* (1985), the story of a group of high school students in day-long detention. In the middle of the franchise boom of the 1980s, John Hughes became a kind of official chronicler of high school high jinks, creating believable high school characters and refusing to pass judgment on them. *Ferris Bueller's Day Off* (1986) had Matthew Broderick portraying the titular character, a legend in his own lifetime for his unmatched skill in skipping classes and getting away with it. In *Weird Science* (1985), two nerdy high school students frustrated at their ineptitude around girls create the ultimate woman in the form of actress Kelly Brock.

But John Hughes was not the only director to achieve critical and commercial success and proving that teen comedies need not be an assemblage of gross out jokes or sexual innuendo alone. Amy Heckerling's *Fast Times at Ridgemont High* (1982) centered on a girl, but portrayed boys in high school with equal empathy, including an unforgettable Sean Penn as stoner dude Jeff Spicoli. Steve Rash's *Can't Buy Me Love* (1987) was more predictable than the Hughes and Heckerling films but appealed to boys with its depiction of a high school student who tries to achieve a patina of cool after inveigling one of the most popular girls in school to date him. The legendary Francis Ford Coppola (director of *The Godfather* trilogy) also took a stab at the teen film genre, even though his was a literary adaptation of author S. E. Hinton's *The Outsiders* (1983) set in a small Southern town in the late 1960s. John Badham's *War Games* (1983) managed to successfully marry the teen comedy to the nuclear scare film in possibly the first box-office success celebrating a teenage computer nerd.

But what really did big business were the franchises, especially as studios could roll out one after the other in a series without having to invest in the development of new characters. Although they did not feature boys, two franchises of the 1980s became boy culture favorites. Both of them starred an actor with limited range of expressions but an enormous range of muscles. Both of them sought to reassure American audiences that, irrespective of the Vietnam War and the Cold War, the United States continued to remain the world's mightiest superpower, as embodied in Sylvester Stallone.

The *Rambo* franchise, starting with *First Blood* (1982), was Hollywood's version of the argument that the Vietnam war was lost because of the blunderings of politicians, and all would have been well if the war had only been left to the soldiers. The first two *Rocky* films had been released in the 1970s, and were both stories about the triumph of the human spirit, but by the time *Rocky IV* came along in 1985, it was all about USA vs. the USSR (as was *Rambo III*, released in 1988). No matter what the ideological orientations behind the films, they were lapped up by young male audiences across the continent. So enduring was the appeal of the characters with the audience that Stallone revived both of them in the twenty-first century, scoring a critical and commercial success with *Rocky Balboa* (2006) but failing with *Rambo* (2008).

Rocky and *Rambo* were not the only franchises that were geared successfully toward boys and adopted wholeheartedly by them. And it was certainly not the case that only franchises with blood, gore, or sex succeeded with boys. *Back to the Future* (1985) put the age old underdog-coming-out-on-top story in a pseudo-science fiction bottle and won the appreciation of geeky, non-alpha males everywhere. Two successful sequels followed in 1989 and 1990, respectively, testimony to how identifiable the title character Marty McFly (played by Michael J. Fox) was to boys.

Another boy icon was created jointly by two of the biggest names in Hollywood, George Lucas and Steven Spielberg. Single handedly making archaeology sexy, Indiana Jones (portrayed by Harrison Ford) was brave and resourceful like all of Hollywood's favorite boys, but he spent far more time under his fedora, bullwhip in hand, escaping motley perils than he ever did at an actual archaeological dig. Starting with *Raiders of the Lost Ark* (1981), followed by *Indiana Jones and the Temple of Doom* (1984) and *Indiana Jones and the Last Crusade* (1989), each of the films in the series grossed more than $150 million. A fourth installment, entitled *Indiana Jones and the Kingdom of the Crystal Skull* debuted in the summer of 2008, motivated no doubt by Hollywood's enduring belief, "Once a boy, always a boy."

Indy was often superheroic, but his appeal lay in the fact that he was often all too human. But what of the character whom boys had looked up to since his advent in the late 1930s: Superman? The first Superman film, released in 1978, was a critical and commercial success, but the subsequent sequels offered diminishing returns to the point that *Superman IV* (1987) hauled in just $15 million at the box office. The hero who embodied hope, above all, was giving none to Hollywood and was in danger of becoming irrelevant to his biggest fans: boys. His pal Batman had become, if anything, even worse than irrelevant. From the original premise of an "angsty" superhero, Batman had been reduced partly by the campy television series of the 1960s into an object of ridicule. Gone was the dark vision of the 1930s Batman as a vigilante, a morally complex figure, with a painfully thin line dividing him from the villains he fought. Frank Miller's seminal comic book *The Dark Knight Returns* (1986) had restored some of the dark aura of Batman. With the abject failure of *Superman IV*, Hollywood realized that perhaps the time was right to bring back the superhero who embodied darkness rather than hope. So Batman was produced and released in the last year of the eighties.

More than the aesthetic qualities of the film, Batman was significant in becoming the first film in which the Hollywood marketing machine came together to impact boys from all directions possible. It was the first film for which action figures were produced and tie-ups with various merchants (called partners in Hollywoodspeak) were concluded a long time before the film's completion so that the various merchants could participate in the advertising. This was a sea change from the days of the *Star Wars* films, where boys desperate to participate more deeply in the film experience would create for themselves light sabers and Luke Skywalker costumes from things they found lying around the house. Or, at best, be content with taking home certificates that guaranteed a Luke Skywalker toy when it was finally manufactured. Now, you had T-shirts and caps and pins and hats and everything else being snapped up by boys (and often their fathers) even before the film was released. Boys could take to a film as strongly as they liked, but more and more their chances of expressing themselves by creating film-related material themselves was being closed off and limited by Hollywood and its partners.

Despite its success, Batman was actually an oddball and not just because it was directed by the eccentric Tim Burton. It was also one of the few non-sequels released that summer of 1989. From *Karate Kid II* to *A Nightmare on Elm Street 5* to *Star Trek V: The Final Frontier* to *Friday the 13th Part VIII: Jason Takes Manhattan* to *Indiana Jones and the Last Crusade*, the summer was crammed wall to wall with sequels and sequels of sequels of sequels. Notably, each of these franchises was a creation of that very decade—and each of them made lasting impressions on boy culture. *The Karate Kid* (1984) was another underdog makes good story, with the added bonus of realizing every boy's secret dream of becoming a martial arts star. The *Friday the 13th* and *Nightmare on Elm Street* franchises drew in huge crowds of young boys (and sometimes girls) with each successive installment, devising wilder and wilder ways of disembowelment and decapitation, and drawing louder cries of outrage from parents and critics. The respected critic Leonard Maltin (2005) summed up the first *Friday the 13th* film as "one more clue to why SAT scores continue to decline." It seemed critics had forgotten rather quickly that once upon a time they were boys too.

1990–1999: Parallel Streams, Differing Depictions

1990 saw, for the first time in decades, the return to center stage of an old Hollywood staple: the family film with a brave and resourceful kid at the center, even if his mischief making leads to him being left home alone when his family flies off to vacation in Paris. Starring the precocious 10-year-old Macaulay Culkin, *Home Alone* (1990) became the biggest box office success of the year, managing to draw in family audiences in droves. The second and third biggest hits that year were, respectively, *Ghost* and *Pretty Woman*, giving boy culture few additional toys to play with. Bringing up the rear were films such as *Kindergarten Cop* and *Teenage Mutant Ninja Turtles*, the former actually trying to soften the hard edges of 1980s boy icon Arnold Schwarzenegger, and the latter resulting in a wave of grade school boys demanding Turtle costumes for Halloween and Turtle gifts for Christmas.

Normal service (at least as far as teenage boys were concerned) resumed the next year with the release of *Terminator 2: Judgment Day* (1991). Whereas Schwarzenegger had played the villain in the original *Terminator* (1984), this time he was back as the protector of John Connor, the character played by the teenaged Edward Furlong, and the ultimate savior of mankind. *Terminator 2* was calculated to appeal to young boys and did not shy away from showing the Connor character stealing money from an ATM machine. But this would be a rare instance of Hollywood depicting what a section of boys in real life were prone to—getting on the wrong side of the law, and sometimes getting away with it. What *Terminator 2* did have in abundance were special effects, the likes of which had never been seen before in film—and a rebellious teenage boy who holds the key to the future of the world. In Hollywood by now, common counsel held that boys did not want to watch themselves on screen and would rather watch what they thought their elder siblings and parents were watching. *Terminator 2* proved that boys would watch themselves on screen as long as they were paired with an older, wiser male figure (even if, in this case, the older, wiser male figure was not even human).

The 1990s were when film studios discovered that audiences other than adolescents and young adults could deliver potent box office results. Romantic comedies and dramas returned for a while to rule the roost, none more potently than the mega blockbuster *Titanic* (1997), which had boys either rolling in laughter or throwing up in their seats—for reasons very different from those that would cause them to throw up during a *Nightmare on Elm Street* screening. The big blockbusters now took on a self-aware mode. As the kids who had grown up on the first wave of tentpoles and franchises became producers and directors, the tentpoles they produced were full of references to the blockbusters they had adored when they were young boys. This ensured that almost any blockbuster, whether it be *Independence Day* (1996) or *Men in Black* (1997), was chock full of allusions to Hollywood successes of the past. Boys who had grown up into men on those past films could once again savor the thrills of their younger days.

Hollywood had discovered that it could make films ostensibly pitched at teenage boys but could attract male audiences much, much older than teenagers, bringing along their male friends and offspring as well. It was the film business' version of having its cake and eating it too. But in the process, the boys lost something themselves, boys for whom films began, in the 1990s, to lose their significance as cultural happenings.

The arrival of the Internet and the technological innovations resulting in advanced video games shifted the locus of boy culture away from the films. In particular, computer games such as Doom, originally released in 1993, made boys feel like the director, producer, and auteur of their own films. The

Internet coupled with the power of online gaming enabled boys to connect to each other even without the communal experience that watching a film in a theater provided. Big-budget spectaculars would continue to succeed at the box office, but films no longer held boys in thrall. As film going became one option among many for boys, into the breach stepped screenwriter Harmony Korine and director Larry Clark with *Kids* (1995), a no-holds-barred look at the sexual (and other) lives of teenagers in the era of AIDS. In many ways, *Kids* was the start of an era of films that showcased just how emotionally wrought navigating the waters of boyhood could be. A completely nonjudgmental look at a group of teenagers in New York, *Kids* provoked storms of revulsion and outrage from many quarters, but also equal measures of praise and acclaim from others. The box-office results, however, were severely affected by the NC-17 rating that the film got before its release—which ensured that there was practically no way in which a film that dealt frankly with the lives of boys could be seen by them. *Kids* was one of a slew of films would deal with boys and boy culture in ways radically different from the norm. The films of Todd Solondz, in particular *Welcome to the Dollhouse* (1995) and *Happiness* (1998), shocked some with their portrayal of boys as outcasts struggling with their identities or discussing masturbation with their fathers, but they also contained some of the most authentic depictions of boyhood in 1990s film.

The nineties were the decade in which the independent film took off. The success of the Sundance Festival of independent film encouraged young filmmakers to take risks in writing and shooting films that went against the very grain of the blockbuster-tentpole ethos permeating most of Hollywood. Young filmmakers, in looking around for subjects, realized soon enough that they did not need to look very far. Their own childhood and boyhood provided rich material for introspection, anguish, and even humor. David O. Wallace's *Spanking the Monkey* (1994), for example, managed to offend sensibilities not just with its titular reference to masturbation but with its incest theme. Sometimes even films that soaked out from the confines of independent film into the larger consciousness portrayed the post-adolescent male as maladjusted and discontent. The multiple Oscar winning *American Beauty* (1999) depicted the boy as alienated from society at large, obsessively filming everything he sees with his video camera (no doubt to grow up later in life to become an independent film director).

While independent film was beginning to look deeper into the psyche of the boy and diagnosing his alienation from society, mainstream Hollywood was turning to cheery depictions of conventional boyhood, in particular that of the mischief-making tyke who was actually only looking for love and affection. *Problem Child* (1990) and *Home Alone* (1990) were typical examples. *The Lion King* (1994), if we ignore the fact that the boy in question was an animated lion, was only the latest in a long line of Hollywood films that portrayed boyhood as largely an uncomplicated zone, free of wrenching doubt and conflict. More often than not, the boy was strangely missing from the most successful Hollywood films of the 1990s, especially the second half of that decade. Hollywood was also busy dumbing down the teen comedy even further in this period. The teen comedies of the mid-1980s—especially those written and directed by John Hughes—managed to appeal to critics and the box office, treating their characters as well as their core audiences with respect. The teen comedies of the 1990s, however, garnered nowhere near the same kind of critical and commercial love, with the possible exception *American Pie* (1999). Adding to Hollywood's general lack of interest in boys as film characters was the fact that most of the high school comedies of the 1990s either featured girls at the center of action or focused heavily on romantic plots and subplots that boys turned further away from (unless, of course, they were coaxed, cajoled, and blackmailed into attending by their dates!).

There were, of course, a number of films that did get boys' pulses racing in this period. If *Jurassic Park* (1993) and *The Lost World: Jurassic Park* (1997) capitalized on the unexplained love that all American boys have for dinosaurs, then *Dumb and Dumber* (1994) and to some extent *Forrest Gump* (1994) validated idiocy as a way to success and became frat house favorites. *Toy Story* (1995) taught boys just starting to fall in love with the Internet and electronic games that it was still cool to love the very material toys that they had spent their entire childhood obsessing about and wanted to disown as soon as they stepped into middle school. But there were precious few films with boys (of any age) at the center of a film, despite the record-breaking success of the first two *Home Alone* films.

It seemed that Hollywood believed that a pre-teenage boy could take center stage in a film only when it was a cheery comedy filled with visual gags, and the boy was an adorable moppet with unruly hair. These notions were firmly put to rest almost a decade after the release of the first *Home Alone* film with director M. Night Shyamalan's *The Sixth Sense* (1999). In it Haley Joel Osment plays a young boy who never smiles, and rather than being adorable often makes the viewer flinch, not least with the memorable line, "I see dead people." *The Sixth Sense*, with its twist ending, went on to become a cultural phenomenon, but it also in some ways spelled the definitive end of the adorable film tyke—a long tradition going as far back to the 1920s with the likes of Jackie Coogan and Jackie Cooper. In the future, such films would continue to be made, but would most often bypass a theatrical release, going direct-to-video or debuting on cable television.

2000 and Beyond: Darker Times, Darker Visions

The first decade of the twenty-first century saw real-life events influence a reappraisal of boys and boy culture. The obsessive media coverage of the Columbine High School shootings of late 1999 led to the recognition that teenage years were fraught with emotional minefields, a terrain that many boys found difficult to negotiate. As the number of school shootings continued to rise, accompanied with strident news media questioning of the role that films and video games played as influencers in these shootings, portrayals of the adolescent or post-adolescent males began to get darker both in independent and in mainstream Hollywood films.

As the last years of the twentieth century leached into the first years of the twenty-first century, films began to present an increasingly darker and nuanced view of boys. In many ways the landmark film of the early years of the new century was Richard Kelly's *Donnie Darko* (2001). The film opened in November 2001, and the national mood at the time immediately in the aftermath of 9/11 was not at all receptive to a dark, head-spinning tale of a schizophrenic teenager, alternate universes, and a giant evil rabbit. A total commercial failure on its original release, *Donnie Darko* became a huge cult favorite on the strength of DVD sales and rentals. For teenagers wondering whether the life they had was the only one possible, and trying desperately to fit into the stereotypical mould of successful high school males, *Donnie Darko* offered empathy, if not absolution.

2001 was also the year when the plucky kid of old Hollywood film made a comeback to center stage of films and national conversation, but in a very new avatar. *Harry Potter and the Sorcerer's Stone* (2001) was the first cinematic incarnation of the Harry Potter stories, and young boys all over started believing that almost anything was within their grasp. The first two Harry Potter films were directed by Chris Columbus, the director of *Home Alone* and *Home Alone 2: Lost in New York,* and if the films appeared cheerier than the books, and one saw flashes of Kevin from *Home Alone* in Harry from Hogwarts, perhaps it was no coincidence. The mood turned darker with *Harry Potter and the Prisoner of Azkaban* (2004) as Harry and his friends faced up to death, betrayal, and the soul-sucking Dementors. In line with the books, the films continued to become more and more complicated as favorite characters perished and Harry began to grapple with difficult choices, huge responsibilities, and sometimes the impact of his own swollen head. By the time *Harry Potter and the Order of the Phoenix* came along in 2007, there was barely a smile to be seen from the late teenaged Harry. It seemed that with every film, Harry Potter was going further and further away from Kevin McCallister and moving closer and closer toward Donnie Darko. In the history of film franchises, especially those targeted at young and teenage audiences, there is no other example of a boy whose emotional growth is so realistically mapped out over succeeding films. Hollywood has always believed that the reason franchises succeed is because audiences, especially younger ones, always want more of the same character. That is the reason why Marty McFly changes little over the course of the three *Back to the Future* films and why the passage of time affects Indiana Jones much less emotionally than it does physically. It is also why the emotional arc of the Harry Potter character seems so realistic even in the middle of the illusory nature of his world.

If there is one actor who has embodied the new face of the boy in the 2000s independent film, it is Joseph-Gordon Levitt. Gordon-Levitt successfully managed to transcend his child actor background (particularly as the youngest alien in the NBC sitcom *Third Rock from the Sun*) to offer the most complex and nuanced portrayals of the American post-adolescent teenager since the days of James Dean in *Rebel without a Cause* (1955). In Gregg Araki's *Mysterious Skin* (2004), Gordon-Levitt plays Neil, a gay hustler abused in childhood by his pedophiliac coach. One of the most critically lauded releases of the year, the film is an uncompromising representation of the dark side of boyhood in small-town America, helped no end by the effortlessly multi-layered portrayal by Gordon-Levitt. If *Mysterious Skin* is a portrayal of boys at the margins, *Brick* (2006) in its own way is no less so. A genre-bending blend of film noir and high school dramas, the characters in *Brick* speak like they have stepped out of the pages of a Dashiel Hammett novel. Gordon-Levitt plays high school student Brendan who has to penetrate the social system of his school and its associated unsavory milieus—including high school drug dealers—in order to uncover the truth behind his ex-girlfriend's death. School in 2000s film is no longer a place where you have can have fun without retribution. No wonder that in *The Lookout* (2007), Gordon-Levitt's overconfident rich-kid high school hockey star is so severely injured in a car accident that he has to get life skills coaching for the rest of his life.

Even as independent cinema was turning out dark visions of boyhood, the empire struck back in the form of George Lucas. He delivered what he had been threatening to for a long time—the three prequels to his original *Star Wars* saga. Boys (and their fathers) everywhere rejoiced and there was brisk trading in Mace Windu and Darth Maul figurines, but the blogosphere was buzzing with cries of disappointment from fans and of derision from critics—not that it prevented the films from raking in a collective $ 2.4 billion at the global box office. The *Star Wars* prequels were all about a boy. The storyline over the three films mapped out the path that the young Anakin Skywalker took to eventually become the evil Darth Vader (even if he paused on the way to stiffly utter some of the most stilted romantic lines in film history). But insight into the boy's psyche, if any, was overwhelmed by the artificial dialogue and gargantuan special effects. For true insight into boy culture, one had to look toward independent cinema in the form of films such as *O* (2000), a high school version of Shakespeare's *Othello*; *Elephant* (2003), a clinical examination of high school shootings; and *Alpha Dog* (2006), a real life inspired story of drug dealing and kidnapping among young adults.

Have the Films Lost Boys Forever?

Thoughtful as these films were, they were ignored by boys, at least as far as theatrical grosses were concerned. It seemed that the old adage about boys not wanting to see their own lives on screen continued to hold true well into the twenty-first century. Boys instead thrilled to Johnny Depp's antics as Captain Jack Sparrow in the hugely popular *Pirates of the Caribbean* franchise (2003–2007). They also gravitated to the slew of film spoofs that began to be churned out with monotonous regularity by the big studios. *The Scary Movie* franchise (2000–2006), in particular, continued to deliver consistent returns at the box office, starting with *Scary Movie* (2000), right up to *Scary Movie 4* (2006). Teenagers who made a success of the original horror films/slasher flicks that this franchise parodied turned up in droves to make a success of their parodic incarnations. No matter what genre was being spoofed, films such as *Not Another Teen Film* (2001), *Date Film* (2006), *Epic Film* (2007), or *Meet the Spartans* (2008), a spoof of historical films, all took the no.1 spot at the box office in their respective weekend of release. It hardly mattered that boys would perhaps not even have seen many of the films that these films spoofed.

All they needed was passing familiarity with the originals and they certainly had that in an oversaturated media environment. The success of these films testified to the fact that by the early years of the new century, boys no longer took films half as seriously as they did a couple of decades earlier. Films were objects of indifference rather than awe. No wonder then that the films had to think up bigger and bigger extravaganzas to impress teenaged and younger boys. As for films impacting boy culture in a significant manner: fugged-aboutit. Boys, who just 20 years ago were in thrall to the movies, were now swayed only by the release of "Halo III" or "Guitar Hero III." Hollywood needed to step back and wonder if it had not lost its most prized audiences for good.

Further Reading

Considine, David. *The Cinema of Adolescence.* Jefferson, NC: McFarland, 1985.

Shone, Tom. *Blockbuster: How Hollywood Learned to Stop Worrying and Love the Summer.* New York: Free Press, 2004.

Maltin, Leonard. *Leonard Maltin's Movie Guide 2006 Edition.* New York: Signet, 2005.

The New York Times Movies Web site, http://movies.nytimes.com. [Online April 2008.]

Allmovie.com Web site, http://www.allmovies.com. [Online April 2008.]

Santanu Chakrabarti

Buffy the Vampire Slayer

Buffy the Vampire Slayer was a television program (1997–2003) well known for its positive and progressive portrayals of female characters and the transgression of gendered stereotypes. Reoccurring male characters on the program also enjoyed an interesting (and in some sense, new) space in popular culture by representing important transgressions of the stereotypical male adolescent character. On the show, male adolescents were continually portrayed as both deviating from and reinforcing stereotypes of what teen boys were and could be.

There were two types of male adolescents on *Buffy:* human and nonhuman (a category that includes demons and hybrids, such as vampires or were-wolves). The human boys on *Buffy* (who are represented in most detail during the first three seasons of the show, when the title character is in high school) at first seemed to be there only as a foil for the powerful main character, as comic relief, and to reinforce stereotypes of "scruffy losers" and "jocks."

Xander (Alexander Lavelle Harris) seemed to be no exception to the scruffy-loser stereotype (a boy who clumsily rode a skateboard, was friends with the geeks of the school, was teased mercilessly by the cool girls and boys alike, and could not get a girlfriend). When he became friends with Buffy (his big crush who saved him and the world from death and certain apocalypse countless times), it is clear that he not only wanted her as a girlfriend (which never happens) but he also wanted to be like her: a hero.

Early in season one, Xander's yearning for cool teenage boyhood and hero status was shown in a particularly telling episode: it begins with Xander on stage at The Bronze (the local club where everyone in Sunnydale, human or not, hangs out). He's playing lead guitar in a loud rock band as Buffy—his friend and chosen slayer of all evil—fights a nasty vampire in the audience. Buffy is too weak to kill the vampire (and, indeed, is almost killed herself) so Xander manages to suavely save Buffy, drive a stake through the vampire's heart, and finish a riotous guitar solo, all within the space of minutes. Of course, this is clearly a dream. Xander wakes to find himself drooling in biology class being mercilessly teased by Blaine, a jock classmate (who seems to better embody strong and sexy bravado more than Xander ever will). Xander's weakness and naïveté is expounded upon as he is seduced by a sexy biology teacher (who plays upon his inexperience with and anxiety of women and who turns out to be a monster in disguise), becoming the key player in her plan to breed with young, virginal males and then kill them. Blaine is also imprisoned by the biology teacher (a She-Mantis), but unlike Xander, he enacts the role of "trapped female in a horror movie" quite well, screaming profusely while Xander tries to think of a way out. It is Buffy, of course, that finally saves these "damsels in distress." In the eyes of the audience and Buffy's gang of friends (affectionately called "the Scoobies"), Blaine's previous hyper-masculine and sexual jock state is relegated to mere fantasy stereotype. Xander, however, is not completely relegated to a weak, side-kick role. He enjoys a moment of power as he destroys the She-Mantis' eggs (the eggs she would have forced him to fertilize before killing him) to raucous guitar chords.

We are always reminded that Xander is an average teen boy, while his best friends are super teen girls: a vampire slayer and a witch who work together to save humans from imminent doom (and who date a vampire and a were-wolf, respectively). Xander is the "normal" one, who offers not brute strength or astute intelligence, but, most often, heart.

When Xander is seen using the tools of strength and intelligence to be a hero, it always occurs due to some kind of fantasy or spell. In the episode, "The Pack," Xander, on a school field trip to the zoo, becomes one of the cool, mean kids in class when he is possessed by an evil hyena. Xander is suddenly quiet, aggressive, thoughtless, impatient, sarcastic, and mean to his friends and the "geekier" set of students at school. When Buffy laments Xander's behavior to Giles, the school librarian and her watcher (her guide through ridding the world of evil), he responds: "Xander's taken to teasing the less fortunate? And there's a noticeable change in both clothing and demeanor? And, well, otherwise all his spare time's spent lounging about with imbeciles? . . . It's devastating. He's turned into a 16 year old boy. Of course, you'll have to kill him." The idea that this isn't really Xander, a concept that relieves both his friends and the audience, is carried through into other episodes where Xander just isn't himself. When he is the victim of a Halloween spell and becomes his costume—a sort of G.I. Joe figure who tries to help save his friends from marauding vampires and chaos worshippers—for all his training and military expertise, Xander can't complete the mission and instead must wait until

Buffy turns from a coiffed, eighteenth-century debutant back into the slayer. Although the audience is somewhat excited at the notion of a new Xander, they are still more excited about the power of the slayer.

In this way, Xander both embodies and subverts a stereotypical adolescent's wishes. He's a normal teenager with an awkward side that real teen boys can relate to, yet he exists—and thrives—in abnormal circumstances. Although his wishes to be a superhero (or villain) are explored on the show, it is clear that these stereotypes—popular jock, G.I. Joe, or rock star—are neither realistic nor fulfilling for Xander. As he enacts fantasy and is forever thrust back to reality, the audience sees Xander's "typical" adolescent state as a sort of thwarted existence, a constant negotiation of what society and stereotypes tell him he should be and the reality of his awkward teenage boyhood.

Although Xander represents the subversion of a typical, fantasical, teenage boy-wonder on television, his nonhuman counterparts play with that stereotype in a different way. The normalcy, humanity, and comedy that Xander often represents are exploded when it comes to the male vampires on the program.

The two main male vampires on *Buffy* are Angel and Spike. Although both vampires are over 100 years old (when Angel is introduced in season one, he is approximately 258 years old, while Spike is a less mature barely 200), they were sired (turned into vampires) when they were on the cusp of adolescence and adulthood. Angel and Spike enact typical superhero fantasies: they are extremely good-looking and sought after, cool, aloof, and, of course, tougher than almost anyone else. Both Angel and Spike will always be 18 years old in body, and sometimes, it seems, through their brooding, selfishness, and bad behavior, it appears they will be 18 years old in their minds as well. In short it appears that the two of them will endlessly explore the notion of perpetual male adolescence. Yet, the two diverge markedly on what that perpetual boyhood could mean.

When we are introduced to Angel, he is a cocky and mysterious figure. Brooding yet completely sure of himself, Angel is the typical loner, vigilante hero. Not only does he want to save the world from vampires, he wants to do so by helping the slayer (who also becomes his lover). Yet to enact this state of righteousness as a vampire, he must ignore and quell the deep and animalistic stirrings of his nature.

For Angel, it seems to be a difficult process of "growing up," this denying or keeping his animalistic feelings and impulses at bay. Angel so desperately wants to be a real man, a human, that he denies himself the pleasures and comforts of human and vampire life, living in an in-between state. This extreme and harsh space that is in neither the human nor demon world stands in stark contrast to the normalcy that is so embodied and subverted in Xander. Although Angel embodies in reality Xander's dreams (the superhero and boyfriend of the slayer), he can never inhabit Xander's realities. He can never be a "normal boy"; he must be a hero, doomed to the shadows, saving people but perhaps never truly loving or being loved by them.

Spike is introduced as the counterpart to "Angel." With a style infused with punk rock and violence (and, often, a slapstick sensibility), Spike is the perpetual bad boy who does whatever he wants and kills whomever he chooses. Spike is the embodiment of unadulterated and untamed action hero. He can be as bad or good as he wants to be (though through most of the seven seasons of the program, he does not often want to be good). In his own way, he is a stereotypical villain. Unlike Angel, Spike doesn't want to "grow up." He wants to fight, create chaos, get the girl (who is also evil), and be triumphant. His desires are not marked by growth but by fame. Of course, this all changes later on when Spike falls in love with Buffy. Although he still wants fame, he also wants a companionship that runs deeper than evil and sex.

It is through these three main male adolescent characters that we understand that boyhood in *Buffy the Vampire Slayer* isn't represented by mere embodiments of stereotypes but by intricate and complex characters and metaphors. The portrayal of adolescents and the way they connect to and enact both the fantastical and the everyday realities transgress what we are taught to think about teen boys.

Further Reading

Pereira, KL. "Kiss of the Vampire: Buffy and the Politics of Queer Identity on Television." *Clamor Magazine*, Issue 35, Vol. 5, January 2006.

Wilcox, Rhonda. *Why Buffy Matters: The Art of Buffy the Vampire Slayer.* London: I.B. Tauris, 2005.

K. L. Pereira

ESPN

ESPN is the most watched sports network in the world, featuring such channels as ESPN, ESPN HD, ESPN2, ESPN Classic, ESPN News, ESPN Deportes, and ESPN U. The brand also boasts *ESPN The Magazine* as well as popular Web sites ESPN.com and ESPN360.com.

ESPN began as the Entertainment and Sports Programming Network on September 7, 1979. A father-and-son team, Bill and Scott Rasmussen, had the idea to start a 24-hour-a-day cable network focused on delivering sports news and content. The channel would feature regular sports programming such as college sports games, but also rather unusual sports such as tractor pulls and the now infamous Strongest Man contest.

ESPN brought to sports fanatics what the daily sports section of the newspaper could not—up to the minute action and news on a variety of sports beyond the local college or professional team. ESPN also created a niche of sports talk that furthered that of radio, including game film and live interviews that linked sports fans and media worldwide. Shows such as *Around the Horn and First Take* bring together sports reporters, athletes, and former athletes from around the nation to offer information and opinions on the top sports stories of the day.

The first and most popular show on the ESPN network, *SportsCenter,* has literally changed the way the nation talks about sports. The hour-long sports newscast, initially featuring such anchors as Chris Berman, Keith Olbermann,

Dan Patrick, and Stuart Scott, brought a new language to the sports arena. Anchors used frank terms in describing sports events and evoked laughter and mimicry with slick, yet vivid phrases such as "just call him butter cuz he's on a roll" and "Boo-yah!" *SportsCenter* is television's longest-running show, airing its 25,000th show in August 2002, and boasting viewership of nearly 88 million people.

Another popular show on ESPN is *College Game Day* in which anchors travel to a different college campus every week and make predictions of the day's game winners throughout the National Collegiate Athletic Association (NCAA). The show brings together the host college's community and collegiate sports fans by providing an informative and comical prelude to the college games to be played that day. The show also displays feature stories on teams, players, and coaches throughout the NCAA.

ESPN features youth programs as well. For children in their elementary school years, the network produces the annual *Scripps National Spelling Bee* and *the Little League World Series.* For older boys, the network's Web site highlights the top rankings of high school teams around the nation and also presents a strong focus on college signing day for high school athletes. As extreme sports became more and more attractive to young boys in the 1990s, ESPN began to cover these sports and began an annual X Games contest, eventually sprouting EXPN and EXPN.com that were totally dedicated to extreme sports.

As the network grew in popularity, the brand expanded to include a variety of networks geared toward nearly every kind of sports fan. In addition to EXPN for extreme games, the company began ESPN Classic, which offers footage of old sports events such as the 1997 WBC Welterweight Title fight between Pernell Whitaker and Diosbleys Hurtado and feature stories on such topics as the 1919 Chicago White Sox. ESPN 2 was specially designed in 1993 to reach the younger sports fan and thus features edgy graphics and some extreme sports. ESPN Deportes is the leading Spanish-language sports brand targeted toward the Hispanic sports fan. ESPN International offers sports news and programming in 15 languages, including Arabic, Cantonese, German, Hindi, Italian, Japanese, Polish, and Turkish.

ESPN U is geared specifically toward college sports, offering coverage of games not shown on its basic cable networks. The network, launched in 2005, is a 24-hour college sports network. Sports coverage includes football, men's and women's basketball, baseball, wrestling, and other NCAA sports. Additional programming on the station includes SportsCenterU, ESPNU Coaches Spotlight, ESPNU Recruiting Insider, and National Signing Day.

ESPN has made an effort to attract younger male viewers by heavily referring to their Web sites throughout their talk shows. Viewers are sent to the Web to get further information on news reports, players, and events such as the NFL Draft. Shows such as *First Take,* ESPN2's two-hour morning show, also incorporate chat messages and blogs into their broadcasts. This way, young viewers feel like they are actually a part of the show. The creation of these interactive instances aids in drawing younger viewers to the ESPN network.

Aside from its many television networks, ESPN also has ESPN Radio, an integrated online media player, publishing divisions, and restaurants. ESPN

Radio has over 700 station affiliates nationwide and includes the NBA, MLB, and college football programming. ESPN's online media player, in addition to its Web sites, provides fans with on-demand video products. The ESPN publishing division distributes *ESPN The Magazine* and several sports books annually. ESPN Zone restaurants are located in Anaheim, Atlanta, Baltimore, Chicago, Denver, Las Vegas, New York City, and Washington, D.C., and offer dining with the added element of sports programming displayed on multiple televisions throughout the restaurant.

Team ESPN, ESPN's corporate outreach program, offers two programs beneficial to young boys: *Play Your Way* and ESPN2's *Cable in the Classroom SportsFigures.* The Play Your Way Web site provides physical fitness materials that offer information on games to play and places to play in order to encourage healthy lifestyles. ESPN2's *Cable in the Classroom SportsFigures* is a commercial-free series available online that teaches physics through sports.

ESPN has become the worldwide leader in sports programming, paving the way for such networks as FOX Sports Network and the SPEED network. Through proper brand marketing and steady expansion, the network has had an indelible impact on the way the world views sports. The network has also made increased efforts to reach young boys who are outside of the network's primary target market—males of age 18–49. With the launching of ESPN2 and ESPNU, the interactive online offerings, and the production of video games, ESPN works to incorporate its sports coverage into the lives of young boys.

ESPN is headquartered in Bristol, Connecticut, and is 80 percent owned by ABC, Inc., and indirect subsidiary of Disney Company. The remaining 20 percent is owned by the Hearst Corporation.

Further Reading

Bryant, Jennings and Andrea M. Holt. "A Historical Overview of Sports and Media in the United States." In Arthur A. Raney and Jennings Bryant, eds. *Handbook of Sports and Media.* Mahwah, NJ: Lawrence Erlbaum Associates, 2006, pp. 21–44.

Freeman, Michael. *ESPN: The Uncensored History.* Dallas, TX: Taylor Publications, 2000.

Mia Long

Little Bill

Comedian, entertainer, educator, writer, and entrepreneur Bill Cosby has been known for encouraging social movements. His work in television and film opened doors for African Americans to create, write, direct, and produce televisions shows that were entertaining and educational for all audiences. These shows have generated imagination and learning for children of all ages, ethnicities, and socioeconomic classes.

In 1997, Cosby created a children's book series that was engaging, entertaining, and educational. *Little Bill Books for Beginning Readers* focused on problems and random encounters that many children face on a weekly if not day-to-day basis. The book series aims to assist young readers between the ages of five to eight in learning and practicing key fundamental reading skills. The *Little Bill* book series focuses on an adventurous and inquisitive five-year-old African American boy, his family, and how they interact in the world. The book series provides fundamental tools for readers to learn how to deal with difficult social situations. The book highlights Little Bill's relationship with his mother, father, siblings, great-grandmother, and friends and how he uses the lessons taught from them to understand how to maneuver in a big and sometimes confusing world.

On November 28, 1999, Nickelodeon aired its first episode of *Little Bill,* the television show. The title of the first show was "Just a Baby" and played during a 30-minute time slot with limited commercials. Through the vision of Cosby, the popular children's book series was transformed into an on-air masterpiece. The show features the voice of Cosby narrating stories about the adventures of Little Bill. Many of the social and moral lessons presented in the book series were transformed to the television series. The show was designed to help young kids understand their everyday experiences and celebrate their unique styles. Viewers of the show understand that what they do in general everyday situations has an effect on how they make a difference in the world. Little Bill helps young boys understand that their presence in the world does matter. One of the major goals of the show is to encourage children to value the love of their family and friends, to increase self-esteem, and to develop social skills. On the show, Little Bill has a signature saying—"Hello Friend"—that symbolizes the importance the show puts on young children developing healthy friendships and relationships. Little Bill, with the help of his family and friends, answers challenging questions about his daily encounters in a healthy manner that gives other children an outlet to learn and adjust.

Some of the characters on the show include Brenda who is Bill's mother. Big Bill is Little Bill's father. Bobby is Little Bill's brother and April is Little Bill's big sister. Elephant is Bill's pet hamster who blinks to indicate that Bill has spoken. Alice the Great is Bill's great-grandmother who tells stories to Little Bill on most every episode. Fuschia is the cousin of Little Bill, and Andrew is Bill's best friend.

Further Reading

Cosby, Bill. *The Meanest Thing to Say: A Little Bill Book for Beginning Readers, Level 3.* New York: Cartwheel Publishing, 1997.
Ennis, Avery, Bill Cosby [Online March 2008]. www.billcosby.com.

Creshema Murray

Masculine Boys in the Media

Manufacturing a man to fit in today's world requires the use of many different, sophisticated, and powerful tools by modern society. More than half a century after the invention of television, the media industry and the marketing industry have joined efforts to use stories, heroes, toys, games, and songs to play an increasing role in the process. Today, corporations with commercial motivations produce most of these tools. Most of these corporations have manufactured and marketed these tools so they could be used to force male children to become something called "real boys," "real teens," or "real men." The way they portray masculinity is profoundly toxic. These tools teach children the qualities that "real" boys must develop to become "real" men. Modern storytellers and marketers include television broadcasters, video game producers, movie producers, and music producers, and most of them have to conform to hidden censorship controlled by powerful media conglomerates.

The entertainment industry creates role models that will transmit values into young male fans and make them wish to become what is portrayed to them as "real" men. After analyzing role models for boys in the media and how these heroes relate with other human beings and with nature, young citizens can (and love to) understand the common ingredients used to manufacture "real" men on a large scale; they can also see the collateral damage of these manufactured role models on education, youth crime, life in society, and public health. Because more parents have been raised into that culture, it makes it hard for most of them to dissociate their way of parenting from the pattern imposed by the media. When some of them try, they are often rejected by their own children who prefer the surrounding culture promoted by the media and peer pressure.

Violent Entertainment

In the view of many, violence is used by the entertainment industry for the purpose of attracting more viewers. Many also believe that films and other popular media take a child's age into consideration only in the sense of taking advantage of their vulnerability and in effect abusing them.

Consider for a moment cultural products targeting children, products such as *Pokemon, Mortal Kombat, Terminator, Doom, Ninja Turtles, Mighty Morphin Power Rangers, Grand Theft Auto, Howard Stern, South Park,* Jackass, Jackie Chan, and so forth. Like hundreds of other popular culture products, these not only attract, entertain, and inspire children and teens across North America, but they also may damage their mental health and social development. They carry and promote values that inspire children's clothing, language, attitudes, behaviors, and also, unfortunately, the way they relate with each other. When boys grow older and become teenagers, such heavily promoted musical entertainers as Eminem, 50 Cent, Marilyn Manson, and Snoop Dog circulate hate propaganda against women. Many are concerned that the music industry promotes such entertainers as rebels, and that they win awards and earn huge amounts of money. Only a minority of teens can understand what many of these role models actually teach: frustration, aggressiveness, humiliation, and hatred. Misogyny, violence, fear, sexism, and racism have nothing in common with freedom and justice.

Before the beginning of the third millennium, the cinema industry had created and marketed violent role models for boys all over the world. In 1998, a global survey by the United Nations Educational, Scientific, and Cultural Organization (UNESCO) highlighted newly found correlation between media violence and youth perception of reality. The survey had been realized in collaboration with the World Organization of the Scout Movement (WOSM). The Scouts' participation in the survey was motivated by UNESCO's program, "Towards a Culture of Peace and Non-Violence," that was close to the ideals of scouting. The Scouts considered the survey as their contribution to the young "whom we help educate by promoting their autonomy and sense of values." At the time of release, UNESCO urged "citizens to react to violence on the screen by exercising their democratic rights as citizens and consumers."

The Global Study on Media Violence was conducted by Professor Jo Groebel of the University of Utrecht in The Netherlands. It was the first and the largest ever intercultural study on the relationship between media and children. Five thousand 12-year-olds in 23 countries were asked to answer questionnaires for the survey conducted between 1996 and 1997 in the following countries: Angola, Argentina, Armenia, Brazil, Canada, Costa Rica, Croatia, Egypt, Fiji, Germany, India, Japan, Mauritius, the Netherlands, Peru, Philippines, Qatar, South Africa, Spain, Tajikistan, Togo, Trinidad and Tobago, and Ukraine.

Ninety-one percent of children in the sample had access to TV at home and spent an average of three hours per day in front of it. This was more than 50 percent longer than with any other out-of-school activity, including homework. TV programs carried 5 to 10 acts of aggression per hour, most of them presented as either thrilling and/or rewarding. The survey showed that *Terminator* was known by 88 percent of children. More than 50 percent living in high-aggression environments wanted to be like the character. In low-aggression neighborhoods, 37 percent wished the same. *Terminator* has what children view as necessary to cope with tough situations. Twenty-six percent of children perceive action heroes as their favorite role models, and 18.5 percent preferred pop stars and musicians.

Forty-four percent of children reported a strong overlap in what they perceive to be reality and what they see on the screen. Fifty percent of children reported that they are anxious most of the time or very often, and nine percent had to flee their homes at least once. Forty-seven percent said they would like to live in another country; in high-aggression areas, 16 percent know many people in their neighborhood who have been killed. In this group, 7.5 percent of children have already used a weapon against another person.

The study showed some regional differences: 34 percent of Asians rank action heroes highest as compared to 25 percent of Europeans and Canadians and 18 percent of Africans, the lowest. UNESCO rang the alarm because they considered that the "acceptable has been exceeded." Parents and educators were asked to guide the children's consumption of media. The report proposed increased public responsibility for politicians and producers. It mentioned that voluntary codes of conduct and self-regulation had been ineffective and still allowed the increase of media violence. When appreciating educational efforts that had promoted critical media consumption among the young, the report saw that "most efforts have been corrupted by the industry." Lobbyists and funds for so-called media literacy helped the industry's PR strategy to blame parents for their individual child's cultural intoxication.

Since the 1998 version of *Terminator,* many other role models have been created and used to appeal to children in movies, including *Spider-Man, Batman, Rambo,* the Jackie Chan films, *Star Wars,* and Harry Potter, just to name a few. Each year, the cinema industry creates new male heroes that have acquired reputations that seem to be more prestigious than those of dads and teachers. These commercial role models have acquired the title of teachers in the global education system. They were created and marketed by unknown people, elected by nobody, and, in the opinion of some, for the sole purpose of increasing benefits of private stockholders.

Results of Children's Exposure to Media

The amount of time children are exposed to television (violent or not) impacts the phenomena of school bullying. Children who spend 3.5 hours daily in front of TV—which an average child does—have a 25 percent increased risk of becoming bullies between the ages of 6 and 11 (Zimmerman, 2005). TV exposure has an undeniably clear independent effect on children's bullying, higher than poverty and parental care.

Troubled Behaviors on the Rise

Massive exposure to violent entertainment is now considered a major factor for the increasing number of children with troubled behaviors. Public data show that since the mid-1990s, schools in the United States have noticed a very rapid increase of the number of children with behavioral difficulties. Authorities mention that the phenomenon was almost nonexistent 10 year before. Is it because they were simply not reported? Is the reporting due to less tolerance by teachers or staff? Should teachers be blamed for lack of tolerance? Look at the data below, which come from different states and provinces.

- California: from 1995 to 2001, assaults nearly doubled.
- Philadelphia: first part of school year 2003–2004, 22 kindergartners suspended.
- Minneapolis: over 2 school years, suspension of 500 kindergartners for fighting, indecent exposure, and persistent lack of cooperation.
- Minnesota: almost 4,000 kindergartners, first and second graders, suspended for fighting, disorderly conduct, etc.
- Massachusetts: between 1995 and 2000, pre-kindergarten through third grade, suspensions doubled.
- Greenville, SC: school year 2001–2002, suspension of 132 first-graders, 75 kindergartners and two preschoolers.
- Québec: from 1985 to 2000, K-6 students with troubled behaviors increased by 300 percent.

Size of Impact

Those advocating for the entertainment industry may try to challenge the size of effect and make it appear a minor problem. They often say that media violence is not the only factor contributing to real-life violence, and they try to diminish the influence of media violence.

As noted above, scientists have measured the correlation between what children watch and how they behave. They found correlations revealing that the effect of media violence is bigger than the effect of exposure to lead on children's brain activity, bigger than the effect of calcium intake on bone mass, bigger than the effect of homework on academic achievement, bigger than protection against HIV when wearing a condom, bigger than the effect of asbestos exposure on cancer, and bigger than the effect of exposure to second-hand smoke on lung cancer. More recent correlations between video game violence and aggression have shown to be higher than smoking and lung cancer. Blaming parents for letting their child be abused by a TV show, movie, or game is part of a public relation strategy. Many parents, educators, and policy makers believe that this tactic diverts the spotlights of public opinion, of governments, and of courts from shining on those who sell violent images that are seen by children. Accusations of censorship are the defense used by those in the popular culture media to neutralize any initiative that limits the use of violence in games, TV shows, films, and other media that children encounter.

Further Reading

Joint Statement to the Congressional Public Health Summit. "The Impact of Entertainment Violence on Children." http://www.aap.org/advocacy/releases/jstmtevc.htm.

Robinson, Thomas N. "Student Media Awareness for Reducing Television" Program (SMART). http://hprc.stanford.edu/pages/store/itemDetail.asp?169.

"The UNESCO Global Study on Media Violence." http://www.unesco.org/bpi/eng/unescopress/98-32e.htm. (For the complete report, see http://unesdoc.unesco.org/images/0011/001178/117881e.pdf.)

Zimmerman, Frederick. "Early Cognitive Stimulation, Emotional Support, and Television Watching as Predictors of Subsequent Bullying Among Grade-School Children." Retrieved on April 4, 2008, from http://commercialalert.org/tvbullying.pdf.

Jacques Brodeur

Military Advertising

Upon viewing a commercial today for the Canadian Forces' (Canada's national defense organization) new advertisement campaign, one might think it is selling a new video game or movie. However, despite the word "dramatization" that flashes once at the bottom of the screen, the rapid-fire images of gunfire and action, fires and floods seem extremely realistic. These images have a clear focus on instilling in the viewer feelings of action and adventure, similar to the adrenaline-rush felt when playing a video game. This technique, usually used to advertise video games or action movies, is now being used as a recruiting technique by the Canadian Forces.

Now imagine these words flash on the screen: "The threats to freedom do not sleep." Images appear of soldiers with guns aimed, traversing a blown-out city. Again, the following words appear on the screen: "The threats to freedom know no boundaries." A burst of images fill the screen with an array of explosions and gunfire and more images of helicopters and bombs. The screen images continue but with the following words "Neither do the protectors of freedom." One lone soldier with a gun silhouetted against a harsh amber background. The Army's Special Forces who defend what is best and confront those who seek to oppress. Join the hundred who will test today and be one of the three to earn the Green Beret.

Recruitment ad? Almost. It is actually an advertisement for the U.S. Army's new video game, America's Army. Watching the commercial, there are times the video game footage and real-life footage are indecipherable; there appears to be both. This advertisement, like the commercial for the Canadian Forces, uses rapid-fire images combined with abrupt sentences. There appears to be little difference between today's military recruitment ad and a commercial for a video game, both of which are geared towards a population of young boys.

America's Army

The video game America's Army came out of an army recruiter's trip to an electronic store with his son. After noticing how many video games depicting armies, guns, wars, and fighting in general there were, this recruiter saw a market the Army could tap into—recruiting young males through video games. According to an article in *PC Magazine* in 2007, almost 10 years later, America's Army has over 8.5 million registered users and 40 million downloads, arguably the most successful recruitment campaign to date (Costa, 2007). This phenomenon has been realized by tapping directly into popular boy culture.

There are many reasons this game is such a powerful recruitment tool. Interestingly, this game has a rating of "T" for teen by the Entertainment Software Rating Board, which means kids as young as 13 are targeted for playing. This is a powerful advantage for the Army because it serves the purpose of educating youth about the Army five years before they can even join, at an age that is very influential, without ever having to make any face-to-face contact. The format alone—the video game—is such a popular medium for males aged 13–24 (within the Army's prime recruitment target age), that America's Army was bound to reach millions of young people, becoming part of their pop culture. However, because this game is "The Official Army Game," the Army, along with the video game, also becomes part of popular culture. One Army study found that among Americans aged 16–24, 30 percent got some of the information they know about the Army from this game. What are these gamers learning about the Army? America's Army purports to be the most realistic game out there about army life on and off the battlefield. However, when you are shot and killed, your game does end, and if you break the rules of war (by firing your gun at nontargets perhaps), you do have a "time-out."

Recently game designers have started using real U.S. Army heroes as characters in the game, blurring the lines between video game and reality even more.

Males as young as 13 playing this game through the Web site www.americasarmy.com do not realize they are being recruited because recruitment is taking the form of a video game, leaving no space for them to be critical of what the game is depicting and how it is depicting the "reality" of war. It has been argued that video games in general do not allow for any critical thinking (despite the fact they no doubt develop problem-solving abilities) because gamers are forced to reason within the confines of the game's operating system. Therefore, games cannot offer the ability to "think outside the box" or be innovative because players cannot change traditional patterns, rules, or even the system itself.

War: America's Favorite Pastime?

Many believe that video game developers and army recruiters have been successful in turning war into a game. Compare older advertisements to today's marketing campaigns: Commercials of the past were about personal skills, learning new technology, gaining personal freedom, and strength. Today's commercials are about action, adventure, and adrenaline and have a much more sophisticated look and feel. Ads of the past were much more obvious in their intent with use of the words, character, maturity, team work; they were also simple, in that their message was easier to digest. One depicts a soldier writing a letter to his father, describing how proud he would be of his son, while another shows a boy in basic training gradually getting better and gaining confidence with the help of his drill sergeant. These ads had the simple job of targeting a young male, who already believed in his country and simply wanted to make something of himself by making his peers and his country proud and proving that he could either get into college or face his fear of heights.

Today's military recruitment advertising faces the challenge of a young man who is increasingly indifferent to the wars being fought around the globe and disconnected from the politics of his country. Therefore, military recruitment ads cannot be as simple and straightforward as they once were. Advertisements for the U.S. Navy Seals clearly criticize the average life of the American male, juxtaposing action-packed clips of helicopters, submarines, and underwater guns with the narration, "And to think—somewhere, some poor guy is buying a minivan." Ironically that same voice says to log onto the "life accelerator" at navy.com, while some take note of the fact that joining the military can actually shorten a life.

What is more is that the Army has not only become more sophisticated with its marketing, but also with its entire training and tactical development. The recent years has seen an uncanny relationship developing between Hollywood and the military. After 9/11 Hollywood writers met with members of the Bush administration to participate in brainstorming sessions on the next possible steps for terrorists; at the same time, Karl Rove met with top Hollywood producers to search for ways the entertainment industry could help with the war on terror. The Army has also built a multi-million dollar facility, the Institute of Creative Technologies (ICT), in which they design and continue to develop their video game, America's Army, as well as develop virtual reality training programs.

Can You Beat the Game?

When advertisements for military recruitment take on the sophistication of a video game, and video games, while they have always tried to assimilate war, now resemble real-life battles depicting real-life war heroes and portraying real-life enemies of America, the lines between reality and the virtual world blur. On YouTube you can find videos that splice together clips from recruitment commercials, video game commercials, and real-life imagery, and it is nearly impossible to tell the difference between the three. This push-and-pull between the reality of war and the world of play seems to be culminating in the world of boy culture, and until commercials and video game characters are able to talk back to the viewer, boys have very little space to be critical and ask important questions such as how real are video games, and how true are the images in a recruitment advertisement?

Further Reading

America's Army: Special Forces [Online March 2008]. The Official Army Game: America's Army Web site. < http://www.americasarmy.com/>
Canadian Forces Recruiting [Online March 2008]. Canadian Forces. <http://www.forces.ca/v3/engraph/home/home.aspx?bhcp=1>
Cooper, Marc. "Lights! Camera! Attack! Hollywood Enlists." *The Nation*, December 10, 2001.
Costa, Dan. "This is No Video Game." *PC Magazine*, October, 16, 2007.
Grossman, Lev. "The Army's Killer App." *Time*, February, 28, 2007.

Nicole Fiore

Rambo

John Rambo is a fictional American soldier created by David Morrell in his 1972 novel *First Blood* and portrayed by Sylvester Stallone in four action films: *First Blood* (1982), *Rambo: First Blood, Part II* (1985), *Rambo III* (1988), and *Rambo* (2008). Rambo is a highly trained Green Beret, a Medal of Honor recipient suffering from post-traumatic stress incurred during his imprisonment and torture in a Vietnamese prisoner of war camp. The novel and especially the movies have been popular with American boys.

The Rambo character of the *First Blood* novel differs markedly from that of the films. Rambo is not given a first name in the novel, which is set in Kentucky immediately after the character's release from a Veteran's Administration hospital where he has been recovering following his imprisonment, torture, and escape in Southeast Asia. The first film's setting is in the Pacific Northwest and the first name, John, is provided the character who is trekking across the United States seeking members of his old squad, all of whom have died either during the war or afterwards from war-related illnesses such as cancer caused by exposure to American chemical weapons (Agent Orange). Author Morrell has stated that Rambo is named after the Rambo apple and the French poet Arthur Rimbaud (pronounced Ram-beau). However, the name also reflects Real American Boy, as well.

In both the novel and the first film, Rambo is harassed as a vagrant by overzealous local law enforcement who drive him over the edge. He takes to the hills and retaliates as first the police and then the National Guard attempt to track him down. Though the first film contains much violence, only one character dies, and that death is accidental (a rock Rambo throws at a helicopter cracks its windshield, causing the aircraft to veer suddenly and pitch a sniper shooting at Rambo to his death). In the novel Rambo kills a couple dozen cops, civilians, and soldiers who are hunting him.

The novel reveals that Rambo was physically abused by his father as a child. The film ends with Rambo arrested after being subdued by his former commander, Colonel Trautman (portrayed by Richard Crenna). An alternate ending of the film, in which Rambo grabs Trautman's shotgun, causing it to discharge and kill him, proved unpopular with early 1980s audiences and was scrapped. The novel ends with Trautman blowing Rambo's head off with a shotgun, an ending Morrell had to address in his novelization of *First Blood Part II.*

With the release of the second and third films, Rambo had become an action hero icon brimming with conservative political implications. "Ronbo" posters and t-shirts featuring then President Ronald Reagan's head on Stallone's chiseled machine-gun wielding body appeared. In *Rambo: First Blood, Part II,* Trautman wins Rambo's release from a federal penitentiary in order for the warrior to parachute into Vietnam and search out American prisoners of war being held since the end of the conflict. The enemies in this 1985 film include the Vietnamese army, their Soviet advisors, and the armchair officer/bureaucrat who stymies Rambo's efforts to free American POWs. Three years later in the third movie, Rambo leaves Thailand where he's been making a living as a stick fighter and journeys to Afghanistan. Aided by the Mujahedin he rescues Trautman from his Soviet captors.

Twenty years separate the release of the third and fourth films. Once again living in Thailand and working as a poisonous snake handler, Rambo leads an international team of mercenaries into Myanmar (referred to as Burma throughout the film) to rescue a group of Christian mercenaries he had earlier reluctantly ferried upriver to aid beleaguered Karen villagers. The film ends with Rambo returning to the United States to his father's horse-farm in Arizona.

Certain themes run throughout the films. Extremely high body counts and powerful weapons mark the later three movies. Rambo's armaments of choice include an enormous survival knife (which he tosses away in a deleted scene of the fourth film, only to forge his own foot-plus long machete); a compound bow complete with explosive tipped arrows; and an M-60 machine gun, which he carries around festooned with links of ammunition. The M-60 is a nearly 25-pound weapon usually serviced by a crew of three soldiers and fired from the ground on a bipod or mounted on a vehicle. Though some soldiers are strong enough to fire and control it from the shoulder, Rambo routinely fires it from his hip. In the fourth film Rambo commanders a .50-caliber jeep-mounted machine gun to terrible effect on the Burmese army. In an extra accompanying the fourth film, it is explained that Stallone (who also wrote and directed this film) was going to bodily heft the 120-pound .50-cal. unit until it was decided this was too unrealistic.

Women play noticeably minor roles in the series. Rambo's love interest in the second film, a Vietnamese warrior guide who he was planning to take back to America with him, is cut down at his side in battle. Also, an attraction between Rambo and a much younger female Christian missionary never develops beyond a platonic relationship, though Rambo risks life and limb and massacres a couple 100 Burmese soldiers to prevent her rape and save her once she is taken captive.

Throughout the films Rambo morphs from a patriotic American serving his country to the embodiment of an aristocratic warrior ethos. In the second film he tells Trautman that he fought in Vietnam to win the love of his country. Trautman, in turn in *Rambo III*, tells Rambo that he must come full circle and not deny what he was born to be, a warrior. By the fourth film Stallone makes clear that the Rambo character kills for neither God nor country but for himself, that when pushed he reverts to what he does best and that his wars and his country's wars are outlets for his warrior nature.

Further Reading

Morrell, David. *First Blood.* New York: Grand Central Publishing, 1972.
Morrell, David. *Rambo: First Blood, Part II.* USA: Arrow Books, Ltd., 1985.
Morrell, David, Sylvester Stallone, and Sheldon Lettich. *Rambo III.* USA: Jove, 1988.

Tony Monchinski

The Simpsons

The Simpsons is the longest-running sitcom and animated television series in the United States. Created by Matt Groening and debuting in 1989, the show broke ground as a cartoon that targeted adults as well as children. It is one of the most popular of the satirical cartoons parodying the working- to middle-class American family (*The Flintstones, The Jetsons, Family Guy, King of the Hill*). The longevity and popularity of the series can be attributed to its sharp and clever writing, its loveably flawed characters, and its many references to popular culture.

Before *The Simpsons* began its prime time half-hour weekly spot on the Fox Broadcasting Company's station, it ran for three years as a series of shorts on the *Tracey Ullman Show.* As of 2009, it has garnered 25 prime time Emmy awards and was voted by *Time* magazine as "the best TV show of the 20th century" (Corliss, 1998). A film version, *The Simpsons Movie,* was released in 2007 by Twentieth Century-Fox Film Corporation and nominated for a Golden Globe Award for best animated film.

Main Characters

The series centers around the Simpsons family living in a fictional town called Springfield. The family comprises Homer and Marge Simpson and their 2.5 children. Homer is the clumsy, crude, lazy, beer-drinking, overweight, and working-class father. Marge is the caring, grounded, and long-suffering housewife. Bart Simpson, the perennial 10-year-old, took on the series' prominent role in its first three seasons as the original "underachiever and proud of it" child. His behaviors are a result of a mischievous and quick mind, a possible case of attention-deficit disorder, and an easily manipulated father. Bart's sister, eight-year-old Lisa, is his opposite: academically oriented, extremely gifted and intelligent, often teased by the popular girls in her class, and a social activist with a strong moral and ethical foundation. Maggie (Margaret) Simpson is the baby of the family. She is generally seen and heard sucking on a pacifier.

Recurring Characters

With the extensive run-length of the series, a number of recurring characters, all based on caricatures of common stereotypes, have evolved into memorable cultural personas. Abraham "Grampa" Simpson parodies the senior citizen. Patty and Selma Bouvier are Marge's twin sisters, avid fans of the television series *MacGyver* and the quintessential in-laws who openly despise Homer. Ned Flanders is the Simpson's next door neighbor and Homer's unknowing rival, a devout, trusting and naïve Christian. Montgomery Burns, Homer's boss, is the rich and villainous owner of the Springfield Nuclear Power Plant. Waylon Smithers is Mr. Burns' personal assistant—a parody of the closeted homosexual, Waylon is secretly in love with his boss. Chief Wiggum is the bungling and obese police chief. Dr. Hibbert is the proficient African American doctor who chuckles condescendingly at mostly inappropriate times. Principal Seymour Skinner is the ineffective and uptight school principal and bureaucrat with a military background. And Apu Nahasapeemapetilon is the Indian owner of the Kwik-e-Mart convenience store, a man who holds a doctorate in computer science and a tireless work ethic.

Stylings and Settings

The voice actors of the show have become uncommonly well-known for their portrayals of Simpsons characters, in particular: Dan Castellaneta as Homer, Grampa, and Krusty the Clown; Julie Kavner as Marge; Hank Azaria as Apu, Moe, and Chief Wiggum; Nancy Cartwright as Bart; and Harry Shearer as Montgomery Burns, Waylon Smithers, Ned Flanders, and Principal Skinner. Phil Hartman played the characters Troy McClure and Lionel Hutz until his death in 1998, at which point the two characters were retired.

The Simpsons has its own distinctive style of animation. The characters' appearances evolved over the first three seasons, but kept their characteristic crude style: heads with no jaw lines, geometric hairstyles, and bright yellow skin. Homer's appearance (bald head, occasionally obese physique, and appetite for doughnuts) as well as Marge's (a beehive mountain of blue hair) are celebrated symbols from the series.

The storylines are generally set in Springfield, often in the Simpsons' home (742 North Evergreen Terrace), the Springfield Elementary School, or the Springfield Nuclear Power Plant, where Homer works as a safety inspector.

Cultural References

One of the series' trademarks is its many guest appearances by eminent celebrities and personalities. Dustin Hoffman played Mr. Bergstrom, the teacher who recognizes Lisa's talents and inspires her to develop a crush on him in "Lisa's Substitute." Meryl Streep played Jessica Lovejoy, the Reverend's manipulative daughter, in "Bart's Girlfriend." Jackie Mason appeared as Krusty the Clown's disapproving father, the Rabbi Krustofski, in "Like Father, Like Clown." Rodney Dangerfield played Montgomery Burns' ungainly son, Larry Burns, in "Burn, Baby Burns." Stephen Hawking played himself in "They Saved Lisa's Brain," as did Tony Blair in "The Regina Monologues." Famous musical guests have included: The Ramones, Aerosmith, Red Hot Chili Peppers, The Smashing Pumpkins, and U2.

The series' characters' catch phrases have also entered into the cultural vernacular, most famously Homer's "D'oh!," Burns' "Excellent," Nelson's "Ha-ha," Ned Flanders' "Okeleedokelee," and of course, Bart's "Ay, caramba!," "Don't have a cow, man!," and "Eat my shorts!"

Bart Simpson

Bart Simpson has taken a significant role in defining what it means to be a boy in the past 20 years. Bart is no doubt a cultural icon and likely the most popular of the mischievous cartoon boys, such as Dennis the Menace, Eric Cartman, and Calvin from *Calvin and Hobbes.* Especially during the series' early years, the storylines focused on Bart. His rebellious, disrespectful, and trouble-making behaviors contributed to the show's controversial reputation, leading parent groups to lobby against children watching the series for fear they be influenced by what was considered a poor role model. The intensity of these petitions dissipated since the early days of the series, and in 1998, Bart was voted 46th in a list of the "100 most influential people of the 20th century," being the sole fictional character in that list.

Bart's speech and appearance are distinctive. His voice is played by Nancy Cartwright, who originally auditioned for Lisa's role. Bart's hair is spiky (unless he's trying to impress a girl), and he is almost always seen wearing a red T-shirt, blue shorts, and blue-and-white running shoes.

In addition to his famous catchphrases ("Ay, caramba!" and "Eat my shorts!"), the opening sequence of each episode shows Bart at the blackboard in his fourth-grade classroom writing lines, such as: "I will not skateboard in the halls," "I will not instigate revolution," "I will not Xerox my butt," "They are laughing at me, not with me," "I will not hide behind the Fifth Amendment," "I am not a dentist," "I will not torment the emotionally frail," "Funny noises are not funny." Bart is also known for repeatedly making prank phone calls to Moe at Moe's Tavern ("Hi, I'm looking for Amanda . . . Amanda Hug N' Kiss").

Bart is a devoted fan of Krusty the Clown—although Krusty has disappointed Bart on occasion ("Bart Gets Famous"). Still, Bart comes to Krusty's rescue twice ("Krusty Gets Busted" and "Krusty Gets Kancelled"). Bart is also a fan of *The Itchy and Scratchy Show*, a gruesome, violent cartoon on the *Krusty the Clown Show*, which parodies the cartoon industry and its writing staff.

However, Bart's viewers are devoted to him because they know that underneath the bad boy persona lies a good heart. As with most long-running programs, Bart evolved from a one-dimensional troublemaker to a more developed and complex personality. In "Lisa on Ice" (1994), Bart faces Lisa in a fierce sibling and hockey rivalry. With four seconds left in the tied game, Bart is set to take a penalty shot on goaltender Lisa. But they each have sudden flashbacks of loving times together and throw their equipment aside to embrace. Lisa may have referred to Bart as "the devil's cabana boy" ("Bart's Girlfriend") but we know their sibling love endures.

And although Bart is loathed by his teachers and nearly fails grade 4 ("Bart Gets an F"), we understand that this is due to a lack of effort—with some insinuations of attention deficit disorder ("Brother's Little Helper"), later refuted—rather than due to a lack of intelligence. In fact, in addition to having an agile mind for mischief, Bart speaks nearly perfect French, Spanish, and Japanese.

Bart's best friend is the nerdy and gullible Milhouse Van Houten. Bart's character is also distinguished from the other boy characters in the show, including the bullies Nelson Muntz and Jimbo Jones; the academically inclined class nerd Martin Prince, who carries pens in his shirt pocket; Ralph Wiggums, the oddball and learning-challenged son of the police chief; and Rod and Todd Flanders, the wholesome Christian sons of Ned Flanders.

With its intelligent writing, memorable characters, and pop culture references, *The Simpsons* has exerted an enormous influence on North American culture. That's 420 episodes and still running—"Ay, caramba!"

Further Reading

Blackboard Openings. *The Simpsons* Archive. Retrieved June 20. http://www.snpp.com/guides/chalkboard.openings.html.

Corliss, Richard. The Time 100: Bart Simpson. *Time Magazine,* June 8, 1998. Retrieved June 28, 2008. http://www.time.com/time/time100/artists/profile/simpson.html.

Gray, Jonathan (2006). *Watching with* The Simpsons: *Television, Parody, and Intertextuality.* New York; London: Routledge.

Malone, Michael (2007). "The Simpsons Do America." *Station to Station,* July 23, 2007. Retrieved June 23. http://www.vtnews.vt.edu/story.php?relyear=2003&itemno=77.

Turner, Chris (2004). *Planet Simpson: How a Cartoon Masterpiece Defined a Genera-tion.* Cambridge, MA: Da Capo Press.

Sandra Chang-Kredl

South Park

Eric Cartman's call to power—"Respect my authorita-a-ay!"—sets the tone for *South Park,* the satirically irreverent Comedy Central cartoon series created by Matt Stone and Trey Parker. Not only does the show depict the antics of four boys, but it is also hugely popular with male audiences.

Premiering in 1997, *South Park* is known for its vulgarity (shit was said a total of 162 times in the episode "It Hits the Fan") and its provocative paro-dying of celebrities (Paris Hilton in "Stupid Spoiled Whore Video Playset" and Tom Cruise in "Trapped in the Closet"), religion ("Jewbilee"); sexuality ("Mr. Garrison's Fancy New Vagina"); disabilities ("Krazy Kripples" and "Le Petit Tourette"); sex education ("Proper Condom Use"); race ("With Apologies to Jesse Jackson"); and environmentalism ("Smug Alert!")—in other words, no subject is sacred in the hands of Matt Stone and Trey Parker.

In the Beginning, There Was Jesus vs. Frosty

Stone and Parker met at the University of Colorado where Stone studied film and mathematics and Parker majored in music. In 1992, while at the univer-sity, they created an animated short called *The Spirit of Christmas: Jesus vs. Frosty.* Comedy Central picked up on this short and asked Stone and Parker to create a series based on the prototype. *South Park* debuted as a weekly series on Comedy Central in 1997 with its first episode "Cartman Gets an Anal Probe." With the success of the series, Parker and Stone released a feature length film musical in 1999, *South Park: Bigger, Longer & Uncut,* to critical acclaim.

Each episode is created through computer animation techniques, but pur-posely maintains the choppy, amateurish look of its prototype, which was originally produced through construction paper and cutout animation tech-niques. A refined end product is not Stone and Parker's goal. The two write, direct, and edit each episode, mostly within a tight six-day production sched-ule, claiming (a) that they are only funny under this type of pressure and (b) that if you think about a joke for too long, you start to hate it.

Watching South Park

South Park is the number 1 cable television program for males 18–34 and third-highest for adults 18–49 (Time Warner Cable, 2008). The program is rated for mature audiences (18 and above) and each episode begins with this tongue-in-cheek disclaimer:

All characters and events in this show—even those based on real peo-ple—are entirely fictional. All celebrity voices are impersonated . . . poorly.

The following program contains coarse language and due to its content it should not be viewed by anyone.

However, it is well-known that teens and pre-teens regularly view the program. *South Park*'s first 11 seasons have been released on DVD, and each episode can be viewed via the Internet.

South Park has been nominated for an Emmy Award seven times, winning in 2005 for the episode "Best Friends Forever" and in 2006 for "Make Love, Not Warcraft." The song "Blame Canada" from the movie *South Park: Bigger, Longer & Uncut,* was nominated for an Academy Award for best original song but lost to Phil Collins. In *South Park* style, Parker and Stone proceeded to lampoon Collins in two *South Park* episodes (in "Timmy 2000," Collins is depicted carrying his Oscar statue in every scene).

The *South Park* Boys

The four main characters in *South Park* are fourth graders who live in the fictional Colorado town of South Park. Stan Marsh, Kyle Broflovski, Eric Cartman, and Kenny McCormick are perennial students of Mr./Ms. Garrison. Since season 7, a fifth boy, Butters (Leopold "Butters" Scotch), has taken on a more central role as well. Each boy depicts a different representation of what a boy is. Stan and Kyle are the two straight men, Eric is the psychopathic antagonist, Kenny is something of a bystander friend, and Butters is the innocent child.

Stan Marsh, voiced by Trey Parker, is loosely designed as Parker's alter ego, with parents who share the same names as Parker's parents, Sharon and Randy. Stan is smart, sensible, and frequently questions adult behavior. In the episode "Stanley's Cup," Stan coaches a peewee hockey team and is expected to save a boy with cancer by leading his kindergarten team to victory over the Detroit Red Wings. When the Red Wings bloody up the preschoolers on the ice, Stan cries in futile protest as the adults in the crowd cheer on. His sensitivity is depicted through his ongoing relationship with his crush, Wendy Testaburger. Each time Wendy speaks to him, he can't help but throw up. Stan almost exclusively wears a brown jacket and red-trimmed blue hat with red pom-pom.

Kyle Broflovski is Stan's best friend—and Matt Stone's alter ego— with parents named after Stone's parents, Sheila and Gerald. Kyle is intelligent, rational, and a good student. Most frustrated and morally outraged by Eric's antics, he is usually able to use his wits to come out on top. Eric frequently refers to Kyle as a Jew, and Kyle calls Eric "fat ass." Kyle's mother, Sheila, is always ready to take up an issue with the school or community, earning her the song "Kyle's Mom is a Bitch." Kyle usually wears an orange jacket and his wild curly red hair is hidden under his green ear-flapped hat.

Eric Cartman is the lewd, foul-mouthed, racist, sexist, self-indulgent, and overweight boy who occasionally dresses as Adolf Hitler and is probably the most often quoted animated character in contemporary television: "Respect my authority!," "No kitty, that's my pot pie!" He carries a distinct loathing toward hippies ("Die, Hippie. Die"), and frequently teases Kenny for being poor ("Too bad drinking scotch isn't a paying job or Kenny's dad would be a millionaire!") and Kyle for being Jewish. His talents include an uncanny business acumen ("Cartmanland" and "Kenny Dies") and an ability to manipulate his mother ("But mo-o-om!").

Eric plays a central role in many episodes as the main antagonist to Kyle and Stan. Kyle and Stan frequently wonder why they play with him, but Eric is the foil, the necessary evil whose antics set off many of the episodes. One of Eric's worst moments is in "Scott Tenorman Must Die," in which he gets back at ninth grader Scott Tenorman for humiliating him by killing Scott's parents, cooking them in chili for a chili cookoff, and then mocking Scott for eating his parents. An interesting mental idiosyncrasy of Eric's is that anytime he hears a part of Styx's "Come Sail Away," he is compelled to finish singing the entire song, a weakness that Kyle takes advantage of. Eric is frequently seen wearing a red jacket and a yellow-trimmed blued hat; however, of the four boys, he is the one who goes hatless the most.

Kenny McCormick is a boy from the lower-class family who, in the first five seasons, was killed in some violent fashion each episode (followed each time by Stan and Kyle's well-known catchphrases: "Oh my God! They killed Kenny!," "You bastards") and resurrected each following episode. Kenny "permanently" died from a muscular disease at the end of the fifth season. Stone and Parker explained that they grew tired of having to kill him off creatively each episode. When Kenny returned in season seven, he seldom died. Kenny's trademark is his unintelligible speech (that only his friends can understand). His head is mostly muffled by the orange parka hood he wears, even on his hospital deathbed. Regularly teased by Eric for his poverty, Kenny has a prolific sexual understanding, and we can infer that much of his incomprehensible speech is of a highly sexual content.

Butters (Leopold "Butters" Scotch) has progressively taken on a more central role in the series. His trademarks are his tuft of blond unruly hair, aqua blue jacket, trusting grin, Southern accent, and a sweet, trusting disposition. At times Butters is capable of profound observations. For example, in "Raisins," he notes that "[t]he only way I could feel this sad now is if I felt something really good before . . . So I guess what I'm feeling is like a beautiful sadness." Butters' parents are exceedingly strict with him, and he has become a particular target and friend for Eric Cartman.

Other boy characters include Token Black, the only Black child who is mocked not for being Black but for being rich. Jimmy Vulver is a physically disabled boy who wears braces, walks on crutches, stutters, and likes to perform stand-up comedy routines. Timmy is a cognitively and physically disabled boy who typically is heard yelling, "Timmy!" He reached fame in "Timmy 2000," when he is recruited as lead singer in the band Timmy and the Lords of the Underworld, taking Phil Collins' place as headliner of Lalapalalapaza. Tweek Tweak is a jittery, nervous child whose parents feed him coffee. Tweek often screams, "GAH!" and "Too much pressure!"

And the girls? Well, it seems that the South Park boys had something in common with Freud: women are a mystery to them. In the episode "Marjorine," Cartman shows the boys a videotape he took of the girls playing with a paper fortune teller, and they, the boys, are convinced that the girls hold a secret power to tell the future. And in "Bebe's Boobs Destroy Society," the boys respond to their classmate Bebe's developing breast by acting like cavemen.

South Park: Controversies and Appeal

Integral to *South Park* is its controversial and insistent pushing of limits of taste and acceptability. The show has been protested against by various groups, including the Parents Television Council, who criticized its provocative material, calling its content offensive. Stone and Parker, however, describe themselves as "equal opportunity offenders." It may be the satirical humor, the controversial material, the characters, the pushing of borders, but whatever it is, *South Park*'s appeal is wide-ranging and strong.

"So come on down to South Park and meet some friends of mine."

Further Reading

Gillespie, Nick and Jesse Walker. "South Park Libertarians: Trey Parker and Matt Stone on Liberals, Conservatives, Censorship, and Religion." *Reason Magazine.* December 2006.

Leonard, Devin. "'South Park' Creators Haven't Lost Their Edge." *Fortune Magazine.* March 2008. http://money.cnn.com/magazines/fortune/fortune_archive/2006/10/30/8391792/index.htm.

Otto, Jeff. "Interview: Trey Parker and Matt Stone." *IGN Movies.* March 2008. http://movies.ign.com/articles/612/612094p1.html.

Poniewozik, James. "10 Questions for Matt Stone and Trey Parker." *Time.* March 5, 2006.

Topel, Fred. "The Puppet Masters." *Wave Magazine.* March 2008. http://animatedtv.about.com/gi/dynamic/offsite.htm?zi=1/XJ/Ya&sdn=animatedtv&cdn=entertainment&tm=381&gps=323_337_1228_841&f=00&tt=14&bt=1&bts=1&zu=http%3A//www.thewavemag.com/pagegen.php%3Fpagename%3Darticle%26articleid%3D25326.

Sandra Chang-Kredl

Star Wars

What started as a movie has expanded to create a universe. The story that began with the battle of Luke Skywalker against the evil Darth Vader "a long time ago in a galaxy far away" has become a multimedia phenomenon and as such serves as a vehicle for boys' identity development through movies, role-playing games, toys, books, and other print media. *Star Wars* has been called a "boy's movie" but it is more than that: it was an iconographic, life-changing media event. It is a synthesis of American myth and archetype in a science fiction universe. The saga incorporates the appeal of the outlaw western with the discipline of the samurai. Every boy can be the hero of this tale—a Jedi Knight, with a trip to the local toy store for that indispensable Jedi weapon, the collapsible light saber. The light saber, like the samurai's sword, embodies the ethos of hero and transformed swordplay and dueling games with the electric buzz of that unique creation. *It is your destiny—feel the power of the Force!*

To the extent that boy culture is a commercial culture, *Star Wars* has been an inescapable phenomenon. The first generation of fans was created between 1977 and 1983 with the first trilogy, and then created anew with the prequel trilogy from 1999–2005. *Star Wars* created a peer culture, important to finding a common ground for cooperative play. Boys on any school playground can engage in play based on the shared knowledge of the culture, artifacts, and language of the *Star Wars* universe. The themes acted out, whether in group or solitary play, may function as fairy tales did for an earlier generation: to give force, context, and meaning to unconscious fears of danger, death, and the unknown.

As a story, a work of fiction, or a narrative, the saga, when internalized, affects identity; as a merchandising phenomenon, the saga affects play. Boys' play toys separated from familiar reality-based objects in the 1980s and spun off into fantasy, largely through the impact of movies and comic books. Fantasy toys are based on merchandised characters and stories, quite the opposite of fantasy. Comic strips and movies provide the narrative for escape and the types for the characters involved. Modern children don't create their own fantasies but adapt those given to them through the mass media. *Stars Wars* pushed innovation in the toy line as well as in film production. George Lucas essentially revolutionized the action-figure toy by inventing the 3-4 inch figurine. Reduced from 12 inches like the standard G.I. Joe, the smaller scale and lower cost allowed Star Wars and Kenner Toys to produce a wide range of individual characters, which made it possible to recreate favorite scenes and episodes from the movies and to engage in creative role playing, set building, and alternative story lines. The small scale also provided for the many extra star ships, creatures, and play sets to accompany the characters. *Star Wars* toys are identified in three releases corresponding to the original movies. Classic Star Wars toys were produced from 1977 through 1985 and are prized by collectors. Neo-classic Star Wars were produced from 1990 through 2000, and the Prequel collection spans from 1999 to 2008. With *Star Wars*, George Lucas created the modern media franchise. The licensing of characters allows for creative control by the corporations that own the images, like Lucas, and they create and sustain a fan base through their products. Science fiction figures, created with *Star Wars*, were warriors in fantasy world setting unlike prior war toys such as G.I. Joes and army men that glorified real war.

The *Star Wars* saga began with the release of *Star Wars* in 1977. Now identified as *Episode IV—A New Hope*, it was followed by *Episode V—The Empire Strikes Back,* in 1980. *Episode VI—Return of the Jedi,* released in 1983, concluded the Original Trilogy. This was the saga as known to the first generation of fans, primarily boys aged from 12 to 16 when the series began. What became know as the Prequel Trilogy would not be seen until 1999. The 16-year gap between the series would be filled with novels, comics, and video games replaying the trilogy and filling in the Expanded Universe of side stories and minor characters. Then finally, *Episode I—the Phantom Menace* was released in 1999, followed by *Episode II—Attack of the Clones* in 2002, and completing the cycle with

Episode III—Revenge of the Sith in 2005. But this was not the end; the Expanded Universe continues with additional series of books and graphic novels. *Star Wars: Clone Wars: 2003–2005*, an animated television series produced by the Cartoon Network studio, is set chronologically between Episode II and Episode III and is available on DVD. At least 200 novels are set in the *Star Wars* universe. Encyclopedias, guides, documentaries, other reference works, role-playing books, graphic novels, comics, and children's books totaling well over 1,500 titles have been published since 1991. There are also at least 50 video game titles for all gaming platforms. *The Clone Wars,* a 3D CGI animated series produced by LucasFilm Animation, was recently released and will be followed by the creation of 100 television episodes.

The extent of its influence may be seen in the obvious merchandise likely to be stashed in some part of every boy's room, but the influence can also be determined by the number of sayings that have entered our cultural lexicon: "The Evil Empire," "May the Force be with you," "You don't know the power of the dark side," "No, I am your father!," " Do, or do not, there is no try," "Let the Wookie win!," "You don't want to sell me death sticks . . . You want to go home and rethink your life," "I find your lack of faith disturbing," and many others.

The wide appeal of *Star Wars* speaks to the pervasiveness of fantasy and play. *Star Wars* toys, role playing with figurines, building race pods or x-wing fighters with LEGO, attacking the Death Star on Game Boy or in computer games, and battling your friends with light sabers, these are the modern forms of play, discovery, and transformation enabled by a common cultural experience, even if it is a manufactured one.

Further Reading

Brooker, Will. *Using the Force: Creativity, Community, and Star Wars Fans*. New York: Continuum, 2002.

Cross, Gary. *Kid's Stuff: Toys and the Changing World of American Childhood*. Cambridge: Harvard University Press, 1997.

Glenn Kenny, ed. *A Galaxy Not so Far Away: Writers and Artists on Twenty-Five Years of Star Wars*. New York: Henry Holt, 2002.

Matthew Wilhelm Kapell and John Shelton Lawrence, eds. *Finding the Force of the Star Wars Franchise: Fans, Merchandise & Critics*. New York: Peter Lang, 2006.

George H. Thompson

Television and Boys of All Ages

TV has always highlighted boys as the central focus in family comedies and dramas. Although other family members were indeed on screen, often a boy (or boys) from the family dominated the screen and focus of attention. Many television shows have revolved around the son, brother, or wayward male cousin from the early 1950s, and boys continue to be the centerpiece of many television shows in the twenty-first century. Globally, the theme of family is predominant in TV shows, and how that family circulates around a boy is often the main plot. Girl characters, whether toddlers, children, tweens, or teens, often rotate around the boy characters, much like orbiting moons to a planet. Along with the traditional boy, from infancy through the teenage years, television constructs another boy, the *dad-boy,* who is a father with many of the characteristics of a boy.

TV boys come in different class structures—urban, suburban, and rural homes— and with or without parents; but in all cases, they do have certain elements in common. Unlike many other characters in family television shows, young male characters have more screen time than other characters. They are "named" personalities—the audience remembers them and often identifies with them. These male characters are the link between the audience and the screen, exhibiting a *wink-wink/nudge-nudge* relationship with the viewer—as if the TV kid was aware that he was both a performer and an audience member. Another television "boy" is the family dad. If the TV show didn't have a visible son/brother/male cousin/next door neighbor character, then often the dad becomes the "boy who never grew up"; some shows contain both the boy and the dad as boy. This *dad-boy* gets into trouble, is impish, usually gets caught doing something bad, and is then disciplined by female characters.

Middle-class Television Boys and Dad-Boys

There wouldn't be television families without television fathers (this is not the case for mothers, as you will find later in this section). From the inception of television, the paterfamilias has been the nucleus of family comedy and drama. In 1952, *The Adventures of Ozzie and Harriet* (*TAOH*) premiered on ABC and aired for 14 years on primetime. Advertised as "America's favorite family," *The Adventures of Ozzie and Harriet* presented an audience-eye view of the famous Nelson performing family. Ozzie, Harriet, David, and Ricky Nelson entered American homes each week with smiles, white angst, and picket-fence dilemmas. Ozzie Nelson, a well-known musician and man-about-entertainment was the center of the family, a dopey dad, always engaged in family affairs, but never quite getting what was going on. Harriet Nelson, Ozzie's former singer turned pearl-laden TV mom, was the voice of rationality and sensibility; always dressed in, well, a dress, Harriet had ironed tablecloths, sit-down dinners, and answers to all issues. David was the not-so-smart older brother, sort of plodding, and a foil for Ricky's antics. And Ricky, not surprisingly, was the impish, cute little brother who knew the answers to everything. America's family literally grew up on television, and viewers invested thousands of hours on the Nelson family.

Ricky's character is an early example of the "know it all" kid who is smarter than his parents and even his older brother. David is an even-tempered character, less likely to get into trouble, and plays to both the grownups and kid brother in the family. Along with David and Ricky, the dad-boy, Ozzie, is seen as an over-grown boy, goofy and bumbling, and often in trouble. Between Ricky and Ozzie, the Nelson men were boys' boys, and the show featured music, especially early rock 'n' roll as a key part of the show as Ricky grew up.

Indeed, Ricky Nelson grew up to be one of rock 'n' roll's earliest legends, and it all began on the television, complete with screaming girls rocking out to Ricky's music at the end of many episodes.

The Nelsons' neighborhood had its cadre of zany neighbors, regular guys, moral-seeking plots, and great kids who came to great parties with the great Nelson parents making great hamburgers and drinking great cokes. The Nelsons did not nag, nor did they try to control the youngsters. Parents discussed issues with the youth, and if either dad or son made a faux pas, resolutions came through humor and logic. Truly, the Nelsons were America's first family, the perfect family. The adventures of the Nelsons were often viewed through the eye of Ricky, the youngest, but obviously the smartest Nelson— somehow, Ricky managed to get things done without getting caught, as opposed to Ozzie, who was always caught red-handed.

Closely following the success of the Nelsons, *Father Knows Best* premiered on CBS in 1954. Originally a radio program, *Father Knows Best* situated the Anderson family in a similar suburban neighborhood as the Nelsons, and imitated similar plot lines to *The Adventures of Ozzie and Harriet,* centering on Mom Margaret and Dad-boy Jim Anderson and the kids. The title misleads the audience with an ironic twist, as it is Mom who usually knows best. Bumbling through life with platitudes and bad advice, Robert Young as Dad manages to be saved continually by his wife's logical worldview. The three children were the outrageous younger daughter and boy-crazy Betty ("Princess"), accompanied by son, Bud (Jim Jr.), not the smartest boy in the world, and irritating but cute Kathy ("Kitten"). The children got into scrapes, but it was Dad who seemed to be the foil in many of the plots, and who never really knew best.

The Donna Reed Show debuted in 1958 and ran through March, 1966, creating a teenage heartthrob in Paul Peterson's character Jeff Stone. A typical TV family, the Stone parents comprised Alex, a pediatrician, and Donna, a housewife. Although the show featured Donna Reed, it was Paul Peterson, and Shelley Fabares (who played sister Mary) who became household names, and, like Ricky Nelson, early novelty rock 'n' roll stars. Not particularly unique, the program was another family comedy that dealt with the loves and losses of teenagers, of dating angst, and of having a smarter sister and a bit of a slacker in brother Jeff.

Generations of viewers will be familiar with *The Dick Van Dyke Show,* which did not begin as a "family" comedy, but still maintained the similar family patterns. CBS aired this successful comedy from 1961–1966. Few can forget the bumbling Rob Petrie, played by Van Dyke, and his sensible, worrying wife, Laura, played by Mary Tyler Moore. While the family was childless for the first seasons, Rob and Laura re-inscribed the traditional TV family roles as bumbling dad and logical, sane mom. When they did become parents, the roles magnified and the Petries became an important television institution. Rob is an eternal dad-boy. Although a married man, he never strays from his boyish nature and ability to get into trouble. Laura will be remembered by her constant expression—"Oh, Rob!"—in response to his latest dad-boy antics.

While the first Hollywood family shows were comedies, they were followed by hour-long family dramas, which were patterned upon their humorous counterparts. ABC's *Family* was a suburban drama, which aired from 1976–1980; a midseason replacement, the show quickly became popular for viewers of all ages. *Family* was a unique program in that the storylines tackled significant issues within the plots. Set in Pasadena, the Lawrence family consisted of Dad Doug (James Broderick) and Mom, Kate (Sada Thompson). The three children were often featured, and Kristy McNichol's character, Buddy, became a teen star. *Family* marked somewhat of a departure from silly/stupid dads and deceit, to more real problems and challenges confronted by a suburban, middle-class family. Still very white and without money problems in its context, the show was critically acclaimed, winning many dramatic awards. Mom Kate remained the stalwart voice of sensibility through her daughter's divorce, son Willie's having a gay best friend, and Buddy's experiences with the homophobic behavior of her school (firing her lesbian teacher). As matriarch, Kate exhibited a strong leadership role in the family, supported by Doug. *Family* created co-parenting roles in Doug and Kate, roles that have seldom been replicated in network television.

Building on *Family's* success, ABC followed with Dick Van Patten in *Eight Is Enough*. Capitalizing on the overwhelming idea of large families, the family lived in an ample suburban home, and the show aired from 1977–1981. Van Patten's character, Tom, was modeled after the newspaper columnist (who had eight children) Tom Braden. Tom was a more serious dad-boy, still leaning toward boyish behavior; he often would suppress his actions in favor of not getting into trouble. The popularity of a book by the same name encouraged ABC to create the show. Lacking any type of social statement, *Eight Is Enough* imitated the tried and true motifs of earlier family television with the goofy but loving dad, sensible mom, and antic-ridden children. The show's topics were safe and lacked the grit of the earlier *Family*. Again, as in previous family shows, the setting was a safely suburban Sacramento, and the home adequate, lacking nothing material.

NBC entered the family stage with the blockbuster *Family Ties* from 1982–1989. For the first time, the children usurped TV roles traditionally assigned to parents. The Keaton family, although middle-class and certainly suburban, consisted of former hippie parents dealing with children who were far more conservative than they were. Michael J. Fox, in his groundbreaking role as Alex Keaton, became the ultimate smart-mouthed son to his bumbling peacenik parents. Alex Keaton is a seminal television boy character. Ironically, the television show originally did not highlight Alex, but within a very short time, producers realized that he was the life of the show. Alex's role as a boy was unusual for a television boy, in that he was not the rebel; rather he was the stalwart stick-in-the-mud kid who kept his wild hippie parents and sisters in line. The ability to laugh at the upside-down political system gave the audience comic relief from the post-Nixon debacle and ushered them into the comforting Reagan years. Often acerbic, *Family Ties* challenged the notion that the children were the ones who needed reigning in.

Suburbanly urban, *The Cosby Show* burst into the scene in 1984 and ran on NBC until 1992. Reproducing suburban comfort, Brooklyn's Huxtables have been critiqued in a large body of work highlighting the first upscale Black family on network television. Although ostensibly set in Brooklyn, the lack of urban challenges is apparent throughout the show. The luxurious brownstone could be Anywhere, USA, but Cliff and Clare Huxtable and their brood took television family to a new level. Although an OB-GYN, Cliff seldom seems to work; Clare's law practice also seems to run itself. Having inordinate amounts of time to interact their children, both parents have a propensity for inserting their opinions at every instant. Again, Dad is the bumbling, comic, and silly dad-boy; Clare, as the voice of reason and sanity, has the final say. The show revolved around Cliff, who does little more than act as a comic foil for the family. Along with Cliff, son Theo is a central male character in the program. Theo (played by Malcolm Jamal Warner) is a salt-of-the-earth type of kid, who is not the smartest of the siblings, but one who is socially aware—he is the strongest political character. Theo is the Black conscience of *The Cosby Show,* and often brings other family members around to acknowledge social issues such as inequities. Underplaying the obvious—that the Huxtables are indeed Black— the show chose to address race only in a peripheral sense; race was more about Martin Luther King Jr. Day or reggae music than about any challenges that Black families may face. Indeed, many scholars indicate that the show had little to do with race and class, but perpetuated the concept that *anyone* can make it in America, if they try. In the attempt to be a "normal family," the Huxtables created a mythical family unit, not only unbelievable for a Black family, but for any American family. Their lack of concern for finances, the ease of the parental vocations, and the compliance of all children create an unreal family depiction. Considered a comedy, the humor lacks originality, and Cliff continues to be the center of any laughs. Theo, as the television boy, remains a strong and ethical centerpiece to the series.

The mid-1980s into the 1990s produced a series of middle- to upper-class suburban comedies. ABC's *Growing Pains* (1985–1992) features the archetypical family themes: the befuddled Dr. Jason Seaver (Alan Thicke), who is the psychiatrist dad who works at home; Maggie Malone, who is Mom-with-her-maiden-name and a newspaper reporter; brainy Carol; the smart but bratty little Ben; and Mike, who is always in trouble. The traditional boy stereotypes played themselves out in *Growing Pains,* and family comedy re-ran the typical household dilemmas. Most interesting was the fact that Dad took care of the kids as Mom was out of the house.

Family Matters was set in Chicago that was, however, devoid of urban trappings. TV's second middle-class Black family focused on the father Carl Winslow, his wife Harriette, and their three children: Eddie (the rebellious one), Laura (the smart one), and little Judy. Viewers will probably remember *Family Matters* best through Steve "Urkel," the ultimate next-door neighbor. Carl is well-meaning, awkward, and pompous; his wife is sensible . . . you know the drill. *Family Matters* includes the dad-boy in Carl, the smart alecky Eddie, who rebels and keeps the family attentive, and the central character, Urkel, who is the boy-neighbor, constantly inserting himself into the home and family antics. Urkel is the more modern Maynard G. Krebs, the buddy, neighbor, friend who seems to have more of a home at the Winslow's—away from his own home.

The popularity of the traditional American family comedy and drama lies in their ability to make the regular appear as more regular on TV; the common more common on TV; the zany just a bit more zanier; the dad-boy really stupid; and the mom really sensible. Its popularity also lies in its inclusion of the elements of a regular household: the smartest kid in the neighborhood (usually boys); a brainy child (usually girls); and a loveable but inconsequential baby or two. Formulaic television families rarely deviate from these characters, and they appeal to American audiences who crave laughs arising from an insular point of view. The American TV family, for 40 years, definitely spoke to viewers seeking a validation of similar lives. However, these mainstream families rarely tackled issues that were on the minds of millions of viewers; it was working-class TV which broke that ground.

Poor and Working-Class Boys

Blue collar work has always been a theme in American media. Early radio dramas often dealt with poor and/or immigrant families. In 1955, television history was made when CBS launched *The Honeymooners.* Not a "family comedy" in the traditional sense, it is included in this chapter because *The Honeymooners* established the repeating themes and motifs that have been re-created for over half of a century in television families. Jacky Gleason's Ralph Kramden was a loud, simple bus driver who felt he was worth more, but certainly didn't prove that in intellect or ingenuity. Alice (Audrey Meadows) played the long-suffering, sensible wife to Ralph's chaos. Ralph and his best friend, Norton (played by Art Carney), were the ultimate grown-up television boys. Never considering the consequences, these dad-boys were continually in trouble, being boyish, and getting chided by their wife-mothers. These roles would be replicated in scores of television families, and many are, in essence, a homage to the original *Honeymooners.*

In 1957, ABC launched *The Real McCoys,* which ran through 1963. *The Real McCoys* were a multi-generational family from the mountains of West Virginia; they had moved to be dirt farmers in California. Grandpa McCoy was played by the eternal grandfather, Walter Brennan, and well-known actor Richard Crenna got his start as the grandson, Luke. The show was different from the family shows of the time, as the grandfather was apparently widowed, and Luke eventually also became a widower. Luke had a young sister, Hassie, and a little brother, Little Luke. Southern and folksy in nature, *The Real McCoys* was an *aw shucks,* often moralistic depiction of dignified poor people and their struggles. The show presented responsible boys in Luke and Little Luke, and many viewers enjoyed the positive role models these boys portrayed. However, role models and comedy don't particularly go together, and TV seems much more successful with mouthy, in-trouble boys and dad-boys.

Working-class television took the reign of programming with plant worker Archie Bunker's debut in 1971 in *All in the Family.* CBS hit the jackpot by casting Carroll O'Connor as the stubborn, bigoted, ignorant, and right-wing father, tempered by Edith "Dingbat" (Jean Stapleton), who was dense, chaotic, and "out there." Daughter Gloria (Sally Struthers) and son-in-law, Michael "Meathead," lived with the Bunkers in a tiny and humble home somewhere in Queens. Nothing was sacred to Archie's rants, sarcasm, anger, and indignation at being poor and working-class. Archie and Michael are the central figures, with Edith and Gloria in the orbiting female roles. Michael provides a counterpunch to Archie's dad-boy personality, and the tension within the family is between these males. Next-door neighbor, Lionel Jefferson, was a secondary character, but brought to TV a young Black youth with serious goals and attitudes much more advanced than Archie's or his own father, George's. With *All in the Family,* television families became politically involved and needled American family sensibility. Viewers quickly identified with members of the family, and even the most conservative of heart felt uncomfortable being cast as Archie. Creator Norman Lear successfully jabbed at the nation's innermost thoughts and made many statements.

Spinning off from *All in the Family* in 1975 was *The Jeffersons.* Archie Bunker had one problem with next-door neighbors George and Louise (Weezy) Jefferson—they were Black. However, Archie became even more outraged when the Jefferson family struck it rich and found themselves "movin' on out, to the Eastside, to a deee-luxe apartment in the sky." Again, a working-class television family brought politics, ethics, morals, and essential issues to the primetime screen via Norman Lear. George Jefferson is the quintessential dad-boy, hopping around, plotting, and getting caught; his boyish loudness and trouble making is constantly chided by Weezy and even Florence, their housekeeper. The Lear television family was harsh, severe, critical, and angry, but the anger was directed to a middle- and upper-class society in general. Television was beginning to make a social difference with these programs, and the family was the site of the sea changes; often it was the male characters that represented rebellion, confusion, or tension within society.

Another Black family moved into CBS territory from 1974 to 1979 to the projects of Chicago. *Good Times* takes place in the low-cost housing apartment of the Evans family. Spun from sitcom *Maude,* the mother, Florida Evans (Esther Rolle), a maid (housekeeper), is married to James, and they live cramped in a rented, humble pre-condo building with their children James Jr. "JJ" (Jimmie Walker), Thelma, and Michael. James is a hard-working man who can't always hold a job. His anger at this position in life is obvious, and as in Norman Lear's other family sitcoms, he is conscious of race and class—a departure from the lack of consciousness of race and class in the middle-class television families. Florida is level-headed, the hearth of the family; Thelma is, well, "the girl"; Jimmie (JJ) is the loud-mouthed comic; and Michael—you guessed it—is the genius with all the answers—the smart aleck. JJ is the nucleus of the Evans family, and his jokes, his mouth, and his physical presence command most of the half-hour episodes. When JJ is not on screen, which is seldom, Michael is often the voice of male reason and control. Even though *Good Times* is not unique in the stereotypes of family comedies, it is edgy and distinctly Black, poor, and working-class.

Family from the Boy's Point of View

One type of television family exists in spite of social class. Although many of the aforementioned shows contain a smart aleck kid, one who reflects the absurdity of parental voice, some TV family shows are created around the omniscient voice of a child. In 1957, Beaver Cleaver's ABC television family became iconic as the quintessential American unit in *Leave it to Beaver.* Airing for six seasons, the show dealt with the adventures of Theodore "Beaver," his parents—Ward and June—and brother Wally. The Cleavers lived in ubiquitous suburban house with two stories. June wore ironed full skirts and pearls, Ward carried a briefcase to and from work each day, and the boys got into scraps. Wally, although the eldest, was none-to-bright, and Beaver's point of view drove the show. Plots were simplistic and life was never difficult, and for over 60 years, American families have been compared to the Cleavers.

In 1959, CBS premiered *The Many Loves of Dobie Gillis,* a quirky teenage television show about a sweater-wearing high school boy (Dwayne Hickman) and his best friend, beatnik Maynard G. Krebs (Bob Denver who would grow to play *Gilligan*). This popular comedy lasted four years, and was narrated by Dobie Gillis, who made his way through life in a befuddled manner (preparing to be a dad-boy). Dobie's narration in the show would begin and end with him sitting in the park, hand on his chin, in deep thought; he would discuss the events of his day with the audience, and this "discussion," which included Dobie's antics and recurring dilemmas, brought a unique view to the viewers and engaged them in a personal manner. Maynard shadowed his best friend Dobie, and is one of TV's first representations of the counterculture in a mainstream environment. Dobie wanted to be popular and attractive to girls, yet never seemed to achieve his goals. His days were filled with many traumas that the audience, however, found hilarious. Maynard's attitude was much different than Dobie's; sloppy and proudly lazy, he saw life as just something to enjoy, to be "cool" about. Dobie's dad was very much a dad-boy, as he was constantly involved in scheming to get rich, and often landed in trouble. Both Dobie and his dad, Herbert, would end up realizing that life just needed to be lived, not manipulated. Many conversations between Dobie and Maynard are humorous, and reveal the teenaged angst that many males are unable to articulate. Two rich boys, Milton and Chatsworth, were Dobie's antagonists, and they always seemed to get what Dobie could only dream about.

Many catch phrases were immortalized by *The Many Loves of Dobie Gillis,* among them, Maynard's voice going high and exclaiming: "Work!" when anyone suggested doing anything constructive; and "You rang?"— Maynard's response when he walked into the scene. The two boys, Maynard and Dobie, created a prototype of boys as lazy best friends, along with many other memorable relationships.

The audience didn't clamor often for a kid's point of view, and in the ensuing years there were few examples of boy narrators. Finally in 1988, ABC premiered *The Wonder Years,* which ran for six years. The show took place 20 years before the current year, so its content covered the years 1968–1973. The series dealt with historical events and political/social concerns of the time. Kevin (Fred Savage) is the focus of the show and deals with his own growing-up challenges. An older Kevin (voice of Daniel Stern) narrates the show in retrospect and discusses his own feelings about what happened at the time, and how he learned from it. This reflective narrative voice allowed viewers to watch a boy and listen to his future voice.

In 1993, *Boy Meets World* became another ABC boy-narrated show, lasting seven years. Cory Matthews observes his young life and loving family—learning lessons and growing. The show continues depicting the sweetness of life as narrated by a young boy. Less sweet was ABC's short-lived, but critically-acclaimed *My So-called Life.* Narrated by Angela (Claire Danes), the show treated viewers to the frustrated soundings of a teenage girl. Dealing with serious issues, the show may have been a bit too cutting-edge, and with a female as narrator/protagonist, it didn't sustain the studio's interest. It is interesting that most audiences indicate that they prefer a boy as the central character in a television family.

In 2000, Fox Television created its memorable family with *Malcolm in the Middle,* which aired for almost seven years. Hal and Lois are saddled with four boys in a tiny home in Nowhere, USA. Malcolm (Frankie Muniz), the narrator, speaks directly to the audience and expresses a smug awareness of both the television medium and his position within the family as the middle child. Hal (Bryan Cranston) is the stereotypical tripping, stupid dad-boy, who is also tolerant and dull, and Lois, his spouse, is continually overwrought and exhausted. Taking cues from *Rosanne,* the Lois character (Jane Kaczmarek) is a screeching, annoying, and crazed mother who is the source of all the fear and loathing in the family. The boys rarely exhibit love, and the working-class family is "stuck" within a Walmartized existence. The show ends with two more additions, both boys, to the family, and genius Malcolm wins every struggle to the bitter end. Caricatured as a homely Cruella DeVille, Lois is the continual loser, while Hal only thinks he is.

Several decades passed before another "hood" comedy was produced. UPN's (produced by CBS) *Everybody Hates Chris* was a retro-narrated family comedy based on the boyhood of comedian Chris Rock. The adult voice of Chris Rock narrates the half-hour show, depicting life in the racially divided New York neighborhood of Bed-Sty, where Rock grew up. The show was unusual in that the narrator was a boy from a lower-class neighborhood, and often articulated a strong race and class consciousness. Tyler James Williams plays 16-year-old and very short Chris; Tequan Richmond is Chris's very tall and cute younger brother, Drew; and Imani Hakim plays younger sister, Tonya. Chris's dad-boy, Julius (played by Terry Crews), earnestly strives to create a better environment for his family. He works three jobs, yet continually is behind, both intellectually and economically. Mom Rochelle (Tichina Arnold) keeps her eye on the family with enormous proclamations. Chris is the genius younger child, who gets into trouble and who gets caught, but narrates his meta-view of the situation and the sociocultural irony within. He is always acutely aware of his lack of popularity and the inability of many people to like him—unlike his siblings, who have many friends but no clue as to their social status within the home, the school, or the neighborhood. *Everybody Hates Chris* is a very honest depiction of how a young boy might see the world, and there are important social and political dimensions woven within the plot. The commentary by the adult Chris Rock includes his observations on racism, society, and authority in general.

Television families from the child's point of view brought a fresh outlook on the concept of family. Taking the "one smart kid/smart aleck kid" prototype and turning him/her into the voice of the family somehow made viewers feel part of the plot; it is interesting how few shows managed to be successful with this model. Class wasn't a denominator in this equation, merely the voice of the child, often in direct conflict with audience expectations.

Motherless Boys and Dads

As has been apparent in the previous discussion of television families, parents figure greatly in the construction of the American family. Until the mid-1960s, television families kept to the Mom/Dad model. The only times a parent became single was due to an actor leaving the show or dying, and the network had to quickly replace the lost spouse. Ratings were clearly higher with two parent families. In the mid-1960s, new themes were created in shows that featured families—a families sans Mom. Common themes are pervasive in most of these shows: the families live in middle- or upper-class homes and money is never an issue; the father (or faux father) is a professional, who is fun, loving, and always has time for the kids; there is a sidekick quasi-dad to take up the slack (grandpa, uncle, brother, butler); the mother is dead and quite forgotten; and it is apparent that a family doesn't need a mom to be successful.

ABC created a sitcom in 1960 about a zany engineer widower and his three sons, *My Three Sons,* which followed Steve Douglas (Fred MacMurray) and the challenges of raising his boys with their maternal grandfather. The show moved to CBS in 1965, where it lasted seven more years, and after Grandpa left, his brother Charley came to pick up the slack. Plots were benign, but the show became one of the most popular shows in television history, second only to the longest-running family show, *The Adventures of Ozzie and Harriet.* Males were central to television shows such as these and the absence of women is barely acknowledged in all the years they aired.

In 1966, CBS created *Family Affair,* which ran for seven years. In this comedy, an uncle raises his brother's three children with the assistance of Mr. French, the butler. Smart and agreeable Cissy (15), and the terminally adorable twins Jody and Buffy ran Mr. French ragged, but he, in turn, ran a tight ship. Devoid of social issues or personal traumas, *Family Affair* continued America's television romance with motherless families. Again, the absence of a female caregiver or characters is not acknowledged, and viewers are secure that the boys can get along just fine without a mother, an aunt, or a grandmother figure.

The Courtship of Eddie's Father was ABC's addition to the motherless family genre in 1969. Starring Bill Bixby as a single father and widower living in Los Angeles, the show focused on Eddie's desire to match his dad up with a new wife. The house was run by Mrs. Livingstone and Eddie and dad Tom spent three years of poignant male bonding, eliciting warm audience sighs. Dad always appeared a bit naïve, and it was Eddie who often brought genuine insights into relationships. It was apparent in the late 1960s that a show with a father and his children, with the mother absent, made for great TV. Like Disney families, television began to promote a romanticized family that flourished in love, comfort, and male bonding with nary a matriarch in sight. And TV family children such as Bambi, Aladdin, Cinderella, Snow White, and Ariel found Mom was easy to forget.

The biological father is not the only person that makes the best father, however. NBC's *Different Strokes* blended orphan Black children from the 'hood with a single, rich, bumbling father, Mr. Drummond (Conrad Bain), who lives in Manhattan. After Mr. Drummond's housekeeper dies, she leaves her two boys, Arnold and Willis (Gary Coleman and Todd Bridges), to Mr. Drummond to adopt. Along with his bright daughter, Kimberly (Dana Plato), smartass Arnold and the slow but steady Willis laugh and play through a life wrought with chauffeurs, Mrs. Garrett, and more money than one can imagine. Much like earlier family shows, *Different Strokes* centered around Arnold, with bumbling dad-boy Mr. Drummond, Willis, and Kimberly revolving around the diminutive tyrant. The one difference with *Different Strokes,* was that the show did not shy away from a discussion of race. Unlike *The Cosby Show, Different Strokes* was eager to engage in a discussion of urban racism and the difficulties of multi-racial families. The characters of Mrs. Livingston and Mrs. Garrett are the exceptions to the no-mom zone in these television shows. However, the two housekeepers, although important in keeping the hearth clean and warm, are not essential to moving the plot or to raising the children, while Uncle Charlie, Mr. French, and other male caregivers are more central to television shows.

For eight years, beginning in 1987, ABC ran *Full House,* which featured Danny—a widowed parent—his best friend, and his (Danny's) brother raising Danny's three daughters. Re-creating the previous dead mom/happy dad shows, the three men fumble their way through idyllic child rearing. NBC joined the widowed bandwagon in 1987 with *My Two Dads.* The show opens with Mom dying and custody of daughter Nicole being awarded to the two men (Paul Reiser and Greg Evigan) who have long vied for her love. The sitcom deals with the awkward issue of the two rivals raising a teenaged daughter. Paternity is an issue not raised in any meaningful way, and the show never resolves who Nicole's father is. Heartwarming and loving, *My Two Dads* is engagingly forgettable.

Two and a Half Men is a long-running CBS show that premiered in 2003. The ultimate dad-boy/boy comedy, this show features three male characters who are boyish and underdeveloped. The motherless plot is a twist in that Uncle Charlie (Charlie Sheen) is invaded by his newly divorced brother, Alan, and little Jake. Upscale and successful, Charlie has to realign his life to accommodate the double-dad approach to child rearing. In one episode Sheen's character expresses doubt in his ability to be a good influence on little Jake's life. Jake responds that, much to the contrary, Charlie is the best father figure a kid could have: he parties constantly, has few rules, and has a different woman over every night. Jake is the dad-boy in training to Charlie's hyper dad-boy character. This is one of the first family shows that articulates separation and divorce as the raison d'être for the lack of a mom on the scene. Again, in these two latter examples, a need for a mother is not highlighted, and the male characters get along just fine without her.

Motherless families bring in big bucks in Hollywood. From the early death of Bambi's mother in the forest, audiences seem to be sucked into a romanticized view of life without a mom. The TV family sitcoms that highlight the "happy without mom" discourse can add to an already alienated societal view and opinion of the importance of a mother to a child. Ironically, and sadly, the alternative is not the case in dadless television families.

Single Moms and Boys

Hollywood found quickly that Moms without Dads don't sell like Dads without Moms. Somehow the romantic notion of a single mother didn't fixate viewers, and few television families lasted with this configuration. It took television awhile to trust a woman to raise her own family. Premiering in 1960 and ending in 1971, NBC's *Julia* was a groundbreaking attempt to address the developments the new Women's Liberation Movement wrought at the time. Diahann Carroll was Julia Baker, a nurse who was widowed when her pilot husband was killed in Vietnam. Although *Julia* was first to depict a Black woman as a lead character (and not a maid) on television, race was not addressed actively in the show. The series was quiet, dignified, and lacked any interest in social causes and politics. The relationship of Julia and her son, Corey, was endearing, and Julia had two love interests, but the "family" unit tended to include her white boss, Dr. Chegley, played by Lloyd Nolan, and her son. Chegley was the voice of reason and the embodiment of a benevolent patriarchy. Unlike most of the TV boys, Corey was neither a smart aleck nor a bad boy; he was a good little boy, who respected his mom. The show lasted less than three years, but was groundbreaking in the depiction of a single mother (of any race), especially a working Black mother, as the lead.

Probably one of the more unusual television family units was created by CBS in *Kate & Allie* in 1984. Originally a midseason replacement, the show was a surprising hit, starring the family of Kate (Susan Saint James) and daughter Emma, and another family of Allie (Jane Curtain) and her two children, Chip and Jennie. Both women were divorced, and dated frequently. Kate and Allie were successful in their careers and not desperate to remarry. This is the one dadless show that did not depict single motherhood has being fraught with frustrations; finances were intact, and the children relatively happy. The mothers played the central roles in the program, and the children did not distinguish themselves in any particular way. The show lasted six years and ended when a newly married Allie had Kate move in with her (as Allie's husband traveled a lot). Evidently family-loving America was uncomfortable with the radical decision to create such a nontraditional unit with nonpathological children.

Blended Boys

In a country with a high divorce rate, one would expect the audience not to feel uncomfortable with the depiction of divorce; however, divorce is not a common theme among any family television shows. Excuses to blend families have been successful, and much like the romantic notion of a momless family, blended families have occasionally titillated viewers. ABC's *The Brady Bunch* is the hands-down winner of blended television families. Airing from 1969 to 1974, the characters—a mother with three girls, a father with three boys, and an ever-present housekeeper, Alice—live on in television memories. The success of the show seems directly connected with the rising divorce rates in the United States in the mid-1960s. However, Mike Brady is not divorced, but widowed, and Carol Brady, well, we never really find out what happened to her former husband. The vacuous show dealt with issues such as getting braces, lost dogs, and spoiled dinners, but never addressed anything social or political, and the Bradys all personified the ease of suburban middle-class life. Even Alice was middle class, and one never questioned her class or value within the family unit.

Fresh Prince 1990

NBC's *Fresh Prince of Bel-Air* aired from 1990 to 1996 and created an unusual type of blended family. Will Smith (also the name of the character) moves in with his wealthy California relatives from his home in urban Philadelphia. An obvious product of "the 'hood," Will is immediately identified as the brains, talent, and humor of the family. Living with his aunt and uncle and cousins, the new member of the Banks family is the focus of the show. Will's cousins are Hilary, who is pretty, not very smart, and very spoiled; and Carlton, who is preppy, a Republican, and a Trekkie. Indeed, Will spends a lot of time describing Carlton as not very Black. Finally, there is Ashley—the cute little one (similar to Rudy in *The Cosby Show*). Although the show is similar to *The Cosby Show,* the collision of a poor Black relative showing up to live with the upscale Banks family sets up many humorous and thought-provoking situations. Will replicates the roles that leading boys had depicted in previous TV shows such as *Good Times, Family Ties, Malcolm in the Middle,* and so forth, but this time, the boy is not an immediate family member, but one who brings the family together.

Step by Step was first an ABC show in 1991, but moved to CBS and stayed on the air until 1998. Imitating the "3 + 3" pattern set by the Bradys, the divorced Frank Lambert, who has three children, marries the widowed Carol Foster, who also has three children. The show deals with the adjustments of a blended family and does not shy away from the apparent "stepness" of each family member. A bit more compelling than the Bradys, the plots were still simplistic, and the show forgettable. Both shows made short use of the blended motif, and television families were more successful with other formulas.

Unique Boys from Unique Families

No discussion of television families would be complete without a mention of some not-so-real families. In 1965, CBS produced the unique *Lost in Space,* which aired for three years. Based loosely on the book, *Swiss Family Robinson,* an astronaut family is marooned in space on an unknown planet. Complete with robots who are smarter than humans, the Robinson family consists of serious parents, with three children—Judy, Penny, and Will. (Besides the family, the show also has a Dr. Smith (a bad-good man) and a Major West.) Will Robinson (played by Billy Mumy) is the heart of the family. Although different episodes feature all the characters, Will gets into more scrapes, gets more attention, and seems to have more of a handle on the entire family and alien world than anyone else. Occasionally, Will confides in Dr. Smith, who usually proves to be untrustworthy; however, Will is his only friend. Will is guarded by the robot, who is known for his warning: "Danger, Will Robinson." Will is the brain of the family like many TV boys, and much smarter than anyone else on the planet.

How can our media history forget the *good night John-boy* hours of *The Waltons* up on Virginia's Walton Mountain? CBS's multi-generational family show began in 1972 and lasted until Hollywood was virtually buried in the thick molasses of family humility, morals, and church-going values. John and Olivia Walton were hard workers who ran a sawmill during the Depression. America was able to grow up with *The Waltons,* just as previous generations did with Ozzie and Harriett. The show encompassed the values that would eventually elect Ronald Reagan: back-to-the-basics, one-room schoolhouse, patriotic values that Americans seemed to crave. The show dealt with human issues, illness, war deaths, light comedy, and tragedy. *The Waltons* became the mythical history of American families. Based on the narratives of John-boy Walton, the family often revolved around the semi-perfect, but flawed John-boy. The entire show is based on the original autobiography of Earl Hamner, a novelist from Virginia.

Animated Boys

Animated cartoon comedies are the most colorful group among American television families. As Disney ducks Huey, Dewey, and Louie follow the military and political changes in the United States in comics, cartoon families parallel human family television shows from the 1960s. Modeled after *The Honeymooners,* ABC's *The Flintstones* was the first working-class Stone Age family. Stupid father, nurturing and frustrated mother, and overly involved neighbors followed the archetypical characters as they wound in and out of deceit and dilemma. Fred Flintstone is the epitome of a dad-boy, Wilma keeps Fred in line (exactly like Alice Kramden), and little Pebbles is cute and sweet. When the neighbors Barney and Betty Rubble's son, Bam-Bam, is born, he replicates his dad's personality as being dimwitted and constantly in trouble.

The Jetsons followed the Stone Age in 1962 on ABC, with a futuristic comedy family that included George Jetson, wife Jane, son Elroy, and ponytailed and irrelevant daughter Judy. Elroy, of course, was the family genius, and the show's plots centered around George and Elroy. George was the dad-boy, getting into scrapes, having run-ins with Mr. Spacely, his boss, and Elroy was a problem-solving imp, smarter than anyone else in the hypermodern society.

The big television animated payoff came in 1989, when FOX Television introduced *The Simpsons,* which has become the longest-running television series in history. Matt Groening's characters magnify the traits discussed within television families in color and in parody. Dull, Duff Beer-drinking dad-boy, Homer, and the sensible and worried mom, Marge, lovingly plod through working-class life with daughter Lisa, a prodigy, son Bart, a smart aleck boy, and Maggie, a pacifier-sucking baby. Although Lisa and Marge are certainly memorable characters, the episodes center around Homer and Bart, and the female characters often orbit them in support, dismay, or worry. No political, social, religious, or sacred issue has been ignored in this parody of American life. Groening lovingly comments on the American family with vision. It is still a vibrant memory—the pulpit warnings about the possible affects that Bart Simpson could have on children when public outrage at the show was great. Mothers recall picking up a Bart doll in the store for a child and having a neighbor pass by in the aisle and chide them about the influence Bart would have on any little boy. Americans were intrigued and frightened by the Simpson family. Other cartoon families have emerged, but it is hard to imagine that anything will surpass this two-decade old television family and its impact on and redefinition of the American family. *The Simpsons* have become the family barometer of television viewers. That which cannot be said is said, and Homer, Marge, and the children get away with it.

In 1999, Fox Television introduced a unique set of boys in *The Family Guy*. In the show, the boy, Stewie, is the twenty-first century prototype of the television boy. Much smarter than his entire family, Stewie (a toddler) is the conscience and the educated voice (with British accent), as well as the ambitious evil genius of the Griffin family. Dad-boy Peter is a buffoon, constantly insulting the world and tripping through self-inflicted messes. The third of the Griffin family trio of males is Brian, the dog, an intellectual ruminator on family situations. Mom Lois is strangely tolerant of Peter, oblivious to the observations of the bad seed Stewie and of the martini-drinking, smoking Brian, and she is constantly concerned about the unpopularity of her teen daughter, Meg. *The Family Guy* has complex plotlines with arcane sociocultural references interspersed with the misadventures of Peter and the grandiose calculations of Stewie. After its first run until 2002, the show came back on the air in 2005. The Griffin boys bring out laughter and anger from different segments of viewers; indeed, much like *The Simpsons* almost two decades earlier, many parent groups and religious organizations "warn" families against viewing *The Family Guy* because of its male characters.

Mike Judge's *King of the Hill* on Fox TV differs from the mold of animated TV families in that the Hill family of the show lives in Texas. Hank, a hard-working, literal-minded "propane and propane products" supplier provides for his family: his wife Peggy (a zealous substitute teacher), his son Bobby, and his airhead niece Luanne. Peggy strives to better herself at every chance, but Hank never gets ahead; he merely plugs on. Bobby is a dull-witted but occasionally smart chubby boy, and Luanne is basically a moron who just wants to be in love. The redneck nature of the program brings a Texas working-class dimension to television, including the depiction of paradoxical efforts for social mobility—Peggy is eager and capable, and Hank, in typical dad-boy form, is slow and unimaginative.

Thanks for Watching

Television families have become our families. Consequently, television dad-boys and the sons/brothers/cousins are now part of America's extended family. Nostalgically its own, the country has adopted these dad-boys and boys. How do we make sense of these depictions and how they affect the consciousness of teachers, parents, and students? Bumbling dads, stern mothers, smart aleck boys make great TV, but what do they say about real families? As we view television boys, we must ask questions about these characters and shows: Why is it that television and film audiences crave stories with dead mothers? Why do families succeed with ease when Mom is gone? Why is it more difficult when there is no father? Who are these families with butlers and housekeepers? Why are most plots of family comedies grounded in white lies and simple deceit? If TV is central to our lives, then why do we not see television families (other than the Simpsons) watch TV?

Further Reading

Jhally, S. and Lewis, J. (1992). *Enlightened Racism: The Cosby Show, Audiences, and the Myth of the American Dream.* Boulder, CO: Westview Press.

Shirley R. Steinberg

Thomas the Tank Engine

Thomas the Tank Engine and the trains of the Railway Series are an imported cultural phenomenon for young boys; they connect young boys' perennial love of trains with morality tales. Trains have historically been a significant play theme for boys; the popularity is attested to by the persistent train mania of many older men. *Thomas the Tank Engine* is the creation of Reverend Wilbert Awdry, who first wrote the stories—based on the Great Western Railway line that ran through his childhood home of Wiltshire, England—to entertain his son Christopher. Reverend Awdry wrote 26 books in the series, which was continued by his son, who wrote 15 more.

The first book in the Railway Series was *Edward's Day Out* published in 1945. Thomas appears in 1946 with *Thomas the Tank Engine.* The popularity of the books in the series was brought to a wider audience when Britt Allcroft created an animated series depicting the adventures of the engines on the fictional Island of Sodor in 1984. The series, narrated by Ringo Starr, and later by George Carlin, made the jump to the United States in 1989 when PBS aired *Shining Time Station.* In 2000, Thomas hit the big screen in his own movie *Thomas and the Magic Railway.*

Central to the stories are the adventures of Thomas and his two coaches Annie and Clarabel. Thomas has dreams to move up from his local branch line to pull the express, which are the more powerful engines such as Gordon and Henry. In the series, we meet all the local engines with their various personalities, including Thomas's best friends Percy, James, Edward, Gordon, Henry,

Duck, Toby the tram Engine, and Bertie the Bus. Thomas strives to be "really useful" and often looks down on the lazy cars and trucks he has to work with.

The adventures center around a matter of pride or pretense leading to an accident of some kind, where either another engine is called upon to aid the abashed protagonist or the railway owner, Sir Topham Hat, must arrange a rescue. Usually the hero is taught a lesson: the value of teamwork, the danger of carelessness, or the importance of helping others. Boys seem to like the accidents best, with all the crashes, rollovers, bridge collapses, and runaway brake failures. They also seem to enjoy the practical jokes and the pastoral excursions.

The popularity of Thomas worldwide has led to a variety of merchandise lines. Beyond the books, which are still popular and have been reissued in replica series as well as collected in anthologies, there are a variety of picture books, counting books, and board books, meant for the very young and young readers. Thomas is most popular with boys between the ages of two and six. Toys are popular in these young age groups and are available in a variety of metal, wooden, and plastic models recreated at various scales. LEGO has produced Thomas train sets, as have major electric train companies such as Lionel. "A Day Out with Thomas" on a real Thomas train is a popular event at selected railway museums and railroads.

Further Reading

Awdry, W. *Thomas the Tank Engine: The Complete Collection.* New York: Random House, 1997

Cross, Gary. *Kids' Stuff: Toys and the Changing World of American Childhood.* Cambridge: Harvard University Press, 1997.

George H. Thompson

Videos of Violence

Sirens wailing, guns blazing, police swarming, bad guys running—the mainstream images of crime that people living in the digital age harbor are connected to the visual representations of crime scenarios on television and in movies. In our increasingly visual world, individuals, consciously or not, rely on the media as the source of knowledge production. One of the foremost means of knowledge production on crime is the music video, especially from the gangsta rap genre, which constructs a type of reality that labels crime as a poor, Black, male, youth phenomenon despite the genre's position as a narrative of the oppressed. For the majority of the viewing populace, these visual texts produce meaning in their representation of crime as racialized, as well as in their portrayal of a particular form of masculinity, that is, a masculinity connected to the hyper-distorted exercise of power. The implications of the creation of meaning through stereotypical representations are dire for young, Black, male youths, as they are adversely affected in their daily lives by this constructed reality.

Gangsta rap music gained popularity in the late 1980s as a response to injustices done to urban Black youth trapped in the depths of poverty. West

Coast gangsta rap emerged as the urban economy underwent devastating changes because of factory closures, unemployment, and dire poverty. The lack of employment amongst Black youth was especially devastating and led to an increasing involvement in the drug culture—a point of access to the economy for many youth at the time. West Coast gangsta rap artists began to address the instability of marginalized peoples' daily lives, using music as a critique of the oppression, with songs directly related to the lack of opportunity for poor Black men because of race and class discrimination. The genre is an autobiographical narrative that expresses the suffering of poor Black male youth; however, while depicting the real lives of the rappers in the ghetto, it has had the adverse effect of racializing and gendering crime as young, male, and Black.

The popular media are largely responsible for the dissemination of information about crime and criminality to the society as a whole. The repeated stereotypical depictions of young, poor, Black men involved in crime become "naturalized" and help to classify this group as criminal—thereby perpetuating their marginalization. The effect that this naturalization process has is it creates distinctions in society between "us" and "them," where individuals that associate with the norms (us) may position themselves as superior to those that defy the norms (them). The mainstream media's depiction of gangsta rap teaches the mainstream "us" to be distrustful of the criminal "them," which leads to further oppression of poor, Black, male youth, despite the genre's intention to shed light on oppression in the ghetto. In the song "Natural Born Killaz" by Ice Cube and Dr. Dre, the "us versus them" dichotomy is evident as the upper-middle class white men and women are terrorized by Ice Cube and Dr. Dre. The video begins with a crime scene investigation and woven throughout is the imagery of the two rappers using guns to terrorize and kill the two white couples. Cube and Dre, as young, Black males, reinforce the stereotype of this group as criminal and dangerous for the mainstream audience.

Music videos not only define which groups are criminal but also reinforce a particular masculinity of marginalized peoples, a masculinity that is associated with violence, strength, power, and aggression. The glorification of guns in many of the gangsta rap videos is a form of exercising power in an environment where the residents have no real power. Easy E's "Neighborhood Sniper" is a clear example of an aggressive masculinity as expressed through the power and control of the gun. The video begins with the viewpoint of a Black male looking down onto a street. The eye of the Black male is portrayed through the lens of a gun, thus connecting weapons and danger to the Black male body. Similarly, NWA's "Alwayz into Something" glorifies violence and gun imagery. Several times the camera pans up the barrel of a gun and ends in the hands of a Black man, which further emphasizes the gun as an extension of the Black male. The gun symbolizes a form of phallic power. Thus, the bigger the gun, the more power one wields.

The construction of a hyper-masculine, criminal, impoverished Black male is an extension of an image that has historically been present in Canadian society. In theory, Canada claims to be a "color-blind" nation where race is not considered; in practice, Canada has a history of "othering" those individuals who do not fit the white Canadian mould. Black people in particular have suffered from discrimination as a result of being labeled the "other" and are subject to racist discourse in the eyes of the criminal justice system. One painful result of all this—and an increasingly common reality for young Black men—is racial profiling, which is the practice of using stereotypes to target specific groups of people as perpetrators of crime. Racial profiling as a discriminatory practice is a theme that gangsta rap artists visit in their lyrics and music videos. "Straight Outta Compton" by NWA begins with a description of the police targeting the residents of Compton, Los Angeles, in a routine gang sweep. This video is a response to the effect of media representations of young, Black males involved in gang activity and crime. Unjust arbitrary policing is an implication of such representations.

The lack of access to a means of expressing injustices for poor Black youth occurs because of the structuring of power in society that leaves this group on the margins. Despite the factors working against them, gangsta rap artists have gained a forum to express oppression in its various forms, as evident in NWA's song "Fuck tha Police." The song is a direct response to the oppressive criminal justice system and its practice of targeting Black people. The lyrics resonate strongly: "Fucking with me cause I'm a teenager/With a little bit of gold and a pager/Searching my car, looking for the product/Thinking every nigga is selling narcotics." These lyrics are powerful and shocking in its truthful depiction of Black youth being targeted because of mainstream stereotypical beliefs that associate crime, drugs, and violence to Black people.

Gangsta rap videos as a site for the construction of truth and meaning is evident through an intersectional analysis of the politics of representation. Definitions of crime and access to power resonate through the medium and directly influence the daily lives of Black men of all classes and ages that experience daily doses of discrimination. Although the medium perpetuates existing negative stereotypes, it also functions as a site for social consciousness and as a forum of dissent against the injustices and inequalities visited upon the marginalized "other." The silenced and invisible are given a voice and made visible through the mass media, all of which sends a strong message, both social and political, about what is real and what is constructed. It can be difficult to distinguish the attempts at voicing discrimination amidst the distorted representations, but a critical analysis of the medium will provide the necessary tools for social awareness and understanding.

Further Reading

James, C. (2002). Racializing Suspects, Suspecting Race. In B. Schissel and C. Brooks (Eds.), *Marginality and Condemnation: An Introduction to Critical Criminology* (pp. 289–307). Halifax: Fernwood.

Kelley, R. (1996). "Kickin' Reality, Kickin' Ballistics: Gangsta rap and Postindustrial Los Angeles." In W.E. Perkins (Ed.), *Dropping Science: Critical Essays on Rap Music and Hip Hop Culture* (pp. 117–158). Philadelphia: Temple University Press.

Anita Menon

SECTION 8

Boys in Print

African American Boys and Two Superheroes: Spider-Man and Superman

Most African American boys living in the United States are more likely to be familiar with the lyrics and hook lines of Tupac's "Keep Your Head Up" (1993) and "Dear Mama" (1995) than they are to recognize the stanzas of poems such as Mother's Goose's "Little Boy Blue" and "What Are Little Boys Made Of?" The identities of African American boys as students, especially Black boys living in urban school communities, are shaped by their status as boy, poor, and Black. Black boys' identities are shaped by traditional American cultural beliefs of the masculine, as well as by urban Americans views of masculinities and femininities. Like the famous rapper, poet, actor, and writer Tupac Shakur, many urban African American males are faced with the complexities of what is expected of them by mainstream society, as well as by what is expected of them by their families, local communities, schools, and peer groups. Larger white middle-class American culture views boys as being naturally aggressive, tough, deceptive, and destructive, while maintaining the belief that the family and school environments can refine and groom those same boys, helping them to utilize their qualities for good.

If we look at typical American heroes, we can easily view how Americans suppress traditional notions of masculinity while also disseminating and valuing ideologies of masculinity. Most, if not all, school-aged boys and girls are familiar with the superheroes Superman and Spider-Man. Spider-Man is characteristically depicted as an adolescent battling with his innermost demons of selfishness and anger, whereas Superman is classically disguised as an adult male who on the surface appears weak and insecure. On the one hand, both all-American heroes represent to most Americans strength, self-sacrifice, patriotism, and advanced intelligence.

Both heroes also symbolize the eternal struggle between what they psychologically and behaviorally desire and what the rest of the universe needs for them to be and to become. In other words, our most revered heroes possess a dual loyalty. Our most beloved superheroes must learn to suppress their own male wants and desires (e.g., fame, female companionship, revenge, etc.) for the good and protection of their fellow citizens. Thus, their loyalty is divided between their selfish heterosexual boyish habits and the nation's need (and other forces beyond their control) for them to embrace manhood. Of course, manhood signifies a sense of sacrifice, self-restraint, and self-control. As is the case with the adolescent Spider-Man more specifically, he is directly encouraged to use his "power for good." Most followers of both Spider-Man and Superman appreciate and revere them for their masculine qualities, while also nearly worshipping them for being able to control their innate aggression and physical prowess to protect the country from urban criminals and alien invaders.

Great American Heroes

Most likely, if a male child is socialized in the United States, he is familiar with these two superheroes, and he understands and reveres their strength and what their power symbolizes—namely, what it is to be a man and boy. Even though most Black boys may not be familiar with mainstream nursery rhymes, they surely are able to recognize the American heroes Superman and Spider-Man. Certainly, like their white peers, they wish to run, jump, fly, and punch like the two superheroes. Maybe they even embrace the idea that they may have to check their boyish ways at the door to become a superhero. Notwithstanding their longing for embodying the ideals that Superman and Spider-Man represent, Black boys struggle with a dualism that might be characterized separately from that of their white middle-class peers. Black boys struggle with their own set of internalized heroes and demons that are also related to notions of masculinity, but their struggles are linked to context, family dynamics, and notions of intellect.

Like the superhero characters Superman and Spider-Man, Black boys live, play, and go to school in urban America. Conversely, Black boys tend to be viewed as part of the problem with urban America, instead of the solution. Like their white peers, Black boys are viewed as biologically wired to be aggressive, destructive, and hostile. However, the mainstream American believes that white boys' biological drives can be changed, but not those of Black boys. In our society, it is believed that schools, religious institutions, parents, and for the more resistant to change, the military or mental health facilities can socialize boys to become more refined men. Historically, African American boys' masculine qualities have been portrayed by the media, science, and the criminal justice system as untamable.

The master narrative reinforces the cultural norm of men: because of the forces of nature/biology (i.e., men are simply created differently), coupled with the lack of prime cultural socialization, Black boys never really have the opportunity to be shaped into useful (masculine) capital. Stated differently, the unspoken assumption is that urban Black male youth do not have the cultural resources and willpower to use their "power" (i.e., innate masculine tendencies) for good. For example, research shows that African American boys tend to receive harsher punishment at school or in the penal system for unwanted behavior or law breaking than their white middle-class peers. When white male youth participate in criminal activity or engage in unwanted behavior it is excused as "boys being boys."

Black boys' unwanted behavior is often viewed as hostile, aggressive, and a potential threat to society. In fact, in the latest Spider-Man epic, Spider-Man's alter ego is a character with a black Spider-Man costume: he is a direct reflection of Spider-Man, except that he is the hero's adversary. The blackened adversary represents Spider-Man's inability to suppress his selfishness and anger. There is much irony to be found in the bad guy being dressed all in black. Black boys' experiences have always been shaped by cultural contradictions. Generally speaking, school-aged boys are expected to behave more aggressively and be more defiant than their female peers. These masculine tendencies are even valued in capitalist societies. U.S. culture values traits associated with masculinity, such as independence, competition, and physical strength. In a patriarchal society these are qualities associated with athletes, corporate leaders, politicians, and soldiers. Some have even argued that men hold such qualities, which is why they dominate sports, the corporate world, politics, and the armed forces. These are highly valued positions in our society, in which workers are expected to think and act quickly, without much contemplation and without much emotionality.

Black Boys and Education

Intelligence is equated with the ability to contain one's emotions and desires. Because of society's belief that African Americans are not as intelligent as European Americans, Black boys are viewed as not intelligent or rational enough to suppress their own selfish needs and desires. By definition, to be irrational is to lack intelligence and to be possibly insane. In America's psyche, because of perceived lack of proper socialization and innate biological drive, Black boys are constructed as irrational and not capable of controlling their impulses. For instance, research shows that African American school-aged boys are more likely to be diagnosed as emotionally disturbed or of having a behavioral problem. Along these same lines, Black boys are more likely to be diagnosed as having a learning disability and being mentally impaired. They are also more likely to be retained a grade in school, suspended or expelled, punished for behavior infractions, or to be verbally or physically abused at the hands of a teacher, compared to others in their peer group. Once larger American society views Black boys as not being able to control their behavior and impulses and contribute to the greater good, then their status as "men" is devalued. Black boys begin to understand their diminished value as soon as they step into the school environment.

Of course, the exclusion and marginalization of Black boys' bodies and spirits in urban school communities are beyond the control of one individual. The inequities are a result of discriminatory school policies, curriculum, teacher attitudes, and classroom practices. White middle-class female teachers are the ones most likely to not understand the experiences of Black boys, but are the ones more likely to have the responsibility to educate Black boys. Therefore,

Black boys' masculine bodies and tendencies are policed both outside the school environment and within the institutional walls of education. Black boys' masculine, heroic wishes and desires are also suppressed and subjugated by the (white) feminine other inside the classroom. Consequently, Black boys are forced to live a dual life, in which they are expected to be masculine and everything that little boys are made of, while simultaneously being mentally and physically regulated by society and other primary socialization agents, such as the school. Ironically, because Black boys are never really allowed to play out their role as heroes, they begin to view the school (and possibly other social institutions) as the enemy. Black boys have higher dropout/pushout rates than their white male peers and white and Black female counterparts. Black males' low graduation rates are considered to be a national crisis for some social justice advocates.

Because of the pressures society places on boys to live out their masculine fantasies and become productive leaders of their families, communities, and schools, it is the responsibility of teachers, parents, policymakers, and community leaders to help Black boys live out their heroic dreams. This call of attention to the needs of Black boys has little to do with proliferating traditional narrow (and often confining) notions of Eurocentric masculinity, but more to do with assisting Black boys in developing to their full potential. Youth who are allowed to dream and establish short- and long-term goals have a better chance of adjusting to adversity in childhood and making a successful transition into young adulthood. All boys will realize one day, sooner or later, that they will never become Superman or Spider-Man. Yet, it is a sense of normality that allows boys and girls to feel that they are a part of the cultural fabric of American society. Thus far, in too many of our schools and classrooms young Black males feel outside of the norm. Consequently, as we make them feel abnormal, while suppressing their dreams and ignoring their realities, we are possibly pushing them to become our nation's adversaries.

Culturally Relevant Superheroes

It is necessary, therefore, to embrace more culturally relevant practices and policies in schools that accept young Black males as boys who are human beings capable of heroism. Lastly, it is important that we socialize Black boys in ways that promote positive images of masculinity (forging new models of masculinity is not going away anytime soon). For example, Spawn and Green Lantern may be reputable superheroes for African American boys. These are superheroes that can be incorporated into our school curricula and literatures. In addition, teachers can teach students how to interpret and analyze the dualism that many male superheroes encounter as characters and have students apply such knowledge to real-life situations a boy or girl may find themselves in in their daily life. For instance, one only needs to think of the X-Men to understand how superheroes can be both outcast and idolized. In this case, the mutants could be described as anything traditionally considered the "other," such as people of African descent, those with disabilities, gays or lesbians, second-language learners, the poor, etc. As a classroom exercise, the teacher could have students discuss how one can be both an outcast and yet a needed and useful protagonist for societal change. Finally, educators can provide boys with real heroes who have struggled with dual identities in society, resisted narrow notions of masculinity, and fought against hegemony, power, and privilege, such as Langston Hughes, Malcolm X, or Tupac Shakur. It is time that the media, parents, and educators turn Black boys away from false heroes who are only invested in whiteness as maleness, or in blackness as thuggery. Instead, we all are responsible for turning Black boys on to relevant superheroes that will possibly assist them in their transformation into real-life heroes.

Further Reading

Noguera, Pedro. *The Trouble with Black Boys and Other Reflections on Race, Equity and the Future of Public Education.* San Francisco, California: Jossey-Bass, 2008.

Kincheloe, Joe, and Kecia Hayes, eds. *Teaching City Kids: Understanding and Appreciating Them.* New York: Peter Lang Publishing, 2007.

Shakur, Tupac. *The Rose That Grew from Concrete.* New York: Pocket Books, 1999.

Malcolm X, and Alex Haley. *The Autobiography of Malcolm X As Told by Alex Haley.* New York: Ballantine, 1964.

Venus Evans-Winters

Books for Boys

Boys typically begin reading on their own around age eight and become more independent and individuated around 12 or 13. Studies show that boys' reading is an endangered activity as reading declines significantly in the teenage years because of competition from other media sources. Although there is evidence that this is true, there is nonetheless a thriving book trade in genres and titles that appeal to boys' interests. Favorite books are often read repeatedly and chosen in spite of parental and educational influence; they are read, in other words, just for fun. These may include media such as comic books and graphic novels as well as traditional works of fiction. Tie-ins with movies and gaming culture are influences unique to the most recent generation of reading boys, although fictional series still prevail, primarily in the genres of science fiction and fantasy continuing a trend in popularity since the 1960s. What follows is an overview of boys' literature from 1965 to 2007, the close of the Harry Potter era, and a determination of what are the best sellers and the persistent favorites.

Young Readers

Reading habits of boys have changed as competing entertainment options displace reading time. Publishers have adapted by expanding titles and themes related to popular movies, television shows, and increasingly, gaming franchises.

For young boys, Mighty Morphin Power Rangers may be an enticement, or Pokemon, a regular feature if movie tie-ins fade. The simple *Bob the Builder* series entertains a large audience of boys who have the traditional interest in all things machine such as trucks, tractors, tools, and construction machinery. The *Thomas the Tank Engine* book series about trains and railroads is another extension of an earlier generation's interests. The most popular of Maurice Sendak's many classic titles is *Where the Wild Things Are,* which generations of boys and parents have memorized from repeated performances. The multitude of works by Dr. Seuss remains the most popular beginning readers' books, as they have been since their introduction. *The Cat in the Hat; Green Eggs and Ham; Go Dog, Go;* and *One Fish Two Fish Red Fish Blue Fish* are perennial favorites, although any book by Dr. Seuss is good. Modern favorites include *Alexander and the Terrible, Horrible, No Good, Rotten Day* by Judith Viorst, and *The Stinky Cheese Man, The True Story of the Three Little Pigs,* and *The Math Curse* by Jon Scieszka. *If You Give a Mouse a Cookie,* or *If You Give a Pig a Pancake,* and others in this series by Laura Numeroff and Felicia Bond stand up tirelessly to repeated readings. *The Magic Tree House* series for beginning readers provides simple short adventures featuring a repeated scenario and ninjas, knights, dragons, and pirates, which boys prefer. Dan Greenburg and Jack Davis created The *Zack Files* series, which provides whacky, humorous tales such as *My Great-Grandpa's in the Litter Box* and *Dr. Jekyll, Orthodontist.*

Animal Tales

One genre that begins in early childhood and flourishes among boy readers is the animal tale. From the easy reading and ever popular Frog and Toad stories of Arthur Lobel, and *Ralph S. Mouse* and *The Mouse and the Motorcycle* stories by Beverly Cleary to the more sophisticated, classic tales such as *Stuart Little* and *Charlotte's Web* by E. B. White and *The Wind in the Willows* by Kenneth Grahame, along with Richard Adams's *Watership Down* and Robert C. O'Brien's *Mrs. Frisby and the Rats of NIMH,* boys explore worlds of action and adventure performed by little creatures that have made lively reading since *The Jungle Books* of Rudyard Kipling. Recent additions to the genre include the award-winning *The Tale of Despereaux: Being the Story of a Mouse, a Princess, Some Soup and A Spool of Thread* by Kate Decamillo, and include the great favorite *Redwall* series of Brian Jacques. Featuring the medieval adventures of the creatures of Redwall Abbey, the fierce badger lords, and the heroic mouse Martin the Warrior, the *Redwall* series of twenty tales pits the peaceful Abbey dwellers against the outlaw Vermin that threaten them from the world beyond the Mossflower Woods.

Classic Themes

It speaks to the richness of our literary traditions that classics such as *The Adventures of Tom Sawyer, Adventures of Huckleberry Finn, Treasure Island,* and *Robinson Crusoe* are still popular. Though older standards of boy's fiction, such as The Hardy Boys, popular from the 1930s through the 1960s, are available, they have not attracted wide readership. Several early genres are still producing new interpretations; for example, Arthurian tales such as Mary Stewart's *The Crystal Cave;* Rosemary Sutcliff's *Sword at Sunset;* and Kevin Crossely-Holland's *The*

Seeing Stone, At the Crossing Places, and *King of the Middle March* are indispensable favorites. Sarah Cooper's *Dark is Rising* sequence employs an Arthurian setting as the Old Ones wielding the power of the Light struggle against the forces of evil known as the Dark.

Rosemary Sutcliff's other popular stories (*The Mark of the Horse Lord, The Eagle of the Ninth, The Silver Branch*, and *The Lantern Bearers*) recreate the world of the Romans and Celts in the Britain of the Roman Empire. Her retellings of *The Iliad* and *The Odyssey* in *Black Ships before Troy* and *The Wanderings of Odysseus,* respectively, sustain young readers until they can master Homer's classics.

Young and older boys alike gravitate to superheroes and comic-book anthologies such as *Superman, Spider-Man, X-Men, Batman,* or *The Hulk.* The graphic novel has become one of the most preferred formats since its origin in the1980s. Some of the most popular are comic based, such as Frank Miller's *The Dark Knight Returns* and other Batman/Dark Knight titles, but with more lavish illustrations and story lines than the traditional comic book. Both Marvel and DC issue many popular series based on the Justice League of America, Superman, Green Lantern, Teen Titans, and the Marvel Universe. Some original graphic novel titles include the *Bone* series by Jeff Smith; *The Watchmen* by Alan Moore and Dave Gibbons; *V Is for Vendetta* by Alan Moore and David Lloyd; *The League of Extraordinary Gentlemen* also by Alan Moore; and *300* by Frank Miller. The best-selling title of all has been Neil Gaiman's *Sandman* series.

Fantasy

The Hobbit and The Lord of the Rings trilogy of J. R. R. Tolkien have been best sellers since 1966, and their popularity has increased with the success of Peter Jackson's film versions. For many boys this is the first and foremost fantasy series, but others have followed in its footsteps. *The Chronicles of Narnia,* by C. S. Lewis, returned to popularity with the film series beginning with *Narnia: The Lion, The Witch and the Wardrobe.* Terry Brook's *Sword of Shannara* trilogy is another favorite, as is Robert Jordan's *Wheel of Time* series.

William Golding's classic *The Princess Bride* is a great swashbuckling tale of a princess, a giant, and the Dread Pirate Roberts. A fantastic movie was made based on this book as well.

A bit easier for younger readers are Lloyd Alexander's *Chronicles of Prydain, Adventures of Taran, The Book of Three, The Black Cauldron, The Castle of Lyr, Taran the Wanderer,* and *The High King.* Additionally, Avi's *Wolf Rider; Crispin: The Cross of Lead;* and *Crispin: At the Edge of the World;* Eoin Colfer's *Artemis Fowl* series; and Joseph Delaney's *The Last Apprentice* series (consisting of *Revenge of the Witch; The Curse of the Bane;* and *The Night of the Soul-Stealer*) are recent additions to this genre.

Since the emergence of the dragon Smaug in *The Hobbit,* the dragon tale has been in a class of its own. Anne McCaffrey's *Dragonriders of Pern* series, beginning with *Dragonflight* and *Dragonsongs,* and Laurence Yep's *Dragon of the Lost Sea* series are among those that have produced best sellers, as is Jane Yolen's Pit Dragon trilogy, beginning with *Dragon's Blood.* The latest favorite addition to this class is Christopher Paolini's *Eragon,* published when the author was 19, and *Eldest,* the second installment, when he was 22.

For older boys the world of fantasy comes alive in video-game–related titles such as *Forgotten Realms* and *Halo.* The *Forgotten Realms* series, with over 200 novels from 1987 to the present, originated as a setting in the *Dungeon and Dragons* role-playing game. Many of the books are written by R. A. Salvatore, including *The Paths of Darkness, The Hunter's Blade Trilogy, The Dark Elf Trilogy, The Legend of Drizzt,* and *Baldur's Gate.*

The most popular series of the decade has been J. K. Rowling's Harry Potter, successful both in print and on the screen. One of the significant facts about this series, aside from having spurred book sales and readership for over 10 years since the debut in 1998 of *Harry Potter and the Sorcerer's Stone,* is that it has been equally popular among boys and girls, which is rare. Philip Pullman's His Dark Materials trilogy—consisting of *The Golden Compass, The Subtle Knife,* and *The Amber Spyglass*—is another emerging favorite and also appeals to both boys and girls.

Silly and Quirky

From serial fantasy to the goofy and the absurd, boys' reading favorites often include the gross, the quirky, the creepy, and the silly. Comic strips have been best-selling favorites since Charles Schultz's *Peanuts* books made the lists in the early 1960s. *Garfield* is among the most popular series ever, placing number 15 in the top 1000 titles held by libraries in 2005. Dav Pilkey's *Captain Underpants* series in graphic cartoon form is popular with early readers, as they follow the exploits of two fourth graders, George Beard and Harold Hutchins, and the superhero they create by hypnotizing their school principal to do battle with the evil Talking Toilets and the Wicked Wedgie Woman. More of the plain silly favorites are Thomas Rockwell's *How to Eat Fried Worms* and Andy Griffith's *Butt Wars, The Day My Butt Went Psycho,* and *Zombie Butts from Uranus.*

The grandfather of the quirky, and one of the most favored and widely read of all children's authors, is Roald Dahl, whose *Charlie and the Chocolate Factory; James and the Giant Peach; Boy: Tale of Childhood; The Witches; The BFG; The Twits;* and *Danny, the Campion of the World* transformed children's fiction. Lemony Snicket continues that tradition in his gothic *A Series of Unfortunate Events,* which—beginning with *Volume 1, The Bad Beginning* and ending with *Volume 13, The End*—follows the adventures of the Baudelaire children, who are suddenly orphaned and subject to the unwanted guardianship of the criminal Count Olaf. Other stories in the gothic tradition include Norton Juster's *The Phantom Tollbooth* and John Bellairs's works *The Face in the Frost; The Eyes of the Killer Robot;* and *The Mummy, the Will, and the Crypt.*

Creepy and Spooky

From the quirky to the creepy, R. L. Stine's Goosebumps books—including the *Ghosts of Fear Street* series, *The Haunted Schoolhouse,* and *The Nightmare Rooms*—delight boys to the despair of teachers and librarians everywhere. Stephen King is a dominant force in young adult fiction as he is in adult popular reading. His numerous novels and stories—including *Carrie, Night Shift, The Dead Zone, Firestarter, Cujo, Pet Sematary, Christine, The Talisman,* and *Eyes of the Dragon*—have left boys sleeping with the lights on for the past 30 years.

The Real World

Realistic fiction has a hard time competing with fantasy and faces the stigma of being assigned reading and required for schoolwork. Nevertheless, there are several titles that emerge as favorites once they are read, even if reluctantly. These include Lois Lowry's *The Giver*; S. E. Hinton's *The Outsiders* and *Tex*; and Katherine Paterson's *Bridge to Teribithia*.

Survival stories, of which Defoe's *Robinson Crusoe* is the originator, challenge boys to think about independence. Like the earlier *My Side of the Mountain,* by Jean Craighead George, Gary Paulsen's *Hatchet, Dogsong, The Crossing, The Island, Voyage of the Frog, Brians's Return,* and *Tracker* stimulate that part of the imagination challenged by being alone. Other titles dealing with alienation, friendship, and other issues of the real world include William Golding's *Lord of the Flies*; J. D. Salinger's *The Catcher in the Rye*; Louis Sachar's *Holes*; Robert Cormier's *The Chocolate War*; *We All Fall Down*; *The Rag and Bone Shop*; and *I Am the Cheese*; and Chris Crutcher's *Chinese Handcuffs*; *Staying Fat for Sarah Byrnes*; and *Whale Talk*.

It is not only serious themes that are treated in a realistic manner. Mysteries and espionage stories for young readers such as *Encyclopedia Brown Takes the Case* and others stories by Michael L. Fleisher are an introduction to one of the most popular adult genres. Favorites include Nicholas Meyer's *The Seven Percent Solution*; Robert Newman's *The Case of the Baker Street Irregulars: A Sherlock Holmes Story*; and Tony Hillerman's tales of the Navajo Tribal Police, such as *A Thief of Time*.

Science Fiction

Science fiction gave rise to fantasy and has always maintained a stable readership among teenage boys. More so than fantasy, science fiction often addresses serious issues and concerns about our relationship with technology, the environment, our families, and ourselves. Issues of individual and global disasters are often raised as well as complex considerations of personality and identity. Pioneering authors such as Ray Bradbury in *The Illustrated Man* and *Fahrenheit 451*; Arthur C. Clarke in *Childhood's End* and *2001: A Space Odyssey*; Isaac Asimov's *Foundation Trilogy*; *Nemesis*; and *I, Robot*; Robert Heinlein's *Starship Troopers*; *Stranger in a Strange Land*; and *Robots at Dawn*; and Frank Herbert's *Dune* series all deal with mature themes in exciting ways that are especially appealing to teenage boys.

Although much of this genre spans from young adult to adult fiction, books with great appeal to preteen and teen readers include Douglas Adams's *The Hitchhiker's Guide to the Galaxy*; Orson Scott Card's *Ender's Game*; William Sleator's *Singularity,* and Michel Crichton's *Jurassic Park* and *Lost Worlds.*

Following the conclusion of the Star Wars trilogy with the *Return of the Jedi* in 1983, the faraway galaxy was revived with Timothy Zahn's *Star Wars: Heir to the Empire, Vol. 1.* It was followed by his *Star Wars: Dark Force Rising,* in 1992, and *Star Wars: The Last Command,* in 1993. Over 200 novels in the *Star Wars* universe, written by various authors, have been published from 1991 to the present, and many have reached the young adults' best sellers' lists.

This brief overview indicates that there are many well-liked and favored works that boys return to again and again. Fortunately, many of the genres boys love continue to be published as adult fiction as well, which allows boys to pursue these interests throughout their lives. Although some decry the influence of movies and television on the pursuit of reading, many examples show that they introduce new readers to ongoing stories or spur interest in pursuing the themes and topics presented. The fictional worlds of *Star Wars,* the Lord of the Rings, Narnia, and Harry Potter are only a few examples in which more complex and creative experiences can be had through books.

Further Reading

Bilz, Rachelle Lasky. *Life Is Tough: Guys Growing Up and Young Adult Literature.* Lanham, MD: The Scarecrow Press, 2004.

Hall, Christine, and Martin Coles. *Children's Reading Choices.* London: Routledge. 1999.

MacRae, Cathi Dunn. *Presenting Young Adult Fantasy Fiction.* New York: Twayne Publishers, 1998.

George H. Thompson

Boys' Adventure Stories in Britain

In 2000, Anthony Horowitz published *Stormbreaker,* the first in his hugely popular *Alex Rider* series. The novels chronicle the adventures of teenage spy Alex, a British schoolboy who works for MI6, as he takes on, outwits, and defeats a number of international criminals. The publication of *Stormbreaker* took place in a climate of anxiety about the lives of many boys: a growth in violence, gang culture, mental health problems, and failing educational achievements during the 1990s and into the new millennium led to debates about boys' lives both in academic research and in the popular press. In some quarters this debate has perceived boys' lives through a lens of crisis.

Specifically in relation to education, examinations at the age of 16 in England and Wales have shown some groups of boys falling behind in certain subjects, with literacy a particular concern. One of the reasons cited for the lack of enthusiasm in reading among boys is a shortage of fiction that interests and excites them. Though this line of argument is open to debate, those who advocate a gendered approach to literature welcomed the arrival of Alex Rider as heralding a new era in literature for boys—although Horowitz himself has never stated that he was writing specifically for a male audience. One of the reasons why the Alex Rider novels have been labeled as boys' literature is their superficial similarity to an earlier genre of fiction prominent in the second half of the nineteenth century, another period during which boyhood was under scrutiny.

Adventure and Empire

The second half of the nineteenth century in Britain was a period of continued expansion overseas, as the project of Empire became more urgent under the banner of imperialism. A spirit of self-improvement along with anxieties about physical degeneracy and lawlessness in the greatly extended, urban, working-class population led to the formation of groups such as The Boys' Brigade (1883) and the publication of Robert Baden-Powell's influential *Scouting for Boys* in 1908. The expanding Empire required men fit to serve their country in all corners of the globe. An Empire serviceman must maintain a strong moral code, demonstrate physical prowess, be independent and self-sufficient, and respond rationally to all challenges he faces. Empire masculinity, to which boys were encouraged to aspire, was visible not only in the social institutions of the day but also in diverse cultural forms, from music hall entertainment to art and literature.

It was in this climate that the genre of adventure stories for boys came to prominence, benefiting from the Elementary Education Act of 1870, which increased the number of children in state education and promoted a growth in cheaper-book publishing, with both education and book publishing reflecting the increasingly gendered nature of society during the Victorian and Edwardian periods. The adventure story offered a medium through which the romance of frontier exploration could be imagined by boys all together. At the same time, the novels exude the ideological belief of the white British male as hero, superior to all others, particularly to women and to the first populations of the colonized lands through which they stride. Although the experience of frontier adventure was beyond the majority of the novels' readers, the masculinities represented in their pages privilege the very specific version of manhood outlined earlier.

It is, however, the characteristics represented in Empire masculinity that have created uncertainty about the promotion of the new version of the boys' adventure story, because they are perceived in some quarters as damaging to the emotional growth of boys by impacting on their ability to form intimate relationships through an emphasis on physical prowess and independence, particularly at a time when problems with aggression and mental health were in the spotlight. Debates that support a specific literature for boys and those that voice concern about the hegemonic masculinity privileged in such a literature reveal the divisions that exist in both academic and popular arenas in relation to men's and boys' lives. However, to approach the debate from such a polarized perspective reduces the possibilities for boys' lives. The new adventure story offers such an example: to understand it merely as a return to the privileging of nineteenth-century versions of masculinity is to give precedence to form over content.

New Adventures

The fictional landscapes of nineteenth-century adventure novels suggest that they were informed by a series of stable ideological beliefs transposed from the culture in which they were produced. Though this may be more illusion than reality, the genre certainly creates an effect of shared beliefs in the enterprise of Empire and the types of men and boys who will succeed in the far-flung corners of the globe. The Alex Rider novels of Anthony Horowitz suggest no such certainty: though Alex is a British schoolboy who takes on and defeats villains from all parts of the world, he is a reluctant and vulnerable hero. Adults, who act as moral guides to heroes in other stories, become manipulators here. Alex is forced to work for the MI6 and has an ambivalent attitude toward his role: he enjoys the power it gives him, but he is also aware of the costs. Separation, which earlier indicated the special place of the hero, is translated into isolation, symbolized by Alex's lack of family or close friends. Though Horowitz's novels offer empowerment to boy readers in that they have a charismatic hero who effectively takes on more powerful adversaries and defeats them, usually by outwitting them, they also represent sites of ambivalence: enemies are charismatic, employers are controlling, moral clarity is uncertain. Simultaneously, the narratives are sites that explore vulnerability and the costs of emotional isolation. The boy reader, then, can be adventurous, heroic, powerful, and also emotionally engaged, vulnerable, in need of support. This emphasizes the changing nature of the adventure genre in the twenty-first century, an elision of adventure and emotion, a representation of flexible masculinities.

The changing landscape of adventure is further evidenced in the novels of Robert Muchamore, represented in his *Cherub Club* series. The first novel, *The Recruit*, published in 2004, recounts the recruitment of James Adams, the series hero, to Cherub, a network of intelligence agents, all aged 17 or under, who are trained and live on the secret Cherub Campus. James becomes a part of Cherub after the death of his mother, while he is living in a children's care home. His younger sister, Lauren, subsequently also becomes an agent. James, however, is not in the mold of previous heroes. He is a working-class boy from an inner-city public housing project, he is physically unfit, he washes himself as infrequently as possible, and he behaves chauvinistically until he is shown the error of his ways by the girls in Cherub who can physically overpower him and tactically outmaneuver him. With time he becomes a successful agent because he is resourceful and loyal and because he learns the importance of teamwork. Though he never becomes a completely exemplary figure, he does represent for the boy reader a flawed but recognizable hero: someone average in school who makes mistakes in his relationships, has doubts and fears, but ultimately saves the day. James, though recognized as the hero of the series, shares his adventures with other Cherub agents, boys and girls alike. Muchamore emphasizes the need for community and cooperation: the isolated hero has given way to group negotiation and recognized the need for shared action. Gender equity is paramount in Muchamore's texts, with both male and female characters represented through a flexible array of both masculine and feminine qualities, which represents a renegotiation of the traditional adventure genre, in which a male hero takes center stage and all evidence of the feminine is erased or banished to the margins. The landscapes of Muchamore's novels are also a long way from the exotic locations of Empire narratives, generally taking place in deprived inner-city streets rife with drug and gang culture where moral ambiguity comes to the fore and the impact of crime is made visible to the reader.

The fragility of life as a traditional action hero and the violence inherent in this landscape is explored in the *Boy Soldier* series of Andy McNab. The first novel of the series, *Boy Soldier,* was published in 2005 and co-written by Robert Rigby. The series follows the life of 17-year-old Danny Watts, whose application to join the army has far-reaching and sometimes catastrophic consequences for his own life and the lives of those close to him. Danny finds himself as a fugitive, on the run with his grandfather Fergus whom he does not know and who is a former SAS officer; initially, the reader is initially led to believe Fergus has betrayed his country. Though McNab represents Danny as becoming expert in surveillance and covert operations, and as physically honed and mentally alert in order to stay alive, he also makes the reader aware of the impact of this lifestyle; the need for secrecy and an itinerant lifestyle leads to both social and emotional isolation. Fergus Watts is represented as a solitary figure, a trained killer who keeps his feelings closed down and is able to offer Danny very little intimacy or emotional engagement. Unlike Horowitz, who uses humor to temper the potentially horrific consequences of Alex's dangerous lifestyle, McNab and Rigby allow the reader to witness the full impact of Danny's life path. He survives and goes on to join the security services at 18; however, this is not without costs.

All three authors offer new versions of the adventure story that engage discussions around what it means to be a hero in the twenty-first century, when confidence in shared cultural beliefs has given way to individualism; when the privileging of the white, middle-class man has come under sustained pressure; and when hegemonic versions of masculinities that support action over intimate engagement have been attacked as detrimental to the growth of emotional literacy. Perhaps the greatest achievement of the novels is to reinstate the adventure hero into boys' reading, to make action acceptable once again, while at the same time updating the hero to incorporate the complexities of being a boy in the new millennium.

Further Reading

Bristow, Joseph. *Empire Boys: Adventures in a Man's World.* London: HarperCollins Academic, 1991.

Connell, R. W. *Masculinities.* Berkeley and Los Angeles: California University Press, 1995.

Rowan, Leonie, et al. *Boys, Literacies and Schooling: The Dangerous Territories of Gender-Based Literacy Reform.* Buckingham, UK: Open University Press, 2002.

Michele Gill

Chip Hilton: All-American Boy of the Mid-Twentieth Century

In 1948, American boys were introduced to a new fictional hero, Chip Hilton, who embodies everything that a hero should be: he excels at football, basketball, and baseball, but he tempers his success with humility. Though he is typically the best player, he never forgets that the team comes first. The series of

24 books written by legendary basketball coach Clair Bee follows Chip's career from his high school days at Valley Falls through his college career at State University. In each book, when the hero is not scoring touchdowns or driving in runs, he finds time to help his friends, foil or convert his enemies, and generally promote truth, justice, and the American way.

Originally published between 1948 and 1965, the series existed within the environment of the Cold War (1946–1991), and Chip embodied everything that an American boy should be in order to keep his nation strong. He has an unfailing moral compass, and he is willing to fight, both with his behavior and his fists, for what was right. He loves his country, and his sense of justice leads him to promote racial inclusion long before the civil rights movement brings these concerns to the forefront. Chip's example served to teach American boys how to grow up willing to promote and defend their teams and their way of life.

Chip's popularity is such that his name graces an award given since 1997 by the National Collegiate Athletic Association to the basketball player who best displays character on and off the court. Through the efforts of Bee's daughter Cynthia Bee Farley and her husband Randy, the series was updated and reissued in 2002 by Broadman and Holman, and so boys in another perilous time can once again learn moral values while reading the very well written adventures of a stellar athlete.

The Author

Clair Bee (1896–1983), the author of the series, was indeed a legendary basketball coach. While coaching at Long Island University (1929–1951), Bee led his teams to win 412 games, losing only 87, a winning percentage of .826, which is the highest of any Division I coach in NCAA history. Bee is also credited with several innovations, including the 1-3-1 defense, the three-second rule, and the 24-second rule in professional basketball. In addition to his fictional series, Bee also wrote several books on the technical aspects of basketball. A three-sport star in high school, Bee also coached LIU's football team until it was disbanded in 1940, and after LIU, he coached the Baltimore Bullets from 1952 to 1954.

Bee's experience provided a real-world feel that many juvenile books could not match. Chip's teams do not always win the big game, and the environment he lives in is not an idyllic "Leave it to Beaver" world. Instead, Chip's stories are full of unscrupulous men, from corrupt baseball scouts to abusive coaches and other bullies who have to be beat down.

Bee also knew about this firsthand. His coaching tenure at LIU ended abruptly in 1951, when three LIU players—including Sherman White, who had been named Player of the Year by the Sporting News—were arrested for taking bribes to throw games. The conspiracy was arranged by former LIU player Eddie Gard and eventually involved 30 players from City College of New York, Bradley University, New York University, Kentucky University, Manhattan University, and the University of Toledo. Although not implicated in the scandal, Bee resigned from LIU, and in an article in the *Saturday Evening Post,* he took full responsibility for not teaching his players moral responsibility.

The Hero

Chip never lets his coaches and teammates down by accepting bribes from unscrupulous men, and in the pages of the *Hilton* series, Bee attempted to teach his young readers how to avoid the troubles that he experienced. In each of the books, Chip and his teammates face moral tests, and pass them all. Chip is typically the leader who shows others the correct path. He helps teammates resolve personal and family crises, makes men out of cowards, and rehabilitates cheaters.

It is not always easy to travel the straight and narrow path, however, and Chip has to struggle against many unscrupulous men, and even against himself at times. In *Dugout Jinx* (1952), Chip is tempted when an unscrupulous scout opens suitcases full of cash to persuade him to give up his dreams of college and sign a professional contract. The hero experiences a moment of doubt, thinking of how the money could help ease his mother's burden, but quickly recovers and sends the man packing. Throughout the series, Chip is presented with challenges such as these, but always chooses right over wrong.

Overcoming corruption often forces the hero to use his fists to defeat his foes. Chip never backs down from violent confrontations, and he displays skillful violence when needed. The hero never looks for a fight, nor does he use violence indiscriminately, but when a teammate needs protecting, he is willing to use force to defend the weak.

Similarly, Chip has a strong sense of patriotism; in one instance he argues that making sacrifices for the love of sport—in this case working rather than accepting a scholarship—was a lot like patriotism. In another story, Chip works at a summer camp whose owner openly instills patriotism in his charges. Sometimes Chip's patriotic fervor is less explicit, but it always hovers in the background.

The Cast of Characters

Though Chip is the star of the series, he has considerable help in traveling the straight and narrow path from a recurring cast of characters. In the early books, the most notable of these is Coach Henry Rockwell, who guides the young star—whose own father dies before the series begins—in all three sports at Valley High, and after local boosters manipulate his dismissal, he follows Chip to State as an assistant coach. Rockwell teaches the X's and O's, but he also serves as a moral exemplar for the young star.

The coach is unwilling to compromise on moral principle, at one point threatening to pull his team from a hotel that would not allow a Black trainer and ballplayer to stay with the team. After the hotel manager backs down, Rockwell feels nothing but contempt for the man who allows expedience to dictate his actions. With such a mentor, Chip cannot help absorbing the intangible benefits that sport is believed to teach.

Chip is also joined by talented teammates, including Soapy Smith, Speed Morris, and Biggie Cohen. Smith is the designated comedy relief of the series, but also steps up whenever the team needs a break, or on the few occasions when Chip needs to be reminded not to believe his press clippings. Morris is the speedy halfback who Chip, the quarterback, hands off to during their victories and defeats. Cohen is a massively strong young man who opens holes, or belts home runs, on the various teams. Cohen is easygoing, but in one story, when an interim coach knocks the ailing Rockwell down, Cohen, protecting those who cannot defend themselves, savagely beats the man.

Women play a much smaller role in the series, with the most visible female being Chip's mother, Mary Hilton. Mrs. Hilton is a single, working mother, which in the 1940s and 1950s was not common for middle-class women. But because her husband died, she has to work to feed her family. As with most of the female characters in the series, Mrs. Hilton stays in the background, and often seems to represent a distraction for Chip. Early in Chip's life, she tried to take some of his athletic focus away by urging him to play the piano, and later by telling him that fighting is wrong, even though his cause is right. A few other females, such as Mitzi Savrill, seem to catch Chip's eye romantically, but those story lines are never fully explored, as young boys in those times are supposed to be more concerned with reaching third base on the diamond, not elsewhere.

Racial Inclusion

Bee did send his young readers a strong message of racial inclusion, however, and there were several Black characters in his books. In many instances, the Black characters were mentioned in passing, such as Miner, a stellar player who is one of Chip's high school opponents. The message in that instance is that a Black player competing against whites is not worthy of any special consideration—talent is what is important, not skin color.

This message is forcefully delivered in *Hoop Crazy* (1950). While watching a PE class, Chip notices Cliff Barnes, a Black student who demonstrates basketball potential. Chip immediately informs the coaches and begins working with Barnes to sharpen his skills. Rockwell adds Barnes to the junior varsity first and then the varsity, and the climax comes when the team plays Southern, where no integrated team has ever played before. Barnes plays well, and eventually wins over the initially hostile crowd with his talent. The message that Bee communicates to his readers is that talent is all that matters in the meritocracy that is the United States. This of course was not so in 1950, and the struggle of the civil rights movement still lay in the future, but Bee sent an early message to boys that racism had no place in sports, or in America.

Jimmy Lee Chung, a Chinese American, also figured prominently during Chip's State career, with a similar theme. In *Ten Seconds to Play* (1955), Chip and Jimmy Lee do not get along, but the hero defends the Asian player to other teammates who doubt that Jimmy Lee is a true American. Eventually the two reconcile after attending church together, and become friends and productive teammates.

In the original series, religion hovers in the background, with occasional mentions of Chip and Soapy going to church, but it is still evident that the boys are following President Dwight Eisenhower's injunction to believe in something. The reissued series contains a more evangelical flavor, its publisher is Christian. In addition, the books are updated to add a more modern feel, referencing the Internet, ESPN, and other features of contemporary life, which includes depicting Speed Morris as an African American.

Respect for Authority

In keeping with the times, Chip also exhibits great respect for authority figures, as long as they deserve it. Coaches, with the exception of the abusive man mentioned above, are respected, even when their styles conflict with the team. But other authority figures also feature prominently in the stories. One of these is J. P. Ohlsen, a leading businessman in Valley Falls who owns the local pottery factory and who built the sport facility used by the high school and the community. Another is H. L. Armstrong, an industrialist who sponsors a semiprofessional baseball team that Chip practices with during the summer while working in the man's factory. Chip also works for John Schroeder and George Grayson, in Valley Falls and at State, respectively. These businessmen help Chip support his family and work his way through college.

The businessmen and community leaders presented in the book are much different from those who form our typical view of these men today. These are positive influences, not greedy abusers. They build recreation facilities and offer profit sharing. They do not send their factories overseas or exploit their workers.

The *Chip Hilton* series both entertained with stories of athletic daring and taught boys how to grow up to be good men between 1948 and 1965, and now it serves the same function for a new generation. In many ways, the world of the 1940s and 1950s was very different from that of today, but many of the situations that boys face today remain the same. Boys who read about Chip's exploits learned the difference between right and wrong, that team was all, that racial inclusion was good for the nation, and that sometimes words must be backed by forceful action; all lessons important for shaping future athletes and citizens in perilous times, both then and now.

Further Reading

Bee, Clair. *Chip Hilton Series.* New York: Grossett and Dunlap, 1948–1965.

Bee Farley, Cynthia, and Farley, Randy. *Hilton Series.* Nashville, TN: Broadman and Holman, 2002.

Defrank, Thomas M. "Comeback Kid: The Return of Chip Hilton." *Weekly Standard,* September 16, 2002.

McCormick, Wilfred. *Bronc Burnett and Rocky McCune Series*. New York: Grossett and Dunlap, 1947–1967.

Nash, Bill. "Times Change, but Book's Lessons Don't." *Ventura County Star,* August 15, 2002.

Russ Crawford

Comic Books

When people hear the term *comic book*, they will agree that it has something to do with the following ideas: something childish, silly, or funny. Many people still connect comic books with the 1960s TV version of *Batman* with the dramatic comic book sound effects flashed in word form across the screen "BAT-

SPLAT!!!" and other such silliness. In fact, the characteristics that make comic books unique are both easily recognized by most of us and at the root of why most people do not take comics seriously. For example, a recent graphic novel of *The 9/11 Report*, adapted and drawn by comic-book veterans Sid Jacobson and Ernie Colón, often creates negative reactions from readers of all ages. Many readers are uncomfortable with the comic-book format because it contrasts with the seriousness of the subject matter covered in the work. For example, the use of "R-RRUMBLE" in large red letters over the crumbling twin towers can be too much of a contrast for readers who view the use of onomatopoeia as comic.

Now, the comic book as a genre is a different form from the comic strip, although artists in both forms share techniques. The comic strip is a brief series of panels, or one panel, that do tend to be humorous and often appear in print as part of newspapers. Many people throughout the mid-twentieth century referred to comic strips in newspapers as the "funny papers." Comic strips that most people still recognize include *Peanuts*, created by Charles Schulz, and *Doonesbury*, created by Garry Trudeau. These are typical comic strips in that they use cartoon artwork and have primarily a humorous intent, from broad humor to more serious forms of satire, whether that satire be directed at the relationship between adults and children or the political world. The comic strip is similar in form and purpose to cartoons, which are comic panels placed into motion. Cartoons have experienced popularity along with the rise of television and include TV shows such as *The Flintstones* and *The Jetsons*, and a wide range of Looney Tunes. In recent years, cartoons have experienced a television renaissance in shows such as *The Simpsons* and *Rugrats*, and the more controversial *South Park* and *Family Guy*.

Both cartoons and comic strips are part of the lives of boys and men, but more broadly, they are also part of all people's lives. When most people look at comic strips, cartoons, or comic books, they see the forms as one genre—not as distinct forms with different purposes, tones, and audiences in mind. The comic book is different in many ways from comic strips and cartoons; however, one segment of the comic-book industry is parallel to comic strips and cartoons. That segment of the comic-book industry is primarily funny and directed at small children, including classic comics that focus on characters such as Archie, Richie Rich, and Donald Duck. But the comic books that many of us know as comics is a world of superheroes, a world that is powerful and dark; these are the comics that are definitely not funny and not for children.

The superhero comic book shares its origin with comic strips and cartoons; however, its form is unique. The comic book is sequential art like a comic strip, but the comic book tends to be many pages of panels and is traditionally published as a freestanding book. Most comic books appear in serial form—a number of separate books of a connected story line focusing on a central character or central characters. The 8×11 comic book with the glossy and colorful single-panel cover and the self-contained story inside, originally published on newsprint but more recently printed on slick paper throughout, is the comic book that we recognize as the form we read, collect, and appreciate.

Whereas the comic strip tends to be the work of one artist who writes and draws the strip, comic books tend to be collaborative art forms—one work of art created by several people. A comic book often involves the work of a writer, an artist (usually called a penciller, because this artist creates rough sketches in pencil), an inker (who finishes the drawing using a black ink), a letterer, and a colorist. In some cases, artists take on multiple roles in their work, such as artists Todd McFarlane and Frank Miller completing writing and artist duties on many of the comic books they create. *Batman: The Dark Knight Returns* is an example of a comic-book series written and drawn by Frank Miller; though this comic book is heavily the work of one artist, it still has an inker and colorist, Klaus Jan and Lynn Varley.

The comic-book form has nearly a century of history and within that history many of the most recognized comics include superheroes, but the form is varied and complex. The comic-book form we will discuss here focuses on the books that include a range of title characters such as Superman, Batman, and Spider-Man. As we will explore further, these characters broadly represent both the male orientation of comic books and the basic types of title characters: Superman has superpowers that raise him above mere mortals; Batman is essentially a mortal, but has refined his abilities through dedication and extraordinary circumstances; Spider-Man is a mortal who gained superpowers through some unusual event. In recent years, the serial nature of comic books, appearing approximately once a month, has evolved into a longer form called the graphic novel, a form that looks like a comic book but presents a more extended story that equals the story line that we would usually find in six or ten comic issues.

Before looking at that history, let us identify the qualities of comics that make the genre recognizable. As mentioned above, comics are driven by artwork, usually a style of artwork that is broadly called cartoons, but can vary greatly. That style involves representing the world through line drawings that outline people, places, and things first through pencil sketches and then finished with pen and black ink. The comic artist often incorporates a range of representations of reality that run from minimal details—usually associated with cartoons and less serious subjects such as the drawing of Matt Groening, who created *The Simpsons* and the early comic strip *Life Is Hell*—to realistic and surrealistic portrayals of reality that are highly detailed and stylized, usually associated with more adult and darker themes such as the artwork by Frank Miller, Todd McFarlane, or Jim Lee. The more realistic and surrealistic styles of superhero comic-book artists typically exaggerate the body structures of the heroes and other people in the story lines; notable is the exaggerated and arguably sexist representation of female characters in comic books such as *Storm of X-Men*.

Comic books are also characterized by their coloring, which traditionally uses the basic four-color process employing black, magenta, cyan, and yellow, but more recently they have been impacted by the coloring possibilities of computers. The distinct black outlining of the artwork and the vibrant colors are classic characteristics of comic-book art along with the muscular and exaggerated body types and movements of the people in those comics. Yet, the most distinct characteristic may be the use of panels in a series over several pages to tell a story. The series of storyboards or panels is driven by the artwork, but comic books also use brief segments of text and the classic dialog balloon to distinguish general narrative from the characters speaking. Though these characteristics are manipulated in many ways by different artists, most comic books share these qualities, and this is why a comic book is a comic book.

When Male Worlds Collide

Generalizations are dangerous, but it is safe to say that comic books are intricately connected with the lives of boys and adolescents. The people who write and draw comics are primarily men, and those buying, reading, and collecting comics are primarily males. The world of the superhero seems to be deeply seated in the minds of males. Why?

Part of the connection between comics and males is certainly the visual nature of the genre. Comics create narrative with text and images. The male mind tends to be highly visual, and the comic book makes demands of a reader decoding words and images in a series of panels (and the rules governing those panels are complex and changing). Because the comic form grew almost exclusively from the minds and pens of men, the way comics communicate is highly masculine in both the language of the text and the language of the images.

Another element of the connection between comics and the male world is the tendency, especially in the superhero comics, for the mythologies to be macho (and even sexist). Probably the most powerful part of comic-book mythologies is the constant tension between good and evil. The stereotype of boys playing cowboys and Indians (despite the politically incorrect language of this activity) has some basis in truth; young boys throughout modern times have turned to play that pits good against evil. One of the many ways that game has evolved is the comic book.

Also involved in the comic world is boys' fascination with their own sexuality and the expectations for their sexuality in the world. Comics range from being subtle (the early Catwoman of *Batman* comics) to being openly sexual in more recent times (Miller's *Sin City*, for example, and his *All Star Batman and Robin*). The worlds of comic heroes are filled with relationship complications—from Superman and Lois Lane to Spider-Man losing Gwen Stacy and having a tumultuous life with Mary Jane.

Finally, the world of superheroes is one separate from but reflecting the real world for boys and adolescents, a place to consider themselves as men. The power and action of the superhero provide one mirror of masculinity for young men; moreover, the muscular and athletic images of the art in comics capture one aspect of how masculinity is viewed. However, comics do not merely stereotype or limit the portrayal of the powerful and muscular male. Many of the primary myths of comics examine a wide range of expectations for males—notably in Spider-Man, as Peter Parker was surviving and excelling because of his mind before his transformation gave him an equally dynamic body.

Comic Books—A Brief History

The comic book, an 8×11 self-contained book of sequential artwork, has its roots in the 1896 publication by R. F. Outcault, *The Yellow Kid.* This humorous beginning in comic strips and cartoons creates some of the confusion today that leads to many people associating comic books with an insignificant genre for children only. Over the next three decades, cartoons as a form of literature and the ability to create publications on newsprint and in mass quantities led to the first comic book, *Funnies on Parade.* This publication looks much like the current comic book does, except for the quality of the paper and the look of the coloring.

Throughout the early 1930s, the reading public became familiar with essentially human heroic characters—some serious and some comic—such as Dick Tracy, the Shadow, and Popeye. In 1936, Lee Falk created the Phantom, a masked hero who stands as a precursor of the comic superheroes we know today. *Detective Comics* #1 hit stands in 1937, establishing the earliest beginnings of DC comics, the first major publisher of comic books.

From the late 1930s to the late 1940s, comic books experienced the golden age of comics, grounded by *Action Comics* #1, the introduction of *Superman* by Jerry Siegel and Joe Schuster. Superman embodies the superhero who surpasses humans; he is an alien and represents the classic pattern in comic books of the dual persona—Superman the superhero and his alter ego Clark Kent, nerdish and bumbling behind his only mask, a pair of horn-rimmed glasses. The year 1939 saw the publication of *Detective Comics* #27, the arrival of Bob Kane's *Batman.* Batman shares with Superman the dual persona and the stylish cape, but Batman stands as unique, because Bruce Wayne, the man behind Batman's cowl, is a mere mortal, although he has tremendous financial resources and is driven by a dark desire to enact revenge because of the murder of his parents.

By 1939 Superman had his own title, and the basic foundation of modern comic books had been established. Superman represents the idealistic good, and Batman a superhero who struggles with madness and his own demons. In 1939, the genesis of the next powerful publisher of comic books arrived in *Marvel Comics* #1, including Bill Everett's *Prince Namor the Sub-Mariner* (a fictional comic book character featured in *Marvel Comics* who resurfaces years later when Marvel Comics takes over control of the industry from DC).

The golden age of comics had drawn to a close by the mid-1940s. The era included the introduction of Batman's sidekick, Robin, in 1940; *Captain America* debuting in his own self-named comic in 1941, the first superhero with such an honor, from the team of Joe Simon and Jack Kirby; and the rise of Will Eisner, with *The Spirit,* and Jack Kirby as two of the giants of the field throughout most of the twentieth century.

The popularity of comic books in the first half of the twentieth century drew a loyal readership primarily among boys, but that popularity also drew criticism, notably from Dr. Fredric Wertham, who declared comic books unhealthy for young people. This backlash coincided with a rise of horror comic books, surpassing the dominance of superhero comics. In 1954, the Comic Code

Authority created a strict code for comics and instituted the comic stamp that many people identify with the covers of comic books. This code system and the charge by doctors and the government that comics were harmful to children brought the golden age to an end and threatened the future of the comic-book form.

The silver age of comics saw a rise of a new publisher controlling the industry. DC's publication of *Showcase* #4, reintroducing the Flash, represents a revival of the influence of comic books, but 1958 held a more important moment for comics—*Strange Worlds* #1, by the creative team of Stan Lee and Jack Kirby. This set in motion the Marvel Age of comics, which anchored the second wave of comic popularity. In 1961 and into 1962, Lee and Kirby took the comic world by storm and moved Marvel Comics ahead of DC with the introduction of *The Fantastic Four, The Incredible Hulk,* and one of the most noted moments in comic book history, *Amazing Fantasy* #15—which introduced *The Amazing Spider-Man,* from the minds and artwork of Lee, Kirby, and Steve Ditko.

The 1960s and the silver age of comics would belong to Marvel Comics with the *Avengers,* the *X-Men,* and a growing list of popular and unique superhero comics. The stories were becoming more sophisticated—clearly not intended only for children—and even the creative process was innovative at Marvel Comics, with Lee giving more power to artists and writers, providing them with valuable training ground within the growing industry. From these years, many comic talents were created and inspired. Marvel Comics also created the first African American characters, beginning with the Black Panther in 1966.

Comic-book historians see the 1970s as yet another transition for comic books—some see it an extension of the silver age, whereas others label it the bronze age. The comics became more sophisticated, dark, and complex. Marvel Comics remained dominant, but DC experienced revitalization because of DC's powerful characters, Superman and Batman (characters who proved to be so popular that their self-titled ongoing comic series help make *Detective Comics* the longest running title in comic history). The bronze age included Marvel Comics introducing Robert E. Howard's pulp character Conan the Barbarian in 1970, and the comic giant challenging the Comic Code Authority with *Amazing Spider-Man #96–98,* which deals directly with drug abuse.

The more adult topics and artwork accelerated throughout the 1970s as comic fans followed the troubled life of Spider-Man/Peter Parker, who lived the life of a superhero and a normal young man—losing loved ones, falling in and out of love, and struggling at work. Marvel Comics also turned the comic world toward the antihero by introducing enduring characters such as Wolverine, introduced in *The Incredible Hulk,* and the Punisher, introduced in *The Amazing Spider-Man.* These characters would find their way to the movie screen nearly three decades later. The mid-1970s also saw the skyrocketing fame of mutant comics, triggered by Marvel Comics' *The New X-Men,* including *Wolverine.*

By the late 1970s, comics were at yet another crossroads, taking a strong shift toward ever darker themes. Frank Miller contributed his writing and artwork to Marvel's *Daredevil* and DC's *Batman,* and by the mid-1980s, the comic-book industry found itself connected to many marketing ventures, including toys and movies. For purists, this marked a decline in the art form, and for the industry, comic books did see a drop in quality and value because too often comics where created purely to generate buzz and revenue—causing the opposite effect on the industry because the flood of comics and related items devalued the items in the collector's market.

The marketing strategies of the comic powerhouses also created superstars in the industry, such as Miller and McFarlane, who generated buzz for the industry through their writing and their stylish artwork on *Batman* and *Spider-Man*. The power some talent gained through the main two publishers, Marvel and DC, helped the rise of independent labels such as Image Comics: McFarlane created his own comic hero, Spawn, and his own comic books and line of toys along with Jim Lee, Marc Silverstri, and other Marvel artists at Image Comics. The 1990s era of comics did spur a rise in the comic-book–based movie industry over the next two decades—from Superman and Batman to a tremendously successful run of Spider-Man movies. Even lesser comic characters have found their way to the movie screen—the Punisher, Daredevil, the Fantastic Four, the Hulk, Ironman. Frank Miller also lent his talent to the rise of the graphic novel, one boom that grew out of the sputtering comic-book industry during the mid-1980s into the twenty-first century.

The Graphic Hero with a Thousand Masks

Throughout his career, Joseph Campbell wrote and spoke extensively about the patterns that myths, religions, tales, and stories of all kinds shared. In his *The Hero with a Thousand Faces*, Campbell identified the hero's journey. Later, in "The Power of Myth," an interview conducted by Bill Moyers, Campbell applied his ideas about mythic patterns to popular culture, specifically the characters and narratives in the *Star Wars* movies. These patterns and that hero's journey are also seen in the hero stories of mainstream comic books.

As noted earlier, Superman, Batman, and Spider-Man represent the basic patterns of comic-book heroes. In Campbell's framework, the traditional hero experiences are a standard cycle of the heroic journey. Though the journey of the hero is not uniquely described by Campbell, here the journey will be outlined and supported within the world of comic books. The hero's journey usually begins with some sort of call to that role of hero, often including the hero losing something or someone valuable. Batman is spawned from the murder of Bruce Wayne's parents, an ordeal witnessed by Wayne as a boy; Spider-Man is created by Peter Parker after the death of his uncle Ben at the hands of a criminal that Peter himself failed to confront before that criminal kills his uncle; and Superman finds himself on an alien planet, having lost his entire world and discovering that the new planet renders him superhuman.

Once the hero has been called to the heroic journey, he or she often resists the call or doubts himself or herself. The comic world is filled with reluctant heroes, possibly best represented by Peter Parker, who persistently fights with himself over his duty as a superhero and his own personal longings. Once the hero commits, some mentor usually intervenes. For Spider-Man, Aunt May provides sage advice. Superman relies heavily on the support of his earthly family, the Kents, who adopt him when they discover him as a baby on their farm. Batman possibly best represents the hero actively seeking the guidance of experts when he commits to becoming a master detective, but Bruce Wayne also has the butler Alfred Pennyworth as his lifelong mentor.

Next, the hero must begin the journey by crossing an initial threshold. In the comic world, that tends to be the first story line for the hero. Superman, Batman, and Spider-Man all have origin stories, initially told in the first issue of the comic in which they appear, but retold throughout the life of the comic character's run. These origin stories include the superhero having some success at the beginning. For Batman and Spider-Man, that origin includes an interesting twist because these characters have tense relationships with the police, with other people in their lives, and with the public inside their comic universe. Once committed and with an adventure behind them, the hero often encounters a helper. In the legend of Batman, this pattern is most evident with the character Robin. To date, Batman has had three separate Robin sidekicks, including losing one to death.

In the traditional hero journey, the quest is linear, moving forward and culminating in some way. For the comic world, the remaining pattern becomes cyclical. In other words, the comic hero tends to be immortal within the comic universe so the remaining elements of the hero's journey repeat throughout the story line. However, these elements are still significant in the superhero's journey.

Once the hero overcomes the initial challenges, the journey often leads to a central cave or abyss. For the superhero, that place is often a lair, and not a dangerous place. Batman has the Batcave, and Superman, his Fortress of Solitude. The concept of the hero having support is counterbalanced with dangers as well. Batman and Spider-Man appear to have personal weaknesses: Bruce Wayne feels unbridled rage and Peter Parker suffers from a deep sense of doubt. Superman has the most famous weakness, kryptonite.

Again, the traditional hero's journey includes a primary challenge, followed by the hero using some additional charm to succeed and return to a homeland. This cycle can include both literal and metaphorical deaths and resurrections as well. Comic-book heroes experience these patterns over and over. Spider-Man lost his girlfriend Gwen Stacy to death, just as Batman lost his second Robin. For all of these superheroes, the ultimate challenge comes in the form of supervillains. The death-resurrection cycle is also common within the comic world. Superheroes can kill their alter ego by quitting their role or by experiencing a change in costumes, as Spider-Man has done. Possibly unique to the superhero journey, in fact, is the masking and costumes of the superhero that allow a dual existence for these heroes.

These patterns suggest that the comic book holds important patterns of storytelling for any reader. These patterns are portrayed in collaboration among several artists, but the value of the comic book is no less than that of traditional literature in many ways.

Twenty-First Century Superheroes—Comics in a Postmodern World

In the last years of the twentieth century, Marvel Comics stopped *The Amazing Spider-Man*, which had run since 1963, and began again with #1. They soon returned the title to its original numbering, but this decision shows the struggle in the comic-book world throughout the late twentieth century. The comic-book universe still looks in many ways as it has since the Marvel Age exploded, around 1960. Comic-book stores are now the place to find favorite comics (not pharmacies), but those stores still prominently display Spider-Man, Batman, and Superman. The enduring superheroes endure.

But the industry has growing pains in the twenty-first century, caused by changes such as the quality of the coloring and the paper. Comic books look more sophisticated now than they did 40 years ago. Moreover, comics still struggle with the problems faced in the mid-1980s into the 1990s. Marketing and the power of comic-book superstars—the people who write and draw comics, and not the superheroes within the pages—have created a market that some fear is ruining a treasured art form.

In 2005, DC launched *All Star Batman and Robin, the Boy Wonder,* a new title written by Frank Miller and drawn by Jim Lee—two of the biggest stars of comic creation working in the twenty-first century. This title represents both the promise and the dangers faced by comic books in a postmodern world. Though the team of Miller and Lee created a huge buzz, the promise left many feeling unfulfilled, because the issues arrived in stores sporadically and late. The series dragged along and many fans criticized Miller for becoming a parody of himself.

This struggle shows that the comic universe has its own model for that world, one where superheroes live lives expected and embraced by the readers. Yet, the comic industry is a business. The tension created between artists and corporations plays out in the marketplace. In other words, those who read and collect comics make commentaries on twenty-first-century comics through their purchases—or lack of purchases. For anyone who collected and read comics in the silver age, *All Star Batman and Robin, the Boy Wonder* is fascinating because the comic has profanity, sex, violence, and even nudity. In the ironic way that the term works, this comic is clearly adult. But for the current market, preteen and teen males, *All Star Batman and Robin, the Boy Wonder* may seem ordinary within the context of the larger marketplace—movies, games, and a whole host of technologies that make the comic-book form appear to be static and tame.

Yet, comic books persist. The venues for buying and collecting comic books have changed along with the coloring and paper quality. But the books are still 8 × 11, and the comic universe in the twenty-first century still remains the domain of Spider-Man, Batman, and Superman.

Further Reading

Campbell, Joseph. *The Hero with a Thousand Faces.* New York: MJF Books, 1949.

Eisner, Will. *Comics and Sequential Art.* NJ: Poorhouse Press, 1985.

Eisner, Will. *Graphic Storytelling.* FL: Poorhouse Press, 1996.

McCloud, Scott. *Making Comics: Storytelling Secrets of Comics, Manga and Graphic Novels.* New York: Harper Paperback, 2006.

McCloud, Scott. *Reinventing Comics: How Imagination and Technology Are Revolutionizing an Art Form.* New York: Harper Paperback, 2000.

McCloud, Scott. *Understanding Comics: The Invisible Art.* New York: Harper Paperback, 1994.

Rhoades, Shirrel. *Comic Books: How the Industry Works.* New York: Peter Lang USA, 2008.

P. L. Thomas

Coming-of-Age in Fiction

Coming-of-age may be defined as the transition from childhood to adulthood and could imply a process or period of physical, social, emotional, legal, religious, and cultural transformation that may be involved in an individual's maturation. Narratives of coming-of-age, and their related themes and characters, have played a central role in fiction about and for Anglo-American boys over the last century. More recently these elements have become significant themes in film, particularly those aimed at teen viewers.

The Novel of Formation

Contemporary coming-of-age books and films about adolescent males are often examples of the bildungsroman, or novel of formation. *Bildungsroman* is a German term used to describe a novel whose subject, according to Abrams, is "the development of the protagonist's mind and character, in the passage from childhood through varied experiences—and often through a spiritual crisis—into maturity and the recognition of his or her identity and role in the world."A bildungsroman consists of characteristic elements that may include a journey triggered by some event, loss, or trauma that moves the protagonist away from home, often through exile or escape; a maturation process that involves struggling against internal and external obstacles; and the protagonist's rebellion against societal norms. Other common elements may include first experiences with love, sex, drugs, and other illicit "adult" activities that usually relate to the protagonist's rebellion or spiritual development.

The first bildungsromans are considered to be the German novels K. P. Moritz's *Anton Reiser* (1785–1790) and Goethe's *Wilhelm Meister's Apprenticeship* (1795–1796). Charles Dickens's *David Copperfield* (1850) and *Great Expectations* (1861) are often cited as early examples of coming-of-age novels in the Anglo-American tradition. These accounts of emotional and moral development from boyhood to adulthood influenced many coming-of-age novels that followed. Mark Twain's *Adventures of Huckleberry Finn* (1884–1885) is one of the classic coming-of-age stories of American boyhood. Distinct from Dickens's novels, the Twain's narrative does not chronicle the protagonist's entire biography; rather, the novel charts a life-changing experience—namely, Huck's journey down the Mississippi River with his friend Jim, a runaway slave. Another influential coming-of-age classic, Robert Louis Stevenson's *Treasure Island* (1883) also focuses on a significant experience in the development of Jim Hawkins, a young man whose discovery of a treasure map begins his coming-of-age pirate adventure. In addition, the young male protagonists of adult fiction such as Thomas Hardy's *Jude the Obscure* (1895), D. H.

Lawrence's *Sons and Lovers* (1913), and James Joyce's *Portrait of the Artist as a Young Man* (1916) were significant influences on the representation of male adolescence in later periods.

Coming-of-Age Classics

J. D. Salinger's *Catcher in the Rye* (1951), John Knowles's *A Separate Peace* (1959), and William Golding's *Lord of the Flies* (1954) are often identified as classic coming-of-age novels with male protagonists. Interestingly, all of these books were not written specifically for adolescent readers. However, with the emergence of young adult fiction as its own genre in the 1960s and 1970s, followed by the rising popularity of the American coming-of-age teen movie in the 1980s, these novels have become models of coming-of-age experience for adolescent males in many books and films aimed at teen readers and viewers.

Salinger's *Catcher in the Rye* (1951) takes place over 72 hours in the life of its adolescent protagonist Holden Caulfield. Written in first person, it follows his experiences in New York City in the days after he is expelled from his college prep school. The portrayal of adolescent angst and the open sexuality and profane language of the novel were extremely controversial at the time of the book's publication. Holden Caulfield has become an icon of teenage rebellion, and many alternative, rebellious, upper-middle-class male protagonists in contemporary fiction and film may be viewed as his descendents. Both Stephen Chbosky's book *The Perks of Being a Wallflower* (1999) and the film *Igby Goes Down* (2002) pay homage to this classic.

Knowles's *A Separate Peace* (1959) focuses on the relationship between Gene, a studious young man, and Finny, his more extroverted athletic friend, at a New Hampshire prep school the summer before they will be drafted into World War II. Over the course of the novel, Gene must come to terms with his guilt over an accident that leaves Finny irreversibly injured, causing him to reflect on loss of innocence and mortality. The protagonist of Judith Guest's *Ordinary People* (1976) deals with similar themes around the death of his brother in a sailing accident.

Golding's *The Lord of the Flies* (1954), about a group of British school boys stuck on a deserted island, may be read as a brutal depiction of how boys, and humans more generally, may act when left in isolation to form a society. It has influenced many coming-of-age novels that followed, particularly in its depiction of leadership and violence within communities of young males. Robert Cormier's *The Chocolate War* (1974) highlights the power struggles among males in school settings through the perspective of a high school freshman who dares to challenge the secret society of older students who control the school through intimidation and abuse.

Coming-of-Age in Times of Trauma or War

Survival novels have a prominent history in literature for young male readers. Farley Mowat's *Lost in the Barrens* (1956) depicts the experience of two teenage boys, one white and one Cree, who attempt to combine their skills of survival while lost in the Arctic. *Hatchet*, by Gary Paulsen (1987), also charts a young plane crash survivor's experience alone in the Canadian wilderness. A recent example of this narrative is Jon Krakauer's nonfiction book *Into the Wild* (1996), based on the extreme wilderness adventures of Christopher McCandless. The book was adapted into a film of the same name (2007) that depicts his ultimately tragic solo journey to live off the land in Alaska.

Numerous coming-of-age novels represent individual struggles of male adolescents during times of war or trauma. One of the first books to link coming-of-age with war was *The Red Badge of Courage* (1895), tracing a 19-year-old's experience during the American Civil War. Many texts follow the experiences of soldiers coming to terms with their role in the terror, loss, and chaos of war. Walter Dean Myers's *Fallen Angels* (1988) depicts these experiences with a group of young men fighting in the Vietnam War. Other books illustrate autobiographical and fictional experiences of victims of war or genocide as part of the coming-of-age narrative. For example, Anne Holm's *I Am David* (1963) describes the experiences of a 12-year-old boy who escapes a concentration camp in Bulgaria.

Coming-of-Age in Fantasy Quests

A number of coming-of-age books in the fantasy genre exemplify the influence of mythological tales, which involve a hero's journey to find a specific object, person, or place. They typically employ male protagonists undergoing a journey or adventure when they become aware of their special powers or inherited status. J. K. Rowling's *Harry Potter* series (1997–2007) may be seen as the most recent of a number of popular fantasy book series that involve a young male hero who must come to terms with his special power, including Susan Cooper's *The Dark is Rising* series (1965–1977), Ursula Leguin's *Earthsea* novels (1968–2001), and Lloyd Alexander's *The Chronicles of Prydain* (1964–1973).

Many fantasy novels fall into a subcategory of the bildungsroman, an *Erziehungsroman,* or "a novel of education," with a focus on training, apprenticeship, or formal education. T. S. White's *The Once and Future King* series (1958), particularly its book, *The Sword and the Stone,* follows young King Arthur's education with Merlin, an eccentric wizard. The relationship between a wise teacher-mentor and a young apprentice can be seen in the relationships between Luke Skywalker and Yoda in Star Wars, Harry Potter and Dumbledore, and outside the fantasy genre with Daniel and Mr. Miyagi in the film the *The Karate Kid* (1984).

Coming-of-Age in Teen Films and Young Adult Fiction

Published when S. E. Hinton was 18 years old, *The Outsiders* (1967) may be seen as one of the first books written specifically for young adult (YA) readers. The book explores coming-of-age themes through the voice of 14-year-old Ponyboy and his experiences of two rival gangs from distinct socioeconomic groups. The novel recounts a series of traumatic events that change his life, including the death of his close friend. The book *The Outsiders* was adapted for film by Francis Ford Coppola in 1983 and became a breakout film for a few American actors, including Tom Cruise, Emilio Estevez, and Rob Lowe.

Many other films from the 1970s onward developed and established the coming-of-age teen film genre. Like *The Outsiders,* many of them focused on an ensemble of adolescent boys. *The Last Picture Show* (1971), *American Graffiti* (1973), and *Diner* (1982) were dramatic films about groups of male friends coming to terms with the end of high school and adolescence. *Stand by Me* (1986) involved a group of young adolescents who share a coming-of-age journey on the quest to find a dead body. *Dead Poets Society* (1989) depicted the relationship between a teacher and his group of male students in a restrictive American private school. *Boyz n the Hood* (1991) showed a group of friends coming of age in a ghetto in South Central Los Angeles. Other films chronicle the individual coming-of-age experiences. For example, *Basketball Diaries* (1995) adapts Jim Carroll's memoir of his experience of teenage drug addiction.

Running alongside this explosion of coming-of-age films, a number of young adult novels have dealt with a range of issues including socioeconomic class, race, and other forms of social exclusion and alienation for adolescent males. Russell Banks's *Rule of the Bone* (1995) is narrated by a 14-year-old homeless boy who becomes involved with drug use and sexual abuse after dropping out of school. Novels by Walter Dean Myers, such as *Autobiography of my Dead Brother* (2005), have presented realistic depictions of coming-of-age as an African American male.

Coming of Age and Sexuality

A surplus of American coming-of-age films, often a mix of romantic comedy and adventure geared at teen audiences, were produced from the 1980s onward. Among the most popular films are *Fast Times at Ridgemont High* (1982), *Ferris Bueller's Day Off* (1986), and *The Breakfast Club* (1985). Many of these films deal with heterosexual dating, romance, and sexuality as their central themes, often focusing on a group of male friends and their first sexual experiences. Recent examples include *American Pie* (1999) and *Superbad* (2007).

Books such as *Then Again, Maybe I Won't* (1971), by Judy Blume, and *The Secret Diary of Adrian Mole Aged 13?* (1982), by Sue Townsend, depict young adolescent males going through puberty. However, young adult fiction has been slower than film to depict sexual experiences of older adolescent male protagonists. Only recent books such as Melvin Burgess's *Doing It* (2004) provide a realistic and irreverent representation of the sexual explorations of a group of diverse adolescent males.

Particularly since the 1990s, many films have specifically focused on gay themes for adolescent males with the experience of coming-of-age presented closely related to the complexities of "coming out." Among these are *Maurice* (1987), based on the E. M. Forster's novel by the same name, which deals with the experience of being gay in early twentieth-century England; *Edge of Seventeen* (1998) is about coming out in Ohio in the 1980s; and *Head On* (1998) explores a young man's negotiation of his gay identity with his Greek background in Melbourne, Australia. The coming-out narrative for gay adolescent males has become an increasingly prevalent theme in young adult fiction. Though some texts represent dark experiences—such as Aidan Chambers's

Dance On My Grave (1982) and *Night Kites* (1985) by M. E. Kerr (one of the first young adult novels about AIDS)—many recent books address gay adolescent dating and relationships in a frank, upbeat, and often hilarious tone such as in David Levithan's *Boy Meets Boy* (2003) and Alex Sanchez's *Rainbow Boys* (2001).

Further Reading

Campbell, Joseph. *The Hero with a Thousand Faces.* Princeton, NJ: Princeton University Press, 1949.

Clarke, B. L., and M. Higgonet. *Girls, Boys, Books, Toys: Gender in Children's Literature and Culture.* Baltimore, MD: John Hopkins University Press, 1999.

Davis, Glyn, and Kay Dickinson, eds. *Teen TV: Genre, Consumption and Identity.* London: British Film Institute, 2004.

Watson, Victor, and Margaret Meek. *Coming of Age in Children's Literature.* London: Continuum, 2003.

Naomi Hamer

Hardy Boys

In North America the characters of the Hardy Boys are synonymous with the juvenile mystery form. *The Hardy Boys* mystery series in its various manifestations is a good example of how American boyhood is expressed through the genre of the adventure story by promoting self-sufficiency through active quest and discovery, and in the case of the two brothers, through a didactic formula that features collaboration with each other and their father.

The Hardy Boys mystery series was conceived by Edward Stratemeyer, the founder of the successful Stratemeyer Syndicate and the inventor of the pseudonym of the author Franklin W. Dixon. Beginning with *The Tower Treasure* (1927), the series was ghostwritten by many writers following specific instructions laid out by Stratemeyer himself. The stories use a formulaic plot whereby Frank and Joe Hardy, sons of a famous detective, solve mysteries in their hometown of Bayport, across the United States, and abroad. Fifty-eight volumes were published by Grosset & Dunlap until 1979 (the first 38 of these were revised between 1959 and 1973) and are considered the "original" texts. Simon & Schuster published new titles in the series from 1979 to 2005, at which time they launched a new series, *The Hardy Boys: Undercover Brother,* and published concurrent series for older and beginning readers, in addition to tie-in titles with Nancy Drew and Tom Swift. The mysteries have also appeared in other media forms such as cartoons, graphic novels, television, films, and video games.

The Stratemeyer Syndicate

The Hardy Boys series forms part of the prolific writing and editing career of Edward Stratemeyer (1862–1930), who wrote dime novels, edited juvenile magazines, and worked with the key pulp fiction writers of the day, notably Horatio Alger. From the outset Stratemeyer appealed to youth, especially to boys, by locating his stories in current events or by using current inventions, although it is important to note that the series is read by both boys and girls. He also appealed to the young readers' desire for personal autonomy by granting his characters freedoms and privileges not associated with a supervised middle-class environment. Beginning with the military school adventures of the Rover Boys (1899) he created other series such as *Bomba, the Jungle Boy* and *Tom Swift,* and for younger children, *The Bobbsey Twins,* and for girls, *The Motor Girls* and *Nancy Drew.*

In 1905 Stratemeyer founded the Stratemeyer Syndicate because he needed a quick way to produce books, and after his death the company was run by his daughters until 1962. Stratemeyer developed new techniques for producing plots and for marketing books, some of which have become staples in contemporary children's and youth mass production of genre fiction. In order to control the characterization and direction of the plots, Stratemeyer developed character cards for each of the main characters and also wrote brief plot outlines for the stories that included formulaic devices such as cliffhanger endings for the chapters. The actual writing, however, was done by contract writers who for a set sum gave up all claim to the characters or profits and who submitted their final stories to the Syndicate for editing. The Syndicate retained copyright and this syndication process took between a month to six weeks. The original ghostwriter for *The Hardy Boys* series was the Canadian Leslie McFarlane, whose autobiography *Ghost of the Hardy Boys* (1976) reveals the silence around the technique.

In terms of innovative marketing strategies, Stratemeyer shrewdly appealed to the collecting instincts of children. Because the process of book production was speedy, Stratemeyer was able to publish books in sets, not singly. Even the first book of a new series was presented along with two other books called "breeders," so the book appeared from the start to be part of a collective. For instance, the inside front cover of *The Tower Treasure* lists the next two books of the series, *The House on the Cliff* and *The Secret of the Old Mill.* In addition, the appearance of the books incited children to collect the series. The books were produced in hardcover format in a uniform style, with distinctive cover art on the paper covers and detailed frontispieces. They were also sold at a low price. Because of the volume of his production methods, Stratemeyer was able to sell his hardcover books at approximately half the price of his competitors. As will be discussed in the next section, Stratemeyer turned the fact that libraries did not hold his books into a positive feature, so children had to buy the books in order to read them.

Critical Reception

The history of the popularity of the Hardy Boys and other Stratemeyer books with their readers is inversely proportional to the history of their critical devaluation by librarians and critics. From the outset Stratemeyer books were very popular with child readers: for instance, in the early days of the Hardy Boys in 1934 it was estimated that 4 million copies had been sold. This was partly due to their low price and also to the fact that public libraries did not hold them. This situation was largely created by the powerful critique by Franklin Mathiews, the official librarian of the Boys Scouts movement. Indeed, the Hardy Boys were published in a climate of long-established moral critique promoted by Mathiews, which was against Stratemeyer's style of publication. This criticism by Mathiews is contained in two key articles, "Blowing Out the Boy's Brains" (1914) and "Fashion in Fiction for Boys" (1929). In the first article Mathiews was alarmed at the outpouring of pulp fiction by the Stratemeyer Syndicate targeting boys and the possible ill effects of consuming such fiction, in which power and authority are ascribed to boys, not men. In his later article, published after *The Hardy Boys* series was launched, it is ironic that Mathiews shrewdly captures the appeal of the series while he is critiquing it, for he understands that the young readers want to retain the state of boyhood while acting like adults and even to show that that they are superior to adults.

Although over time the bias against libraries holding series mysteries has lessened, the attitude toward Stratemeyer series books was only finally completely lifted when the present owners of the Syndicate, Simon & Schuster, gave some of their materials to the New York Public Library in 1993. At the same time the later manifestation of the Syndicate retained other items such as the character cards, which are still in use, to create continuity in the way the young detectives are presented.

Contemporary Manifestations

One strategy of the Stratemeyer Syndicate, as with other long-lasting popular culture artifacts for young people, has been to alter the books according to the changing attitudes and conventions of the times. The revision of the entire series between the 1950s and 1970s is a case in point. On the one hand the revised books have a simpler vocabulary, less characterization and description, and a more rapid pacing—they are intended for a middle-school reading audience of 8- to 11-year-olds. On the other hand the Syndicate was responding to the political tenor of the times, and many sexist, racist, and class-biased material was removed. Since 1987, *The Hardy Boys* have also had to keep pace (and be in competition) with more action-oriented texts. Thus, in *The Hardy Boys Casefiles* series, written for a slightly older audience, there is a greater emphasis on terrorism and espionage. The boys are more interested in girls and their daring exploits now include the use of electronic technology in solving mysteries. From 2005 onward, the series *The Hardy Boys: Undercover Brothers* features Joe and Frank as part of an organization called A.T.A.C. (American Teens Against Crime), giving them a new role within a both action-oriented and activist agenda for young people. This series is also characterized by the use of first-person narration. In keeping with the emergence of a new genre of literature, the graphic novel, Hardy Boys adventures are also now part of the *Undercover Brothers Graphic Novels* series. Within contemporary manifestations, the Hardy Boys have also joined up with Nancy Drew in the *Nancy Drew and the Hardy Boys Super Mystery* series (from 1988 to 1998) and since 2007 in a new series called *Nancy Drew and the Hardy Boys Super Mystery* series, a series that uses the first-person narration characteristic of Girl Detective and Undercover Brothers. The crossover texts also include the Hardy Boys teamed up briefly with Tom Swift in the *Hardy Boys and Tom Swift UltraThriller* series.

In addition to the various book series involving the Hardy Boys, there have also been a number of tie-in television shows and films associated with the Hardy Boys. These include an animated TV series for ABC that appeared from 1969 to 1971, in which the Hardy Boys were part of a rock band, through to the *Hardy Boys & Nancy Drew Mysteries* prime-time series, which aired briefly, to a TV show, *The Hardy Boys* (1995). In 2008, Frank and Joe Hardy were featured in an interactive PC adventure game, produced through JoWooD and The Adventure Company.

Further Reading

Billman, Carol. *The Secret of the Stratemeyer Syndicate: Nancy Drew, The Hardy Boys and Million Dollar Fiction Factory*. New York: Ungar, 1986.

Deane, Paul. *Mirrors of American Culture: Children's Fiction Series in the Twentieth Century*. Metuchen, NJ: Scarecrow Press, 1991.

Johnson, Deidre. *Edward Stratemeyer and the Stratemeyer Syndicate*. New York: Twayne, 1993.

McFarlane, Leslie. *Ghost of the Hardy Boys*. Toronto: Methuen, 1976.

Mitchell, C., and J. Reid-Walsh. (1996). Reading on the Edge: Serious Series Readers of Nancy Drew and Hardy Boys Mysteries. *Changing English* 3(1), 45–55.

Mitchell, Claudia, and Jacqueline Reid-Walsh. *Researching Children's Popular Culture: The Cultural Spaces of Childhood*. London: Routledge, 2002.

Jacqueline Reid-Walsh and Claudia Mitchell

Harry Potter

Since J. K. Rowling's *Harry Potter and the Philosopher's Stone* was published in Great Britain in 1997, "Pottermania" has changed reading. Harry Potter has become a cultural icon. The Harry Potter phenomenon asks questions such as, why is Harry Potter so beloved by children?, and what made this the best-selling children's book of all time?

Why do boys love Harry Potter? What does Harry have that draws them into reading such long books? It is not like this is the only book in which a male is the main character or where there is a lot of action and adventure. What is it that makes Harry so popular with boys?

The *Harry Potter* series includes seven books chronological in order. Each book is one year in the life of the series' protagonist, Harry Potter. The main setting of books one through six is the Hogwarts School of Witchcraft and Wizardry. There Harry and his classmates learn how to perform magic, outwit evil forces, juggle relationships both personal and professional, and how to struggle and succeed. In some respects it is a coming-of-age story in which the main characters learn about life. Harry and his two best friends, Ron and Hermione, struggle through their adolescence like many of us do: making difficult decisions while still trying to stay true to themselves and not compromise their standards or beliefs.

In *Harry Potter and the Sorcerer's Stone* Harry learns that his deceased parents were wizards and that they were murdered by Lord Voldemort, the most evil of all wizards, which is why Harry has the lightning bolt scar on his forehead. Voldemort tried to kill Harry as well as his parents, but was not able to. Harry has never be able to forget this fact because of the scar. Harry soon leaves his miserable life at his aunt and uncle's house and embarks on his new life at Hogwarts School of Witchcraft and Wizardry, where he learns how to be a wizard. He befriends Ron Weasley and Hermione Granger and for once in his life he has real friends. The three soon realize that evil lurks around every corner. Harry must come face to face with his parents' murderer, Lord Voldemort, in a quest to save everyone from letting Voldemort gain much needed power from the Sorcerer's Stone, which he needs in order to become as powerful as he was once.

The second book in the series, *Harry Potter and the Chamber of Secrets*, deals with Lord Voldemort trying to regain power by reincarnating himself through memories that he stored within a diary. When students at Hogwarts begin to turn up petrified, Harry realizes that Voldemort is behind it, but many of his peers and professors believe Harry to be doing these awful deeds. Harry soon finds himself in the Chamber of Secrets, which is underneath Hogwarts, accessible through the girls' bathroom sink. Harry must save Ginny Weasley, Ron's sister, who has been abducted into the Chamber by Tom Riddle, Voldemort's given name before he changed it to Voldemort.

Harry Potter and the Prisoner of Azkaban is the third installment in the Harry Potter saga. Harry is now in his third year at Hogwarts and believes to be in danger from an escaped convict known as Sirius Black. In order to protect Harry and the other students, the Ministry of Magic, which is the governing body of the magical community, has placed dark, life-sucking creatures called Dementors at posts surrounding the schools. Instead of protecting the students, they seem to be out for Harry and on one occasion come very close to killing him. It is interesting to note that this is the only book in which Lord Voldemort does not play a key role.

Harry's fourth year at Hogwarts is chronicled in *Harry Potter and the Goblet of Fire*. In this installment Harry finds himself entered into the Triwizard Tournament, which is a potentially fatal contest. In it, students from three wizarding schools must participate in a variety of dangerous competitions. The book follows Harry through the competitions, also asking the question of who entered Harry into the tournament to begin with. In the end Harry finds out that it was Lord Voldemort who entered him in order to ultimately kill him. The book ends with Voldemort killing another tournament participant, one of Harry's friends at Hogwarts, and Harry telling everyone who would listen that Voldemort is indeed back in power.

In *Harry Potter and the Order of the Phoenix* Harry must try to make the wizarding world at large believe that Voldemort is back. Many do not believe him and thus do not feel the need to protect themselves. Harry's friends and family know the truth, though, and begin hiding out at Sirius Black's family estate, where they form the Order of the Phoenix, which is a group of wizards and witches who do not want Voldemort back in power and who are willing to fight against it. Because the Ministry of Magic does not believe Harry's accusations that Lord Voldemort has regained power, they appoint Dolores

Umbridge as the director of Hogwarts to keep an eye on the students, making sure they do not perform magic of any kind. In this book we come closer to finding out the connection between Harry and Voldemort.

The sixth book, *Harry Potter and the Half-Blood Prince,* delves into the life of Lord Voldemort more than previous books do. In order to preserve himself and live forever Voldemort has splintered, or broken, his soul up into parts called horcruxes. The horcruxes are everyday items that have something to do with Voldemort's past, but which have been enchanted with evil spells that must be broken in order for the horcrux to be destroyed. Harry and Dumbledore set out to find and destroy the multiple horcruxes and ultimately kill Voldemort. The book ends with the murder of Dumbledore—by Professor Snape, whose loyalty has been in question since the first book—and his subsequent funeral.

The seventh and final book in the series, *Harry Potter and the Deathly Hallows* begins where the sixth one left off, with the death of Dumbledore. Unlike the other six books, the *Deathly Hallows* does not take place at Hogwarts. Instead of finishing their final year at school, Harry and his friends decide to search for the horcruxes, which Harry and Dumbledore were unable to find, in order to destroy Voldemort, who has now taken control of the Ministry of Magic. In the end, the battle between Harry and Voldemort, which all seven books had been leading up to and foreshadowing, occurs. Harry finally kills Lord Voldemort, allowing peace to come back to the wizarding community. The book ends with Harry and his friends at the train station many years later, sending their own sons and daughters off to Hogwarts for their first year.

A Good Role Model?

Many boys discuss Harry Potter and how they relate to the character. They focus on things and emotions that would not be socially acceptable for them to say in the public arena otherwise. There is so much pressure on boys to be "masculine," as society has defined it, that they do not allow emotions to enter their lives, much less run their lives. It is not acceptable in our patriarchal society to have our boys talk about their emotions because emotion equals weakness, and boys are not allowed to show any signs of weakness. Our society would much rather have boys, and men for that matter, be prisoners within their own psyches. Therefore, boys have to suppress their emotions and feelings because society has deemed them fraudulent. Harry Potter is an example of a young boy who has to battle his inner emotions and feelings. Reading Harry Potter allows young males to connect with someone else, albeit a fictional character, who is going through something similar.

Being Able to Relate

The *Harry Potter* series definitely allows its readers to be part of a magical world in which good does triumph over evil and into which boys of all ages can escape and find a little or a lot of themselves. Previously unenthused readers now read with zest and determination. Harry Potter has brought forth a new generation of readers who by the end of the series have read a total of

4,100 pages and maybe have learned that they are not alone in their feelings and experiences—Harry is there with them. Harry Potter has great mass appeal; there is something in the books for almost everyone, young and old alike. People can relate to Harry.

Further Reading

Mayes-Elma, Ruthann. *Harry Potter: Feminist Friend or Foe?* Rotterdam: Sense Publishing, 2007.
Mayes-Elma, Ruthann. *Females and Harry Potter.* Maryland, MD: Rowman and Littlefield, 2006.

Ruthann Mayes-Elma

Magazines

Adults and children in today's world are very familiar with magazines. They are on every newsstand and in every library and are delivered into many homes by subscription. More recently, e-zines self-published by boys have been found online. Magazines are periodicals published on a regular schedule with articles that focus on particular topics and interests and tend to target particular audiences. The word *magazine* is derived from the French word *magasin,* which means "storehouse." Historically, magazines were a male genre, a place where literate men could publish their points of view in essay or satire form for a wider audience. Daniel Defoe began publishing the first English-language magazine, *The Review,* in 1704. In 1731 Edward Cave published *The Gentleman's Magazine,* which is thought to have been the first magazine for the general public, still targeted at men.

Today's magazines have standard pages that are 8 × 11 inches and usually contain from 24 to 48 pages in a glued spine format. They usually have glossy paper covers and include stories and articles and attractively colored pictures and illustrations. Magazines contain a table of contents that organizes the articles and provides readers with a guide as to where to find the articles that they might find the most interesting. They are, for the most part, more affordable than books and relatively accessible for boys.

Magazines are published on a wide variety of topics, and boys can usually find a magazine that reflects their personal interests, such as computers; digital, figurine, and card games; wildlife; sports; geography; and motor vehicles (cars, trucks, quads, and motorcycles). Magazines devoted to guns, humor, music, and satire are also popular among boys, including *Hockey News, Disney, Comic Zone, Sports Illustrated, National Geographic for Kids, Reptiles, Big Buck Magazine, Time for Kids,* and *Trucks.* Digests and comics also fit in this genre that appeal to boys. For the most part, these formats and genres do not appeal to girls, so the boys see themselves as a part of a guys' literacy club. They see their dads, uncles, and older brothers reading them, and that makes it cool.

More recently, the Internet has spawned e-zines, or electronic magazines, for readers and writers. These are popular because they can be self-published quickly and can focus on a specific topic. There are currently few actual e-zines for boys. However, a number of magazines are online versions of existing print magazines. For example, *SIKids* is the online version of *Sports Illustrated*, and *Time for Kids* is the online version of *Time*.

Boys look for visuals when they pick magazines to read, they are drawn to pictures. Both the digital texts and the graphics are important parts of the magazine. Boys are drawn to the color photographs and cartoons. One teenage boy said, "As you are flipping through the magazine the pictures often catch your eye and make you want to read the articles, if it wasn't for the pictures you might not read many articles." The timeliness of magazines appeals to them because the current topics and images reflect their life and times or imagined life and times. Magazines represent a form of popular literacy in an up-to-date fashion. The font sizes and shapes vary, and interesting combinations of text and pictures are used to create special effects. Frequently, the written text and visuals overlap and cover two pages, which provide a more expansive, panoramic view.

Magazines have a certain appeal to boys in that they can be carried easily in a backpack or stored in a desk or locker. To some boys, carrying a magazine does not have the same stigma as carrying a novel, and thus they avoid the risk of being labeled a "school boy." Magazines may be read at home, at school, or on the bus, and they take only a few minutes to read. One boy said "They are always short articles so they are quick and easy to read." This accessibility and short time span fits well with boys' views of what can be fun about reading.

Many boys have a keener interest in reading magazines than in reading books because schools do not usually sanction this trendier form. Magazines are more likely part of their out-of-school reading. Teachers frown upon them and see them as less scholarly than books, and some boys see this as a type of resistance to the teacher's perspective. With magazines it is perfectly acceptable to browse back and forth rather than reading in the more linear fashion that novels and informational texts demand. Although they are paper texts, the reading of magazines more closely resembles the reading of digital texts. Some boys are not as intimidated by magazines as they are by books, and magazines might more easily help them to see themselves as readers in that they are able to turn pages, sample text that interests them, or study the visuals—and it is reading. This type of reading appeals to them, and they see themselves as more successful as readers.

Magazines also include a great deal of advertising aimed at attracting the reader, and the advertisements may be as visually appealing as the articles. Print infomercials such as the classic "I was a 98-pound weakling" advertisement aim at catching their attention, and even if boys see it as cheesy, it still sparks their interest. What might be censored in other publications is permitted in the advertisements in magazines. They also give boys a way to see themselves as acquiring things for themselves, which puts them in a guys' world.

Some magazines include pullout posters of personalities, animals, and vehicles, or charts of sporting statistics that boys display on their bedroom walls and bulletin boards. Some contain trading cards that they can collect to form a set or exchange with friends. Collecting and trading posters and cards appeals to boys.

The information in magazines is usually more timely and up-to-date than what is found in other sources. Magazines do not demand an academic form of writing, and authors may use a more popular conversational voice and tone that contrasts with the more formal academic tone usually found in novels or information texts required in school literacies. Magazines also represent some connections to other aspects of boys' world and allow them, for instance, to mirror what they see on television or in movies. For example, World Wrestling Entertainment gives background information about popular wrestlers and tournaments, and the boys can follow wrestling competitions. Some boys may even decide to attend wrestling events or join a wrestling club. Magazines are also where a lot of boys get caught up on their latest news. Reading up-to-date articles on their interests makes them current and smart when talking to their friends.

Magazines also appeal to boys because they represent the freedom to choose based on their personal interests. The act of purchasing and owning a magazine may contribute to boys' seeing themselves as readers and as masters of a text form. They may see magazines as a form of social literacy when they share a magazine with friends or talk about what they have read. Finally, boys can enjoy magazines as one form of literature that they have the freedom to read for pleasure, interest, and fun without the worry of academic assessment.

Further Reading

Cox, Ruth E. (2003). From Boys' Life to Thrasher: Boys and Magazines. *Teacher Librarian*, 30(3), 25–26.

Martino, Wayne. (2001). Boys and Reading: Investigating the Impact of Masculinities on Boys' Reading Preferences and Involvement in Literacy. *The Australian Journal of Language and Literacy*, 24(1), 61–74.

Scieszka, Jon. *Guys Write for Guys Read*. New York: Penguin Group, 2005.

Smith, Michael, and Jeffrey D. Wilhelm. *Reading Don't Fix No Chevys: Literacy in the Lives of Young Men*. Portsmouth, NH: Heinemann, 2002.

Brenda Kelly and Heather Blair

Manga and Anime

Manga and anime have become increasingly popular in America, especially with boys. Manga originates from Japan, and the word *manga* literally means comic. Manga are similar to comic books and graphic novels, and are typically printed in black and white. The most popular manga are those with fantasy or action/adventure story lines, though the plots can be romantic, historical, dramatic, or even related to sports. *Anime* is short for the Japanese word for animation (*animeshiyon*) and refers to an animated adaptation of manga. In America, the term *anime* usually refers to a cartoon from Japan or a cartoon designed to look like a Japanese cartoon. Anime features stylized characters with large, expressive eyes and distinctive facial expressions. The style of the characters differs between animes, from the less detailed art of a series such as Nintendo's *Pokémon* to the stylized art of a series such as the Namco Bandai's *Cowboy Bebop*.

Anime and manga were introduced to American audiences in the 1980s. Keiji Nakazawa's manga *Barefoot Gen* was published by Shueisha and later by Chuokoron-Shinsha. It chronicles the author's experiences during the Hiroshima bombing of World War II. For many Americans, it was their first exposure to manga. The anime movie *Akira*, which was released in America in 1988 by Orion Pictures, laid the foundation for anime's popularity in America. *Akira* was written by Katsuhiro Otomo and Izÿ Hashimoto and tells the story of a young man named Shotaro Kaneda whose best friend Tetsuo begins to display superhuman powers. Tetsuo's powers grow beyond his control and Kaneda tries to rescue him while he uncovers the mystery surrounding a boy named Akira who displayed powers similar to Tetsuo's. In addition to the film's detailed animation style, one reason for its popularity was that it explored many issues faced by adolescent boys that American cartoons did not. Tetsuo has extremely low self-esteem. The discovery of his powers drives him to a point where he cannot control them and nearly destroys Japan, which may reflect an underlying fear of growing up and entering adulthood.

Manga and anime often explore issues that are important to boys but are not openly discussed in social settings. The subtext of many manga and anime series touches upon fears, fantasies, and concerns that boys have about their personalities, their desires, and their movement toward adulthood. In that sense, anime and manga validate concerns that are important and prevalent for boys. In Rumiko Takahashi's manga *Ranma 1/2*, which was originally published as a serial manga in Shogakukan's magazine *Shōnen Sunday*, beginning in 1987, the main character Ranma Saotome transforms from a boy to a girl every time he comes into contact with cold water. There is an indication that the series is an exploration of adolescent boys' fears of being labeled feminine or girly. Such fears and insecurities are common, especially as boys enter adolescence and feel increased social pressure to define and assert themselves. *Ranma 1/2* touches upon those fears, gives them voice, and validates the audience's similar concerns.

Yoshiyuki Sadamoto's manga *Neon Genesis Evangelion*, published by Kadowaka Shoten in *Shōnen Ace* beginning in December 1994, tells the story of Shinji Ikari, an insecure and passive boy who must pilot a large robot known as an Eva to fight against creatures called Angels. The manga explores Shinji's dysfunctional relationship with his father. Many of the other characters in the series are metaphors for different aspects of Shinji's consciousness, resulting in a series that explores his psyche while also telling an adventure story. Many of Shinji's challenges are ones that are common to adolescent boys: Shinji does not know how to relate to or form a healthy relationship with his father, he is attracted to multiple girls who excite different parts of his personality, and he struggles to define himself amid pressures to be the person he believes others want him to be.

The experiences of male characters in manga and anime are common to boys and young men. However, concerns such as defining oneself, becoming a powerful and respected person, and being confident in one's gender identity are not as openly discussed among boys as they are among girls. As a result, part of the popularity and significance of anime and manga for boys may be that the themes and conflicts experienced by the main characters resonate with them. The difficulties the characters face are challenges that boys and young men will encounter in their lives. These challenges are presented in a way that allows the audience to enjoy manga and anime as entertainment; the challenges also validate very real and complex questions and issues boys have about their identities, growing up, and their places in society. The validation of these concerns and the entertaining qualities of manga and anime are two reasons these forms of entertainment have become so popular among boys.

Further Reading

Fulford, Benjamin. "Anime Opens on Main Street." *Forbes Magazine,* October 18, 1999.

Patten, Fred. *Watching Anime, Reading Manga: 25 Years of Essays and Reviews.* Berkeley, CA: Stone Bridge Press, 2004.

Poitras, Gilles. *Anime Essentials: Every Thing a Fan Needs to Know.* Berkeley, CA: Stone Bridge Press, 2001.

Meghan Guidry

SECTION 9

Boys and Tunes

Androgyny in Music

What is it about boy bands that attract some people? Equally, what is it about boy bands that repel some people? Because, let us be honest, we often listen and watch with a mixture of fascination, anguish, and fear at the perverse sounds and sights that mix in perfect pitch harmonies. The boys seem so grown up, but act like kids. On the surface the "boys" in the band are full of fun and throw away pop music, breaking their moves in synchronicity. Yet there is often something else going on. Is it their innocence? Is it that we do not quite know if we should be drawn into their world of innocence that hints at complexity? Somewhere within the sea of boy band performances there is a question mark. It is not the question mark of The Clash: "Should I Stay or Should I Go?" It is the question mark of a deeper uncertainty: Why do I like this? The answer to this and the questions posed above can be found in thinking about how boys in society are portrayed: as men in the making. This stereotype of boys-to-men contrasts with the complex innocence of the boys in bands who often appear not as men, but as a cross section of sex and gender possibilities. In fact, the public circulation of images of "boys" in boy bands is marked by a recent development in which gay culture and queerness have become a regular part of public discourse and are seen as the boys who are androgynous.

Androgyny in boy bands is about hearing and seeing sexuality as neither male nor female. So though science has shown us that males and females are clearly identified by their chromosomes (XX and XY), what happens in the social world does not fit the easy categories of genetic measurement of chromosomes. The question that the androgyny of boy bands raises is how gender operates in a society, beyond the certainties of science. This is more challenging when we consider how ideas circulate through the interpretative systems of meaning human beings use to understand the world around them. For most of us, our interpretive systems of meaning are created through our daily interaction with media. In fact, our social interactions are mediated through sound recordings, and increasingly, through visual media based on television and cinema. For many millions of people, especially young people, that visualization has moved to the Internet, desk-based video monitors, and handheld devices.

Hidden Codes in the Unconscious

What information about our sexuality are we getting through the media? How do we process that information to become a significant part of the knowledge resources that adult human beings rely on to make informed and ethical decisions? To answer these questions it is necessary to recognize that there is no perfect interpretation of an image, or for that matter, a boy band. There are almost as many interpretations of what the boys mean as there are people watching and using the images. We know they invest themselves in the imagery, the music, and the experience of the band with varying intensity. Fans respond in a powerful way, becoming members of an active audience. As audience members and fans, they are linked to the image and ideas about the band. Their emotional connections generate and reproduce a shared sense of authenticity about the realness of the music, which also creates a sense of empowerment as they move into the cultural "space" created by their relationship with the band.

Hidden codes bring boy bands and their fans together. Hidden codes have been part of the long history of the study of human consciousness and, equally important, of the unconscious. This area of research, known most commonly as psychoanalysis, was initiated by the Austrian psychiatrist Sigmund Freud in the late nineteenth century in modernist Europe. According to Freud—whose key works are gathered in the 18 volumes of *The Complete Psychological Works of Sigmund Freud*—and the school of analysts known as Freudians, our attitudes and behavior are informed by our unconscious: ideas about ourselves that are closely tied to experiences during our development as embryos through our formative years in childhood and continuing into adulthood. Freud's theory of the unconscious was closely tied to sexual development within the family. In growing into adulthood, a person moved through stages of development. In essence, Freud produced theories that were often wildly creative and controversial in the rapidly changing era in which he was working. This controversy continues today in the field of psychoanalysis, as analysts across the disciplinary fields seek to gain an understanding of how human behavior can be interpreted. Yet his ideas are valuable because they help us understand the forces at work that determine our character: why we do what we do. Though it is possible that Freud placed too much emphasis on the relationship between sexual development and adulthood, his ideas offer a way of extending our understanding of sexuality.

Of special relevance to boy bands is Freud's idea of infantilism. This idea was at the center of Freud's theory of development, which, at its boldest, suggested that the range of sexual possibilities open to us as infants is very wide indeed, but society and its institutions—especially the family—repress the choices that are available to us. Freud's view of infantilism was negative, reflecting the times and the emergence of psychoanalytical theory as a way of explaining human behavior. According to Freud, our infantile impulses lead us to not want to leave the security of home and the difficult choices that it involves. Furthermore, homosexuality and bisexuality were a manifestation of immaturity, Freud argued, writing during a time when queerness was considered a serious medical condition to be cured. If we cannot develop to maturity and discover our sexuality, we cannot move beyond infantilism—a stage in which the individual's sexuality is always in question. Infantilism became a way of describing the refusal of an adult to mature: "One cannot remain a child forever," Freud said. If a person refuses to mature, Freud argued that this was evidence of the repression of our sexual realization. Infantilism painted a picture of a person who could not find a confident sexual orientation and who may, despite being a man, behave as a woman, and vice versa. Why, asked Freud, was there this confusion, this "inversion" about male and female behavior in some people?

Infantilism is the ultimate expression of this immaturity and should be discouraged because, in a uniquely generous twist, Freud wanted illusion to give way to a mature understanding of the adult as a rational, moral decision maker. Of course, he was also suggesting that the nonstraight person—the "queer," as we would say today—was infantile. It is clear that today's liberal society has moved beyond this intolerance of queerness, of the immature and infantile. In a contradictory sense, to Freud the mature person would be confident of their sexuality, not retreat back to the warmth of the family, where dependency and the illusions of childhood are the norm.

Boy Groups

Boy groups are part of a complex set of related concerns that make up the interpretive systems of meaning and consist of struggles between genetic codes of gender identity and the way those identities are muddied when they are mediated. When we watch boy bands on television or hear them sing, questions about their sexual identity emerge as a central aspect of their performances. Understanding how boy bands become part of this muddied reality brought about mostly by television's mediation requires tools that can confidently equip consumers of boy band music and images to make sense of them. Cultural theory is a tool that helps make sense of these muddied meanings.

Arguably one of the most influential schools of thought and action has been the interdisciplinary field of cultural studies. Although there are now many fields of cultural studies, the one that offers the most productive tools is the critical approach. It seeks to empower users and creators of culture to understand who they are and how they can identify the knowledge they are producing and using as part of their everyday experience. In so doing, the critical approach places knowledge in a meaningful position within the larger fabric of everyday life. The critical approach also encourages the active interpretation of mediated sounds and images about which producers and consumers often care very deeply, even if those around them may not care at all about those same sounds and even resist them. The critical cultural studies approach recognizes and encourages the realization of individual identity within the larger field of social identity.

If we try a thought experiment that is probably a real-life example for many people, it is possible to see how this collision plays out. If we say boy bands are about gay culture, such a statement would be objectionable to many heterosexual people sitting at home watching music videos by The Backstreet Boys and 'N Sync on their televisions or listening to them on the MP3 players and CDs. This interpretation allows us to say that the reaction to gayness is an expression of the dominant idea of boys as young men and recognize that the status quo is heterosexist. It prefers to reproduce the dominant view of sexual identity, as being about relationships between male and female—XX and XY. This view is known as unexamined identity, according to which the dominant ideas about sexuality and gender alternatives to heterosexual life are unquestioned, uniform, and ignorant (Hardiman, 2004).

In contrast, critical cultural studies endorses the muddied aspect of this scenario by saying that the reading of the text is open: the gay can interpret the text differently as empowering and providing encouragement. Likewise, it reaffirms the individual by seeing and hearing his or her gay identity being reproduced. The heterosexual is also celebrated for the pleasure he or she finds. It may also be possible, in a truly liberal and tolerant society, for each identity group to enjoy the other, without any feeling of anxiety, fear, or shame—the heterosexual will celebrate the gay content of the band and the gay will celebrate the straight's enjoyment of the gayness (if indeed the straight sees any gayness). Objections to the "hidden codes" come from people who are not liberal, not tolerant. Such people and their way of seeing the world are considered fundamentalist and conservative because they recognize only one way of interpreting a cultural artifact—a song and its music video or a concert—and because they often resist the possibility that the text would offer them pleasure.

Everybody's Free to Feel Good

Since the rise of the promotional television video in the early 1980s, boy bands have offered a way for society to experience infantilism. This risk free infantilism means that the multiple codes of sexual orientation are encoded in the videos and songs, offering a range of sexual possibilities for the audience to decode. This is an expression of the liberal and tolerant role of media in society. Contemporary media brings infantilism from the psychoanalyst's couch to the video monitor, the MP3 player, and the television, where it is possible to enjoy diverse expressions of sexuality on the pathway to maturity. The unconscious is being revealed.

Further Reading

Freud, Sigmund. *Collected Works of Sigmund Freud*. New York and London: Bibliobazaar, 1920 [2007].

Hardiman, D. L. "White Racial Identity Development in the United States." In *Race, Ethnicity and Self*, edited by E. P. Salett and D. R. Koslow. (2nd ed.). Washington, DC: National Multicultural Institute, 2004.

Jamieson, Daryl. (2007). "Marketing Androgyny: The Evolution of the Backstreet Boys." *Popular Music*, Vol. 26, no. 2, pp. 245–258.

Marcus Breen

Bow Wow

Where do young boys learn that being a man means looking and acting tough? It would be naïve to state that media culture, in particular hip hop, is the root cause of tough masculinity; however, it is not naïve to state that hip hop has influenced the normalizing of tough manhood images in the minds of young boys. Adult male hip hop artists such as Dr. Dre and 50 Cent have drawn condemnation from parents and teachers, but there appears to be an absence of critique regarding teen male artists of the genre. Even though the underlying messages of teen artists very much resemble adult contemporary hip hop, there appear to be factors that make their music videos gentler, more acceptable, and thus less controversial. These factors include the infusion of familiar and nice images of childhood/teen life. Teen male hip hop videos may influence adolescent male perceptions and behaviors of gender through the dissemination of a narrow masculinity presented in music videos. Adolescent boys, who regularly view the representation of tough masculinity depicted there, may come to consider this type of gender performance as familiar and normal, establishing a dichotomy of what is acceptable and unacceptable male behavior. This narrow image of tough masculinity may influence how young boys act and think.

Bow Wow is one of the most noted teen hip hop stars around. At the age of 13, "Little" Bow Wow released his first album entitled *Beware of the Dog*, under the label So So Def Records. Under this label he received his first hit single "Bounce with Me." By the age of 16, he had released his third album, entitled *Unleashed*, with the release of the single "Let's Get Down." The videos of both of these songs offer representative examples of a teen hip hop artist performing tough masculinity through a softer and gentler adolescent lens.

When an adolescent hip hop artist has yet to develop in physical strength and size, style of clothing becomes a key factor in helping these artists achieve authenticity as tough males. Teen male hip hop artists walk a tightrope between earning street credibility as tough males and appearing as innocent young boys for their adolescent fan base. In cultural theorist Stuart Hall's discussion of representation, meaning has multiple potentials, and it becomes fixed with a particular meaning within a context. Currently, the meaning of the white tank top, worn by the majority of men in the hip hop world, has come to represent (or be read) as a marker of violence toward women. The *wife beater,* a term used when referring to the white tank, has become a part of the vocabulary in the hypermasculine world of hip hop. The white tank projects an image of toughness helping to create a hard appearance. While Bow Wow is seen wearing a symbol of violence in "Bounce with Me" (2000), his actions and behavior come in direct conflict with what is an acceptable image for him.

Interestingly, one might observe that the images are softened when 13-year-old Bow Wow is wearing the "wife beater" tank, compared to when he is not. For example, the only instance when his hair is not in cornrows is when he is wearing that tank. It is here that his hair is left unbraided, the length coming close to his shoulders, creating a more feminine and thus softer appearance.

Bandanas have also become a code of tough masculinity because within the context of crime it has become one of the signifying clothing items worn by gang members. Bow Wow, at age 13, is seen wearing several different bandanas. Once again this image is softened with him riding his bicycle around the neighborhood, an activity reminiscent of childhood. The background images of children engaged in childhood activities such as riding bikes, playing with toys, and reading books help moderate a softer reading of the bandana worn by Bow Wow as he walks through the neighborhood. Despite his small stature, Bow Wow is able to present an image of tough masculinity through his style of clothing.

Teen artists lacking in physical strength are also able to reveal their toughness through physical postures and gestures. In "Bounce with Me" (2000) Bow Wow, a short and thin 13-year-old adolescent, is seen crossing his arms, standing in a wide stance, and thrusting his body into the camera while rapping out his lines. He continuously uses his hand gestures, which are forcefully directed toward the lens, to pronounce his presence in a way that his physical body is unable to at this time. Furthermore, his facial expressions appear aggressive, as he is seen frowning and scowling, helping to create an image of a tough male. Interestingly, at the age of 16 Bow Wow's body posturing becomes even more aggressive. As his physical strength increases, he is able to use his muscular body to enhance his tough masculine image. In his video "Let's Get Down" (2003) the camera zooms in on Bow Wow wearing a tank jersey that reveals his bicep muscles. He also positions his body to reveal his side profile so that his tattoo, which lies prominently on his left shoulder, is visible to the audience. The significance of the tattoo lies with its representation; tattoos are one physical indicator that can reveal an individual's threshold for pain. Thus, the bigger the tattoo, the tougher an individual is perceived. Tough masculinity has become inextricably linked with tattoos as witnessed by the tattoo-armored body of 50 Cent, a notable hypermasculine hip hop star. Bow Wow continues to soften his image by flexing his biceps only in the shots that capture him in the Department of Motor Vehicles, where he is taking his driving test, much like any 16 year old would. This helps to soften his behavior as it draws the viewer back to a familiar teenage rite of passage.

Being teenagers, it is difficult for these artists to exert power through physical violence, because most of their market is made up of adolescents. Therefore, they must acquire and maintain power of a different type. Economic power becomes a key factor in reinforcing tough masculinity. Accessories, in particular jewelry, have come to represent an aspect of power and success in the hip hop industry. Jewelry symbolizes a person's wealth, prestige, and success in the world of hip hop. Tough masculinity can be viewed through the overabundance and indulgence in jewelry, as the amount and size become key factors in assessing an individual's real manhood. In "Bounce with Me," Bow Wow is seen holding his large diamond pendant in better view of the camera as well as physically accosting the camera by thrusting his pendant toward the camera lens. Meanwhile, young kids are seen in the background skipping rope and riding scooters. As he matures, his car also becomes a symbol of his economic wealth. Taking his driving test in a red convertible sports car reveals a different level of power because he is able to indulge in more extravagant purchase than most other teenagers. However, this image continues to be softened as the viewer watches Bow Wow navigate the streets during his driving test. Thus, teen hip hop artists draw on economic power to establish themselves as tough and powerful males.

The construction of tough masculinity as a cultural norm cannot be simply blamed on the hip hop industry. In combination with images of manhood that are displayed in music videos, films, and on television, a young boy also learns what it means to be a real man through family, school, and other networks. The script of the tough masculine male is introduced at an early age, which may be evidenced by my own students' responses to my question, "What does it mean to be a man?" This script, or discourse, of hypermasculinity continues to be recycled and reused, sustaining the message that in order to be considered a real man, young boys must act and look tough. In order to begin challenging this cycle of socialization and allow spaces for alternative images of masculinity to have equal play, we must consider the ways in which the phrase "real man" can encompass qualities such as vulnerability, emotion, and compassion, and how it can do so without seeping into the script of a wimp or a sissy. What it means to be a man must be rewritten so that adolescent boys come to emulate and respect the qualities of men who will not engage in tough masculinity to assert their manhood.

Further Reading

Bow Wow. "Bounce with Me." *Beware of the Dog*. So So Def Records, 2000.

Bow Wow. "Let's Get Down." *Unleashed*. So So Def Records & Sony Records, 2003.

Hurt, B. "Hip-Hop: Beyond Beats and Rhymes." Media Education Foundation, 2006.

Jhally, S. "Stuart Hall: Representation and the Media." Media Education Foundation, 1997

Jhally, S. "Tough Guise: Violence, Media, and the Crisis in Masculinity with Jackson Katz." 1999.

Raj Sanghera

Boy Bands

Very few aspects of popular music have ever unified boys and critics as much as boy bands. This of course was an agreement forged in common disdain directed at boy bands, but it did seem for a few years in the 1990s that boy bands would prove to be the salvation of the music business.

It is not as if the 1990s were the first decade in which boys came together to form bands. Many of the best-known groups in rock and pop were composed of four or five young men barely out of their teens—for example, The Beatles. What distinguished the typical boy band of the 1990s was that *none* of the members of the band showed any great proficiency in composing their own music, writing their own lyrics, or even playing their own instruments. Their proficiency lay chiefly in vocalization and harmonies and in appealing to young girls and teenagers. Even more significantly, they were generally not a group of four like-minded friends or acquaintances marking adolescent rites of passage by forming a band. They were usually assembled by an impresario or music producer, more as a visual package that would appeal to multiple audiences than as a musical force. Musical ability was a desirable (though not critical) plus.

Credit for being the first American boy band to achieve significant chart success must go to the Boston-based New Kids on the Block, who were put together by producer Maurice Starr in 1984. They achieved significant success in the United States, but their success did not translate into a trend of any sort. By the early 1990s, they were on the wane even as grunge, alternative, and punk sounds were staking a claim to mass popularity. A few years later, an aviation entrepreneur named Lou Pearlman, inspired by the success of New Kids on the Block, put together a group of clean-cut youngsters under the name Backstreet Boys. The Backstreet Boys initially failed to find success in the United States, but soon became one of the biggest bands in the world. Their nonthreatening image was as appealing to teenage girls as it was comforting to the parents of those teenage girls. They were designed to be different from typical rock bands whose live performances suggested an aggressive sexuality and whose audiences predominantly were young males who identified with the performers' talent and power and enjoyed live performances as an essentially communal experience. Boy bands on the other hand appealed directly to female audiences who responded to the band members' needs. Listening to boy bands was always an individual experience for girls, no matter how big a crowd they were listening in.

Spurred on by adoration of their female audiences, the Backstreet Boys delivered one hit after the other. It was a common sight to see row after row of bobbing female teenage heads at their concerts with only the occasional male head popping up. Most boys refused to have any truck with them, preferring to find solace in grunge, alternative, and more importantly, rap and hip hop. In a still predominantly hetero-normative sexual culture, boys' disavowal of boy band music was based not so much on aesthetic judgment but on sexual jealousy, and a perceived inability to measure up to the standards of impossibly sensitive romanticism that boy band lyrics connoted. No wonder then that the *New York Times* declared that boy bands such as the Backstreet Boys had extracted revenge on the typical boy by teaching girls to prefer sensitive choirboy types over the football-playing kind.

It mattered little that boy band music was directed to and appealed mainly to girls. The phenomenon was growing bigger every minute. Backstreet Boys soon had competition at the top in the form of 'N Sync, another act assembled by Lou Pearlman in 1995. With Backstreet Boys and 'N Sync inundating the airwaves with inoffensive pop declaring love or mourning the loss of it, there was no lack of boys trying their hand at becoming the next big thing, even if boys themselves turned a deaf ear to their music (or at least kept their love for such music very guilty secrets).

The entertainment industry fell over itself to cash in on the so-called boy band craze. Boy bands developed online alter egos and played the Super Bowl. Television networks got into the act with the omnipresent Lou Pearlman. ABC aired the reality show *Making the Band* in 1999, which ultimately spawned the boy band O-Town. The show delivered ratings strong enough to warrant a second season featuring the band's further adventures, though this time on MTV. The bigger the boy band juggernaut grew, the bigger the target they presented for their detractors. The überboys of the *South Park* cartoon mercilessly mocked the boy band craze on an episode first aired in July 2000 entitled "Something You Can Do with Your Finger," as did *Saturday Night Live*. Live tours, greatest hits compilations, and court battles by band members against their management added spice to the boy band story.

By early 2001, as the economy took a turn for the worse, the boy band phenomenon began to draw to a close. The second season of *Making the Band*, which started in 2002, was no longer looking to assemble a boy band but a hip hop group. By the middle of the decade the only relevance of boy bands seemed to be as objects of sometimes fond parody, as in the musical *Altar Boyz*, the satirical story of a Christian boy band with lyrics such as "Jesus Called Me on My Cell Phone" and "Girl, You Make Me Wanna Wait." As the first decade of the twenty-first century came to a close, there was news that New Kids on The Block were attempting a comeback even as most of the 1990s boy band superstars were languishing in semiobscurity—except for Justin Timberlake of 'N Sync, who had managed to transform himself into a multimedia superstar. Timberlake notwithstanding, boy bands had all but disappeared from the musical scene by the end of 2007. Boys across America were no doubt fervently hoping things would stay that way forever.

Further Reading

Brown, Janelle. "Sluts and Teddy Bears." Salon.com. http://archive.salon.com/mwt/style/2001/02/05/teen_aesthetic/index.html (accessed April 2008).

Frith, Simon. "Youth Culture/Youth Cults." In Charlie Gillett and Simon Frith, eds. *The Beat Goes On: The Rock File Reader.* East Haven, CT: Pluto Press, 1996, pp. 143–152.

Powers, Ann. "Three Heartthrob Material Boys Threaten to Burst Bubble Gum." *New York Times*, March 6, 2000.

Strauss, Neil. "How a Pop Sensation Came Undone." *New York Times*, August 18, 2002.

Zinomani, Jason. "Beyond the Boy-Band Trend, Where the Altar Boyz Are." *New York Times*, December 23, 2005.

Santanu Chakrabarti

The Clash

The Clash are an English punk rock band formed in London in the mid-1970s consisting of Joe Strummer (vocals, guitar), Mick Jones (guitar, vocals), Paul Simonon (bass), and a rotating cast of drummers (most notably Nicky "Topper" Headon, who would be the drummer on many of the band's most important releases). Though not the first punk band, they would become the most successful and the favorite among punks and non-punks alike. Yet, despite being the public face of punk, the band would experiment with a variety of genres, including rap, rockabilly, and reggae, forging a durable sound that drew raves from critics. And even though the band would become known for the same rebellious nature and hard-living lifestyle for which punk had become notorious, they quickly abandoned the movement's nihilism to become one of the more politically aware rock bands since the late 1960s.

The Clash was formed when Jones, Simonon, and guitarist Keith Levene recruited Strummer away from his band (the 101ers) and found a stable drummer in Terry Chimes. Their first gig was to open for the Sex Pistols in July 1976. Soon after, the band signed a contract with Britain's CBS records and went into the studio, but not before firing Levene for failing to show up to practices. The self-titled debut (released in 1977) was a success in the United Kingdom, but their label refused to release it in the United States, doubting the prospects for success in the more radio-friendly U.S. market (though the album would become the highest-selling import in history there). Wanting a sound that would sell well across the Atlantic, the band gave in to pressure by their label and produced *Give 'em Enough Rope* in 1978, which featured a slicker, cleaner sound. It was also at this time that Chimes left the band and was replaced by Headon, a talented multi-instrumentalist who would help to fill out their sound. Though some of the band's faithful fans would disagree with the more polished result, the album reached #2 on the UK charts, but still failed to break through into the American market.

That began to change in late 1979 with their third release, the critically revered double album *London Calling*. A wide-ranging record that incorporated elements of reggae, ska, and rockabilly, and with a decidedly leftist political bent, the album almost immediately went gold in the United Kingdom and reached as high as #27 on the U.S. album charts. They followed up the success of *London Calling* with an even more sprawling triple album in 1980, entitled *Sandinista*. But this time the band reached too far afield for musical inspiration, and the album's mix of children's choruses, gospel, and country was too eclectic for most reviewers, though the record sold reasonably well.

International commercial success finally arrived in 1982 with the release of *Combat Rock* and the single "Rock the Casbah," about the Iranian censorship of Western music, which became a top 40 hit in the United States. The band opened up for The Who on their reunion tour the following year, and though they were booed at nearly every appearance, they were at the height of their popularity and commercial success.

But though the band was enjoying larger audiences than ever, internal problems began to pull them apart. Headon was fired just after the release of *Combat Rock* (with Chimes coming back briefly to take his place), and fighting between Jones and Strummer resulted in Jones being fired from the band in 1983, when he would go on to form his own band, Big Audio Dynamite. The Clash staggered on for one more album (the universally panned *Cut the Crap*) before formally disbanding in 1986.

The Clash's influence on the independent rock scene was enormous. Their fusion of punk with early rock created a resurgence of interest in rockabilly, and their incorporation of a variety of Black music forms beyond the blues—such as soul, reggae, and ska—helped to break down genre walls and encourage experimentation. But far from just being musically progressive, the band was politically progressive as well, and brought leftist politics back to rock music after the band had been mostly absent during the 1970s. Not only did they play music created by Blacks, they also headlined the Rock Against Racism concert, which sought to break down color barriers in the real world as well. Their rebellious politics were underscored by a number of run-ins with the law for a variety of minor offences, and the band's outlaw image became a rallying point for bands throughout the 1980s looking to resist the right-wing politics of Thatcher and Reagan.

Further Reading

Gruen, Bob. *The Clash*. London: Vision On Publishing, 2001.
Tobler, John. *The "Clash."* London: Omnibus Press, 1984.
Topping, Keith. *The Complete Clash*. London: Reynolds & Hearn, 2003.

Ehren Gresehover

The Cure, Post-Punk, and Goth Music

The Cure is an English rock band that is principally the work of vocalist and multi-instrumentalist Robert Smith working with a variety of regular contributors in various combinations, most notably drummer and keyboardist Laurence Tolhurst and bassist Simon Gallup. The band's sound has changed significantly from album to album, starting out as post-punk on their first record and occasionally coming through as straightforward pop. But the sound most associated with the band is a dark, spare rock dirge with moody, existentialist lyrics. It is this sound that helped to form and popularize the Goth style of music and subculture, though the band frequently resisted being associated with either. They were also one of the earliest and best-selling (along with REM) examples of the budding alternative rock phenomenon, and helped break down the barriers between independent music mostly listened to by college students and mainstream radio.

The Cure was formed when Smith, Tolhurst, and Michael Dempsey (who were friends at a middle school in southeastern England) began playing together in a variety of bands, eventually ending up as a trio in the band Easy Cure, winning a talent competition and a recording contract with the German Hansa label. Though several demos were recorded, none were released and the relationship was dissolved. They then recorded their first single, the jangling post-punk song influenced by Albert Camus's *The Stranger,* entitled "Killing an Arab," and released it on the independent Small Wonder label, just as Chris Parry of Polydor Records began to express interest in signing them to his own imprint, Fiction Records.

Fiction re-released the single and the band then released their debut album, *Three Imaginary Boys* in 1979, which featured more of the edgy rock sound of their first single. The band booked a slot opening up for Siouxsie and the Banshees, with Robert Smith taking over guitar duties for the headlining band when theirs quit halfway through the tour. Smith's experience with the Banshees led him to steer the band's sound in a new direction, writing stormy, haunting dirges filled with layers of dense guitar. At this point, Simon Gallup joined the group, but Dempsey was unhappy with the new material and in a sign of things to come, was fired by Smith prior to the release of their followup, *Seventeen Seconds,* in 1980.

What followed were two more records of deepening gloom, 1981's *Faith* and 1982's *Pornography,* before Smith began to get restless with the darkness of their sound. Gallup departed, and Smith took time off from the band to play with the Banshees again, speculating openly about the possibility that the Cure would no longer exist. At the urging of Parry, though, Smith reformed the Cure with a new lineup. This new incarnation of the band would record albums that would alternate between their older, more melancholy sound with more upbeat and pop-driven numbers, which was the beginning of their way to the singles charts.

In 1992 the band would release *Wish,* their most popular (and most pop) record to date, which offered two smash hits, "Friday I'm in Love" and "High." But the lyrical sunshine also blinded many of the Goths that formed the core of their fan base, who began to feel as if the band had lost its way. That seemed to be the case with the long-delayed release of *Wild Mood Swings* in 1996, which disappointed critics and fans alike, and sold poorly compared to previous releases. After another four-year break, the better regarded *Bloodflowers* was released, earning the band a Grammy nomination. Though it was thought to be their last recording, the self-titled *The Cure* was released in 2004, and at the time of writing the band was planning a 2008 world tour, proving that they were still very much alive.

Even more than the new sounds introduced to the world of rock, Robert Smith brought a whole new style to the cultural landscape. Though boys wearing makeup were nothing new in rock culture, Smith gave a whole group of boys and young men license to craft a theatrical image for themselves, and made sensitivity and introspection a form of rebellion. Though claims that the band promoted suicide will always dog their legacy (especially after a fan stabbed himself as they took the stage at a concert), with no other band does the natural moodiness and introspection of adolescence find so natural a home as with Smith's Cure.

Further Reading

Carman, Richard. *Robert Smith.* Shropshire: Independent Music Press, 2005.
Sutherland, Steve, and Robert Smith. *The Cure: Ten Imaginary Years.* London: Zomba Books, 1990.
Thompson, Dave. *In-Between Days.* London: Helter Skelter Publishing, 2005.

Ehren Gresehover

DEVO

The electronic rock band DEVO gained mainstream fame during the 1980s. DEVO are known for their independent political message, which has been summarized as a critique of modern industrial society, not dissimilar from the messages embedded within the punk rock music of the Sex Pistols and the Dead Kennedys. This somewhat aggressive critique has been linked to the sensibilities of boys being socialized in a patriarchal society. However, rather than transporting their analyses on the thunder broom of punk rock, DEVO employed the uplifting and happy sounds of pop rock. This aspect of their art found appeal not in those boys drawn to hyperaggression, but in those intrigued by complexity and irony. The visionaries that were DEVO have been described as observers, and they named what they observed de-evolution—DEVO—that is, a resurgence in white, right-wing conservatism, the redistribution of wealth upward through trickle-down economics, an intensified propaganda machine, the de-industrialization of much of North America, heightened military interventions against democratically elected governments in the developing world designed to bring stability for investors, which combined, paved the way for the post–Bretton Woods globalization of neoliberal capital.

This context of de-evolution was to be represented in the sound of their music, the content of their lyrics, and the look and imagery of the band. In other words, DEVO strove to create the auditory and visual experience of things falling apart, but in a postmodern, hyperreal, plastic-smile way. That is, DEVO strove to capture the ironic image of the boss's premeditated upbeat pep rally song crudely designed to distract our attention from the all-too-obvious inability to demand democratic accountability, and in turn, prevent the capitalist leaders of industry from externalizing the costs of production to those who rely on a wage to survive manifested in the intensification of human suffering and misery—again, de-evolution, or DEVO.

Their image was that of the robot. They sarcastically wrote the script for their robotic selves as predetermined to entertain the corporate life forms as they were genetically programmed to do. Rebellion was futile, they mockingly proclaimed, because the immutable Darwinian laws of survival of the fittest govern the world. They critiqued the social Darwinist ideology the ruling elite used to justify the hierarchies of class-based societies that was becoming vastly more barbaric as the limitations and regulations on the mobility of speculative capital were lifted, by posing as caricatures of the biologically determined performers who calm the oppressed and exploited masses for the bosses.

The band members were all roughly the same size, stature, and build, contributing to their robotic, manufactured, and emotionally cold image. They always dressed in uniform. DEVO's costumes were typically a space-age or disco-flared working-class jumpsuit or lab coat accessorized with black sunglasses and their trademark red helmets. The members were clearly true performers and actors inspired by theatrical themes.

The band began independently recording and self-producing their own records in their Akron, Ohio, garage. After gaining some overseas popularity and cult status, they ended they stint with independent recording after signing with Warner Brothers in 1978. They made it to the pop charts in 1980 with "Whip It," a dance floor favorite. DEVO's use of ironic theater and critical social analysis continues to influence independent artists today.

Further Reading

Coupe, Stuart, and Glenn Baker. *The New Rock'n'Roll: The A–Z of Rock in the '80s.* New York: St. Martin's Press, 1983.

Curry Stephenson Malott

Hip Hop Culture

If ever there was any doubt regarding hip hop's current popularity among boys of the *me* generation, a stroll down the hallway of most North American high schools would likely reveal a similar visual landscape and soundtrack: searing loud bass lines emitted from iPods, mp3 players, and cell phones, stuffed into standard-issue phat pants, or ill-fitting polyester-blend uniforms. While either holding their collective breaths until puberty hits, or shaping their newly minted moustache-soul-patch combos, these boys are learning a lot about male identities through hip hop, thanks to MTV, YouTube, and record companies such as Def Jam and Death Row Records.

A historical recounting of the climate in which hip hop emerged in North America reads something like an old story recalled by your great-aunt Ida: it is long winded, sometimes sad, peppered with random characters, and seldom predictable. And unlike those stories that have been frozen in time with the help of a few dusty Polaroid's and some 8-track soundtracks to accompany them, hip hop has not remained untouched in your mama's vacuum cleaner. Since emerging from the soil of Black American culture of the early 1970s, hip hop's draw began by attracting and keeping the attention of some of the roughest and toughest kids of New York City's Bronx borough, who were looking for a place to broadcast to the rest of the country what was happening in their own backyards.

Get Skooled!—The Roots of Hip Hop

Before New York was ever considered cool, and before the hip hop MC reigned supreme, folks were walking to a different beat than the boom-bap so familiar to rap music. The hip hop MC is a descendent from the eighteenth-century African griot: a traditional storyteller who peppered his tales with rhythmic chanting and body movement. The griot's shout-outs were a form of self-expression, and a way to express out some of the pain and grief of slavery. The griot laid the foundation for the hip hop MC, who would come to deliver their tune to a different beat, and would soon learn to cultivate the "skillz to pay the billz."

For youth growing up in poor urban areas in the United States in the early 1970s, hip hop was the cool kid on the block who got invited to all of the wicked parties. Young Bronx residents of the late 1960s witnessed one of the worst periods of poverty and crime in New York's history up until that point, and they were desperate for something fresh. So come Monday morning, when all the cool kids are talking in the schoolyard about the throw-down that happened last Saturday night, and everyone wanted to be able to say that they were there.

All past and current hip hop heads agree that what we now refer to as hip hop—the combined elements of the DJ, the MC, break dancing, and graffiti—began in the early 1970s, in the Bronx, in New York City. Three DJs from different parts of the 'hood—Kool Herc, Afrikaa Bambaataa, and Grandmaster Flash—gathered groups of mostly Black and Latino youths together to make music and art, and to "kick it old skool style" by break dancing on split open cardboard boxes. Part of the appeal of these three DJs for their youth fans, was that they came from the same difficult, socioeconomic conditions as these kids. Through their efforts at reaching the young and disenfranchised from the Bronx, these DJs endeavored to transform the hopelessness of poverty into a creative force. The birth of hip hop, and the success of these DJs, represents an important period in Black history, by bringing successful Black male role models into the public sphere, from which they had often previously been absent. While coexisting in the same poor urban ghettos as their young fans, Herc and others managed to achieve financial success by sowing the seeds of a culture that responded to poverty with a vibrant cultural movement.

Like reggae music production in Jamaica, rap music originated from the voices and experiences of mostly lower-class Black people living in city slums and reflected influencing elements from artists such as Cab Calloway, be-bop singers, and the man who gave power to the people with his political slam poetry of the 1960s and 1970s, word-siren Gil Scott-Heron. Some key players from that early period in hip hop were the break-dancing Rock Steady Crew, who are still going strong in 2008. Also, the first commercial rap song, "Rapper's Delight," by the Sugarhill Gang, is still being played on the radio.

Also in need of representing are the ladies, who though often get left out of hip hop's story, were also holding it down from the beginning. For instance, although not much is known of women's contributions to the origins of the hip hop movement in the 1970s, female rapper Ms. Melodie claims that though males were the first ones to record rap, women were as involved in bringing the culture and music to life. Though current female black rap artists such as Foxy Brown and Lil' Kim are often on the receiving end of harsh criticism for their sexualized lyrics and videos, Queen Latifah and MC Lyte, two hugely successful female rap artists of the 1980s, continue to represent powerful female role models for the hip hop generations past and present.

The Birth of the Hip Hop Gangsta

Of all the subgenres within hip hop, such as conscious rap and southern rap, gangsta is perhaps the one that raises the most eyebrows. The critiques directed toward gangsta rap music and culture largely stem from its public image: hordes of scantily-clad dancing women, the portrayal of gangs, violence, and jail sentencing as commonplace for Black men, are common themes in the music and videos. And though some of these videos and lyrics from artists such as 50 Cent and Three Six Mafia may indeed reflect some of the harsh realities of these artists' lives, it remains that when examining male archetypes as portrayed through gangsta rap culture, we are left with a very limited perception of what men are, or could be.

When LL Cool J told the world that he was hard as hell in 1985, hip hop had no idea what was coming. Gangsta rap emerged on the scene during the late 1980s, with West Coast notables such as Ice-T and NWA at the fore. The hard-hitting lyrics and in-your-face posturing of these gangsta artists, punctuated by song titles such as "F—— Da Police" (NWA), and "Cop Killer" (Ice-T), conveyed a message to the world that these men were angry and were not going to take it sitting down. Around the same time as the rise of gangsta, hip hop also witnessed the rise of California rap group 2 Live Crew's song "We Want Some P——." With the rise in popularity of gangsta, and the continual use of women's bodies as props in rap videos, the original hip hop script was flipped beyond recognition. While Ice and his ilk were working their "gangsta thang" on the West Coast, New York heavyweights such as The Beastie Boys, Run DMC, and the politically charged lyrics of Public Enemy were still "keepin' it real" on the East Coast.

Boys Will B Boyz

The notion of hardness and masculine posturing has always been present in hip hop. The emergence of gangsta, however, birthed a fresh, hypermasculine construct, with mostly Black men doing the representing. Gangsta rap artists such as 50 Cent, Papoose, and Three Six Mafia, for example, draw huge numbers of young male fans, and they can be seen in their videos lauding diamonds and guns, and driving expensive cars; and they are always surrounded by a plethora of scantily clad, sexually ready women. At its worst, gangsta rap music personifies the most grossly exaggerated stereotypes of Black American male identity today, such as the Black hypersexualized uneducated gang member and street thug. And yet, on the other hand, the culture does provide its young male fans with successful and hugely visible Black masculine role models. Gangsta rap's influence on its young male fans presents lots of complications. Though the culture can be criticized for its portrayal of women and its glorification of violence, it also shows successful Black men making it big in the music industry. Especially for its youth listeners, many of whom come from the same challenging socioeconomic circumstances as the first wave of hip hop fans, gangsta rap is very influential on these young male fans.

As gangsta's popularity is continually on the rise, the question remains of how it continues to affect the way its male young listeners receive, interpret, and perform the cues gleaned through and from the culture, and how that affects the ways in which they construct their masculine identities as they come of age. As the spread of global hip hop culture piggybacks on the behinds of globalization, it continues to attract young male listeners who are drawing on various aspects of the culture to construct and define their identities, and giving new meaning to the old hip hop adage of "keepin' it real."

Further Reading

Chang, Jeff. *Can't Stop, Won't Stop: A History of the Hip-Hop Generation.* New York: Picador, 2006.

Kitwana, Bakari. *The Hip-Hop Generation: Young Blacks and the Crisis in African American Culture.* New York: Basic Civitas Books, 2002.

McKinnon, Matthew. "Tougher than Leather: Masculinity in Hip-Hop Culture." CBC Web Site. http://www.cbc.ca/arts/film/leather.html (accessed February 2008).

Jacqueline Celemencki

Led Zeppelin

Led Zeppelin was an enormously influential and wildly popular English band from the 1970s who are credited with popularizing and defining the musical genre heavy metal. Their sound was a mix of overdriven blues, psychedelic rock, and British folk, powered by heavy, slightly behind-the-beat drumming, and screeching, high-pitched vocals. As their career progressed, they would also incorporate English folk elements and reggae into their sound. Lyrically, they borrowed heavily from the blues, but incorporated mythological themes and references to J. R. R. Tolkien's Lord of the Rings fantasy series. Described by many (including the band members themselves) as the biggest band of their era, Led Zeppelin spent the 1970s dominating the Billboard charts (all eight of their albums were in the top 10 on the Pop Album charts) and selling out arenas, breaking attendance records set by the Beatles. They also became the biggest proponents of Album-Oriented Rock (AOR), the idea that the album as a whole was an artistic statement, rather than merely serving as a collection of singles. The band was made up of Robert Plant on vocals, Jimmy Page on guitar, John Bonham on drums, and John Paul Jones on bass. Their lyrical obsession with swords, sex, and sorcery; reticence with the press; and dynamic, muscular sound created a type of rock star that was as much pulp fiction hero as musician, a model that has proven irresistible to generations of teenage boys.

In the late 1960s, Page had joined the Yardbirds for their final record, having a significant influence on its sound. When the band broke up in 1968, Page found himself the sole remaining member, and recruited Jones, Plant, and Bonham to fulfill the Yardbirds fall touring commitments. The band stayed together after the tour, renamed itself Led Zeppelin (based on comments made by The Who's Keith Moon and John Entwistle), and went into the studio immediately. In just 35 hours they recorded their first album, *Led Zeppelin*. The record was released in January 1969 on Atlantic Records, which gave the band a $200,000 signing bonus (the largest of its type at the time) and unusually unrestricted artistic freedom.

The first year of the band's existence found them completing four concert tours in the United States and Europe and the release of their second album, *Led Zeppelin II*, which was even more commercially successful than their debut, becoming the band's first #1 album on the Billboard charts. But despite this success with fans, the music critics were dismissive or even hostile to the band, and as a result the band rarely gave interviews to the press for the rest of their careers.

The band followed *Led Zeppelin II* with the largely acoustic *Led Zeppelin III* in 1970, and critical reaction was once again extremely negative. As a direct response, the band released their fourth album without a title, the name of the band, or any identifying information at all, save for four rune-like symbols chosen by each of the band members. Known unofficially as *Led Zeppelin IV*, many consider the album to be their best. It was also their most commercially successful album, having sold over 23 million copies in the United States alone. The album also contained the song "Stairway to Heaven," one of the most popular rock songs to have ever been recorded, though it was never released as a single.

Led Zeppelin would continue to release records throughout the 1970s, though they toured less rigorously, in part because of a serious motorcycle accident involving Plant and his wife in 1975 and the death of their son Karak in 1977. They started their own record label, Swan Song, and began to experiment with elements of funk and reggae. They also filmed a documentary film, which cut together footage of live performances at Madison Square Garden with fictional fantasy sequences showing the band members and their manager inhabiting various heroic roles.

On September 24th, 1980, Bonham, a depressive alcoholic, was found dead in his home, having choked on his own vomit after an intense bout of drinking. Before the end of the year the band announced that they were breaking up, with the remaining members all embarking on successful solo careers, though none of these projects would approach the success of their original band.

Throughout the years, Page and Plant have worked together on a number of projects, including a set for MTV's *Unplugged* series in 1994. The surviving three members (with various guest artists replacing Bonham) have also reunited under the Led Zeppelin name—including a 1985 Live Aid concert, a 1988 performance celebrating Atlantic Records 40th anniversary, and in 1995, when they were inducted into the Rock and Roll Hall of Fame. In December 2007, the band reunited for a concert in London that received glowing reviews, and subsequent comments from the band hinted at a full-fledged tour for the following year, with the chance that the band might also enter the studio to record material for a new album.

The band's breakup only deepened their already impressive mystique, giving the band an almost legendary status. "Stairway to Heaven" became a cultural touchstone for a whole generation of boys, as can be seen in the coming-of-age movie *Fast Times at Ridgemont High*, when one boy insists that the most important way to ensure romantic success with a girl was to play side one of *Led Zeppelin IV.*

The band's hostility to critics and the recording industry (they refused to release any songs as singles), their artistic aspirations grounded in a macho swagger and sexuality, and their fondness for heroic fantasy all endeared them to boys looking for ways to rebel against authority and to escape the occasionally difficult and awkward world of adolescence.

Further Reading

Cole, Richard, and Richard Trubo. *Stairway to Heaven.* New York: HarperCollins Publishers, 1992.

Davis, Stephen. *Hammer of the Gods.* New York: W. Morrow, 1985.

Fast, Susan. *In the Houses of the Holy.* Oxford, Oxfordshire: Oxford University Press, 2001.

Ehren Gresehover

Metallica and Heavy Metal

Metallica is an American heavy metal band that formed in 1981 in Los Angeles, when James Hetfield (vocals, guitar) and Dave Mustaine (lead guitar) responded to an advertisement placed by drummer Lars Ulrich in a local paper. After some personnel changes (including a bitter split with Mustaine, who went on to form Megadeth), the band moved to San Francisco and picked up Kirk Hammett (lead guitar) and Cliff Burton (bass). Later, Jason Newstead would replace Burton after a fatal traffic accident, and then Robert Trujillo would in turn replace Newstead when he left the band in 2001. The band became famous for pioneering a fast, aggressive style of heavy metal known as thrash metal, and for mostly avoiding the science fiction and fantasy clichés and operatic vocals for which the genre had become known. As a result of their less theatrical style and critically acclaimed music, they would cross over to mainstream radio and become one of the best-selling bands in the world, topping over 100 million records sold worldwide.

In addition to making some of the most musically intelligent and powerful heavy metal records of the 1980s, they also eliminated a lot of the eccentricities of the genre, making the sound more approachable to the average rock listener and, as a result, popularizing the whole genre. And in their use of rage as a primary force in their music, they provided their fans (most of whom were adolescent boys) with a cathartic release that they could not find in the new wave or rock and roll on the radio.

With James Hetfield's growling, angry vocals, Hammett's intricate guitar solos (working from Mustaine's work with the band early on), Ulrich's thunderous, yet complex drumming, and Burton's innovative work on bass, Metallica members were unlike most of their peers in the early 1980s metal scene, who, like their idols, Led Zeppelin, tended to favor fantasy themes, high-pitched vocals, and concept albums. Metallica, on the other hand, seemed to replace much of that artifice with rage and power, and together with Anthrax, Slayer, and Megadeth created a new genre known as thrash metal.

They developed this style over the course of two records released on the small, independent Megaforce Records, their debut *Kill 'em All*, and its follow-up, *Ride the Lightning*, regarded by many as one of the best metal recordings. It was the strength of *Ride the Lightning* that drew attention from major labels, and as a result they signed to Elektra to release their third studio album, *Master of Puppets*, considered by many to be their best. The record sold more than half a million copies upon its release in 1986, and that without any radio play or a music video on MTV.

But with Metallica seemingly on the verge of real commercial success and touring Europe to support their recent release, the band's tour bus skidded out of control and flipped, killing Burton. The band continued to carry on, hiring Newstead (formerly of Flotsam and Jetsam) to take over on bass, and recorded *. . . And Justice for All* in 1988, whose single "One" would become a video and radio hit and would catapult the band into the mainstream. Though the album would be their first in the top 10, there were already complaints that the band was changing their sound to become more popular, a criticism that would only intensify with their self-titled follow-up (sometimes called "the Black Album"), which debuted at number one on the Billboard charts. The album's sound was slower than that found on their earlier albums, and the songs were shorter and more radio-friendly, picking up thousands of new fans, at the expense of some of the metal fans that had been part of their original core audience. A 2000 lawsuit and publicity campaign against the peer-to-peer file sharing service Napster over piracy accusations would further tarnish their image as being down-to-earth, and eventually the band dropped the suit.

Now a chart-topping rock band, Metallica found themselves cutting their hair, contributing songs to blockbuster action movies and continually moving to a more alternative rock sound. By the time the went into the studio to record 2001's *St. Anger*, the band was suffering deep fissures (depicted in the documentary film *Some Kind of Monster*), resulting in Hetfield completing a rehab program for alcoholism and Newstead leaving the band to pursue other projects. At the time of writing, the band had hired Suicidal Tendencies bassist Robert Trujillo and was again at work on a new album.

Further Reading

Chirazi, Steffan. *So What!* New York: Broadway Books, 2004.
Crocker, Chris. *Metallica.* New York: St. Martin's Press, 1993.
Pillsbury, Glenn. *Damage Incorporated.* New York: Routledge, 2006.

Ehren Gresehover

Mosh Pits

(Editors' Note: The following is a first-person account by Joseph Carroll-Miranda and Ernesto Rentas-Robles about the highs and lows of the "pit," a raucous group crowded together, typically in front of the stage, at a live concert. A description of the pit experience and the typical cast of characters and actions follows.)

Then, suddenly, there was chaos: fists, running in circles, legs everywhere, blood, sweat, and tears, euphoric chants, screams and laughs, all composing a harmonious cacophony. How can we materialize, in this text, the synchronicity of asynchronicity, the ordered chaos, the full-blown explosion of youth inebriated with testosterone, a blank state of mind controlled by mechanisms of sheer survival as it deals with menacing expressions of uncontrolled violence? This is not another gory movie that systematically comes out of Hollywood every summer; this is the tale of a 20-year-old music scene born, bred, and raised in the humid heat of the Caribbean.

Both of us know what a pit is, but if you ask us to explain it, then we fall into the realm of multiple interpretations and experiences intertwined with distinct noncategorical social dynamics. To some, the actions in the pit may appear as childish games, immature tantrums, a testosterone fest that may bleed as a homoerotic scene from the movie *Fight Club*. How do we see it? It depends. Is it a fight? Is it a dance? Is it a celebration? Is it a ceremony? A ritual? A rite of passage? It's very hard to define and also describe what a pit is. Such difficulty forced us to engage in prolonged dialogue, as we established the best way to expose what a pit is. Under specific musical scenarios, we concur that the answer to the following question shall guide our venture: who are the different characters that we may encounter in a pit?

The Cast of Characters and Glossary

The best way to illustrate the pit is to share some of our most memorable experiences that attest to what we have lived.

1. Little Grasshopper: a person who goes to a pit for the first time.
2. Agent Provocateur: experienced pit dancer who incites the pit to come alive.
3. Cherry Boy: a pop culture fan who gravitates towards the scene.
4. Masoko-Bag: person who gets all banged up and continues to stay in the pit, loving the pain.
5. Model-Thrasher: metal head who defies all odds and never leaves the pit.
6. Las Nenas: scene girls just ripping it up like La Femme Nikita.
7. Jock aka Beef-Brutus: a serious muscle head.
8. Riot Squad: a crew of agent provocateurs who need to appease the violence they created.
9. Korillo: the crew from the scene.
10. Fresitameter: a sixth sense that identifies new blood on the scene.

11. Jaws Syndrome: Experienced dancers who circle around the new prey, little grasshopper, cherry-boy, and jocks.
12. Testometer: level of testosterone in a pit.
13. False Manpride: an airbag who boasts toughness, but never does anything.

The first rule is there are no fights in the pit-fight!

To the untrained eye, pits may appear as a center of uncontrolled violence. In our experience, nothing could be farther from the truth. As strange as it may sound, pits have a golden rule: fights are not allowed in a pit. The reason is extremely simple: if there is a fight, there is no show. Shows and pits are the life of our scene. Without shows we are nothing. The anticipation of a show is not necessarily to go and see a band. Good bands guarantee good pits, but not always. What the reader needs to understand is that the show is a pretext for meeting and hooking up with like-minded people that coincide in a time and space. The mood of the night determines the nature of the pit.

The golden rule is flexible. Sometimes, an incident instigated a fight, while at times the same incident provoked general laughter. It all depends. For instance, one time a jock was disturbing the groove of Las Nenas as he was dancing. Ironically, at a bar called Punch Bar, the jock was introduced to a good old fashion boot party executed by Las Nenas. As the beating ensued, nobody broke it up, nobody felt sorry, and nobody cared. There was just a general acknowledgment that the jock needed to chill.

During a 25 ta Life show in Ponce the electric excitement of the show had everybody in a seriously joyous mood. Nothing was going to impede this show from being a full-blown success. As soon as the band started playing, the pit just spontaneously combusted. Fists were flying, stage dives were elegantly orchestrated, bodies were flying and dropping to the ground, bodies that were quickly being picked up by those within the pit. Within all that violence there was a strong sense of camaraderie. The violence was controlled violence. Out of the blue, a fellow skin falls to the ground and instead of being lifted up, a Krishna starts kicking him while the skin is on the ground. Fellow skins become aware and run to the site. One of them grabs the Krishna by the back of his neck, and in a cradle like fashion, punches him with a pinky ring in the middle of the forehead. The Krishna was tattooed with the ring as he was being repeatedly punched and interrogated by one of the skins: "Ain't your faith supposed to be peace loving?" All weary, the Krishna acknowledges: "yes." "Then why are you kicking this man on the ground?" Dumbfounded, the Krishna realizes what he just did and apologizes. Paradoxically this fight guaranteed that no other fights took place in this legendary show.

Battle Wounds

All of those who have been inside the pit have had their share of battle wounds. After every show, it is customary to meet up and talk about what the pit was like. "Check our my fat lip," "Look at this bruise under my armpit," "Man, I twisted my ankle," "Trip out on the bump on my forehead," "Ufff, it was buck wild tonight!," were statements heard after show, gossip that looked for a sense of validation that this was a good pit. These were our battle wounds. As such, we flaunted them as we reconstructed and deciphered with joyous dialogue the pit experience that had just transpired. A momentary pause infused with calmness, nod, and smiles affirmed bonds of complicity within the Korillo.

The pit is not the show itself, but it is undeniably the best part of it. It is a time and space where you do battle with yourself, you test yourself, you meet yourself, you conquer yourself, and you become aware of self and embrace it. In the pit you learn your strengths and weakness and your virtues and your flaws; in the pit you are both loved and hated. It is hard to explain. You need to be there.

You need to breathe in the smell of blood, sweat, stale beer, and cigarette butts on the floor. You need to feel sweaty bodies bouncing, slamming, hitting one another, the punch in the face, a kick to the side, and the thud as you hit the floor. You need to experience being lifted up from the floor by 10 hands in a fraction of a second. You need to feel the comfort of being carried by the crowd after a stage dive. You need to feel how there is no fear, but rather confidence, security, and solidarity in the air. You need to learn how you die in the pit, as you shed all your problems and worries. You need to see how people take care of one another. You need to see how the strong protects the weak. You need to see how the Agents Provocateur grabs a Little Grasshopper and forces him to survive. You need to see the Little Grasshopper inebriated by his adrenaline as he celebrates his debut. You need to experience how you can leave a pit a completely different person, somehow stronger and more confident to face society's ills.

Only after seeing, smelling, feeling, touching, and experiencing the pit can one understand why it can be considered a beautiful thing. Then, and only then, can one understand how violence can control violence. This "violence" can become a beautiful dance. Like Kung Fu, the dance of death, it is beautiful to see. Trying to make sense of what you just read will give you an insight in how a pit can become a rhythmic fight club. When you become conscious of how the pit can be considered a beautiful thing, then you are prepared to internalize the beauty of the pit. Step into our world, so you can understand how instant the pit starts; if you are in the middle, it hauls you. You have no choice: it just sucks you in. Why? You want it to. Why? It just feels good! ¡OI! *y punto.*

In loving memory of Manteca, Cristy, and Guido.

Further Reading

Goméz, G. (2007). *La Escena.* DVD Documentary.
Letts, D. (2005). *Punk: Attitude.* DVD Documentary.
Rachman, P. (2006). *American Hardcore.* DVD Documentary.
Spooner, J. (2003). *Afro-Punk.* DVD Documentary.

Joseph Carroll-Miranda and Ernesto Rentas-Robles

Nirvana and Grunge

Nirvana is an American rock band formed in Aberdeen, Washington (though the band is most associated with the city of Seattle) in the late 1980s by Krist Novoselic (bass), Kurt Cobain (vocals, guitar), and Dave Grohl, the last in a string of drummers employed. Though they made only three official studio albums, they were one of the most influential and successful bands in the history of rock, having sold over 50 million records worldwide. Despite (or perhaps because of) their aversion to stardom, the band was often placed at the forefront of youth culture, and Cobain was frequently treated as a type of spokesperson for his generation. This prominent status would be tragically magnified upon his death by suicide in April 1994, resulting in the dissolution of the band. They were known for being the most prominent band of the grunge rock subgenre, but their sound owed as much to heavy metal, punk, and straightforward pop melodicism as anything else.

Novoselic and Cobain met in 1985 and bonded over a shared love of punk rock, particularly the extremely heavy punk band the Melvins. After forming several short-lived bands with a variety of personnel, they settled on the name Nirvana and on a drummer, Chad Channing. This trio released their first single, "Love Buzz/Big Cheese," in 1988 on local record label Sub Pop, which also released their first album, *Bleach,* in 1989. The sound of this early record was a mix of the sludge punk of the Melvins, the jangly grunge of local band Mudhoney, and the hard rock of Led Zeppelin and Black Sabbath. It sold a modest 38,000 copies, but garnered heavy radio play on college stations and attracted some high-profile fans, particularly bands such as Sonic Youth and Dinosaur, Jr.

Frustrated with Sub Pop, they followed Sonic Youth's advice and became their label mates at DGC. They also replaced Channing on drums with Grohl, whose DC punk band Scream had just broken up. They went into the studio with well-known producer Butch Vig to record their first release on a major label. The result was *Nevermind,* which boasted a much more slickly produced sound, ample pop hooks, and their first and biggest hit, the top 10 song "Smells like Teen Spirit." The video, which featured a dingy, punk rock version of a high school dance with a rather apathetic Cobain brooding over the proceedings, was a runaway sensation and became nearly ubiquitous on both MTV and radio stations nationwide. The album was released in the fall of 1991, but by the end of the year it was selling 400,000 copies a week in the United States alone, bumping Michael Jackson's comeback record, *Dangerous,* from the top spot on the Billboard charts.

Unfortunately, the band, especially Cobain himself, seemed unprepared for their stardom. The band took to mocking the very publicity machines that were turning them into front page news, wearing dresses in public, refusing to play their instruments on television shows that featured lip syncing, and saying confrontational things to the press. All of this just fed into the world's view of the band members as the unofficial spokespeople for all young people, the so-called Generation X, with Cobain absorbing much of the adulation and scorn alone as the band's charismatic antihero. Perhaps as a result of the pressure, Cobain became a heroin addict, and would have several covered-up overdoses. Also during this time, Cobain would marry the controversial front woman of rock band Hole. The two would have a child together, Frances Bean, in 1992.

The band continued this confrontational attitude toward their stardom in the studio, hooking up with indie rock musician and producer Steve Albini to produce their raw and aggressive third album *In Utero*. Despite songs such as "Rape Me" and the feedback squall of ironically titled "Radio Friendly Unit Shifter," the album would be a major success. Because of all that had been going on in Cobain's life, the album was not released until 1993 (with a stop-gap rarities record called *Incesticide* slaking the fan's thirst in 1992), and they followed it up with a performance for MTV's *Unplugged* series, playing a number of cover songs and unreleased material.

But touring life once again put strain on Cobain, and heroin, tranquilizers, alcohol, and depression (along with a chronic stomach condition) seemed to drive him further into melancholy. Eventually, on April 4, 1994, Cobain killed himself with a shotgun wound to the head. When his body was discovered days later, fans and television crews began to descend on his home, making him the biggest topic in the news and furthering his mythic status.

After Cobain's death, Novoselic and Grohl went their separate ways, occasionally coming together to haggle with Love over Nirvana's legacy (box sets and live recordings were released after Cobain's death). Novoselic would go on to play in a number of bands, but he seemed to have the most success as a political activist, forming the organization JAMPAC to fight for musician's rights. Grohl started his own band, The Foo Fighters, who would go on to have massive commercial success of their own.

Though Cobain seemed to be uncomfortable as a stand-in for an entire generation, it is clear from the reaction to his death that many young people felt that he did speak for them, and his brand of angst and apathy would inspire the lyrics and attitude of a multitude of bands that would come after.

Further Reading

Azerrad, Michael. *Come As You Are*. Garden City, New York: Doubleday, 1993.
Cross, Charles. *Heavier than Heaven*. New York: Hyperion, 2002.
True, Everett. *Nirvana: The Biography*. New York: Da Capo Press, 2007.

Ehren Gresehover

Pink Floyd

Floyd (whose name was derived from the names of two U.S. blues musicians, Pink Anderson and Floyd Council) was an English rock band that actively toured and recorded from the mid-1960s through the mid-1990s. The five musicians most associated with the band are Syd Barrett (guitar, vocals), Roger Waters (bass, vocals), David Gilmore (guitar, vocals), Rick Wright (keyboards, vocals) and Nick Mason (drums), though all five were only part of the band for a brief time in 1968. Though the band is often strongly associated with marijuana, black lights, and spacey, atmospheric music, Pink Floyd's musical output was remarkably diverse and complex, reflecting the most dominant tastes and inclinations (if any) of the band's members at the time. Despite the band's experimental and changing sound, they were one of the most successful rock bands in the history of the genre, selling more than 200 million records worldwide.

Pink Floyd's effect on music is unquestioned, with bands such as Yes, Genesis, and Radiohead borrowing their approach to music and their techniques. In addition, their intensely introspective lyrics, frequently dealing with themes of depression, alienation, and insanity (seen even in the history of the band itself) provided the soundtrack to the lives of disaffected boys for the next two decades.

Pink Floyd began as a psychedelic rock band focused largely on the work of Barrett, who both wrote all the songs and sang them, with Bob Klose preceding Gilmore on guitar. They released only one record during this time, *Piper at the Gates of Dawn,* though it is widely considered to be one of the most important and influential psychedelic albums ever produced. Soon thereafter, Barrett became crippled by mental illness (caused or aggravated by intense LSD use), often going catatonic during live performances. Klose left the band and was replaced with Gilmore, who was also expected to take over vocal duties from Barrett, who was deemed unfit to tour, though they still hoped to be able to continue making records based on his songwriting. Unfortunately, Barrett's mental health deteriorated rapidly, and the remaining band members were forced to collectively write their follow-up, *A Saucerful of Secrets,* themselves. The result was a unique and bracingly experimental sound, with all members having a chance to contribute. Though the records they released during this period were uneven, their relentless use of studio tricks, new technology, and science-fiction–inspired lyrics ensured that they maintained the respect of critics while gathering an increasingly large fan base.

This egalitarian arrangement did not last, because Waters's lyrical preoccupations and inclinations toward epic songwriting began to dominate the band, at the same time as they broke through to mainstream success with *Dark Side of the Moon* in 1973. This album, which was hailed as a studio masterpiece (thanks in part to the engineering of Alan Parsons), used innovative recording techniques and state-of-the-art technology (including early use of synthesizers) to create a clear, precise sound that had not been heard on a rock album previously. *Dark Side of the Moon* became the ultimate record for audiophiles and encouraged a generation of rock listeners to put together high-fidelity stereo systems capable of hearing every detail of the album's intricate sound.

The next 12 years found the band becoming increasingly popular, as it was also becoming more exclusively the expression of Waters's lyrical preoccupations, which included a distrust of women and relationships, authority figures, and even his own fans. Though music critics and fans would find that Waters's social sloganeering and introspection were taking too much away from the music on the records *Animals* and the *Final Cut,* the formula worked well enough on "Wish You Were Here" and the concept album *The Wall* to give the band a legion of fans and their own feature film, written by Waters and starring Bob Geldof. *The Wall* also featured Pink Floyd's only #1 single, "Another Brick in the Wall (Part 2)," an anthemic critique of the mechanistic public school system whose refrain "we don't need no education / we don't need no thought control" and portrayal of women as shrill and controlling would serve as a rallying cry to millions of teenage boys oppressed by the high school world around them.

But Waters's dominance of the band would prove too much for any of them to take. Waters fired Wright after *The Wall*'s release (citing a cocaine addiction and insufficient participation), and Waters himself left the band in 1985 to pursue solo work. Gilmore and Mason continued on (eventually hiring Wright back on) to record two albums of new material (*A Momentary Lapse of Reason* and *Division Bell*), mostly bluesy guitar albums written in part by outside writers and primarily reflecting Gilmore's sensibilities. Though the records sold reasonably well, most critics considered the output substandard and uninteresting.

The band eventually disbanded for good in 1995, though they have come together for partial reunions without Waters since then. The full band did memorably reunite for the Live 8 concert in 2005, apparently reconciled.

Further Reading

Mason, Nick. *Inside Out*. London: Phoenix, 2005.
Schaffner, Nicholas. *Saucerful of Secrets*. New York: Harmony, 1991.

Ehren Gresehover

Punk Rock Culture

Popular culture can be understood as language, customs, preferences, manners, intellect, and other influences on human behavior that are intended for, and thus common among, the general population. Because punk rock embodies its own unique preferences, customs, and the like, it is often viewed as a form of popular culture. Punk rock culture has long attracted boys (and girls) who want to challenge the conventional culture in an aggressively derisive way. Within punk rock culture, for example, it is a common practice (custom) for punk rockers to sarcastically name their bands that which they resist, such as the British punk band The Exploited, whose name represents a form of protest against the state of being exploited. However, there are at least three ways in which scholars have tended to theorize popular culture, summarized below in regard to their usefulness for understanding punk rock.

In practice, punk rockers that make it their mission to fight the bosses are often limited by the fact that they were themselves socialized (raised) in the same system that they are against. Because of this, sometimes punk rockers do not realize it when they are supporting the system. For example, when punk rockers think that to be punk is to be against everything, including those who are different (sexually, racially, etc.), they have misunderstood what it means to be against, and as a result, they wind up supporting the very system they think they are fighting.

Punk Rocker's Revolution, by Malott and Peña (2004), outlines the complex and contradictory ways in which punk rock has both resisted and accommodated the dominant, white supremacist, homophobic, patriarchal society. This work looks at the ways in which punk rockers have failed to overcome their mainstream socialization, while at the same time celebrating the ways in which they have been successful at fighting the bosses. For example, when punk rockers are able to bring many people from all walks of life together united against large systems such as capitalism that cause many people and the natural environment to suffer greatly, they are demonstrating an awareness of what it means to be against, in the name of what is typically called social justice. At its finer moments, therefore, punk rockers have put their culture to work against injustices and human suffering.

The Sex Pistols, who broke up more than 30 years ago (1979), was one of the first groups to be known around the world as a punk rock band. The Sex Pistols were formed in London, England, with Johnny "Rotten" Lydon, sporting his bright orange head of Irish hair, as the lead vocalist. Their songs, such as "God Save the Queen," were very anti-English and, if primarily only by suggestion, pro-Irish. Being both visibly pro–Irish Republic and anti-English at the time in London was radical and dangerous because of substantial anti-Irish racism in England. The Irish had been colonized by the English for hundreds and hundreds of years and had always struggled for their independence. During the 1970s many Irish in Ireland were using violent force to expel the English. The Sex Pistols, in this context, were ridiculed and often viewed as terrorists (Share, 2003). The band only made one album, but their influence on punk rock music has been extraordinary. For example, The Clash was formed in the late 1970s in England by lead singer and guitarist Joe Strummer and a group of musicians after hearing the Sex Pistols play their new style of music, punk rock. The Clash, following the Sex Pistols, also made social protest music. The Clash, however, made many records and protested against racism, war, and other injustices. Together (along with other bands such as Sham 69 and The Dead Boys), The Sex Pistols and The Clash influenced many social justice punk rock bands in the United States (D'Ambrosio, 2004; O'Hara, 1999).

Perhaps the most popular U.S. punk rock social justice band that was influenced by the British scene was The Dead Kennedys, who were from San Francisco. The Dead Kennedys put out their first record in 1979 on Alternative Tentacles Records, which was created by the band as a vehicle to distribute their music, and ultimately, the social justice messages of their lyrics and artwork. Although The Dead Kennedys broke up in 1986, their lead vocalist Jello Biafra continues to make music and to give talks on music censorship, war, and many other topics while continuing to run Alternative Tentacles Records as a way to promote artistic freedom and radical politics (Blush, 2001).

Biafra has emerged as arguably one of the leading advocates of punk rock that is truly against the bosses. For example, after scientifically analyzing message trends over time in Punk Rockers' Revolution (2004), it is clear that Alternative Tentacles has become more socially just over time. The amount of content coded as "resistant" remained relatively consistent between the 1980s and 1990s (around 80%), but the message presenters became less white and less male (Malott and Peña, 2004). As a result of these findings, Malott and Peña began talking about punk rock not so much as defined by a particular musical style or way of dressing (aesthetic), but as an increasingly democratized cultural space. Surprisingly, it has been the spoken-word record that has opened up new possibilities within spaces created by punk rockers. Alternative Tentacles, in collaboration with AK Press, has published dozens of such records by revolutionaries from all walks of life, from Earth First! activist Judi Bari to former Black Panther Party and Communist Party USA member and current University of California at Santa Cruz professor Angela Davis.

Further Reading

Blush, Steven. *American Hardcore: A Tribal History.* New York: Feral House, 2001.
D'Ambrosio, Antonino. *Let Fury Have the Hour: The Punk Rock Politics of Joe Strummer.* New York: Nation Books, 2004.
Malott, Curry, and Milagros Peña. *Punk Rockers' Revolution: A Pedagogy of Race, Class and Gender.* New York: Peter Lang, 2004.
O'Hara, Craig. *The Philosophy of Punk: More than Noise.* San Francisco: AK Press, 1999.
Share, S. *If I Should Fall From Grace: The Shane MacGowan Story.* DVD. Mvd Visual, 2003.

Curry Stephenson Malott

Queercore

Queercore is a form of punk that is concerned with challenging the sexist conventions of heterosexuality, and the spectacle of mainstream, uniform homosexuality. This movement addresses issues such as hetero- and homo-normativity, sexuality, alternative sexual and gender identities and behaviors, and gay rights (Halberstam, 2003). Its emergence resulted from queer youths in the punk scene who were dissatisfied with the homophobia present in both mainstream society and punk culture, as well as with the segregated and fashion-oriented norms of the dominant homosexual community.

Though queercore moves against the homophobia and aggression of hardcore punk, it is still located within punk's culture and values. These values involve subversive and alternative social, political, and ethical principles that are manifested through the practice of DIY (do-it-yourself) music, art, dress codes, and other cultural production methods, all of which combine to form a way of life. In this way, queercore uses punk as a vehicle for voicing alternative sexualities and genders.

Queercore, otherwise known as homocore, originated in the early 1980s, during the heyday of the early hard-core punk movement (Spencer, 2005).

Though the initial punk movement left room for play with gender and sexuality, and diverse expressions of defiance, the hard-core movement favored rigid norms of aggressiveness, dominance, and masculinity, which included the acceptance of homophobia and sexism. Those who were queer sought to create their own scene within punk. Queercore's beginnings are marked by the advent of a handful of bands and several zines (self-published print works of minority interest). One of the most renowned zines was *JDs*, created by Bruce LaBruce and G. B. Jones in Toronto, Canada. One of the first statements to declare the perspective of queercore was *JDs* manifesto, wherein LaBruce and Jones challenged the hypocrisy of punk's rebellion by asking, "If you're fighting against how the majority tells you to act, then how can you act like the majority when it comes to sex-type-stuff? . . . Who says girls can't be butch? Who says boys can't be fags?"

What followed from these early expressions is a network composed of various methods of communication and production, such as music and writing, which both asserted and played with sociosexual identity (Dechaine, 1997). Some influential queercore punk bands include Pansy Division, Limp Wrist, Tribe 8, and G.B. Jones' Fifth Column. Zines continue to be dynamic and essential to queercore; among them are such titles as *Homocore, Bimbox,* and *Fertile LaToyah Jackson*. Music, text, clubs, conferences, dialogues, and performances all create the network that draw together individuals of alternative genders and sexualities to encourage communication and assertive self-expression.

Queercore is a community that is sincere, playful, welcoming, dissident, and a source of strength for many adolescent and young adult men. It provides lads with a social network where they can find camaraderie and support, and it has equipped them with means for expression. As a movement, it has created a space where sexual identity is more than a product of mass consumerism, and it has encouraged creative exploration of one's identity within the context of social awareness and sexual diversity.

Further Reading

Halberstam, Judith. 2003. What's That Smell: Queer Temporalities and Subcultural Lives. *International Journal of Cultural Studies* 6, 313–333.

Spencer, Amy. *DIY: The Rise of Lo-Fi Culture*. London: Marion Boyers, 2005.

Teixeira, Rob. Punk-Lad Love, Dyke-Core and the Evolution of Queer Zine Culture in Canada [Online March 2008]. Broken Pencil Web site. <http://www.brokenpencil.com/features/feature.php?featureid=51>.

Maya A. Yampolsky

Reggae

Reggae is an internationally popular and enormously influential style of music that originated in the Caribbean island-nation of Jamaica in the late 1960s. Reggae's influence on male youth culture since the 1960s would be difficult to overestimate. It began among disaffected youth (the Rude Boys of Kingston, Jamaica) and has not only remained popular in its original form but has also played a prominent role in punk and hip hop, two of the most widely influential cultural forces for young men and adolescents all over the world. And with the massive popularity of reggaeton, it seems poised to once again renew its popularity with yet another generation of rebellious youth looking for a music and a culture to call their own. Reggae's mix of sexuality, politics, and toughness (helped out, no doubt, by the place of honor accorded to marijuana smoking) provides the perfect mix for many boys, and it can be found on the speakers and headphones of wealthy college students at Ivy League universities and impoverished teenagers in the poorest of Third World cities.

Musically, reggae is a slower form of *rock steady,* which itself was a slightly slower form of *ska* (though reggae is sometimes used to refer more generally to all Jamaican music), a blend of American rhythm and blues with a native Jamaican music form called *mento.* Like ska and rock steady before it, reggae can be most easily distinguished by an emphasis on the offbeats in a standard 4/4 time signature, creating a distinctive loping rhythm. Lyrically, the music deals with a variety of political topics such as poverty and oppression, the philosophical tenets surrounding the beliefs of a religious group known as the Rastafarians, in addition to a variety of more personal subjects. Reggae is in fact so closely connected with the Rastafarian movement that the cultural trappings of the religion (such as dreadlocks, smoking cannabis, and the color scheme red, green, yellow, and black) are also strongly associated with the culture of the music, even where the religion is not practiced. Though initially popular only among the urban poor, reggae became quite popular first in Jamaica and then around the world, thanks largely to the success of its most famous performer and recording artist, Bob Marley. Though the genre is still popular today in its original form (known as roots reggae), it has also evolved into several other distinct musical forms, in particular dub, dancehall, and reggaeton. In addition to these, reggae has influenced a wide variety of other modern musical genres around the world.

Jamaica is a small Caribbean island-nation in the Greater Antilles, located approximately 100 miles south of Cuba, and approximately 120 miles west of Hispaniola. Columbus claimed it for Spain on his voyage to the Americas, but it was a British colony from the mid-seventeenth century until 1962, when it finally gained its independence. The music that developed in this environment was a mix of West African drums and chants brought over by slaves from their homelands and the European music of their colonial masters. This music, called mento, was similar to the calypso heard elsewhere in the Caribbean, without the strong reliance on Latin rhythms. After the advent of radio, Jamaicans began to receive signals from stations in the United States (most notably New Orleans), with jazz and then rhythm and blues becoming popular with traveling dance bands (called sound systems) that would play the singles in concerts in public places. But as American audiences shifted toward rock and roll in the 1950s, Jamaican band leaders and musicians moved to fill the demand for new R&B dance floor singles. The first studios and pressing plants were built, and Jamaican musicians went into the studio to create new R&B singles, often just recording new versions of singles already imported from the United States. By the late 1950s, though, a new form of music (known as ska) was being produced that was a combination of R&B and the more traditional mento, that used a 4/4 time signature with a walking bass line, horns, and most importantly, an emphasis on the offbeats (usually 2 and 4) known as the skank. Ska music caught on not only in Jamaica but also in England, where young people who were attracted to its fast, danceable rhythms appropriated it. After Jamaica gained its independence in 1962, a group of teenagers and young men who were called rude boys began to distinguish themselves from the rest of society through their pessimistic attitude toward the new government, fashion, and ultimately, music, preferring a cooler, slower version of ska that came to be called rock steady. Rock steady flourished for a short period in the mid-1960s, before it was slowed down even further, creating the music known as reggae.

The origin of the word reggae is uncertain, but *streggae* (the torn clothes of a prostitute), *rege-rege* (a quarrel), or a Spanish term meaning "the king's music" have all been put forward as possible etymologies. Regardless of its origins, the word appeared as both a dance style and a variation on the rock steady genre before the first actual reggae singles, as seen on the Maytals' 1968 rock steady hit "Do the Reggay." At about this time the first true reggae singles started to appear, beginning with "Nanny Goat," by Larry Marshall. Among the first reggae songs to appear on U.S. charts were Neil Diamond's "Red, Red Wine," in 1967, and Johnny Nash's "Hold Me Tight" in 1968.

Many reggae artists were already successful rock steady and/or ska musicians who made the transition to the sudden popularity of each new genre. Most notable of these are The Wailers, who were a successful ska band influential in creating rock steady by slowing down the frenetic ska beat with their single "Simmer Down," subsequently finding themselves at the vanguard of the reggae movement. The band consisted of Bunny Livingston, Peter McIntosh, and Robert Nesta Marley, but they are much better known by their stage names, Bunny Wailer, Peter Tosh, and Bob Marley. Though all three members would go on to have successful solo careers, it was Bob Marley who proved to be the most successful, and who indeed became one of the most successful artists in the history of popular music. Marley's success (with such hits as "Get up, Stand up," "No Woman No Cry," and "I Shot the Sheriff") helped to popularize reggae internationally, as well as spread the Rastafarian culture with which it was linked. In fact, Marley grew to be revered as a guru as well as a musical legend, a status that was only enhanced by his untimely death due to cancer in 1981, at the age of 36. As an outspoken defender of the rights of the poor, a vocal proponent of Rastafarian beliefs (which hold that the Ethiopian king Haile Selassie is divine and will ultimately create a paradise for all people of African descent), and the most widely listened to reggae artist, Marley is almost synonymous with the genre.

Reggae's musical influence looms large in popular music. Ska and reggae were both wildly popular in England during the 1970s and 1980s, contributing to the creation of much original music in these genres and to the nascent punk movement. Bands such The Clash and Madness ensured that Jamaican music and punk would be closely related for many years, and even into the new millennium bands such as No Doubt and 311 would continue this tradition. Similarly, in the 1970s DJs in Jamaica began speaking over the top of instrumental reggae songs, a phenomenon called toasting. This lead to a new drum-heavy genre of music known as dancehall that spread to New York City (which has a sizable Jamaican population) and formed one of the most important influences on the creation of the new music form that would become hip hop. Another offshoot of reggae called dub would rely on electronic sound effects and tape loops to create new versions of existing reggae songs. This spirit of experimentation would go on to heavily influence early electronic music artists and dance club DJs alike, and would also set the precedent for the practice of remixing popular songs. Currently, reggae exists both in its original form as roots reggae (with active reggae scenes in as unlikely places as Russia, Japan, and New York's Hasidic community), as dancehall (as well as a more electronic subgenre of dancehall called ragga), and dub. But perhaps the most popular new hybrid of the music is reggaeton, a combination of hip hop, reggae, and various Latin American musical forms such as samba, merengue, and bachata. It began in Panama, but it is mostly associated now with Puerto Rico and is popular throughout the Americas.

Further Reading

Barrow, Steve, and Peter Dalton. *The Rough Guide to Reggae*. New York: Rough Guides Limited, 2004.

Bradley, Lloyd. *Bass Culture*. Harmondsworth, UK: Penguin, 2001.

Manuel, Peter, et al. *Caribbean Currents*. Philadelphia: Temple University Press, 2006.

Ehren Gresehover

REM

REM is an American rock band formed in Athens, Georgia, in 1980, consisting of Michael Stipe (vocals), Mike Mills (bass, guitar), Peter Buck (guitar), and Bill Berry (drums and percussion). The band became famous for Buck's distinctive arpeggiated, chiming guitar sound and Stipe's plaintive, enigmatic vocals. They were one of the most influential bands of the 1980s and 1990s, helping to create and popularize the genre known as alternative rock, but more importantly, they achieved their success without adopting a theatrical look or compromising their artistic sensibilities, creating a template for independent musicians of all types to follow through the end of the century. Eschewing both the overwhelming theatricality of new wave and the swaggering machismo of hard rock, REM provided a template for a new generation of rock stars, one that was intelligent without pretension and tough without being aggressive, and in the process gave millions of boys a more realistic ideal of masculinity to live up to.

REM began in the town of Athens, Georgia, where all the band members attended classes at the University of Georgia. Within a year of writing songs and playing together, they had settled on the name REM (short for rapid eye movement, the type of sleep during which most of our dreaming takes place, though the band would insist that the name was chosen by opening the dictionary to a random location), and recorded their first EP, *Chronic Town.* Though major labels made offers, the band chose instead to go with a smaller, independent label, I.R.S. Records. Though I.R.S. tried to direct them toward a more contemporary sound, REM was able to convince the label to allow them to continue to use their producer from the first EP, Mitch Easter, and to forego the guitar solos and synthesizers currently in style. The resulting debut album, *Murmur,* garnered massive critical acclaim (*Rolling Stone* picked it as the album of the year), but reached relatively moderate sales.

The band continued on in this fashion until they finally achieved a measure of commercial success in 1987, with the Scott Litt–produced *Document,* which gave them both their first million-selling record and their first top 20 single ("The One I Love"). They were now being played not only on college stations, but also on mainstream rock stations and top 40 radio as well. With their new-found success, they left I.R.S. and switched to Warner Brothers, releasing *Green* in 1988 and *Out of Time* in 1991, which was their first record to top the charts, selling more than 10 million copies at the time of writing. It also generated the smash hit "Losing My Religion," whose impressionistic video garnered numerous awards. The group followed this up with *Automatic for the People,* which marked the band's commercial and, in many critics' opinions, artistic high-water mark, with three top 40 singles and sales of 10 million records.

Though the band would go on to achieve some success with their 1994 follow-up, *Monster,* it was clear that the band had started to decline. Berry left the band shortly before they began work on their next album, and continuing as a three-piece (rather than audition a new drummer, the band chose to use a drum machine), they have failed to place another single in the top 40. The band continues to record and tour, though, and their 2008 release, *Accelerate,* was seen by many critics as at least a partial return to form.

The band's legacy is hard to overstate. They began at a time when college radio was a marginalized musical subgenre and MTV had just gone on the air and played mostly concert videos, but as a result of their efforts, college rock would become known as alternative and would take over the airwaves, and videos would improve in sophistication to become more akin to short films. They also paved the way for small college bands to achieve success on the radio and out on tour.

Their refusal to change their appearance or create any type of mystique influenced a legion of young musicians, most of them boys, and acted as an antidote for the elaborate fashion and high concept of the 1980s new wave art bands, or the bluster and bravado of heavy metal. Interestingly, Michael Stipe is one of the few male rock musicians who publicly identifies himself as gay. REM has shown that all you needed to find an audience is good songs and enthusiastic performances, creating a sort of anti–rock-star model that would be the norm for young rock bands.

Further Reading

Buckley, David. *REM Fiction.* London: Virgin Publishing, 2002.
Fletcher, Tony. *Remarks Remade.* London: Omnibus Press, 2003.
Platt, John. *The R. E. M. Companion.* New York: Schirmer Books, 1998.

Ehren Gresehover

Rock and Pop Music

Popular music has always been the music of youth, created by, for, and of, the youth. Even the music of Mozart composed almost 250 years ago was at his time the music of commoners—young as well as old—as composed by a young man. But when rock music emerged from the womb of rock 'n' roll (the music form identified with the likes of Chuck Berry, Little Richard, Jerry Lee Lewis, and Elvis Presley, to name but a few), it screamed out loud to everyone that this was music meant solely for the young, especially the male under 18. It became commonly accepted that musical tastes froze by that age, so any musician or group seeking to be popular had to appeal first and foremost to that age group. That is the reason why almost all of rock 'n' roll music and much of rock music in the initial years were songs about love and girls, and then about angst and alienation. No rock song worth its salt would ever concern itself with the travails of working in an office and feeling stifled in a suit!

It was 1965 and while revolution was not yet in the air, rebellion against parents and everything of that generation certainly was. This rebellious attitude of rock was perhaps best summed up that year by the defining line from the song "My Generation" by The Who, with the line: "I hope I die before I grow old." In North America, the British invasion was in full swing. Led by the greatest rock band in history, The Beatles, quickly followed by The Rolling Stones, The Who, The Yardbirds, and many other now legendary bands, the continent faced an onslaught of creativity from across the Atlantic. The United States responded with its own distinctive talents. The Beach Boys started out as superb purveyors of classic boy songs about beaches and hot rods, but by 1966 had crafted one of the most significant albums in rock history, *Pet Sounds.* On the West Coast, bands such as Grateful Dead, The Doors, and Jefferson Airplane were dabbling in what was being called psychedelic music. Canada followed with Steppenwolf, and later, The Guess Who. It was music to which the flower power generation swayed, while spreading messages of peace, love, and universal understanding. Bob Dylan was upsetting his folk music fans by turning to rock with a vengeance. But this was rock music like no one had heard before, with allusive, playful, and often bizarre lyrics, and music that pushed the boundaries of what was possible and what was not. Boys had never had it so good—especially when it came to confounding parents' expectations of just what a good boy should be inspired and influenced by.

As rock music continued to grow more and more complex, in the UK and on both coasts of the United States, it became more and more acceptable for older listeners to gravitate to the form. Suddenly older listeners were not just listening to classical music and jazz, they were—horror of horrors—grooving to rock. As rock music—at least some bands and albums—began to get recognized as an art form in its own right, boys recoiled from the pretentiousness that accompanied it all and looked for music they could still call exclusively theirs. Heavy metal typified by loud instruments, pumping rhythm, and driving beats—owing a great debt to blues and rock 'n' roll—burst on to the scene. Bands that merely rocked very, very hard, such as Led Zeppelin and Deep Purple, gave way to bands that combined loud, insistent music with often dark and nihilistic lyrics. Black Sabbath and Judas Priest begat Iron Maiden, Motorhead, and AC/DC and marked a decisive rift in the musical relationship between boys on the one hand, and their parents and the critical establishment on the other. While older audiences moved to the soft-rock of the likes of Bread and James Taylor or the bombastic stadium rock of Pink Floyd, boys all over risked serious damage to their eardrums and their sanity by headbanging wildly to offshoots of heavy metal with evocative names such as speed metal, thrash metal, and even death metal.

But by the end of the 1970s it seemed even heavy metal was in danger of being appropriated away from boys. The time was ripe for the emergence of punk music, typified by The Sex Pistols and The Clash in the UK, and The Ramones in the United States. Punk music stood against the hyperbole and excesses of mainstream rock music and was marked by an "anyone can do it" attitude. Even as punk music was alienating music critics and endearing itself to boys, it was splitting off into various subgenres such as glam punk, horror punk, and so on.

As the 1980s arrived, it brought to the fore the two biggest acts in mainstream popular music, the two M's: Michael Jackson and Madonna, the latter endearing herself to boys not so much for her music as for her blatant sexual public image. Still filling arenas at this time were heavy metal bands such as Kiss, Megadeth, and Def Leppard, but many boys turned away from the two M's as well as the monster acts of the 1970s. Older boys, especially those at college, were supporting a different genre—more accurately a different ethos—of music largely through college FM stations. Initially called college rock, the genre soon came to be known as alternative music. Alternative music, in turn, gave birth to possibly the last avatar of rock that was lapped up by a vast cross-section of boys: grunge. With angst filled lyrics, grunge seemed to speak directly to adolescent boys. Some of the grunge bands crossed over into the mainstream with "Nevermind" by Nirvana and "Ten" by Pearl Jam becoming multimillion selling hits.

But that was in many ways the last gasp of rock as a musical marker for generational difference between boys and their parents. Rock was a genre declining ever so surely in importance among boys. In fact, music itself was occupying boys less and less. As early as 1992, the respected *Wall Street Journal* was declaring that rock had lost its place as a cultural force. A late 1990s survey conducted by researchers at the University of Illinois listed talking, TV viewing, paid labor, sports, and household chores as the top activities consuming teenagers' time. There was no mention of music at all. Music, leave alone rock, was simply not a priority for teenagers any more, even if you assumed that most music was played in the background of boys' daily activities and therefore failed to find separate mention in surveys and the like.

By the late 1990s FM stations were putting so-called classic rock from the 1960s, 1970s, and even 1980s in the category of "oldies," indicating the complete disdain young listeners now had for the founding fathers of rock. As the music industry got more and more fragmented with practically a new genre of rock music sprouting every day, it seemed there was no longer a form of music that could cut across boys spanning all kinds of geographical, age, and social fault lines. It was at this moment that boys discovered two related genres of music that seemed to have only faint connections to rock: rap and hip hop. Cultural critics speculated that what attracted boys to hip hop and rap was the promise of a highly organized familial structure that these genres promised—with their cliques and mentor-protégé relationships—even as boys' own family relationships grew more and more strained. What attracted boys more to these genres, especially to the aggressive strains of rap music such as gangsta rap, was that however popular they got, the genres never did win the approval of their parents. A survey conducted by *USA Weekend* magazine in 2002 asked 60,000 U.S. teens what kind of music they would choose if they could choose only one type of music to listen to. Twenty-seven percent indicated their preference for hip hop/rap, and 23 percent for pop. Rock was a distant third with only 17 percent of the votes. The music that was only 40 years ago the music of rebellion was effectively dead. The Who would have been glad: they—and all their peers—were in fact dead and buried long before they got really old.

Further Reading

Cox, Meg. "Rhythm and Blues: Rock Is Slowly Fading As Tastes in Music Go Off in Many Directions." *The Wall Street Journal,* August 26, 1992.

Danesi, Marcel. *Forever Young: The Teen-aging of Modern Culture.* Toronto: The University of Toronto Press, 2003.

Gilmore, Mikal. *Night Beat: A Shadow History of Rock and Roll.* New York: Doubleday, 1998.

Santanu Chakrabarti

Rock 'n' Roll Culture

Rock 'n' roll has had staying power in the lives of boys for over five decades. Today's vision of rock has little to do with rock 'n' roll's 1950s pioneers, but rather with the hard rock of the long-haired bad boys that emerged in the late

1960s and into the 1970s. The rock stars that resonate in the lives of contemporary boys are, to a great extent, heroin-chic, skinny boy lead singers and lead guitar players, with their bare chests, bulging crotches, drug habits, and groupies.

One band whose music has best withstood the test of time in boy culture is Led Zeppelin. Most likely a testament to the quality of their sound, Led Zeppelin set a standard. Robert Plant and Jimmy Page balanced the two sides of the rock star ledger: Plant was the center of attention, the "chick magnet" who did not seem to possess a shirt with buttons—a tall, thin macho rock god who boys wished they could be, or be like; Page, on the other hand, stood back a little from the center of the stage, but he was the ultimate guitar whiz, a technical genius who demonstrated the difficulty of his art by making it look easy. Today, boys learning the electric guitar are challenged to follow Jimmy Page's lead guitar solo on "Stairway to Heaven," and young boys can be found grunting the lyrics to "Whole Lotta Love" well before they understand the meanings of the song.

This type of heavy rock permeates our culture. Whether because of exposure to the musical tastes of their parents, the ubiquitous classic rock stations, or rock songs embedded into the soundtracks of movies, new generations of rock fans and rock musicians have emerged. Rock 'n' roll t-shirts, usually black and ideally with a tour list on the back, have withstood fashion's capricious changes. The garage band is still a fixture in boy culture and some young prodigies step up into actual rock 'n' roll careers. The original bad boy rockers of the 1970s have been followed by a parade of newcomers, new trends, and new styles of rock, but the formula of the drum kit, bass guitar, electric guitar, and lead singer is the rough standard still followed today.

Rock stars, the demigods among mortals, play a powerful role in popular culture. Cameron Crowe's *Almost Famous* (2000), a feature film that portrays the rock star through the eyes of a teenage journalist, is littered with realistic anecdotes of the lives of rock stars and their fans, a world of hard-living musicians that thrive on the adulation of their audiences.

A new twist in the old tale is the emergence of rock 'n' roll video games. The same cast of characters that wowed the boys through the 1960s, 1970s, and 1980s is back in contemporary boys' lives in the form of Guitar Hero and Rock Band, the wildly popular, interactive video games. Available on a number of different consoles, these games do little to enhance the musical talents of the players, but a lot in terms of bringing hard-driving rock 'n' roll into the hearts and minds of the participants. For the most part, they involve mimicry and the emphasis is on coordination and timing. Players use facsimile instruments to imitate the sounds they hear over the speakers, striving to perfect sequences, beats, and rhythms. The lead singer in Rock Band uses his or her own voice, hence the correspondence between the real and the virtual is closer to a live act, but, for the most part, these games do more for motivating young people as fans and musicians, than instructing them to play real instruments.

The irony, or wrinkle, in the world of rock 'n' roll is the graying of the rock star. Whether it is dinosaur rockers tottering on stage for one more draw on the public purse and one more whiff of the cheering crowd, or health nuts such as Mick Jagger reforming the myth of the drug-addicted rock and roller, the world has changed, and rock with it. Already anthems of another era such as Led Zeppelin's "Rock and Roll" and the Beatles' "Revolution" have been used in advertising (by Cadillac and Nike, respectively). And today it is common to find audiences looking for some "Satisfaction" or "Rocking in the Free World" at corporate-sponsored community events. To some extent, although the pulse of rock 'n' roll remains, some of its soul has gone missing. But that is for the new young rockers and fans to decide for themselves.

Further Reading

Frith, S., Straw, W., & Street, J. (Eds.) (2001). *The Cambridge Companion to Rock and Pop*. Cambridge: Cambridge University Press.

George-Warren, H., Romanowski, P., & Pareles, J. (Eds.) (2001, 3rd edition). *The Rolling Stone Encyclopedia of Rock & Roll (Revised and Updated for the 21st Century)*. New York: Fireside.

Marcus, G. (Ed.) (2007, 2nd edition). *Stranded: Rock and Roll for a Desert Island*. Cambridge, MA: Da Capo Press.

Michael Hoechsmann

Run DMC

Run DMC, the pioneering hip hop group that surfaced in the 1980s, have been credited with breaking hip hop into the mainstream. This group comprised of three African American males who were socially conscious rappers, promoting equality and justice among the Black community. Even though the group is no longer producing new material, due to the death of one of the members, their legacy will forever live on in the history of hip hop.

Joseph "Rev Run" Simmons, Darryl "D.M.C." McDaniels, and Jason "Jam Master Jay" Mizell made up the group Run DMC All three men grew up in Hollis, Queens, in New York City and this bond of being neighbors and their collective love of music forged an unbreakable unit between music pioneers. The group signed their first deal in 1981 to Profile Records and have been creating hits every since. The group has been credited for the development of hip hop into the mainstream while staying true to the roots of the underground hip hop music founders.

Through the years the group has been credited as the only rap group to have reached several number one accomplishments. They are the first rap act to have a number one rhythm and blues charting rap album, as well as the first rap group to earn RIAA gold, platinum, and multi-platinum albums. They were the first rap group to appear on the cover of *Rolling Stone* magazine. Other firsts include beating other rap groups to a Grammy Award nomination, having a video added to MTV, and the first rap act group to sign an athletic endorsement deal. Their performances were legendary and aided in them being the only rap act to perform at Live Aid in 1985, and the first rap group to appear on *Saturday Night Live* and *American Bandstand*. These accomplishments are few and far in between the foundation that this group paved for other African American rap artists that followed after them. The hard work and dedication of Run DMC has led to worldwide recognition and fame.

Their first album, entitled *Run DMC*, was release March 27, 1984, and was certified gold. This album produced hits such as "It's Like That" and "Rock Box." In January of 1985 they released the album *King of Rock*, which was certified platinum and featured hits such as "Can You Rock It Like This" and "You Talk Too Much." One of the most notable songs, "Walk This Way," which was a collaboration with rock group Aerosmith, was a song off of their 1986 album entitled *Raising Hell*. From 1988 to 2001 they released four additional albums: *Tougher than Leather, Back from Hell, Down with the Kings*, and *Crown Royal*. Each of these albums garnered immense success and recognition for the group.

In 2002 Jam-Master Jay was shot and killed while working on an album in a music studio. His untimely death led to the official retirement of the group. The heart and determination of these men illustrate that through hard work and dedication anything is possible. They had a dream to create a new genre of music that would leave a lasting legacy on hip hop. Without their contributions it would be very difficult to assess the state of current mainstream hip hop.

Further Reading

The Official Run-D.M.C Web site [Online March 2008]. www.rundmc.com.
Ogg, Alex. *The Hip Hop Years.* New York: Fromm International, 2001.

Creshema Murray

Rush

Rush is a three-piece Canadian rock band whose most long-lasting line-up consisted of band members Alex Lifeson (born Alexander Zivojinovich) on guitar, Geddy Lee (born Gary Lee Weinrib) on vocals, bass, and keyboards, and Neil Peart on drums; Neil was also the principal songwriter of the group. The band was formed in the late 1960s (with original drummer John Rutsey) and released their eponymous debut record in 1974, but the band cemented their sound and their image with the addition of Neil Peart that same year. His accomplished drumming fit in well with the musicianship of Lifeson and Lee and gave the band a reputation for virtuosic playing, but it was his cerebral songwriting (drawing on his interest in science fiction, fantasy, and philosophy) that truly defined the band and set them apart from their peers. Despite critical indifference and only sporadic airplay, Rush nevertheless managed to sell millions of records, becoming one of the best-selling rock bands of all time. More than almost any other rock band, the group has always been strongly identified with boys, especially those for whom their mix of strong rock sound and intellectual lyrics dealing with suburban isolation rang particularly true.

Rush came together (with Rutsey on drums) in Toronto, Ontario, in 1968, but didn't release their first single, a cover of Buddy Holly's "Not Fade Away," until 1973. Failing to secure a recording contract, they followed this up with a self-produced debut the following year on their own label Moon Records. Again, their music failed to gain many fans. Soon, however, their song "Working Man" began to get radio airplay in the Midwest, which forced Mercury Records to take a second look at the band, signing them to a contract and re-releasing their debut. But Rutsey, who was reluctant to adopt the touring lifestyle of a major recording artist, left the group shortly after they were signed. After an open audition, Peart was hired as his replacement in the summer of 1974, and took over as the band's lyricist as well.

Their next three records (*Fly by Night, Caress of Steel,* and *2112*) found the band creating the style that they would become most identified with, slowly drifting away from the straight-forward blues rock of their first album toward a more complicated sound, with longer, sprawling compositions taking up entire album sides, punctuated by Lifeson's complex guitar work. In addition, Peart would begin to establish a lyrical style that would explore science fiction and fantasy themes, and draw heavily on the work of novelist and philosopher Ayn Rand. Though their label discouraged longer songs and esoteric subject matter, the formula seemed to work for the band, and by the end of this period, the band had their first platinum certification in Canada.

After the success of *2112* in 1977, Rush began to experiment with their sound and arrangements, incorporating new instruments (and an increasingly dominant use of keyboards for the melody lines) and influences as varied as reggae and new wave. Peart's songwriting also continued to evolve, gradually shifting away from the future or the imaginary past to offer commentary on the contemporary world, though retaining his interest in ethics and metaphysics. The band also continued to grow in popularity, peaking with 1981's *Moving Pictures,* which reached number 3 on the Billboard 200 and going quadruple platinum in the United States. This album also generated their most well-known song, "Tom Sawyer," though it did not chart in the United States.

As the 1980s drew to a close, the synthesizer-heavy sound of new wave fell into disfavor and the guitar rock of grunge began to appear on the horizon, and Rush found themselves moving with the times and returning to the hard rock sound of their mid-1970s output with the albums *Presto* (1989) and *Roll the Bones* (1991), both of which received mild critical approval and a somewhat warmer response from their fans. Sadly, this slight return to form was interrupted by tragedy, with the death of Peart's two daughters (car accident) and wife (cancer); the tragedy caused the band to go on hiatus in the late 1990s.

Peart worked through his grief by traversing America on his Harley-Davidson motorcycle (eventually writing a book about the experience), and returned rejuvenated and back with the band in 2001. During the time of writing, the band had released two more well-received albums, and they continue to tour.

Though the band were never superstars on the order of Led Zeppelin, they sold remarkably well to a mostly male demographic during their most popular years. More important, they built and retained a core audience that stuck with them throughout their career. They were drawn to the sort of cerebral lyrics—which dealt with the alienation of the suburbs, the perils of being different from one's peers, and the difficulties in having a strong moral code in a world that was inherently corrupt—that were not found in rock music of the time. For a generation of boys from this time period, Rush provided a strong, confident voice of intelligent dissent with the status quo, along with a defense of unapologetic intelligence and professionalism, both taboo topics in youth culture in the 1970s and 1980s.

Further Reading

Banasiewicz, Bill. *Rush Visions.* London: Omnibus Press, 1988.
Collins, Joe. *Rush: Chemistry: The Definitive Biography.* London: Helter Skelter Publishing, 2005.
Popoff, Martin. *Contents under Pressure.* Toronto: ECW Press, 2004.

Ehren Gresehover

Russell Simmons

Russell Simmons, often referred to as the godfather of hip hop, is credited with giving hip hop its cross-cultural appeal. He is the owner of Rush Communications, which oversees such brands as Phat Farm clothing, Phat Footwear, Russell Simmons Music Group, and Def Jam Mobile. His success in the music industry and his ever-growing entrepreneurial skills have led to the development of several companies targeted to youth.

Simmons was born on October 4, 1957, in the Hollis neighborhood of Queens, New York, as the second of three sons to Evelyn and Daniel Simmons. He learned the value of entrepreneurship early in life, selling products in high school years to raise money to buy clothes. Simmons quickly acquired two of the secrets of a successful business—supply and demand, and buying for less to sell for more. In 1977, he dropped out of City College of New York and began to pursue his passion—music. Simmons planned to make his money by promoting something he loved: a new breed of music that was hitting the streets of New York—hip hop. He attended many live events and loved the beat that this new grade of music provided to listeners. That same year, he began his career as a concert promoter, producer, and artist manager.

Simmons's name began to spread throughout the New York music community. Bitten with the hip hop bug, he continued to look for ways to better market local artists. One of the first artists Simmons managed was the legendary rapper Kurtis Blow. In 1979, he released his first record with Kurtis Blow's *Christmas Rap.* Three years later, he released the album of another group he managed, Run-DMC, in which his younger brother, Joseph (Run), was a lead rapper. The Run-DMC album went gold and Simmons saw a way for hip hop to reach beyond the African American and Latino communities. His musical success continued to spread and in 1986, Simmons made hip hop history by producing a single featuring Run-DMC and the rock band Aerosmith. In addition, he gained a major sponsor deal with Adidas for Run-DMC's national tour and talked MTV into airing Run-DMC's rap video for "It's Like That," a first for the station. This marked the beginnings of Simmons's quest to take the hip hop culture to mainstream America.

In the early 1980s, Simmons also had the opportunity to meet another young man making history in the production and management of hip hop artists, Rick Rubin. Rubin was a white college student who managed groups such as the Beastie Boys and operated his company out of his dorm room. Simmons and Rubin joined forces to create the Def Jam record label, managing such artists as LL Cool J, Public Enemy, and DMX. Though Simmons and Rubin eventually parted ways, Simmons held on to the Def Jam label, later selling it in 1999 for over $100 million.

To extend his reach beyond the music industry, Simmons founded his own company, Rush Communications, in 1990. Rush Communications became a media conglomerate that currently includes publishing companies, a movie production company, clothing lines, and an advertising agency. The company was designed to carry the hip hop culture to the masses and create entertainment that would engulf American youth culture. It was the springboard for such successful productions as HBO's *Def Comedy Jam* and *Def Poetry Jam*.

One of the major companies under the Rush Communications umbrella is the Phat Farm clothing line designed for boys and men. The clothing lines are watched very closely by Simmons who himself is known to dress in casual hip hop gear even in business meetings. He wants to make sure that the clothes are of high quality and authentic to the nature of hip hop culture. In 2003, Simmons sold Phat Farm for $140 million, but still maintains managing control of the company.

Outside of his music, television, and clothing ventures, it is important to Simmons to be involved in and give back to the community. In doing so, Simmons founded two organizations that directly or indirectly benefit young boys. In 1995, Simmons founded The Rush Communications Philanthropic Arts Network with his brothers. The foundation is specifically aimed at providing disadvantaged youth with greater access to the arts. The company has been reported to give more than $300,000 annually toward this effort.

The Hip Hop Summit Action Network, founded in 2001, is a nonprofit, nonpartisan coalition of hip hop artists, entertainment industry leaders, education advocates, civil rights proponents, and youth leaders united in the belief that hip hop is an enormously influential agent for social change that must be responsibly and proactively utilized to fight the war on poverty and injustice. One of the programs of the network is the Hip hop Summit Youth Council (HSYC), which has positioned itself to become an effective voice for youth on a host of issues that confront them daily. HSYC uses the positive influence of hip hop for the social, political, and economic empowerment of youth.

From music to social empowerment, Simmons has had quite an impact on the lives of young boys. His drive in the music industry provided a new type of music for boys in the 1980s that remains among the top-selling genres each year. In the 1990s, Simmons created a clothing line whose success became a catalyst for the many fashion lines of musical artists that we see today. Near the start of the twenty-first century, Simmons launched the prepaid Visa Rush-Card with Unifund Corporation and the Hip hop Summit Action Network that financially and politically empower youth.

Other companies owned by Simmons include, but are not limited to, Rush Productions, Rush Artist Management, Simmons-Lathan Media, Run Athletics, DefCon3 Energy Soda, and Phat Farm mobile phones. Simmons has also produced such films as *The Nutty Professor* and *Krush Groove.*

Simmons married model Kimora Lee Simmons in 1998, though the two later separated and then divorced in 2009. The couple has two daughters, Ming Lee (2000) and Aoki Lee (2002). Kimora Lee Simmons operates the Baby Phat clothing line, an extension of the Phat Farm clothing line specially designed for girls and women.

Further Reading

Oliver, Richard, and Tim Leffel. *Hip hop, Inc.* New York: Thunder's Mouth Press, 2006.
Dingle, Derek T. *Titans of the B.E. 100s: Black CEOs Who Redefined and Conquered American Business.* New York: John Wiley & Sons, Inc., 1999.

Mia Long

The Who

The Who are a British rock band originally consisting of Roger Daltrey (vocals), Pete Townsend (guitar), John Entwistle (bass), and Keith Moon (drums). They formed in 1964 in London, but have continued to tour and record material through the time of writing (though at a much slower pace than in their heyday in the 1960s and 1970s). They are known for their hard rock sound, snotty attitude, and explosive live shows, which from the earliest days have featured the smashing of the band's instruments as a key component. All of these elements would be a significant influence on the punk rock scene to come, leading many to call the band the godfathers of punk. Just as important to their sound and at odds with their image as a swaggering forerunner to punk are the melodicism of Townsend's songwriting, coupled with his fascination with concept albums and experimentation, perhaps nowhere best scene as on The Who's most well-known release, the rock opera *Tommy.*

In addition to their contributions to music, there is perhaps no other band that has so occupied themselves with the unique problems, delights, and confusion of being an adolescent boy. In such songs as "Pictures of Lily," "Squeeze Box," and of course "I'm a Boy," the band wrote from the perspectives of young boys dealing with the issues of growing up. Without embarrassment, Townsend wrote about masturbation, jealousy, and love with all the snickering, angst, and joy that accompanied these new experiences, and without playing down the innocence at the heart of every coming-of-age story.

The band began when Daltrey met Entwistle, who was walking down the street carrying his bass on his arm. Daltrey asked him on the spot to join his band, The Detours. Before long Entwistle brought in Townsend, who he had played with in a Dixieland band. Before long, personnel changes resulted with the other Detours band members departing, and the band changed their name to The Who shortly before adding Moon to drums, completing the line-up (though they would play some early shows under the name The High Numbers). Their first single was a Kinks-inspired tune entitled "I Can't Explain," released in 1965, followed shortly thereafter by "Anyway, Anyhow, Anywhere," the first song to feature a guitar solo with feedback. Their first album, *My Generation,* contained a number of other singles, but none was as big a hit as the title track, about how the adults cannot understand the motivations and desires of contemporary young people. Written for a particular youth group known as the Mods (who favored high Edwardian fashion and R&B music), the track featured a swaggering, stuttering vocal by Daltrey and would go on to become one of the most covered, referenced, and written about rock songs ever, coming in at number 11 on *Rolling Stone* magazine's list of the 500 greatest rock songs.

The Who would continue to record hit singles throughout the 1960s and build a reputation for a ferocious live show, powered by Daltrey's thuggish menace, Keith Moon's hyperactive drumming, and Townsend's trademark windmill guitar playing. But perhaps the most notorious aspect of their live shows was their penchant for demolishing their instruments on-stage, which started when Townsend accidentally broke the neck of his guitar on the low ceiling at a show in 1964. To stop the snickering of some members of the audience, he demolished what remained of his damaged guitar and switched to a 12-string for the rest of the show. At the next show, Townsend didn't smash his guitar, but Moon demolished his drum kit, establishing what would become a standard part of their early shows, and a destructive disregard for their equipment and hostility to their fans that would become an integral part of the punk movement in the next decade.

At the same time as they were developing a reputation as a muscular singles band with an exciting live show, Townsend was becoming increasingly interested in pushing his songwriting into new territory. The early song "A Quick One, While He's Away" consisted of several sonically distinct segments, and serves as perhaps the earliest instance of the genre known as progressive or prog rock. Later, Townsend would go even further with his rock opera *Tommy,* a musically adventurous double album that would eventually become a movie (starring a who's who of rock musicians) and a Broadway musical.

By the end of the 1970s and despite some internal strain about the direction of their music, The Who were one of the biggest musical acts in the world, selling out arenas wherever they went. Then in 1978, Moon, whose reputation had gone from fun-loving prankster to alcoholic wild man, died from an overdose of Heminevrin, a drug that ironically enough was prescribed to help him combat the symptoms of alcohol withdrawal.

PART IV
Games, Toys, Tech, and Schools

SECTION 10

Boys Play, Boys Learn

Action Figures

Actions figures are posable plastic toys manufactured and marketed primarily for boys that often feature characters from films, comic books, and cartoons.

The toy company Hasbro released the first action figure, G.I. Joe, in 1964 in an effort to capitalize on the success of the Barbie doll, first released by rival toy-maker Mattel in 1959. Hasbro coined the term "action figure" to promote the G.I. Joe toy to boys, distancing it from the term "doll" and any of its feminine connotations. The first line of G.I. Joe dolls were 11-½ inches tall, made from molded plastic, featured 21 movable parts, and were outfitted with cloth fatigues. Each figure had detailed features on its face, including a trademark battle scar on the right cheek, but the bodies of the figures lacked detail. Hasbro produced a wide variety of accessories for G.I. Joe figures, including vehicles, a space capsule, and a range of weapons. The toy was an enormous hit among boys, and became the standard for all action figures throughout the 1960s, when several competing toy manufacturers introduced innovations into the action figure market.

Mego Corporation, a toymaker that had specialized in manufacturing inexpensive toys for dime stores in the 1950s and 1960s, began competing for the action figure and doll markets in the 1970s. Mego introduced the Action Jackson figure to compete with G.I. Joe in 1971 as well as the Dinah-Mite doll to compete with Barbie in 1973. Action Jackson and Dinah-Mite were shorter than their competitors, standing at 8 inches tall, and their smaller size made them less expensive.

Mego planned a very aggressive television advertising campaign to promote Action Jackson, but made the mistake of using stop-motion animation to make the figures seem more life-like. This violated a television industry rule in place that prohibited toymakers from advertising toys performing actions they were not realistically able to do. As a result, Mego was unable to air the Action Jackson commercials and the toy line was unsuccessful. Without an aggressive marketing campaign, the Action Jackson toy line was discontinued in 1973. However, the failure of Action Jackson prompted Mego to develop an innovation that quickly became critical to the future of action figure manufacturing: the company took Action Jackson bodies and added new heads and superhero costumes to create their successful World's Greatest Superheroes toy line in 1972. By using the same basic body with interchangeable heads and costumes, Mego discovered that they could manufacture and market multiple characters very inexpensively. The original World's Greatest Superheroes included Superman, Batman, Robin, Aquaman, and was quickly expanded to include Spiderman, Captain America, and Tarzan. Mego continued to successfully license comic book characters throughout the 1970s, even spinning off a Supergals Assortment line that included Supergirl, Batgirl, Wonder Woman, and Catwoman. Their success with comic book heroes led Mego to produce toys based on films and television shows, including *Planet of the Apes, Star Trek,* and *Buck Rogers in the 25th Century.*

Mego also introduced a new type of packaging for the superhero lines that quickly became the standard for all action figures. Prior to this, action figures were primarily sold in solid boxes that did not display the actual toy, a challenge for retailers. Mego pioneered the Kresge card, named for the Kresge line of retail stores that originally sold the new packaging, which showcased the action figure in a clear plastic bubble in the middle of a piece of promotional cardboard, allowing shoppers to see what the action figure really looked like. This style of packaging is also commonly called the "Mego Bubble Card" and is very similar to the packaging used to sell action figures today.

In 1978, the standard for action figures changed again when the toy company Kenner Products introduced the wildly popular line of *Star Wars* action figures and play sets. Kenner introduced a traditional, 12-inch set of action figures complete with clothes and accessories. But due in part to the oil crisis, which made manufacturing much more expensive, the company also produced a much smaller set of toys and accessories. These 3 ¾ inch action figures had much less detail than their larger counterparts and their costumes were made from the same molded plastic as the body instead of real fabric. The smaller toys were much cheaper, and quickly became more popular than the taller figures, prompting Kenner to phase out the 12-inch line altogether. As a result of the *Star Wars* figure success, nearly every action figure maker would adopt the 3 ¾ inch size going forward.

Action figures were primarily marketed through print advertising in the 1960s and then through television commercials in the 1970s. Television ads often featured boys acting out exciting scenarios with multiple characters from the same toy line along with their accessories. Rare exceptions to the exclusive portrayal of boys playing with action figures in commercials included advertisements for the Kenner *Star Wars* line, many of which featured a girl playing with the Princess Leia action figure. All of the commercials included a voice-over informing children and parents that each action figure or accessory was "sold separately."

The action figure market changed radically in 1983, however, when the Federal Communications Commission (FCC) began allowing toy manufacturers to license cartoons and children's programming based on toy lines. The FCC had banned all television programming that was associated with any toy lines since 1969, mandating that all children's programming had to be primarily educational. The landmark 1983 ruling allowed toy lines to market directly to children through cartoons and other television shows. This prompted a wave of daytime cartoons with their own toy lines, starting with Mattel's highly popular *He-Man and the Masters of the Universe* show and toys in 1983. By the mid-1980s, almost every cartoon produced for children had an action-figure tie-in, including G.I. Joe, Thundercats, Transformers, Silverhawks, and the Teenage Mutant Ninja Turtles. Most of the figures were 3-¾ inches and had a wide range of accessories, as well as other toy lines that included board games, posters, comic book, and video games.

In addition to becoming prominent cartoon characters, action figures of the 1980s are notable for their increasing muscularity. Until the 1980s, most action figures—12 inches tall and 3-¾ inches alike—shared the original G.I. Joe's lack of body detail. Although some action figures had evolved to include more prominent and detailed muscles, they were minor in comparison with the *He-Man and the Masters of the Universe* toys. He-Man ushered in a new body type for action figures, with oversized muscles that bulged beneath his costume. Other figures followed suit, and the majority of toys produced since the 1980s have featured extremely unrealistic, hypermasculine body types.

In the late 1980s, the perception of action figures as children's toys shifted to include their value as collectibles, and a secondary market of adults (as well as some children) began buying action figures to collect and preserve instead of to play with them. Action figure collectors keep their toys in original packaging to preserve their condition and increase their value, and have developed numerous collectable magazines, Web sites, and conventions to showcase and market their collections. Toy companies have responded to the popularity of action figure collecting by producing more expensive, highly detailed collector editions of figures, increasing the number of figures produced, and promoting more film and television tie-ins.

Although there have been action figures produced and marketed specifically for girls, including She-Ra: Princess of Power, a spin-off of the He-Man toy line, action figures have primarily been marketed to boys. The original G.I. Joe figure was notable because it encouraged boys to act out dramatic scenarios using doll-like toys. Action figures based on comic book and film characters further encouraged boys to imagine and play out hero fantasies, reinforcing the importance of pop culture male role models ranging from Spiderman to Luke Skywalker. Despite the imaginative possibilities offered to boys through action figures, the toys themselves reinforce very rigid ideals of masculinity, including an unrealistic, hypermasculine male body type.

Further Reading

Marshall, John. *Action Figures of the 1960s.* Atglen, PA: Schiffer Publishing: 1998.
Marshall, John. *Action Figures of the 1980s.* Atglen, PA: Schiffer Publishing: 1998.

Tammy Oler

Airsoft Guns

Guns and gunplay continue to be sites of fascination and pride for young males. In the suburban woodlands and empty lots of America, Asia, and Europe, young men are testing their tactical knowledge and armed courage. The "sport" is called Airsofting because the weapons used in this backyard combat exercise are Airsoft guns that fire a 6–8 mm plastic projectile. These weapons of simulated annihilation are the modern form of the BB gun that many young males, now adults, used to possess. Prior to the Airsoft phenomenon, paint ballers in plastic armor and tactical gear were running through the woods firing orbs of paint at one another. The paintball guns (called markers) are noticeably different from the Airsoft weapons. Paintball markers are designed in colorful metallic finishes with plastic extensions and accessories. These features make the paintball marker look like a futuristic fantasy weapon. A young male building a rig for his markers is like adding aftermarket parts to his favorite automobile. It is part performance and part extensions of ego and style. Airsoft weapons, because of their similarity to real firearms, are far more dangerous objects of young male bonding and play.

Gunplay and boyhood are intimately intertwined; however, Airsoft weapons introduced a new factor in this on-going debate about violence, combat games, and boyhood. Young males wrap a great deal of self-importance in the acquisition of their Airsoft guns. The make, model, and style of gun are important indicators that identify hunters, snipers, enforcers, soldiers, or hooligans. Organized groups of young boys gather in battles that follow various formats (the death-match, rescue and recovery, capture the flag, king of the hill, escort, point to point, and close quarter battle simulation). As with most things, the problem is not when knowledgeable people use these objects responsibly, following Airsoft gun safety rules, under controlled situations, but when young males are waving these toy guns at their friends in playful aggressive behavior or posting images and videos online for all to see, images in which they pose, as well as act out scenes of violence that look "real."

Criminals are also giving the leagues of Airsofters a bad name. The news is uncovering numerous reports where people are using these replica firearms to threaten the public into submission. The laws are as varied as the guns themselves; in some cases the guns are destroyed and the boys are simply warned about their "bad behavior," yet in some extreme cases the actions surrounding the gun play constitute a felony offense and charges are filed against the threat. Police departments are reported as saying that some of these guns are so realistic that, as experts, they have difficulty knowing if the firearm is real or not. In an ironic twist, real guns are also being painted to look like toys by criminals in order to gain the upper hand in confrontations with security officials and police. Play is a complex activity governed by engaged people, designated spaces, and appropriate times. The objects of play are the unconditional elements that require us to constantly mediate the activity for responsibility and safety.

Further Reading

Fruehling Springwood, C., ed. *Open Fire: Understanding Global Gun Cultures.* United Kingdom: Berg Publishers, 2007.

St. George, D. "Line Blurs Between Play, Gunplay: Popularity of Replicas among Adults and Kids Alarms." *The Washington Post,* June 22, 2008, A01.

Roymieco A. Carter

Boys and Play

Play includes all activity in boys that satisfies a need for movement but does not directly serve the drive to preserve life or the self. Because, in our culture, boyhood covers at least two decades, play takes on many forms in boys' lives, ranging from activity for its own sake (functional pleasure), to participation in organized sports, to enactment of elaborate scenarios. Boys are playing when they allow their bodies to enjoy the stimulation of events around them or stimulate themselves; move for the sake of moving (running and jumping, strumming a guitar); repeatedly carry out a skilled or semi-skilled series of movements (throwing or kicking a ball); play games with or without rules; make believe; take part in a team sport; or engage in virtual play (video games, play-fighting). Certain psychomotor and cognitive activities such as drawing, assembling a puzzle, building a model, or even solving a geometry or arithmetic problem are venues for play in boys, especially given their known competence in visualizing spatial relations.

Play in children was first systematically studied by the ethologist Karl Groos (1901) and continues to produce a vast literature. It is not clear that there are gender-specific forms of play, although psychoanalysts such as Erik Erikson have suggested that boys' play is centripetal (moving up and out from a center) while girls' play tends to contain and form enclosed spaces. He cites some cross-cultural evidence for this. Other psychodynamic psychologists have suggested that given any object (a "feminine" doll or a "masculine" toy truck), boys will hurl it through the air while girls will hold it and seem to protect it.

Play has been seen as a means of nonverbal communication of thoughts and emotion and is used by child psychotherapists to elicit expressions of inner conflict. During adolescence, playing with words forms an intermediate stage between play as recreation and work, including creative activity. Donald Winnicott understood certain toys and performances he termed transitional objects (blankets or soft toys) and phenomena (tunes hummed or whistled) to represent a kind of object having the qualities of both imagined entities and real things. Playing with such things provides comfort by reminding the very young child of his mother, and consolation as the child increasingly becomes independent. Overall, in the psychodynamic tradition, the ability to play is considered a sign of maturation, indicating that a boy has found means of expressing physical and emotional energy. Finally, Jean Piaget developed a series of stages in the development of play practices that paralleled cognitive development.

It is not clear that boys play more than girls, but only that they are encouraged to do so. Extensive vigorous play in boys may be a result of evolution and represents the result of an early division of labor between males and females in which the young male had to acquire skills needed for hunting and fighting off predators. But this would not be consistent with most mammals (and would not be consistent with all cultures) as we would expect play to be just as vigorous in girls, given that in many species the females hunt. Boys' play has also been related to the male's more active thrusting role in sex and to a competitive urge for sexual dominance over other, usually older males in pursuit of available and accepting females. But attestation to this is based on written documents and works of art preserved for us and therefore represents a selective reading of history. Another basis for the sexual thesis is Sigmund Freud's assumption of a preliminary (oedipal) stage for later, post-adolescent heterosexuality in which a boy fights with his father for possession of his mother. Boys' rough-and-tumble play has been related to such a spirit of competitiveness and is invoked to explain play as an early form of fighting, so that play between boys is seen to easily segue into competitive group sports and, later, to the martial arts, hand-to-hand combat, and the use of firearms alongside and against groups men in war. All of these so-called explanations are, however, perhaps only rationalizations of socialization practices. Our practices are changing dramatically as nationalism is succeeded by a global humanity, and soon traditional warring will be as obsolete as hunting down prey and fighting for access to sex in the technological West. As girls increasingly take the lead in forming sexual relationships with males and are empowered to control how they develop, and now participate in nearly all organized competitive sports (as well as in some areas of the military), it is becoming clear that we need a more fundamental understanding of boys' play. A re-evaluation of all boyhood play in view of these changes is just beginning. In general, it makes most sense to understand play in boys primarily as compensatory behavior, and vigorous play may be as much a phenomenon of flight as of fight, or an escape from maternal dominance toward independence—beginning in infancy and away from the earliest partial identification with the mother that all babies form.

Older boys have already begun to fashion ways of negotiating these cultural changes and engage more and more in what I term virtual play, where the scenario is often noisy, but only *seemingly* driven by anger and aggression related to stereotypes of *machismo*. Three examples will have to do: playing rock music, playing video games, and play-fighting. Belonging to a band is taking the place of belonging to a gang, the traditional precursor of the military unit in the West. Performers take turns standing out from the group to demonstrate individual skills, and although there is a lead, every player is considered equally notable. In the end, however, there is harmony. The themes and tone of hard rock are often vigorous, but they are not violent. Mosh pit dancing and raves allow for intense physical contact, but the boys spot each other as they do in gymnastics. A band's performances are rehearsed (even choreographed) and contained by the structure of the improvisation or set piece (song). Playing video games, boys vicariously participate in scenes of violence modeled on the reality of our culture, but most do not anticipate becoming soldiers or gangsters. Instead, they experience battles and other fighting much as earlier generations did reading comic books or watching television and movies. Boys fully understand the difference between real violence and fictional violence.

In play-fighting boys have found the most ingenious means of enacting what earlier generations acted out: wrestling and fist fights. Play-fighting allows boys to take on the roles of villain and victim in a melodrama of good vs. evil or the imposition of power over other males. Inspired by professional wrestling entertainment, the moves of these play fights are well choreographed and the participants are careful to partner each other's moves. In this way, they make each other's performances more realistic and exciting. Once again, play-fighting is clearly distinguished from real fighting and only very rarely deteriorates into the latter. It is usually carried out in front of an audience, which also acts as a safety net if the excitement becomes excessive. Play-fighting is very likely boys' way of satirizing the fighting traditionally used to impress females or to please a handful of senior males. It replaces gangs with ironic performances of roles boys realize they no longer need to play in society and certainly are not destined to play as males.

Further Reading

Erikson, Erik. *Childhood and Society.* New York: W.W. Norton, 1993. First published in 1950.

Groos, Karl. *The Play of Man.* New York: Appleton, 1901. Available online: http://www.questia.com/library/book/play-of-man-by-karl-groos-elizabeth-l-baldwin.jsp.

Piaget, Jean. *Play, Dream and Imitation in Childhood.* New York: W.W. Norton, 1962. Originally published in French in 1945.

Piers, Maria. *Play and Development.* New York: W.W. Norton, 1977. Originally published in 1972.

Winnicott, Donald W. *Playing and Reality.* New York: Routledge, 2005. First published in 1971.

Miles Groth

Erector Sets

Erector sets are construction toy kits consisting of various parts of metal and, in later models, plastic and rubber. A typical set features steel beams, nuts and bolts, pulleys, gears, and wheels. Erector sets were sold in numbered kits that ranged in numbers of pieces and what could be built from them. Early sets included plans for buildings and structures, while later famous sets built a walking robot, a carousel, a Ferris wheel, and airplanes. Current sets come in age-related designs (the models for four years and up, for example, have more plastic and feature softer edges than the eight and up and "advanced" designs), almost exclusively feature vehicle designs, and some feature radio control and even Internet uplink capabilities.

Erector sets were first produced in 1913 by A. C. Gilbert (1884–1961), a Yale-educated doctor and an Olympic gold medalist in the pole vault, who was also a producer of magic trick sets when he invented the Erector set. Erector was not the first construction set of its kind. Indeed, it competed fiercely with

Meccano, a brand imported from England. Gilbert's set, though, had innovations that made it stand out from others. Erector had flanged pieces—that is, the edges were folded over—that made them much stronger than competing sets, and, more innovatively, each model year had at least one set with a motor to animate it.

Much of Erector's success is often attributed to its marketing and advertising campaigns. Inspired by media and community concerns over the welfare of boys at the turn of the twentieth century, Gilbert sought to market Erector as a productive and educational pursuit for boys particularly. He advertised in magazines read only by parents and claimed that Erector could give wayward boys direction and teach them engineering skills at the same time. Gilbert also developed a newsletter, *Erector Tips,* which featured his own boyhood reminiscences, prize contests, new ideas for models to build, and a chance for boys to send in their own ideas and have their pictures in the newsletter.

The combination of marketing and quality made the A. C. Gilbert Company well known and financially successful, turning a profit in excess of 20 million U. S. dollars a year throughout the 1950s, largely due to the Erector set. After Gilbert's death and that of his son, Al, the company eventually sank into bankruptcy and the Erector brand was sold several times. Currently, Nikko America, Inc. produces and sells the Erector brand, both new models and reissued classic sets.

Erector sets have a continuing nostalgic value, and the name has come to refer generally to any construction toy. Also, a collector culture has grown up around Erector. Groups and individuals around the world host Web sites and hold conventions; they have also established a network for buying and selling sets and parts.

Further Reading

Cook, John. Girders & Gears [Online February 2008]. <http://www.girdersand gears.com/erector.html.>.

Nikko America. Erector [Online February 2008]. <http://www.erectorusa.com/ index.html>.

Watson, Bruce. *The Man Who Changed How Boys and Toys Were Made.* New York: Viking, 2002.

Marcus B. Weaver-Hightower

G.I. Joe

G.I. Joe is an action figure toy line that was introduced by Hasbro in 1964, and has become one of the most successful and recognizable toy brands in American history. As a toy line that is primarily marketed to boys, G.I. Joe is a representation of idealized masculinity, and the evolution of the line over the past four decades reflects changing ideas about the type of manhood to which American boys should aspire.

Hasbro introduced G.I. Joe in 1964 at the American International Toy Fair in New York as "American's Moveable Fighting Man." Named after a film about an American Army unit in World War II called *The Story of G.I. Joe,* the toy line had 75 different products in divisions designed to represent each brand of the armed forces. G.I. Joe was available as a soldier, a sailor, a marine, and a pilot. The molded plastic dolls were 11-½ inches tall, came dressed in olive green fatigues, and featured 21 movable parts. The right cheek of each doll had a faded battle scar, a distinctive feature designed to protect the brand's trademark. Hasbro introduced G.I. Joe just five years after Mattel released the Barbie doll (1959), and coined the term "action figure" to market the toy to boys who would be less than eager to play with dolls. G.I. Joe quickly became as popular with boys as Barbie was with girls, and Hasbro supplemented the action figures with a wide array of accessories over the next several years, including an array of weapons, a Five Star Jeep, and a Mercury Space Capsule. The original G.I. Joe, inspired by images of World War II heroism, represented a rugged, wartime masculinity to boys. In 1967, Hasbro attempted to market the toy line to girls with the introduction of the G.I. Nurse Action Girl ("American's Movable Action Girl"). Girls did not respond, and, as the doll was immensely unpopular among boys, it was discontinued almost immediately.

Hasbro began updating the action figure in the 1970s to reflect changing American ideas about conflict and masculinity. In 1970, Hasbro scrapped the traditional army man and introduced the G.I. Joe Adventure Team (1970–1976), complete with a new "AT" logo to distinguish them from their military predecessors. Responding to the vigorous anti-war sentiment of the decade, Adventure Team dolls were designed and outfitted for jungle and desert adventures. Instead of battling humans, this brand of G.I. Joe would battle lions, tigers, and ecological disaster. Hasbro also introduced several innovations with these figures: the dolls had "life-like" hair and beards (reflecting men's changing fashion styles) and hands with a "Kung Fu grip" that allowed the dolls to hold any number of accessories. Among the nine Adventure Team action figures were two African American dolls. Hasbro also introduced the short-lived Mike Power, Atomic Man, and Bulletman figures to compete with the Six Million Dollar Man toy lines.

In 1982, the doll changed again, this time in size as well as theme. The Real American Hero (1982–1994) action figures were scaled down to 3-3/4 inches size to compete with the popular *Star Wars* action figure line, and were made entirely (outfits included) of molded plastic. The Real American Hero dolls are also notable for their idealized hypermasculinity, including disproportionately bulging muscles. G.I. Joe transformed from being the name of a soldier to becoming the code name for an elite anti-terrorist military unit whose enemies were a fantasy terrorist organization named COBRA. All of the Real American Hero action figures produced, including several COBRA characters, had their own name, identity, and history that were featured on the backs of their packaging. Popular characters in this line included Snake Eyes, Duke, Cobra Commander, and Scarlett, a popular new female G.I. Joe character. Hasbro licensed the extremely popular line to Marvel for a comic book series and to Sunbow (1985) and DiC (1989) for cartoons, both titled *G.I. Joe: A Real American Hero*. The cartoons featured large amounts of fighting and violence, but no deaths. For instance, when a fighter plane was destroyed in combat, its pilot would always be shown parachuting to safety. In this way, G.I. Joe moved from the civilian context of The Adventure Team back to a wartime context, but unlike the World War II–inspired original toy, this new G.I. Joe was a fantasy character. The cartoon also featured now-famous public service announcements with safety lessons for children. The Real American Hero line was produced until 1994.

In the 1990s, Hasbro produced several less-popular lines: the G.I. Joe Eco-Warriors, Sergeant Savage and His Screaming Eagles, and G.I. Joe Extreme. All of these lines were extremely short-lived due to decreasing demand. By contrast, reissued G.I. Joe lines became very popular. Hasbro produced several 12 inches collections: Hall of Fame (1992–1994), Masterpiece (1996–1997), Classic Collection (1995–2004), and Timeless Collection (1998–2003). The three and three-fourth inches figures were also issued: Real American Hero Collection (2000–2002), G.I. Joe vs. Cobra (2002–2005), and 25th Anniversary (2007–2008). One more additional line, Sigma 6 (2005–2007), was released with a new 8 inches size, mixing new characters with the existing Real American Hero characters. In 2009, Paramount Pictures released the live-action film adaptation of the cartoon, *G.I. Joe: The Rise of Cobra*, to theatres internationally.

In addition to the *Real American Hero* comic book and cartoon, the toy line generated additional merchandise, television series, and games—almost all designed to appeal to boys. G.I. Joe also has a notable history of video game adaptations, including Cobra Strike (Atari 2600, 1983), G.I. Joe and G.I. Joe: The Atlantis Factor (Nintendo, 1991 and 1992), and G.I. Joe (Konami Arcade Systems, 1992).

G.I. Joe is an enduring, multi-generational figure of archetypal masculinity and heroism for boys: he epitomizes strength, fortitude, and aggression, often blended with images of patriotism and military service. The introduction of G.I. Joe created a new play pattern for boys, actively encouraging them to play out fantasies of war and combat (or adventure and tomb-raiding, during the 1970s) through doll-like figures. G.I. Joe was both toy and role model, encouraging boys to build qualities such as character and identity into war games that had previously been populated with featureless toy soldiers. At the same time, G.I. Joe has continued to reinforce conventional notions of masculinity.

Further Reading

Bellomo, Mark. *Ultimate Guide to G.I. Joe, 1982–1994.* Fairfield, OH: Krause Publications, 2005.

Michlig, John. *G.I. Joe: The Complete Story of America's Favorite Man of Action.* San Francisco, CA: Chronicle Books, 2005.

Santelmo, Vincent. *The Complete Encyclopedia to G.I. Joe.* Fairfield, OH: Krause Publications, 2001.

Tammy Oler

Hot Wheels

Hot Wheels are a series of die-cast toy cars produced by Mattel that has become one of the most enduring and popular toy brands for boys. According to Mattel, there are over 15 million boys ages 5–15 who collect Hot Wheels cars, and the average boy collector has at least 41 Hot Wheels cars in his collection. Mattel has expanded the Hot Wheels brand to include numerous toy lines and play sets as well as collectibles for adults and promotional tie-ins with professional racing circuits.

Mattel released the first Hot Wheels cars in 1968 to compete with the popular Matchbox car toy line being produced by British manufacturing company Lesney. While Hot Wheels shared some qualities with Matchbox cars, Mattel's toy cars were sleek and highly customized, featuring metallic spectraflame paint, a metal collector button, redline tires, and black roofs painted to look vinyl. All were designed to be 1:64 scale replicas. The original line-up of 16 cars included the Python, Barracuda, Camaro, Corvette, Cougar, El Dorado, Firebird, Fleetside, Mustang, T-Bird, Deora, Ford J-Car, Hot Heap, Beatnik Bandit, Silhouette, and a custom Volkswagen. Hot Wheels released the Custom Corvette toy car several weeks before General Motors unveiled the actual third-generation Corvette on which the toy was based, giving boys who bought the toy a sneak peek at what would become one of the most popular Corvette designs ever produced. One of the most important features of Hot Wheels, though, was low-friction wheels that allowed them to be raced on orange plastic Hot Wheels tracks that could be made into ramps, jumps, and loops. These specially designed wheels allowed Hot Wheels to claim the title of the fastest metal cars in the world. Mattel and other toymakers would battle for this title in the next few decades, introducing new axle designs and tires to make their toys move faster and handle curves better, echoing the design war waged among real-world automobile manufacturers.

Hot Wheels became an immediate hit, and Mattel quickly increased its line to 40 cars in 1969. The toys capitalized on the growing popularity of automobiles and car racing among boys, allowing them to build exciting racetracks indoors. Hot Wheels also gave boys the opportunity own scale replicas of high-end custom cars and emulate cool, hot rod drivers. As the cars evolved, so too did the racetracks and play sets. Tune-up stations, racetracks with double lanes, and other innovations were added, further encouraging boys' car fantasies. In addition, Hot Wheels were actively marketed as collectors' items, inspiring boys to purchase as many cars as they could afford in each series.

Almost immediately, Mattel licensed the toy line to produce a cartoon show based on it. *Hot Wheels* followed the teenage leader of the Hot Wheels Racing Club, Jack "Rabbit" Wheeler, who got involved in a wild car race in every episode. In order to address parental concerns that *Hot Wheels* might encourage reckless behavior and risk-taking among their viewers, producers included driving safety tips at the end of each episode. The cartoon inadvertently became part of a landmark ruling what would impact the toy industry for over a decade. The Federal Communications Commission (FCC), insisting that all children's television programming had to be educational, ruled that

Hot Wheels constituted little more than a commercial for the toy line, and demanded that all references to the popular toys be removed. They also banned all cartoons and children's programming that were associated with toy lines from the air, a ruling that was in effect until 1983. Stripped of its toy tie-in, *Hot Wheels* had a short television run, but its demise did not affect the popularity of the toy line.

Mattel has produced over 10,000 Hot Wheels models and numerous play sets, accessories, and related merchandise since the original line-up. The company has released new car models nearly every year, and promoted the brand with multiple cross-promotions and special editions. In 1975, Mattel introduced the first motorcycles for Hot Wheels, which were later dropped until 1997. In 1982, the company issued cars through McDonald's to promote the brand. In 1984, the "Ultra Hots" line was introduced and marketed as the fastest Hot Wheels in history. In 1985, Mattel teamed up with Kellogg's to issue cereal cars. The first price guide for Hot Wheels was issued in 1987, and the first collectors' convention was held in Toledo, Ohio, later that year, cementing the brand's perception as a valuable collectible. In 1991, Mattel produced their one-billionth car and released special gold-plated Corvettes, and the 25th anniversary of the toy followed quickly in 1993 with a special toy line released exclusively through Toys "R" Us. Mattel continued to innovate throughout the 1990s and into the 2000s, releasing high-end limited editions designed to appeal to collectors as well as pro-racing inspired models. In 1997, the toy manufacturer made the leap to actual auto racing, sponsoring driver Kyle Petty in the NASCAR Winston Cup. Mattel has since become involved with nearly all racing circuits, including NASCAR, Formula One, CART racing, and the NHRA.

The toy line's enduring popularity resulted in a growing population of adult collectors. In response, Mattel launched HotWheelsCollectors.com in 2001. The online portal gives toy collectors access to information on news and limited releases as well as discussion boards.

Although generations of girls did actually play with Hot Wheels cars, the toy company did not design or manufacture any car toys with girls in mind until 2007, when they released their Polly Wheels toy line. Throughout their history, Hot Wheels have been actively marketed and advertised to male children, reinforcing the importance of cars and car-related culture to the experience of boyhood.

Further Reading

Leffingwell, Randy. *Hot Wheels: 35 Years of Speed, Power, Performance, and Attitude.* Motorbooks International, 2003.

Tammy Oler

LEGO

Formed from the Danish words *leg* and *godt* meaning "play well," LEGO was founded and owned by the Kirk Christiansen family in Denmark. Ole Kirk Christiansen began making hand-crafted wooden toys in the 1930s and the family-run company has evolved to include hi-tech programmable computers, robots, and action toys. LEGO first made the plastic blocks in 1949, and in 1953 launched their first play system with the Town Plan line. LEGO quickly proved superior to other building block sets, perfectly made and indestructible. LEGO may now accompany a boy from his playpen to the university classroom where they are used to study robotics.

The interlocking bricks as we now know them were developed in 1958, and innovations came regularly, adding wheels in 1961, the DUPLO line for younger children in 1968, and human figures in 1974. After developing plastic gears and cogs and multiple connection forms, LEGO launched the TECHNIC series in 1977, allowing for the complex technical development of machines and motorized models. Horses, castles, pirates, and space stations followed through the 1980s. LEGO MINDSTORMS was introduced in 1998, which made building computer-programmable robots possible.

The core of LEGO toys' attraction has always been that they enable the builder to take a set of bricks and reconstruct and repurpose it according to the builder's imagination: combining blocks and sets and themes as creatively as desired skeletons on pirate ships or knights in castles, and dragons in space. LEGO play encompasses both role-playing games and creative, imaginative construction, engaging the player in dimensional awareness and spatial cognition.

Perhaps one of the most captivating story lines developed with the Bionicle series in 2001. It has since evolved into at least four generations of characters in the good and evil playing out the grand mythic narrative of the Toa fighting for freedom from the darkness of Makuta with the help of the Kanohi Masks of Power.

LEGO quickly adapted to the digital age, adding CD Rom games, such as LEGO Chess, LOCO, CREATOR, and LEGO Island. Through licensing agreements, LEGO capitalized on the popularity of movie and entertainment themes, producing extensive production lines of Star Wars, Harry Potter, and Indiana Jones themes. LEGO branched out with the Toa into digital movies and games for console systems. Some of the story lines were expanded into book series for early readers.

The LEGO company develops ever more complex models and themes, and yet as toys they retain the simple joy of building a square house, a wall, or a car, even allowing you to recreate your family with the interchangeable body parts and characteristics of LEGO people—furthermore, the earlier sets never become obsolete.

Further Reading

Cross, Gary. *Kids' Stuff: Toys and the Changing World of American Childhood.* Cambridge: Harvard University Press, 1997.

LEGO.com, the official Web site of LEGO products [Online]. <http://www.lego.com>.

Pickering, David, Nick Turpin, and Caryn Jenner, eds. *The Ultimate LEGO Book.* New York: DK Publishing, 1999.

Wiencek, Henry. *The World of LEGO Toys.* New York: Harry N. Abrams, 1987.

George H. Thompson

Miniature Wargaming

In miniature wargaming, two or more players confront either each other as individuals or in groups with miniature armies. The idea for war games comes originally from classic conflict simulations. There is also a strong connection to role-playing games, with the rules and game play, as well as to board games, especially for war games that are played on a predefined game board (e.g., a gridded terrain).

The dominant aspect of miniature war games is strategy, even though many games contain randomisers that are controlled by dice rolls. Many games are based on fantasy or science fiction or even a mixture of different genres. There are also historic miniature war games that reference particular epochs and represent armies or regiments that actually existed. A creative and artistic aspect of these games is the creation of an army mostly made up of figures that must be assembled and painted by the player.

The figures made of plastic, tin, or cardboard are often only a couple of millimeters tall; this is especially true for historic games. These figures have been designed simply and often act in formation. Other game systems are based on a few figures that are a couple of centimeters tall. These figures are complex and can either act alone or represent whole units. How the figures are designed correlates closely to the game mechanic. In games such as Battle Tech (1984)—later known as Mech Warrior—as well as Lord of the Rings Strategy Battle Game (2001) and Confrontation or Warmachine (2003), a few figures battle against each other; this is the skirmisher level. In other games, the action is based on entire armies or groups of people or mythical creatures. An example of this is Warhammer, which, like the other examples, takes place in a fantasy world. Warhammer 40,000 makes use of elements from science fiction, and Chronopia is a mixture of both genres—science fiction and fantasy. The armies have different equipment and various strengths and weaknesses. Their weapons have different ranges and effects. This puts all players at a more equal position at the beginning of the game.

During the battle, units advance toward one another and attack. Individual units or figures have different abilities that can hurt and affect the opponent in different ways. The opponent then reacts to the attack according to his abilities and/or possibilities. An element of chance is introduced and used in order to evaluate how effective each individual action is; also a ruler is used to check if the attack's range was sufficient to hit the opponent. These methods are used to make the events of the battle seem more realistic. The games are played in rounds that are split up into different phases. Certain actions are only allowed in certain phases, that is, troop movements, actions from individual figures (e.g., magic), ranged attacks, or close combat. This is where the different tactics come into play: a figure's or unit's advantages and disadvantages become exceedingly important. More complex ways of playing are possible, with figures that can be deployed in different ways. Important for deciding a winner is the weakening or loss of troops of the opponent, and, in many games, such a decision is expressed in points.

New figures, armies, or editions come out regularly for various games, which are often based around new stories or rules. Besides being a useful marketing tool for works of fiction and having strong connections to computer games, manufacturers create complex background stories and develop illustrations and possible game scenarios based on these ideas. Local hobby stores and gaming clubs as well as Internet forums are the meeting places for players where they can discuss and play war games.

Further Reading

Eastern Chapter, Historical Miniatures Gaming Society [Online]. <http://www.hmgs.org/index.htm>.

Miniature Wargaming Web site [Online]. <http://www.miniaturewargaming.com>.

Maren Zschach

Motors and Masculinity

The invention of the car and motorcycle during the mid to late nineteenth century is undoubtedly one of the greatest advancements in technology and transportation. Although these inventions have left their marks on social institutions such as the economy, the family, the government, and the military, cars and motorcycles have also spawned a culture that has historically drawn males—both men and boys—into its fold. Although many people merely see cars and motorcycles as a means of transportation—I just want a car that will take me from Point A to Point B, as is the common saying—many others immerse themselves in subcultures whose primary goals may include racing, showing, or just simply enjoying the looks and speed of cars and motorcycles. Inherently competitive events, racing and showing are important aspects of car and motorcycle culture, and individuals compete against others for best time or best in show; in many ways, these competitions also extend beyond the car or motorcycle itself, becoming expressions of masculinity of the man or boy behind the wheel (or at the handles) as well.

Many men report that they did not suddenly develop an appreciation for cars and/or motorcycles during their adult lives. Rather, this interest stemmed largely in part from participating in car/motorcycle-related activities, such as a show, a racing event; from regularly reading car or motorcycle magazines; or from fixing and/or modifying cars and motorcycles in a father's or a friend's garage. Although many girls and women are active participants in car and motorcycle culture, the vast majority of participants are indeed boys and men. Historically, this trend is the result of cars and motorcycles first being marketed toward men, who were usually the only individuals with the means to purchase such expensive modes of transportation in the first place. The question is, then, why are males drawn to cars and motorcycles, and why does this appreciation begin at such a young age?

Car and motorcycle culture is intricately linked to a culture of masculinity. In this way, boys develop a sense of understanding about their gender based on their participation in a particular subculture that defines hegemonic, or proper, masculine ways of behaving that stereotypically should include an appreciation and active interest in cars or motorcycles. Thus, not having an interest in cars or motorcycles is seen culturally as un-masculine or effeminate. Many fathers understand the importance of their sons developing in ways that affirm their masculinity, so oftentimes male members of families establish a bond through participating in car and motorcycle culture. By using car and motorcycle culture as bonding time for fathers and sons, fathers effectively pass on culturally acceptable socialization skills that involve a relatively intricate understanding of various types of cars or motorcycles, knowledge of different parts of the car or motorcycle, and, at the very least, the knowledge of how to fix simple car or motorcycle problems.

As younger boys grow into their teen years, many are expected to have a sophisticated understanding of the difference among various types of cars. Many teen boys also develop a particular appreciation for specific cars: domestic or foreign/import cars; manual or automatic transmission; front-wheel, rear-wheel, four-wheel, or all-wheel drive; 4-, 5-, 6-, 8-, 10-, or even 12-cylinder engines; normally-aspirated or forced induction. As car and motorcycle enthusiasm grew during the latter half of the twentieth century, a number of companies began offering after-market products for numerous types of cars and motorcycles in order to enhance their appearance and/or performance.

There are obvious differences between cars and motorcycles. Although cars offer many more creature comforts and relative safety compared to motorcycles, the latter is generally less expensive to purchase and maintain. Car culture, for various reasons, draws a larger crowd than does motorcycle culture. Stereotypically, motorcyclists have been labeled as more reckless, as danger seekers, and as less law abiding than their automobile enthusiasts, despite the fact that in many instances, there is an overlap of people who participate in both cultures. As cars are more likely to be the first means of transportation that teenagers encounter, car culture becomes more accessible and more popular among youth.

Hollywood and popular culture have also contributed to the rise of car and motorcycle culture, particularly during the 1950s and 1960s as a group of young actors emerged to become Hollywood's first true car guys. These post-war actors, including James Dean, Paul Newman, James Garner, and Steve McQueen, devoted personal as well as screen time to car and motorcycle culture before it caught on as being fashionable in the United States.

Actor, racer, and car and motorcycle collector Steve McQueen most likely best personifies the male enthusiast. Known throughout Hollywood and popular culture as the King of Cool, McQueen is also associated with car culture through his title character in 1968's *Bullitt*, the movie known mostly for what is still considered to have the best car chase scene in all of movie history. Some of his other films such as *The Great Escape* (1963) and *The Thomas Crown Affair* (1968) demonstrate McQueen's skill as a motorcyclist and his passion for exotic cars. Described by many of his biographers as intensely competitive and hegemonically masculine, McQueen truly epitomizes the link between American masculinity and car/motorcycle culture.

Cars and motorcycles are sure to capture the hearts and imaginations of boys for generations to come, and have proven to be a staple of most boys' means of masculine socialization. With cars and motorcycles hugely dependent upon gasoline, neither mode of transportation has gone out of favor, even during times of economic strain. During the gasoline crisis of the 1970s, car companies such as Ford began offering their popular Mustang model with a turbo-charged 4-cylinder engine as opposed to its seemingly less fuel-efficient V8 engine in order to draw in consumers who were becoming increasingly aware of the link between engine performance and efficiency. However, the oil embargo of the early 1970s had lasting effects on the evolution of car culture well into the 2000s. The epitome of car "tuner" culture in the 1990s through today is represented by the Honda Civic, which is often compared to the 1955 Chevy in terms of its complete personalization capabilities and performance/style customization.

Although the Civic arrived on U.S. soil from Japan in the late 1960s, it was not until the gas crisis in the 1970s that Honda was able to break through the domestic U.S. car market and establish itself as the dominant import car company, even above Volkswagen, Toyota, and Nissan (originally Datsun). Because of the "tuner-readiness" of the Civic, many of these cars were able to challenge (and beat) American muscle cars through horsepower and overall performance, while still being practical—Civics were and are still known to be reliable, "everyday driver" cars. Thus, car culture and tuner culture widely overlap—those who are interested in cars and motorcycles are often interested in how to modify such vehicles as well.

Tuner culture picked back up in the 1980s once gas prices fell, and cars were again judged and valued by their horsepower ratings and personal modifications. High-performance cars were featured in numerous television shows such as *Knight Rider,* which ran from 1982–1986 and featured a sentient Pontiac Trans Am with artificial intelligence. Another popular show was *Miami Vice,* which ran from 1984–1989 and featured, among various exotics, the Ferrari Daytona and Testarossa. Both television shows have been resurrected within the past few years—*Miami Vice* was remade into a popular U.S. film in 2006, and a new *Knight Rider* series has been on television since 2008.

The demand for horsepower went down in the 1990s, both on television shows and in consumer buying habits. However, it was not truly until the summer of 2001 with the release of Universal Pictures' *The Fast and the Furious* that tuner culture was exposed and the "horsepower race" emerged again. This series of movies has showcased newer tuner gems beginning with the Civic in the first film, following with cars (and various superbikes) such as the Toyota Supra, the Nissan Skyline, and the Mitsubishi Evolution, all import tuner culture favorites.

In the third movie of this series, 2006's *The Fast and the Furious: Tokyo Drift,* the protagonist, Sean Boswell, begins by street racing and totaling a hand-modified domestic car, the 1971 Chevy Monte Carlo. After being sent to Japan to live with his father, he immerses himself in drift racing, a type of racing popularized by light, rear-wheel-drive cars from Japan and only recently gaining in popularity in the United States. Sean ultimately builds a domestic-import hybrid in order to race—his car is a 1967 Ford Mustang fastback (widely assumed to be a nod to Steve McQueen's custom Mustang in *Bullitt*) with a Nissan Skyline engine. A trend with import car enthusiasts is to take a classic Japanese car and transplant a new high-performance engine; however, it is virtually unheard of to swap a Japanese-made engine into a classic American car, making Sean's car very unique within tuner culture. Symbolically, Sean's car bridges the domestic tuner culture with the import tuner culture, creating a vehicle that many car enthusiasts either love or despise for its mixing of domestic and imported components. With no end in sight for this popular series (the fourth installment, titled *Fast & Furious,* was released in 2009), young boys and men—and increasingly women as well—will continue to immerse themselves in car culture and the more popularized, accessible, and affordable domestic and import tuner culture.

Currently, with gasoline prices on the rise over the past decade and with the new economic downturn, cars and motorcycles continue to be wildly popular among boys and men while car companies continue to evolve according to consumer and enthusiast demand.

Further Reading

Connell, Robert W. *Masculinities.* Berkeley, CA: University of California Press, 1995.

Paradise, Alan. *Civic Duty: The Ultimate Guide to the World's Most Popular Sport Compact Car—the Honda Civic.* Cambridge, MA: Bentley Publishers, 2000.

Pierson, Melissa Holbrook. *The Perfect Vehicle: What it Is about Motorcycles.* New York: W. W. Norton, 1997.

Stone, Matt. *McQueen's Machines: The Cars and Bikes of a Hollywood Icon.* St. Paul, MN: Motorbooks, 2007.

Thorne, Barrie. *Gender Play: Girls and Boys in School.* New Brunswick, NJ: Rutgers University Press, 1993.

Lauren Sardi Ross

Poker

While its American origin can be traced to the riverboats of the Mississippi delta in the early 1800s, by the early twenty-first century, poker has turned out to be a global phenomenon. Although Americans of all walks of life have been fascinated by the game, the mythos of poker culture has always been distinctly masculine. Poker's early history is marked by stories of young male outlaws, hustlers, and cultural rebels of dubious character and quick calculation playing dangerous, high-stakes games for big money. The game has long captured the imaginations of many generations of American men, particularly in their youth.

In the new millennium, professional poker events such as the *World Series of Poker* and the *World Poker Tour,* as well as entertainment-oriented shows such as *Celebrity Poker Showdown* featuring American celebrities playing poker for charity are regularly televised on networks such as ABC/ESPN, The Travel Channel, Fox Sports, and NBC/Bravo. In this age of multimedia, the simplicity of the game of Texas Hold'Em—a popular form of poker today—makes it able to provide content for media platforms such as film, television, video games, and even mobile phones. Poker has even become a popular theme for adventure and mystery stories directed toward boys who enjoy reading fiction.

But nowhere is the recent popularity of poker—particularly Texas Hold'Em—more evident than in the rise of Internet poker over the past decade. In 2002, estimates suggested that 40 million players paid buy-ins of over $1.1 billion to Internet poker sites. On average, 32 hands of poker and $1,454 are waged per second on one single Internet poker site. Today, there are well over 2,400 online poker sites. Worldwide revenues for online poker gaming are $15 billion per year. It is predicted that such revenues will climb to $24 billion by 2012 (O'Brien, 2006).

Poker has also become a more prominent part of the culture of American boys and young men through the rise of Internet poker (and gambling) sites. According to the Annenberg risk survey of youth in 2004, 11.4 percent of male students said they played poker in the last year, up 84 percent from the previous year. In an American era marked by rampant desires to get rich quickly, and with the easy availability of credit to college students, young male collegians have become a key target for the marketing efforts of the poker industry, particularly online casinos. These casinos tempt young men through grand prizes such as a free semester of tuition. Poker is further popularized to boys and young men through media stories featuring the exceptional stories of young men who win big money through the game.

The rise of online poker has generated some public fears over boys and young men becoming addicted to gambling at earlier ages than ever seen before. Addiction experts are concerned about the nature of gambling online, where money seems less "real," games can be played at any hour of the day, and new rules speed up play to increase profitability for Internet poker sites. Although, at this time, these experts do not currently know the long-term effects of online poker on boys as they mature into men.

Further Reading

Araton, Harvey. "Fold 'Em Before Poker Can Hold 'Em." *New York Times,* November 4, 2005.

Caswell, Jim. "Listening to Their Stories: Students' Perspectives About Campus Gambling" [Online April 2008]. Wiley InterScience Web site <www.interscience.wiley.com>.

Grotenstein, Jonathan. *All In: The Almost Entirely True Story of the World Series of Poker.* New York: Dunne/St. Martin's, 2005.

Holden, Anthony. *Bigger Deal: A Year Inside the Poker Boom.* New York: Simon and Schuster, 2007.

O'Brien, Timothy. "Is Poker Losing Its First Flush?" *New York Times,* April 16, 2006.

Schwartz, Mattathias. "The Hold-'Em Hold Up." *New York Times Magazine,* June 11, 2006.

Kyle Kusz

Role-Playing Games

Role-playing games (RPG) are arranged interactive game-playing activities involving at least two people. Contrary to the familiar, spontaneous role-playing games of children, pen and paper, table top as well as live and computer role-playing games have subsequently become particularly established among young people. Pen and paper, and table top role-playing games are generally based on prearranged specific rules. An important component is the imagination as the players take over the role of a fictitious character, which interacts with those of the remaining fellow players. This exclusively happens in the form of a conversation.

Role players usually meet regularly, often over years, in order to play a game with a progressive plot or story. At the beginning of a game each participant selects a character from a collective imaginary world (in the RPG called a setting), which they would like to embody. Common imaginary worlds are often from the fantasy genre. In addition, modern variants are also played, such as science fiction or mixed categories within a game, called multi-genre games.

In particular, fantasy role games have been inspired by literary models such as Tolkien's *Lord of the of Rings* or the Conan series by Robert E. Howards. RPGs can be played without guidelines as freeform role-playing games, although numerous rules and procedures exist too. On the one hand, there are gaming systems such as the Generic Universal Role Playing System, created by Steve Jackson (1986), or the d20 system, which is freely available on the Internet as an open Gaming License. These procedures are quite general and can be related to different genres or campaign settings; on the other hand, there are special commercial gaming systems, such as Dungeons and Dragons (D&D), developed in 1974 by Gary Gygax and Dave Arneson, which are more concrete. Based on D&D and d20, various campaign settings have also been developed, such as Blackmoor (1970), Greyhawk (1975), Dragonlance, and Forgotten Realms.

Besides these game systems, initially produced by Tactical Studies Rules, and later by the Wizards of the Coast, there are further gaming systems created by other publishing houses, systems such as Shadowrun (1989), Middle earth (1994), and The Lord of the of Rings (2002), as well as various Star Wars RPGs (1987 and 2000).

These are based on the idea that a player chooses a particular character at the beginning of the game. This procedure of character creation refers to the allocation of the gaming figure of a certain species, and also allocates various attributes and skills that such a gaming figure may possess, corresponding to the respective character in question. The strength of the respective character is usually decreed by dice, and all the attributes of the character subsequently noted on a character sheet. Most gaming groups select a gamemaster, who takes over the role of the storyteller, while simultaneously managing as well as refereeing.

During a game a character meets those of other players (in the RPG called player characters), as well as nonplayer characters who are not personified by fellow players, but embodied by the gamemaster. During the game process the gamemaster describes various scenes using objects and/or creatures, which the players meet or may come up against. The player's characters react to such tasks of the gamemaster, and either act alone or together as groups (in the RPG called a party). This could, for example, involve overcoming obstacles or fight situations. Such situations can be determined with special dice, in particular a 20-sided cube (d20). Since 1968, the most important event for game enthusiasts is the annual Geneva Convention, named after Lake Geneva, in the U.S. state of Wisconsin.

Further Reading

Mackay, Daniel. *The Fantasy Role-playing Game: A New Performing Art.* Jefferson, NC: McFarland & Co, 2001.

McLimore, Guy. What is a Role Playing Game?, 1997. [Online April 2008]. Plaid Rabbit Productions <http://www.rpg.net/oracle/essays/whatisrpg.html>.

Rilstone, Andrew. Role-Playing Games: An Overview. [Online April 2008]. <http://www.rpg.net/oracle/essays/rpgoverview.html>.

Williams, J. Patrick, Sean Q. Hendricks, and W. Keith Winkler. *Gaming as Culture: Essays on Reality, Identity and Experience in Fantasy Games.* Jefferson, NC: McFarland & Co, 2006.

Maren Zschach

Scouting

Robert Stephenson Smyth Baden-Powell began the scouting movement in England in 1907. The lieutenant-general was a British war hero who had written a manual on reconnaissance and scouting, titled *Aids to Scouting*, which was widely read by boys in his home country. He devised a plan to introduce his teachings to male youths in a paper, titled *Boy Scouts—A Suggestion*, which he sent to like-minded men. And in 1907, he put his plan into action by taking a dozen boys on a camping trip on Brownsea Island in Poole Harbor. The trip was successful and led to the publication of *Scouting for Boys,* the first Boy Scout manual, in 1908. Both his original book and his revised edition for boys were very popular and led to the establishment of many scout troops across Britain.

William Dickson Boyce founded the Boy Scouts of America in 1910. Boyce, a Chicago publisher, visited London on business and lost his way in the fog. A British Boy Scout helped him find his way and refused a tip from Boyce by saying it was his duty. Boyce, so impressed by the act, sought out the boy's scout leaders to learn more about the organization. When he returned to the United States, he founded the Boy Scouts of America. The boy, whose name and identity remain a mystery, became known as the Unknown Scout.

Boyce may have founded the organization, but two other Americans had a great influence on the Boy Scouts. Artist and naturalist Earnest Thompson Seton, who grew up in Canada but gained citizenship in America, founded the

Woodcraft Indians in 1902. The Woodcraft Indians had their own merit badges and a manual titled *The Birch Bark Roll,* which influenced Baden-Powell's own writings. Another American influence was author and illustrator Daniel Carter Beard, who founded the Sons of Daniel Boone in 1905. The Sons of Daniel Boone had their own uniform and a manual titled *The American Boy's Handy Book.* Like many Progressives of their day, Beard and Seton worried that boys were losing many self-sufficiency and outdoor skills in the nation's drive toward urbanization. They created their organizations to answer such concerns. Both men's groups would be folded into the Boy Scouts of America, and both men would assume leadership roles in the organization.

The Boy Scouts emphasize character building. Scouts are taught to be good citizens, to be helpful, to be strong physically and mentally, and to possess strong morals. Such qualities are highlighted in the Scout Oath and Scout Law, which have been integral parts of the organization almost since its inception. The American version of the oath and law were revised from the original British versions to sync them more with American values. Some of those revisions reflected a religious influence, which has led to strong ties between scouting and churches in this country. For its heavy emphasis on character, scouting is sometimes seen as a supplement to the education provided by schools. And there is some overlap between the methods and content taught in scouting and in schools. Thus, there has been a long tradition of partnership between the Boy Scouts and the American education system.

The Boy Scouts of America boasts a membership of roughly 2.8 million boys and young men. Membership extends from the Tiger Cubs at age 7 to the Venturers at age 20. Although the Boy Scouts emphasize character, education, and citizenship, the club also still emphasizes physical activity. The organization sponsors three "high-adventure bases" where members can go backpacking, or canoeing, or participate in aquatics. And troops still participate in local camping trips as well as regional and national jamborees.

Further Reading

Boy Scouts of America National Council [Online April 2008]. The Boy Scouts of America <http://www.scouting.org/>.

Peterson, Robert W. *The Boy Scouts: An American Adventure.* New York: American Heritage, 1984.

Townley, Alvin. *Legacy of Honor: The Values and Influence of America's Eagle Scouts.* New York: Thomas Dunne Books, 2007.

Wyland, Ray O. *Scouting in the Schools: A Study of the Relationships Between the Schools and the Boy Scouts of America.* Concord, NH: The Rumford Press, 1934.

Robert Andrew Dunn

Tonka Toys

The Tonka brand is best known for a line of toy trucks and construction vehicles marketed particularly for boys' play. The signature yellow Tonka dump trucks and cranes grace sandboxes all over the world. The Tonka Toy Company grew into a global leader in toy manufacturing in the 1980s, with additional toy lines such as the GoBots (vehicles that could be turned into robots, like the later and more popular Transformers toys) and Pound Puppies (stuffed animals). Recent years have seen the addition of computer games, infant track toys, lunch boxes, clothes, books, and even home decorations with the familiar Tonka logo and vehicles.

Tonka trucks were first manufactured in 1947 by Mounds Metalcraft Inc. of Mounds, Minnesota, a company originally founded by Lynn E. Baker (1899–1964), Avery F. Crounse (1880–1960), and Alvin F. Tesch (1915–2000) to make metal tie racks and garden equipment. The word *tonka* is a Dakota Sioux word meaning "great," and it pays homage to Lake Minnetonka, next to which Mounds is located. With Tonka a household name in toy trucks, the company changed its name to Tonka Toys Incorporated in 1961. Production of Tonka in the Mounds plant ceased in 1983, when production was moved to Texas and Mexico to reduce costs for the company. In 1991, Tonka Toys was sold to Hasbro Toys, which still makes the trucks and other licensed products.

Tonka's line of toys grew immensely popular because of their rugged construction, their low price, and their detail and accuracy to the real-world vehicles on which they were based. From the crane and clam digger design that started the line in 1947, Tonka produced hundreds of other vehicle designs, from the Road Grader, to the Allied Van, to 1956's Fire Pumper that could be hooked up to the garden hose, to perhaps Tonka's signature vehicle, 1964's Mighty Dump Truck.

Though the company throughout much of its history often preferred to use the generic term "children" in advertising for its vehicles, the majority of the marketing focused on boys. Boys were most often shown in photos playing with the toys, ads frequently addressed "tough guys," and Tonka toys for girls were explicitly feminine, like the Jeep with pink canvas top and the metal doll bed. Tonka was especially appealing to boys and their parents, for the trucks allowed boys to play in traditionally masculine ways, with the tools of masculine work, in masculine rough-and-dirty play.

In 2007 Tonka began a controversial advertising campaign that had no pretense of catering to girls: "Built for Boyhood." The campaign drew on stereotypes of boys as messy and highly active. The Tonka Web site also began offering "parenting advice for boys," advocating rough-and-tumble play (with toy cars and trucks, of course!).

Like other toy brands, a vast collector culture has developed around vintage Tonka toys. Collectors pay hundreds of dollars for rare vehicles and trade replacement parts for restoring older models.

Further Reading

David, Dennis, and Lloyd Laumann. *Tonka*. St. Paul, MN: MBI Publishing, 2004.
Hasbro. *Tonka Toy Trucks* [Online March 2008]. <http://www.hasbro.com/tonka/>.

Marcus B. Weaver-Hightower

Toy Soldiers

In 1903, an article in the juvenile paper *The Boy's Own Paper* declared that boys had a natural interest in military pursuits and were attracted to toy soldiers. Traditionally made by German companies, in 1893 the aptly named company, Britains, stormed the British market with inexpensive, hollow-cast alloy miniatures; by 1900, millions had been sold. The availability of these 54 mm tall, brightly painted soldiers coincided with Britain's global imperial expansion that precipitated countless wars. These were reported and glorified in the new mass-market newspapers, journals, and novels. The resultant interest in warfare and toy soldiers led the fiction writer H. G. Wells to write a book of war gaming rules called *Little Wars,* which he believed would satisfy the natural martial impulses of boys, men, and "girls of the better sort." Published in 1913, Wells hoped his book would contribute to avoiding real war. He was wrong. In 1914–1918 and again in 1939–1945, Europe and the world fought the largest and most destructive wars in history. Despite these world wars, and innumerable conflicts that have occurred since, the interest in military pastimes in boys' (and men's) culture persists. Indeed, highly sophisticated military and combat-themed computer simulations and games are extremely popular. However, the toy soldier and the historical miniature war game have survived into the twenty-first century. Far from undermining the popularity of these tactile activities, the computer and the Internet have supported the hobbies that developed commercially in the 1960s.

The type of toy soldiers collected by Wells and by the men and boys of the early twentieth century are still available today, but these military models are less playthings than collectables. Their place in boys' culture has been supplanted largely by realistic scale models or smaller miniatures designed for war gaming. Until the 1960s, the distinction between toy soldiers for play and those for collecting was largely nonexistent. More recently, collecting toy soldiers seemed polarized between the collector of valuable prepainted metal miniatures and the modeler who displays his finished pieces or plays with them in war games. Due to the cost of the toy soldiers, the former has become the pastime of adults with adequate means to collect the original nineteenth and early twentieth century models, or the hand-painted figures produced today. Although some of these collectors enjoy painting the lead-tin alloy models in the simple fashion made popular by the old manufactures, it is more common for toy soldier collectors to seek out the finished product. Indeed, the paint schemes of the original Britains models were sometimes the only thing that differentiated the generic castings, and small variations can enhance the desirability and value of the pieces. The young collector is more likely to be interested in the cheaper plastic or metal "scale model" soldiers that are finished by the collector/modeler in a more realistic fashion.

Assembling and painting model soldiers (and military vehicles) are well-supported pastimes. These intricate scale models made of polystyrene, pewter, or resin are usually historically accurate and scrupulously detailed. Specialized reference books, Web sites, and publications such as *Military Mod-*

eling and *Fine Scale Modeler* provide support and inspiration to those who seek to impart a realistic finish to these models that typically range in size from 20 mm to 120 mm. For the dedicated collector and hobbyist, the artistry of the sculpting and the painting is paramount, and displaying the final product is the ultimate goal. For other toy soldier enthusiasts, displaying their finished pieces is not enough. Toy soldiers are for playing with, and, after World War II, war gaming developed from being a specialized training tool for military officers using map, pen, and paper to a commercially supported hobby played with models.

The modern origins of war gaming comes from the *Kriegspiel* (literally "war game") used by the Prussian General Staff in the nineteenth century to train their officers and to test plans for future wars. War games continued to be used for training and planning through the world wars, and this continues today, albeit as computerized simulations as opposed to "games." Popular war gaming takes many forms and ranges in complexity. Sophisticated board games, such as those produced by the U.S. company Avalon Hill in the 1970s and 1980s, surrendered to computer simulations. Because of the social and aesthetic appeal, the use of toy soldiers has more successfully weathered the fluctuations of interest in war gaming. Regardless of theses varieties of form, the purpose of the game is generally consistent: to represent some of the decision-making problems faced by commanders and soldiers in battle and to use a set of rules to govern the effects of those decisions in an entertaining fashion.

War gaming is often compared to the oldest military game: chess. Like chess, each type of playing piece in a war game (representing different types and numbers of soldiers) has distinct abilities. So, like a chess "knight" and "bishop" that have different movement options that are used in coordination to achieve a desired outcome, war game models that represent miniature units of infantry, cavalry, and artillery also have different abilities to move and fight that the player-general must combine to gain advantage.

Despite this basic similarity with chess, war games are different in a number of ways. First, the playing surface is usually covered in a miniature landscape—the terrain—that affects the defined movement and fighting abilities of the miniature military units. More important, war games are distinct from chess in that the role of chance and morale are accounted for. Reduced to a numerical value, the combat worth of a unit of soldiers represented on the playing surface is modified to account for physical and psychological circumstances that develop during the simulated battle. This modified value is also affected by the throw of dice that adjusts the combat results to represent chance.

Modern war gaming owes much of its development to the military and H. G. Wells, but the current form of the hobby stems from the books, rules, and toy soldiers produced by a small group of enthusiasts who popularized the hobby in the 1960s and 1970s, particularly in Great Britain. Brigadier Peter Young and Donald Featherstone wrote introductory books such as *Charge! Or How to Play Wargames* (1967) and *Battles with Model Soldiers* (1970), respectively, that explained the concepts and provided rules for play. Charles Grant achieved much the same with *The War Game* (1971), as did Terence Wise with his *Introduction to Battle Gaming* (1971). What all of these books shared was a passion for military history and the aesthetic satisfaction of using toy soldiers, just as Wells had recommended. What differed from Wells was that these books introduced the abstraction of mathematical values and dice to the commercial game, in addition to instilling a greater sense of historical context; the rules for ancient warfare, for example, were different than those used for the American Civil War.

More sophisticated and historically variegated games required more accurate and diverse toy soldiers with which to play. Britains and other "toy soldiers" had become too expensive to use and the 54 mm size was too large to represent "battles" that involved thousands. To address this need, new ranges of model soldiers became available, models designed for the war gamer and the scale modeler that were realistic in detail and inexpensive. Initially, soft-plastic soldiers were manufactured by firms such as Airfix and Matchbox. However, the limited variety of soldiers and vehicles produced by these larger companies still failed to keep up with the diverse historical interests of war gamers. To fill this market niche, a cottage industry developed, providing war gaming soldiers in smaller sizes most commonly ranging from 30 mm down to 5 mm in height, cast in pewter. Armed with history books, rules, purpose-made models, and a profound enthusiasm for their hobby, war gaming has a small, but worldwide, following. Although traditionally supported by home-based clubs with loose regional and national affiliations, the hobby is now regularly promoted through publicly accessible conventions; dedicated hobby magazines such as *Miniature Wargames* and *Wargames Illustrated;* and by a lively Internet presence that connects the relatively small community of dispersed enthusiasts.

Most recently, historical miniature war gaming has benefited from the products and reference materials produced by the fantasy and science-fiction gaming company, Games Workshop. Started in 1982, this English firm has successfully marketed their miniatures and rule systems (Warhammer) around the world. With franchised shops in malls and high-streets, Games Workshop gave toy soldiers and war gaming—albeit representing battles of "Orcs" or "Space Marines"—a commercial and cultural profile that the cottage industry–based historical hobby lacked. This profile was further enhanced with Games Worskshop producing the gaming products for the feature film adaptations of the *Lord of the Rings* trilogy. Since the late 1990s, Games Worskshop has supported a new venture: Warhammer Historicals. While earlier generations of war gamers found pleasure in the labors of doing historical research and developing the rule interpretations of military history, the comprehensive and lavishly produced Games Workshop guides to war gaming have supported a crossover from fantastical to historical war games using the shared rules interface of Warhammer. These "how-to" books lead the hobbyist through the whole process of collecting and finishing their miniatures to fighting their war game battles.

After a century of popular development, the toy soldier and the war game have evolved from Wells' parlor game with Britains models to a more sophisticated representation of warfare crafted by amateur historians and modeling enthusiasts. Compared to the vastly more popular and immediate stimuli of computer-driven entertainments, the toy soldier collector and miniature war gamer might seem an anachronistic novelty. However, the tactile and intellectual qualities of these pursuits have retained their place in boys' culture.

Further Reading

Grant, Charles. *The War Game.* London: Adam & Charles Black, 1967.
Henry, Harris. *Model Soldiers.* London: Octopus Books, 1972.
Opie, James. *The Great Book of Britains: 100 Years of Britains Toy Soldiers 1893–1993.* London: New Cavendish Books, 1993.
Wargames Illustrated, 1985-.<AUQ: Please provide full reference information.>
What is Wargaming? [Online January 2008]. Historical Miniatures Gaming Society (USA) <http://www.hmgs.org>.

Christopher Leach

Trading Card Games

Trading Card Games or Collectible Card Games are games for two and more players, competing against each other with individually arranged (therefore not identical) sets of cards (so-called decks). The length of a game can often be quite short, lasting from 20 minutes up to 1 hour at most. Developed by Richard Garfield in 1993, the concept of the game is based on the combination of three different elements: collectible cards, card games, and role-playing games.

Collective or ensemble images, which companies have added to their products for reasons of advertising since the nineteenth century, have usually been related to the topic of sports, and were often already appropriate for use in card games. Trading Card Games, however, are not only solely card games, but are also collectable items that are generally stored in albums. Extremely rare cards exist, which, as individual objects, can lead to auction prices of up to U.S. $4000. Additionally, specially designed cards (foils), which have a higher value for collectors, are also available. Normally the actual value of a trading card is based on the rarity of its existence, which is categorized as common, uncommon, and rare. Rare cards are also usually qualified to be of higher value within a game.

The kind of duels that take place during the game is based on standard role-playing games, where fictitious creatures duel with each other. As in role-playing games, the player tries to put a certain strategy into operation according to the arrangement of the cards in his or her deck. The combination and format of the cards, where different categories include similar colors or symbols, as well as the elements of the course of the game are based on the concept of common card games.

Before the game, each player constructs his or her individual set of cards; the so-called deck. This process is based on various packages, which are sold in booster packs ranging from 9 to 15 cards, or in tournament packs, starter, or theme decks with around 40 to 60 cards. Each pack contains a random selection of cards and cannot be viewed before purchase. However, desired cards, which are required for a particular strategy of deck construction, can be obtained through card exchanges, or be bought individually, that is, at Internet auctions.

The deck becomes the draw pile, also called the library, from which each player repeatedly draws cards for his or her own hand, cards that are gradually included into the game. Some cards are permanents and can be activated at each turn (so-called tapping). In many Trading Card Games the player obtains a certain number of life points at the beginning of the game, which will decrease according to attacks made by the opponent. For this purpose, cards can be played in ways that may harm an opponent or repulse the opponent's attacks. When during one turn no further actions are possible, the cards go from the stack to the discard pile (graveyard) of each player and a new turn follows. The player who subsequently loses all of his or her life points loses the game.

The first Trading Card Game published was Magic—The Gathering of Wizards of the Coast (which today belongs to Hasbro) in 1993. Since then many more Trading Card Games have been developed, even as merchandising products from cartoons, such as Pokemon, Duel Masters (the Trading Card Game of Yo-Gi-Oh!), Dragonball Z, or Naruto. Additionally, Trading Card Games based on popular movies or TV series also exist. Many Trading Card Games can be played online, and books and comics are also published regularly, which add stories and figures to the various games themselves.

A financially important, and, from the perspective of young players, also problematic aspect of Trading Card Games are tournaments. At organized tournaments players construct their own decks as normal, but as older cards are not allowed, players have to buy new cards regularly. Also at limited tournaments, cards have to be bought at the actual tournament. Such practices are regulated by the companies that produce such cards and have a strong influence on the consumer behavior of the players.

Further Reading

Owens, Thomas S., and Diana Star Helmer. *Inside Collectible Card Games*. Minneapolis, MN: Millbrook Press, 1996.

Williams, J. Patrick. "Consumption and Authenticity in Collectible Strategy Games Subculture." In J. Patrick Williams, Sean Q. Hendricks, and W. Keith Winkler (eds.), *Gaming as Culture: Social Reality, Identity and Experience in Fantasy Games*. Jefferson, NC: McFarland, 2006; pp 77–99.

Maren Zschach

SECTION 11

Boys and Technology

Blogging

With millions of new bloggers emerging in the blogosphere each month, tweens, teens, and young adults have been inculcated by digital practices—practices that produce both a physical and virtual existence for individuals as well as a form of identity unknown to any other generation before them. From among the hundreds of thousands of free programs, games, networking sites, music and video downloading, and messaging boards available, blogs (first named in 1997)—or Weblogs, in Web 1.0-speak—are one of the oldest forms of new media. For some youth, 11-year-old technology is practically prehistoric in digital history. Regardless, blogs were not a dying fad, as many media theorists once believed they would be. Blogs continue to offer Web users of any age with Internet access a unique online format to create their own personal Web space. Bloggers control who can view and post comments on their blog, and what information, opinions, and media expressions are most interesting and important to them and their online audience. The most popular blogs are those expressing informed opinions that adhere to particular principles or ideals held by a blogger's audience. The blogger's ability to write well, and infuse wit, humor, and critical thinking skills are crucial to gain an online audience and sustain popularity. This popularity is often gained not by word of mouth, but by pasting of hyperlink—sending links to others, and in turn, creating online affiliations.

In their December 19, 2007, report entitled "Teens and Social Media," researchers Lenhart, Madden, Macgill, and Smith found that 93 percent of all teens use the Internet; 64 percent between the ages of 12 and 17 have participated in content-creating activities, 33 percent have created their own Web pages, 28 percent have created their own blogs, and 26 percent have remixed content they find online (p. i). Sixty-four percent of online teens have been involved in one of the five mentioned online practices, which is about 59 percent of all American teens according to this study; 55 percent of online teens have a personal profile on social networking sites such as Facebook and MySpace; and 14 percent of online teens have posted videos (p. i). Lenhart et al. make several observations based on their data (p. v):

- Girls continue to lead the charge as the teen blogosphere grows; 28 percent of online teens have created a blog, up from 19 percent in 2004.
- The growth in blogs tracks with the growth in teens' use of social networking sites, but they do not completely overlap.
- Online boys are avid users of video-sharing Web sites such as YouTube, and boys are more likely than girls to upload.
- Digital images—stills and video—have a big role in teen life.
- Posting images and video often starts a virtual conversation. Most teens receive some feedback on the content they post online.
- Most teens restrict access to their posted photos and videos—at least some of the time. Adults restrict access to the same content less often.

Unlike writing for school or academic purposes alone, blogs continue to gain popularity among boys (though they lag behind girls) because they are driven by the possibility of gaining immediate responses from a wide range of viewers/readers. Those viewers may include members of their immediate peer group or range the entire digital planet, because any cybercitizen with access to the Web who conducts a search using keywords tagged in their blog postings may find a link to their blog, view it, and perhaps even post commentary. Teachers and educational researchers are starting to finally tap into this digital media phenomenon as well, designing and implementing creative, meaningful, and productive learning experiences for their young digital users.

Blogs foster four key elements of participatory culture: (1) affiliations, both formal and informal depending on the blogger and whom he allows to view or post to his blog; (2) expressions, as bloggers reinvent what and how postings appear on their blogs by infusing music, embedding video, and forming other aesthetic elements and creations unique to blogs; (3) collaborative problem solving, by responding to issues and tasks that impact their personal, social, and/or communal lives in the physical realm; and (4) circulations, in that bloggers have determined and shaped the flow and popularity of media in and beyond the digital realm, having an impact on their physical communities, television and radio productions, political campaigns, and school policies. More poignantly, blogs are the media mode of choice for critiquing other media productions by naming distortions, outing false reports, and identifying misinformation by major news media conglomerates. In effect, blogs have given voice to individuals otherwise lost or unheard in the physical world.

In schools, blogs offer boys virtual hallways to participate in social and learning communities in salient ways otherwise unavailable to them before the evolution of this new media. By having far greater control over how and who perceives their virtual identity, boys categorize and situate themselves or maintain anonymity altogether according to their virtually constructed and perceived differences among other individuals who express viewpoints more or less popular or meaningful to them. In this way, blogs serve as a virtual backchannel to the social and cultural communication occurring in their physical school hallways and classrooms. For this reason, the power structures often implied or expressed relating to popularity and social control among teens have been disrupted because of youth participation in digital backchannels such as blogs. In more unfortunate cases, those already in social control may exacerbate dominating practices as they become more adept at manipulating and producing digital events that serve to marginalize or ridicule others.

But the intrinsic benefits of blogging continue to appreciate among boys who create and share their writing with others, sometimes carefully choosing who can read and post responses, sometimes soliciting and gaining the popularity of their entire school or of hundreds, thousands, and even millions of members of the global digital community. As young bloggers continue to establish affiliations with members of the blogging community, foster circulation of their own knowledge as they scaffold the knowledge of their peers (both physical and digital) and their teachers, create circulation of their expressions, and solve problems in ways that develop new knowledge, teachers and researchers are beginning to reevaluate and reinvent curriculum and pedagogy that taps into the benefits of blogging and other forms of digital media. By embracing media practices traditionally deemed deviant or pathological, these teachers and researchers are changing the way learning is officially defined and implemented.

Further Reading

Jenkins, Henry, Katherine Clinton, Ravi Purushotma, Alice Robinson, and Margaret Weigel. "Confronting the Challenges of Participatory Culture: Media Education for the 21st Century." *Building the Field of Digital Media and Learning: An Occasional Paper on Digital Media and Earning.* MacArthur Foundation. http://www.digitallearning.macfound.org/atf/cf/%7B7E45C7E0-A3E0-4B89 -AC9C-E807E1B0AE4E%7D/JENKINS_WHITE_PAPER.PDF.

Lenhart, Amanda, Mary Madden, Alexandra Rankin Macgill, and Aaron Smith. "Teens and Social Media: The Use of Social Media Gains a Greater Foothold in Teen Life as Email Continues to Lose Its Luster." Washington, DC: Pew Internet & American Life Project. http://www.pewinternet.org/pdfs/PIP_Teens _Social_Media_Final.pdf (accessed February 2008).

John Pascarella

Computer Technology and Gender

Computing technology has been in the realm of boys and men in North America for over 60 years. It was developed by elite white males to promulgate their economic, military, and political interests. In the early 1940s, the United States military sponsored the research of John Mauchly and J. Presper Eckert, who sought to develop a technological device to count the trajectory of ballistics during World War II. By the end of World War II, male military, economic, and political powerbrokers' collective computing use parlayed into a closed systems discourse, where the computer became the hierarchical symbol for analyzing human behavior.

Computing Technology and Male-centered Visions

The unprecedented economic growth that took place in Western societies after World War II came to an abrupt halt by the early 1970s. The United States and Western capitalistic societies faced an economic crisis, which was caused mainly by an overproduction of goods and a disruption in the supply of oil. Western political and economic leaders sought to overcome barriers that inhibited their ability to maximize profits by liquidating their organizations, social relations, ideologies, and imperatives to the so-called Third World regions.

Computing technology served as the linchpin in the globalization of capital and the commodification of many aspects of social life. It has aided in coordinating transnational corporations' overseas investments, in continually moving their operations to the most economically advantageous locations, and in marketing their products on a continual basis to consumers worldwide. This technology has also allowed male corporate leaders to find additional ways to feed their companies' coffers. For instance, computer technologies have allowed business leaders to eliminate information labor in various industries, such as banking, communications, and other service industries. Concomitantly, some male corporate leaders' desire to amass wealth and power, aided and abetted by computing technologies, has generated stark economic realities for most global citizens. During the neoliberal era, people in developed nations have lost either their well-paying jobs or have dealt with prolonged bouts of joblessness, while at the same time, men, women, and children in most developing countries were economically exploited, toiling long hours in unsafe work conditions and living amid poverty, pollution, and hopelessness.

Unmasking the Gendering of Computing Culture

The perpetuation of computing as a white male domain has been reinscribed in many social contexts in North America, such as schools, the business world, homes, and media culture. This accounts for the normalcy of males being perceived as technological experts and the technological patriarchy structuring social relationships across the globe. For instance, many white male corporate leaders generate policies and practices designed to cater to the interests of mostly male IT professionals. Businesses that rely on computer experts to manage key parts of their operations have sometimes instituted male-centered activities, such as pizza nights, video game nights, and overtime sessions, which tend to foster a men's locker room atmosphere. Most male IT professionals prosper when working in an environment that caters to their interests and needs. Not coincidentally, men are far more likely than women to use computers in expert jobs in the business world and hold positions in academic departments that focus on preparing college students to design or create computers. Some male IT professionals may also be guilty of imagining only men as technological experts and are reluctant to hire female IT professionals who are just as equipped as their male counterparts to design, create or repair computers.

Over the past 15 years, a variety of new teaching machines have also rein-scribed the notion, to peoples across the globe, that computing technology and power are associated with maleness. Video and computer games have become one of the most persuasive forms of entertainment among boys and men. The cadre of white middle-class males who design these games recognized that many boys and men will gravitate to spaces that are not fraught with the day-to-day uncertainties and anxieties that are all-pervasive in our physical and social lives. Computer and video gaming is also appealing to many boys and men because of the presence of male-centered adventures, sexual fantasies, and violence.

The video-gaming gap that exists between boys and men and girls and women also plays a key role in many boys' early attachment to computing technology. The constant play that boys have with computer and video games leads them to view computing, at an early age, as a fun activity. Consequently, boys are much more likely to tinker with their "toy" to determine how it works, whereas girls tend to view computers as a "tool" to complete tasks, such as e-mailing friends, purchasing goods or services online, or completing school-based writing assignments.

Boys' gaming also conflates with their computer tinkering to lead parents, teachers, and students to believe that boys are inherently computing experts. This gendered stereotype is a guiding force in how boys and men and girls and women are positioned vis-à-vis computing technology. This is witnessed in many households across North America, occurring when adult caregivers unconsciously assume boys have a penchant for playing with computers. They act on this gendered stereotype by placing computers in male-centered spaces, such as the boy's bedroom.

Like their adult caregivers, many transformative scholars have noted that K-12 schoolteachers often unwittingly assume their male students are com-puting experts and cater to their interests. They are much more likely to ask their male students to help them fix computer glitches, to allow male students to control the classroom's computer equipment and mentor their peers on how to use specific technology programs, or to trust them with the intricacies behind how computers function. They also frequently implement male-centered edu-cational software into the instructional process, which further piques male students' interest in gaming and attachment to computing technology.

Even outside of typical, academic classrooms, boys are positioned as com-puting experts. Computing labs have often served as safe havens for geeky white boys. The labs often provide a safe space for the socially awkward, brainy boys, where they are free to socialize, demonstrate their computing expertise, and interact with one another without the physical and verbal threats foisted upon them by jock students. Even though computing labs serves as empowering spaces for boys, they reinforce to girls that computing is a shallow activity, something that only dislocated, computer geeks do because their effeminate bodies position them to be verbally and physically abused in schools. Because most IT professionals and school administrators in K-12 schools are men, a surreptitious message has been continually sent to students and their colleagues: men and boys are more equipped to determine how computers should inform instruction and to solve technical problems, and more versed in keeping computer systems up and running.

Not only have video games configured computing as being associated with the masculine, but advertisements designed to sell gaming products and computers have represented gender in very conservative ways, locating the white male as the dominant computer user. Men are generally depicted as actively engaged with computing technology, manipulating it for their own pleasure, whereas women are generally left out of the computing picture, just as they are in most activities or occupations that confer wealth and status in the wider society. On the rare occasion that feminine images appear, they are designed to position women as passive computer users incapable of using computers with skill or power.

Computing Technology and Creating a Democratic Computing Culture

Although computing technology has functioned as boys' toys for the past 60 years, some believe that allowing male political and economic powerbrokers to eliminate labor costs, further their military agendas, and unleash their tensions and aggressions in the virtual word has promoted and normalized this computing culture as a masculine activity. Yet, many also believe it is still possible to alter the dominant visions surrounding technology and generate a computing culture predicated on the ideas of equity, justice, and democracy. We must guide our youths and their caregivers, in-service and pre-service teachers, and university students and their professors to recognize as specious the claim—made by political pundits, educational leaders, and corporate executives—that computing technology is an omnipotent artifact that solves social and economic problems in its context of use. Rather, they must come to understand that computing is a social practice wedded in systems of power that are bent on extracting the world's labor power and resources for mainly white male corporate and political leaders.

However, just helping various social actors recognize the factors responsible for computers promulgating corporate and military interests and fueling a computing culture that is aligned with the interests of men and boys, will not by itself alter how computers are typically used or formulate symmetrical computing relationships. Many believe that educators at all levels of schooling must also illustrate to students how computing technology can be employed to challenge the economic and political structures that dominant computing practices which support the interests of those in positions of power, rather than function to build a society predicated on developing the intellectual, social, and emotional needs of all citizens. For instance, many socially conscious groups have harnessed computers to formulate pockets of resistance that challenge policies, practices, and arrangements that are linked to corporatizing and militarizing life; have created academic organizations, such as Computer Professionals for Social Responsibility (CPSR) to envision new ways of using computers to promote equity and social justice in society; and have developed online learning communities in which youth and their teachers from across the globe reflect on what policies and practices are responsible for causing violence, war, poverty, and injustice.

Further Reading

Bromley, Hank, and Michael Apple, eds. *Education/Technology/Power: Educational Computing as a Social Practice.* Albany, NY: SUNY Press, 1998.

Cockburn, Cynthia, and Susan Ormrod. *Gender and Technology in the Making.* New York: Sage Publications, 1992.

Millar, Melanie Stewart. *Cracking the Gender Code: Who Rules the Wired World?* Toronto, Canada: Sumach Press, 1998.

Brad J. Porfilio

Handheld Electronic Gadgets

For many young children today, handheld electronic gadgets are taking up a sizable portion of their toy collections. These include branded devices, such as the Go Diego Go laptop, and devices such as the One Step Ahead Record-A-Voice cell phone, which give children a "feel" of what it is like to use a laptop or a cell phone without actually offering the same functions (for example, a child cannot go online or make a phone call). However, there are also devices created specifically for children that perform the same functions as their versions for adults: for example, the TicTalk by Enforma is a gray wristwatch device that combines the ability to play educational games and receive phone calls.

These gadgets obviously reflect the fact that our culture has moved into the digital, handheld age. But there is more to it: these gadgets tap into a long-standing tradition of "cool gadgets" used mostly by strong male characters in books, TV shows, and movies. Since the 1950s, when the James Bond books were first written by Ian Fleming, many boys have grown up idolizing the digital goodies given to James Bond by Q (and the present-day M). Starting in the 1960s, the crew members of the Starship Enterprise on *Star Trek* have remained in contact with one another using the Communicator. Both Inspector Gadget and Batman in his many incarnations have all had cutting-edge gadgets.

Marketers have tapped into this inherent "coolness of the gadget" and by following standard gendered marketing practices. These gadgets are specifically designed to appeal to both genders: manufacturers will typically offer their devices in a "boy" color (blue, grey, black) and in a "girl" color (typically pink). They may also engage in parallel branding: for example, VTech has created a Go Diego Go laptop, which is supposedly intended for boys, and a Dora the Explorer laptop, which is supposedly intended for girls. However, devices such as remote controls, drills, walkie-talkies, calculators, and game consoles have all been marketed particularly to boys.

It seems the handheld gadget that remains the most popular among boys is the cell phone. According to a recent study on cell phones and boys, in 2006, 13-year-old teen boys with cell phones accounted for about one million subscribers, over 40 percent higher than the 12-year-old teen boy segment, and the number of 16-year-old teen boy cellular subscribers in 2007 numbered over 1.6 million, almost 30 percent higher than the 15-year-old teen boy group (US Teenage Girls, 2008).

In 2004, Motorola started selling their RZR phone, which combined sleek style and digital functions, including a photo/video camera, video games, MP3 ringtones, and wireless Bluetooth technology. The original RZR was targeted at boys, and shortly after the release of this phone, a hot pink version of the same phone was released for the female chatters. In 2005, Cingular started selling its Firefly cell phone, a phone designed to be used by children as young as eight, which was only available in blue (other models are now available in dark grey or pink, but the original model is still only available in blue).

Then, along came the iPhone. Named invention of the year by *Time Magazine* in 2007, the Apple iPhone became the must-have gadget for young men and women alike. However, soon after the launch of Apple's iPhone and iPhone 3G, some female users accused Apple of gender discrimination, because the phone is not suited to young women who have long fingernails (Parfitt, 2008). It seems that the inventors of the iPhone did not consider this as a possible obstacle for their users, which might indicate that they had a primarily male audience in mind for the iPhone.

Further Reading

Arceneaux, Noah, and Anadam Kavoori, eds. *The Cell Phone Reader.* New York: Peter Lang Publishing, 2006.

Caron, Andre, and Letizia Caronia. *Moving Cultures: Mobile Communication in Everyday Life.* Montreal: McGill-Queen's University Press, 2007.

Castells, Manuel, Mireia Fernandez-Ardevol, Jack Linchuan Qiu, Jr., and Araba Sey. A *Mobile Communication and Society: A Global Perspective.* Cambridge, MA: MIT Press, 2006.

Ito, M., D. Okabe, and M. Matsuda. *Personal, Portable, Pedestrian: Mobile Phones in Japanese Life.* Cambridge, MA: MIT Press, 2006.

Multimedia Intelligence Web Site. "US Teenage Girls Mature with Mobile Phones Earlier than US Teenage Boys." http://www.multimediaintelligence.com/ index.php?option=com_content&view=article&id=113:us-teenage-girls -mature-with-mobile-phones-earlier-than-us-teenage-boys&catid=37:front pagetitleonly&Itemid=129 (accessed December 2, 2008).

Parfitt, Ben. "Apple Accused of iPhone Gender Discrimination." Mobile Entertainment Web Site. http://www.mobile-ent.biz/news/30740/iPhone-accused -of-gender-discrimination (accessed December 2, 2008).

Giuliana Cucinelli

Hyperspace Heroes

Gone are the days of toy boxes filled with social indexes of boyhood. We no longer find the low-slung leather gun belt holding the two-chrome six shooters with faux ivory handles. It is just as difficult to find the military action figure with vehicles and necessary weapons removed from the collector's box actually being played with by young boys. The guns, action figures, and rugged utility vehicles once made for a good day of boyhood fantasy play. What has taken their place?

Boys replaced toy boxes with the Xbox, Playstation, Gamecube, and personal computers. These gaming platforms are filled with objects and avatars of fantasy just like the toy box. Sports, player versus player (pvp), military action, and role player adventure games (rpg) are the new testing fields for boys to engage and challenge intersections of the personal, social, and material worlds. The trials of boyhood were bound to change with hordes of gaming companies targeting the understimulated minds of young males as primary audience for millions of games sold each year. Not all these games are blood and gore; the gaming landscape is full of complexity through hybrid forms of interaction and innovative problem-solving scenarios. Boys barely get techniques mastered before the next generation of games are developed. The feverish cycle is intended to keep young males anxiously awaiting the "new thing." This is not to minimize the arguments about how games glorify aggressive behavior, decrease emotional empathy, and create inability to assess consequence. At the same time it cannot be denied that the video game industry has proven its staying power and declared itself a key part of our interactive sociocultural future. Why do these game experiences create player euphoria and spectator anxiety?

The cultural expansion of games evolves from the system of community based-role play. A cliché analogy applies here: it is a new frontier defining itself and its footprint on culture simultaneously. Advertising companies are convincing clients to place their brands in front of unsuspecting eyes, the military is building arcade forms of training simulators for kids' play, and automobile companies are building driving experiences for boys who cannot even see over dashboards of the latest models. Video games impact everyday life, and efforts are made to make it the ubiquitous medium for entertainment, learning, desire, and identity aspirations of all boys. Many are enticed by the old slogan "It's just a game."

When boys stopped spending endless Saturdays feeding a stream of quarters into arcade machines and brought the arcade home in a console, the irreversible quest for in-depth video game experiences began. Its growth was first restricted by technology and computing power. Serious gamers played text-based role-playing games that perpetuated virtual heroic identities, yet self-representations resided in the gamers' imaginations. The Sega Dreamcast, Sony Playstation, and Nintendo 64 expanded the base of serious gamers. The desktop role-playing genre boom preceded the console by almost a decade, though. Here limits were not on graphics, but on the Internet's bandwidth, which slowed the desktop's growth within gaming communities. Boys lived out their heroic fantasies in front of television sets and backlit digital monitors. The genre of games grew to match the variety of gamers. Characters in video games mimicked great heroes in classic historical epics. Gamers knew their favorite character's back stories, creating the illusion that characters preceded game play. Mario, Lara Croft, and Solid Snake were all prefabricated heroes of choice. Faster computers, higher resolution monitors, cable modems, and high-speed connections provide current hyperspace heroes to be better captured in detail and played online. Heroic illusion is at an all-time high, boys log in and choose the character class/guild that most reflects how they desire to play, be, and be seen by others. In character-based network gaming experiences, gamers play the roles of characters in a temporally fixed world organized by game developers or game facilitators. The developer's role is to provide a cast of nonplayable characters (NPC) that offer interaction and in-game support for live players. Gamers in conjunction with developers create collaborative, immersive storytelling experiences. The classic character-centered narrative with its dependence on plot and motive is still the foundation for gaming experience and fantasy, even though video game storylines are affected by the unpredictable behavior of gamers. Both narratives and storylines depend on one basic thing, the hero. The hyperspace hero is represented through four main groups: ballers, slayers, soldiers, and healers.

The Baller

All over the world young men are calling themselves ballers, and for every young man there is at least one cringing adult not understanding his testosterone-driven proclamation. Adults wonder, is he referring to his budding vitality or just being weird? Whatever the rationale, adults often prefer not to engage young people and may retort with a "don't say that." A simple "what does that mean?" or "what makes you a baller?" can reveal a new understanding of the young male self-image. He is letting everyone know he is the "king, mac, playa, pimp, g, and bomb" of his current environment, company, and/or action.

The most popular genre in console gaming platforms is sports. It provides us with the first heroic persona, the baller. The image is connected most readily with boys who demonstrate game on the basketball court, taking on all comers, beating his opposition, and putting aside any notion of "good" sportsmanship. It is not within the nature of a baller to see anyone as his equal; he is superior. The baller character is a well-known figure in popular and street culture, simply and publicly proclaiming excellence at anything. Ballers are the ultimate show-offs. He exclaims the battle cry, "I'm a baller!" after proving his supremacy on the battle field and waiting for his next challenger.

This type of hero brings every bit of his street swagger into the virtual world. The sports gaming genre is his primary hunting ground. He is also found lurking the shadows of his favorite first-person shooter (FPS) game. There is a common thread between the two game genres. Sports games such as golf, tennis, or racing place the individual against formidable competition that force him to prove his supremacy. The first-person shooter exercises a similar competitive model. How does this work in the team sport scenario? We all have been told that there is no "I" in team. If this is true, how does our hero maintain his shine as a member of the team? Simple: the game designers understand the need of the baller to be the center of the action. They have designed team games in which the baller can control the key decisions for everyone on the team. If the team wins, it is by his will and his alone.

The Slayer

Another hero persona that embodies a similar aggressive attitude is the slayer. The competitive supremacy lends itself to the virtual expression of physical combat. Warriors, barbarians, vigilantes, gangsters, rogues, and assassins are the primary slayer characters. The slayer is easy to identify inside and outside of the virtual world. He is driven by his male ego, attitude, and his need to fulfill his personal values of honor and glory. The slayer's aggressive attitude places him in situations that are only resolved by a hostile physical act.

People not accompanying the slayer on his quest misunderstand this hero. His brashness and arrogance is heroic because he is usually acting on behalf of a weaker character incapable of defending himself or herself against an overwhelming opposition. He asks nothing in return and is generally offended if offered praise or thanks. His act is his duty and a matter of honor, nothing more. The slayer distances himself from others around him to mask his vulnerability. This weakness is a source of his personal conflict, adding depth to his motivations. In his supermasculinity the slayer can never allow himself to feel comfort and love. If he entertains the happiness that is the by-product of comfort and love, he risks letting these emotions overwhelm him, and loose his will to be an unapologetic champion.

The Soldier

Soldiers, on the contrary, must know the love for others. It validates any and all of his actions. The great defender looks on the slayer with pity and remorse. He is perplexed that the slayer operates as protector but does not allow any gratitude for his protection or salvation. The soldier is performing a job and does not see it as his destiny to fight. He is employed for a task during a finite period of time and his behavior is part of a predetermined matrix of war. The soldier goes into the fight knowing the rules for both parties involved. Etiquette is a strange condition for the battlefield. The soldier not only expects it, he requires this civilized mask in the face of savagery. He prepares for the enemy's performance of battlefield etiquette and depends on the loyalty of his brothers in arms. Game environments are perfect for the soldier because their limits and parameters are set and unaffected by emotion. Conflict is reduced to a series of objectives, and once the online soldier meets the criteria defined by the commander, the game is over and he is free to pursue his personal desires. Soldier discourse is unforgiving and eternally binding. After the job is complete, soldiers look back at their unit's performance and service. The objectives are checked off like a grocery list and understood as untouchable examples of dignity and honor.

The Healer

Our last heroic persona is the healer, the great redeemer of hyperspace. All sins in game play can be generously wiped away by this character class. The strength of the healer is epic because it is realized through others, not him. He becomes a conduit for possibility, a martyr for other heroes. The healer is a hero to heroes. His ability to resurrect the dead signifies the importance of his role in the group, designed to prove him a powerful prerequisite. His knowledge is highly respected, and he has an air of mysticism about him. The shaman, cleric, medic, monk, priest, and paladin gain satisfaction from making sure others are able to perform at their highest levels. Where most hero classes are concerned with honor killed and damage done, the healer is fulfilled by facing the challenge with his team in tow and by having everyone perform their best while he removes poisons, shields, and heals any damage his team endures in the throws of battle. The enemy is defeated indirectly and falls with no casualties. Our hero stands proudly knowing a job well done. No more and no less is considered necessary.

In order for hyperspace heroes to thrive, game developers must continue to create bridges between material and virtual worlds. This allows the gamer to play center stage and confirm hero status throughout the virtual experience. Are young males aware that their gaming choices are part of a larger system of market values and game theory? The gaming industry makes no apologies for telling young ballers, slayers, soldiers, and healers "you are the hero," "you make others do the things you desire," and "you will gain the wealth and materials of your dreams" without regard to work, craftsmanship, or interpersonal relationships. In all game genres, gamers are made to believe they are the sole heroes getting an individualized experience, holding the keys to improvising what fantasy and limited restraint has to offer, but the reality is that anybody playing the game is led to believe the same heroic, solitary experience. Game managers (GM) operate as invisible sentinels of the world. They support gamers while maintaining a sense of order in a world of self-appointed heroes run amuck, negotiating with and colliding into each other throughout the virtual experience.

Game experiences that are based on the heroic model of game play are not won or lost. These are based on the engagement and activity that gamers experience from the game. Video game culture is notable as an innovative form and as a tool for creativity, communication, and confrontation. The realism of digital simulation, the speed of digital technologies, and the ubiquity of digital culture make it necessary to understand how the video game culture is impacting new definitions of boyhood.

The definitions and practices for engagement between game developers, digital culture, and boyhood are changing with every next-generation game. The traditional goal of the gaming experience was to win by simply having a higher score than your opponent; however, in a growing number of game genres the score is irrelevant or, at the most, incidental. Game builders make countless assumptions about the nature of heroics and its connections to boyhood. But no matter the genre, story line, or console the hyperspace hero is and will continue to unfold as a multifaceted practice of masculinity.

Further Reading

Howard, Jeff. *Quests: Design, Theory, and History in Games and Narratives.* Natick, MA: A K Peters, Ltd, 2008.

Taylor, T. L. *Play between Worlds: Exploring Online Game Culture.* Cambridge, MA:
    MIT Press, 2006.

Roymieco A. Carter

Online Environments

A great number of online activities, conducted by men and women, girls and
boys, can be classified as various forms of self-presentation. Theories of Erwin
Goffman, dating back to the year 1959, that were first coined for the off-line
environment have become very useful when talking about presenting the self
in an online context. Goffman was the first to emphasize the importance of
impression management, meaning that people often consciously and unconsciously engage in specific activities in order to influence the perceptions of
others about themselves. According to Goffman's theory, these impressions
are formed through interpreting two types of sign activity: the expression
given and the expression given off. The former is mostly expressed during
verbal communication; the latter, presumably unintentional and largely
uncontrollable, is expressed through one's looks in general. In order to find
out what type of qualities and features are thought to be sought by potential
partners, a person may have to perform several acts before receiving the
approval they were looking for. Goffman also states that individuals tend to
accentuate and suppress certain aspects of the self, depending on the context
of the situation. Whenever other persons are present, people tend to accentuate these aspects of the self that typically correspond to norms and ideals of
the group the person belongs to, or wishes to belong to.

Sociologist Ann Swindler has suggested that people mainly choose their
strategies of action based on the relationships with others, the most influential
of whom being their peers. Young people's identity constructions are especially vulnerable to peer pressure. In the new media environments, these types
of pressure may result in switching from the real to the online identity to form
more favorable impressions among one's peers. Therefore, in online communication, the impression management is formulated through constant worry
about how to construct one's virtual identity so that it would be appreciated
and accepted in one's peer group. By formulating a virtual identity, people
interacting online can learn aspects about the offline identities of their fellow
participants in an online community. This is important so that different messages about oneself could be sent out to the right audience. Furthermore, these
playful performances need to be modified according to the received feedback,
so that the messages given off could be read out as impressions the person was
trying to convey.

Youngsters communicating online are, thus, influenced by the online community and by the norms and values that are important for that community
while constructing their virtual self. For example, children engaged in role-
playing games based on science fiction narratives such as *The Lord of the Rings*
try to act and talk in the same way the characters from the books and the
movies do. The players who cannot stay true to their chosen character are

often given hints and suggestions by other players for reforming the character in order to best suit the needs of the community. Children also learn the adequate behavior while lurking around the community and looking for the activities of other members, either by reading their posts or looking at their role playing.

Computer-mediated communication (CMC) is unique in that it also diminishes a number of social clues that are present in the everyday face-to-face context. We cannot hear the person laughing at our jokes or making faces to our negative comments while socializing on the Internet, therefore an important part of the information is being left out of the event of communication. Teens, however, have found a way of to overcome such facelessness when communicating online. Angela Thomas proposes in her book *Youth Online* that in online communities a new type of body is created. The self-produced virtual body that is made up of different textual as well as visual elements becomes the center of attention while communicating in the virtual worlds. Aspects such as one's nickname and avatar selection, netspeak use, and profile creation all function to give birth to the virtual body. Unlike the off-line body, virtual body parts can be easily modified and even erased if necessary.

Social Networking Sites and MUDs

A number of scholars have reached an understanding that in the case of online communication the majority of expressions of self are given rather than given off, that is, they are uncontrollable. This notion is very well applicable to social networking sites, where the self-presentation is limited because of the already pre-given fields in the profile. A person has to fill in the fields of a profile about one's preferences, about one's professional and personal life, and about one's worldview; however, the answers to these fields are often already limited by the network itself. These limitations also lead to greater control over the self-presentation in an online context than in the off-line world, and therefore most of the identity performance on the Internet could be considered, in Goffman's terms, front stage. Profiles form a public face of the person, whereas additional identity clues can be seen only through private communication. In order to form a more thorough impression about the others, youngsters search for additional information about the other members of the community. For instance, the nickname used, the poster's e-mail address, the links on a person's profile, and so on become important while assessing each other because these small clues are generally regarded as uncontrollable and can therefore give a better picture of the person.

The same types of issues of intentional self-presentation also appear in different text-based forums on the Internet. Participants of online forums or MUDs (multi-user domains/dimensions/dungeons) are very well aware that the information presented by others can intentionally be presented as misleading. They rely on their gut feelings while searching for uncontrollable clues such as mistakes in spelling, the time of sending the posts, and so forth before forming their impressions of other posters. Nevertheless, as Lori Kendall has pointed out in her book *Hanging Out in the Virtual Pub,* most of the posters are still unlikely to fully trust someone unless they meet face-to-face.

Virtual Identity as a Conscious Choice

In many instances young people are simultaneously engaged in different tasks while sitting in front of the computer. They may be doing their homework, sending instant messages with numerous friends, being engaged in a role-playing game, MUDding, and talking to their parents in the next room all at the same time. These types of simultaneous actions, however, need a lot of careful identity management by the teens. All of these tasks emphasize different aspects of the identity; therefore, whenever they change a task they are performing, the action has to be followed by a quick and spontaneous change in their identity. Young people are especially talented in this type of multitasking. For example, switching roles from being a student doing one's homework, to being a Warrior King conquering the land of the Dwarfs, to being a boyfriend flirting with one's partner needs a lot of skillful identity management, which can be achieved only through constant practice.

Identity management is easier, if certain rules of conduct and information sharing are provided. These rules are also important for differentiating between the members of the community and outsiders. Different attitudes toward the identity consistency and self-disclosure circulate among the forums, MUDs, social network sites, and dating sites' users. These attitudes are generally formed according to the social norms of the given community. In role-playing games, for example, people are used to adopting characters and acting in ways that do not resemble any of the aspects from their own off-line lives. In some MUDs people are happy in their state of anonymity, whereas in others participants are, on the contrary, open about their off-line personae and expect the same honesty in the representations of others. As Kendall's research suggest, carried out in a MUD called BlueSky, many online communities share an opinion that an online persona should match the off-line personality. The more people become interested in forming a close personal relationship with their online companion, the more eager they get to know aspects about each other's off-line lives. Therefore, although sharing intimate fictional details can be fun for a short period of time, close personal relationships in online environments can only be formed when there is mutual trust between the personae and consistency in their online identity.

The need to reveal a true off-line self is especially important when there is a chance of meeting face-to-face. People using dating Web sites and social networking sites should be most concerned with the fact that their online identity has to bear resemblance with their off-line life. Performing as a good-looking 29-year-old banker can definitely be fascinating and could draw attention from many possible love interests, but if the reality is far too different from the portrayed picture, the consequences may end up working against the lonely heart. Many youngsters communicating online do not see their online identities as fluid or separate from their off-line identity altogether. For example, although one is allowed to adopt whatever identity one chooses in virtual environments, studies have shown that men and women still tend to present themselves with the help of stereotypical gendered codes, that is, their virtual identities contain a number of attributes that are thought to be sought by the opposite sex. These gendered scripts that are used for constructing the virtual selves are formed according to the prevailing values and norms of the society. For example, according to the research by Christine A. Smith and Shannon Stillman about the representation of women's personal ads (2001), women were found to be foremost describing their physical characteristics in order to form favorable first impression to potential partners. This belief was supported by the results of Julie M. Albright's study (2001), which found that men visiting online communities were interested in finding physically attractive partners. Fatima Jonsson's cyber-ethnography about the identity play of boys in online games (2005) suggests that in these games young men are often engaged in typically masculine actions such as power abusing other characters or showing off their skills.

Constructing the Virtual Masculine Self: Virtual Identities

Screen names (also known as nicknames or nicks) can be said to be the cornerstones of online identity because they are mainly used for creating first impressions of the character. Therefore, choosing a nickname needs a lot of thought, and a conscious decision has to be made of what impressions one wants to convey and what aspects of oneself (for instance, gender, age, ethnicity, location) one wants to reveal to others. Selection of a nickname is also important because the name starts to act as an identifier for the person making the character unique among the others. This uniqueness is also the reason why many people have never seen a screen name identical to their own. As nicknames are so carefully chosen, people remain true to their nicks for a long period of time and do not even try to change them when entering another virtual place. However, if there is a need for youngsters to change their nickname, they usually still hold strong ties to their previous selections.

Lois Ann Scheidt's results from her 2001 study of nicknames give a reason to believe that the virtual world does not differ that much from the real world because in both cases young people want to be seen as they are and to be known for their true selves. This is also the reason why the character's gender is often revealed in the selection of the nicknames, which carry strong gender signs or stereotypes (for instance, cyberboy15, JustaGuy, and show-go-man) or by using the actual name, nickname, or a diminutive of the person. In that way the true identity of the person will not be hidden. Additional flavor to the character can, however, be added by using various versions of typography (for instance, matt, JaKOB, Taaviiii, and EddyEddy). Some names such as Hotgrungeboy, sexyitaliano, and PLAYBOY function as sexually suggestive, that is, these playful names are selected in order to attract potential partners. Quite often self-character traits (for instance, dj-rex, THESWEDE, and cool-mann) or age-related nicknames (such as Nice guy18 and sexyboyy1985) can be found as nicks used by boys. Less frequently famous people or groups (for example, jordan100, MEtallica, and Arsenal) and different literature, film, or fairy tale figures find their way into boys' nicknames (for instance, james007, TERMINATOR123, Frodo, POTTER, and snoopy19).

In case the nickname does not conceive any information about the character's gender, they can be viewed as statements of identity, something that the person wants to convey about oneself or something they want to become or be (for example, Cool-n-quiet, SmartCookie, or Happy-go-lucky).

Profile Construction

Social networking sites (SNS) have become immensely popular among teenagers. Hundreds of thousands of youngsters bombard SNS such as Facebook and MySpace in order to present themselves and keep in touch with their friends. Having a profile up on at least one of these sites is practically a must for a teen to be accepted as someone part of the group. In order to appear appealing to other users, profile owners have to decide what aspects of the self they want to reveal and what to emphasize. For instance, people usually feel a need to give an overview of their interests and hobbies in their profile. While comparing the interests of young men to those of young women we may come across quite typical gender patterns. Research carried out by Malin Sveningsson in Sweden in 2006 shows that boys are more likely to mention aspects that have to do with technology, sports, or motor vehicles rather than declare being interested in relationships, cooking, work, education, and animals or expose their feelings in general. The social networking site profiles of young men also often show them being interested in practical things and physical activities, that is, in positioning themselves as proper masculine beings. Even more so, boys also feel a need to bring up aspects that would strengthen their masculine selves—for example, confirm their interest in politics or declare their sexual orientation to be heterosexual. As for the characteristics that were presented as aspects of the self on the profiles, young men stressed qualities such as independence, intelligence, and strength as part of their identity. However, experience, status, and (hetero) sexual desire were also valued identity markers. All in all, regardless of the much talked-about liberating aspects of the Internet, the profiles of boys send powerful messages about the prevailing stereotypical masculine norms.

Photos for Social Networking Sites

On most social networking sites, people can also add photos to their profiles that have a very specific role in the online self-presentation context. Nicole Ellison and her colleagues found in their study about self-presentation in online-dating environment (2006) that people use photographs not only to visualize their looks but also to strengthen the textual claims made in their profiles. For instance, they claimed that a photo showing a man without a shirt on and another photo showing the same man standing in front of the wall where his diplomas were displayed, function on many levels. On the one hand, the photos are supporting the discursive claims made in the textual part of the profile; on the other hand, they are giving an overview of a person's self-concept and physical characteristics. The study also confirmed that people are very conscious of their selection of photos and even the different poses and behaviors they are portraying on them are formed according to concrete rules, which are also used for assessing the photos of others.

Visual analyses made on the photos on the SNS profiles have found that young men play with many different gendered images of themselves. They either use different social distances (between themselves and the imagined viewer) and locations for taking the photo or pose with various people in order to create favorable first impressions for different audiences. Nevertheless, several studies made by Andra Siibak (2005–2007) also support the idea that young men are even eager to combine two contrastive masculine types, the Macho Man (that is, someone who holds stereotypical values true to the hegemonic masculinity) and Mr. Nice Guy (that is, a metrosexual who is ready to show one's feminine side), in the selection of their profile photos. The age-old image of the Macho Man can, for example, be seen in photos where boys are posing near a car or a motorbike to show their strength and manliness, or exposing their bare athletic body to everyone to see. Mr. Nice Guy, however, may appear gazing dreamily into the horizon near a lake when the sun is setting, playing with golden leaves in a park, or sitting on a sofa, stroking lovingly the head of his pet. The photos of this new type of a guy are therefore taken so as to show him as sensitive and romantic, the qualities that would hopefully make him irresistible to potential partners. In both cases, however, the young men in these photos seem to be concerned only with their good looks because on most photos boys are just posing passively without being engaged in any purposeful activities. Furthermore, rather than look the viewer straight in the eyes, the young men prefer to gaze away from the camera, a habit that leads to a strong tendency to be objectified. In order to emphasize themselves as proper idealized exemplars of masculinity, numerous young men also have the habit of posing without their shirts on, so that their muscular bodies are shown.

Netspeak

The language used on the Internet is usually referred to as netspeak, or cybertalk. Netspeak consists of traditional linguistic forms as well as nonstandard forms and slang that are seldom used in the off-line environment. Acronyms (afk = away from keyboard, OMG = oh my god, JK = just kidding), graphic symbols made of punctuation (:D) that are used for conveying emotions (called emoticons), and variations of words (kinda = kind of, anywaz = anyways, s'pose = suppose) are all elements of netspeak.

Netspeak becomes an important part of virtual identity performance as youngsters combine the use of certain words, phrases, and emoticons with the concrete characters they play. Children also make conscious decisions about choosing the language they use. The choices are based either on the need to perform a concrete character type or to create an image of oneself as an educated and friendly person. Youngsters vary their netspeak also to be able to differentiate between their various virtual selves.

Netspeak of males does not differ much from their face-to-face conversations, that is, males still tend to be more impersonal, resolute, less polite, and even aggressive in their online discussions. Just as in real life, adolescent boys also tend to hide their feelings and disguise their emotions while talking online. Their unwillingness to be emotional is visible in the lack of emoticons used in their netspeak. Although emoticons, especially flirty ones, can be used while talking to a girl online, there is a tendency to avoid expressing one's emotions through emoticons while talking to another man. Kendall states in her book *Hanging Out in the Virtual Pub* that an accompanying element to netspeak used especially in male-dominated discussion forums or MUDs is humor. As the use of emoticons is rare among men, the varied use of humor compensates for the feelings of joy and mutual satisfaction gained from the conversation as well as for the feelings of disappointment or anger (for instance, "blow me!"). Sometimes humor or jokes can also be used for strengthening the masculine group identity. For instance, making degrading comments about women such as "Didja spike her?" or calling the potential sexual interests "babes" may be used to stress the comradery among members of the group. Discussions that include making mock sexual suggestions to one another, friendly insults, horseplay, and derogatory comments about women all are used to provide evidence both of mutual friendship and understanding between men online, as well as to enforce men's need to stress stereotypically masculine identities.

Furthermore, Kendall's observations as a participant in the male-dominated MUD lead us to believe that the most frequent topics for discussion by men tend to evolve around technical issues (for example, computers), women and sex (dating, girlfriends), or ignorant people (annoying co-workers, weird acquaintances). These topics can be viewed as typical examples of guy talk that together with the accompanying tone and slang also emphasize masculine identities.

Nevertheless, it should be still noted that because the Internet environment is more flexible and allows more freedom in terms of language usage, the netspeak of females rather than males can be seen as changing. The language used in blogs can be classified as androgynous rather than gender specific, as stated by David A. Huffaker and Sandra L. Calvert in 2005.

Avatars

Another component of netspeak are avatars, that is, graphical icons that are used to represent actual persons. Just as nicknames, avatars are extremely important aspects of the online identity performance. Compared to the off-line world, in which we have quite a limited control over how we look, we make a conscious choice of how we would like to show ourselves while choosing an avatar in the online world. Furthermore, we can always change and modify the avatar whenever we feel like it.

In *Youth Online,* Thomas discusses her findings based on the visual analysis of avatars. She claims that boys often create avatars that do not look directly in the eyes of the viewer but more likely offer themselves to be looked at by gazing somewhere in the distance. They either cover their eyes with sunglasses or hats, or just look away from the viewer to signify psychological withdrawal from the social context.

A study by Scheidt made in 2001 found that young boys tend to choose avatars that stereotypically convey messages of masculinity and boy culture.

For example, male avatars often wear baggy clothing, a pair of sunglasses on their nose, or a trendy hat. Sometimes their trend consciousness can also be visible on their cyberbody as different logos or brand names are used on the avatar. Typically, masculine physical features are not that often emphasized, although avatars whose muscles are visible through a buttoned-up shirt can also be found.

Boys and Online Masquerade

Online environment provides many opportunities for online masquerade and deceit that sometimes it is difficult to understand whom you are talking to. The problem is more relevant in MUDs or role-playing games that do not have strict rules about registration, therefore allowing the participants to easily change their character or use more than one character at the time. In some cases MUD characters may even be usurped by another player, either by password stealing or by spoofing. One may also come across instances in which two or more people represent the same character, though this is rare.

Pretending

Although one can practically be whoever one wants to be on the Internet, young people use the opportunity of experimenting less often than grown-ups. Most of the studies conducted about pretending in an online context report that youngsters mostly prefer to stay true to the self.

Usually, young people pretend as a joke, to trick their online friends when passing as someone else. In some cases hiding one's true identity online can be connected to the need for privacy or the need to skip some online restrictions.

Elisheva F. Gross's study from 2004 reports that the most often used method of pretending for young men is trying to appear older than they actually are. This quite innocent way of pretending is used mainly to appear more appealing and interesting to others communicating online, or may just be seen as a future identity exploration, trying to behave the way one could actually be in a few years' time. However, trying to be younger than one's age may turn out to be much more difficult than expected. Studies have proven that compared to older people, youngsters brought up as the Internet generation have exceptional skills in making the right guesses about each other's age after exchanging just a few sentences.

Gender Swapping

Online interaction has often been associated with a possibility for gender swapping or gender bending, that is, behaving as someone from the opposite sex. The importance of knowing the gender of other participants is often visible as soon as one logs on to different chat rooms, discussion boards, or MUDs. New members of the community, so-called newbies, are constantly asked questions such as, "Are you male or female?" (amof?, in netspeak) to form the first ideas about how to interact with each other.

It has been said that female characters often get much more attention online than their male counterparts. Wanting to get that type of attention is one of the reasons why some young men act as women online. It has been noted that whenever women online behave in a way that is exaggeratedly feminized, for example, or if they are too shy and polite, and use a lot of adjectives or tag-questions, the characters are quite often played by males, instead. The same tendency is reported if female characters start to act out sexually, to send sexually suggestive messages, or to behave in a manner that is sexually aggressive. These sexually promiscuous women are usually also played by men. In online forums, MUDs, and role-playing games, youngsters can explore and experiment the values our society is used to associate with each gender. Young men can experience for themselves, rather than just observe, what it feels like to be female when behaving like one in the virtual world.

Although gender swapping may appear to be a fun and playful activity that would probably attract many teenagers, a number of studies have found that it is not actually that common among adolescents. Rather than behaving as someone from the opposite sex, young people and children are more likely to exaggerate aspects of their own gender in the characters they play.

Reasons for Masquerading

Researchers have mainly brought out three different reasons for online masquerade. The first and most often mentioned reason for masquerading among adolescents is self-exploration. For example, while behaving as a girl, boys not only learn what it feels like to be a totally different persona, but they also actually learn a lot about their own identity. In that way they get a chance to explore their inner sense of self. Youngsters strive to know how their peers would react and what behavior is anticipated from them. Performing as a girl online may give him a better picture of what to do and how to behave to become popular among girls. In this way masquerading may also be used for trying out new behaviors that would later be used also in their off-line lives.

Online masquerade is tried also in order to overcome shyness. Thanks to the relative anonymity of the online environment, youngsters are more willing to take social risks and behave the way many of us would not dare to in our off-line lives.

Finally, online masquerade is tried for receiving social facilitation. For many youngsters, it is much easier to form relationships online than in their off-line lives. They feel more at ease and are not afraid to open up with people they get to know online. This readiness to share may lead them to tell their most intimate secrets to total strangers as well as to say things to their friends in online settings that they would be scared to reveal off-line.

Conclusion

The available research suggests that boys actively use virtual environments to explore and play with their identities, to learn more about social norms and rules through constant feedback from peers, to overcome shyness, and to receive social facilitation. Although boys sometimes play with many different gendered images of themselves and may even combine contrastive masculine types (for instance, the Macho Man and Mr. Nice Guy) in constructing their virtual selves, different aspects of boys' online behavior (such as self-reported interests and qualities in social network site profiles, discussion topics in MUDs, displayed muscular bodies on photos, actions in online games, netspeak, and avatars) still tend to send powerful messages about the prevailing stereotypical masculine norms. Moreover, regardless of practically unlimited possibilities of pretending to be someone else on the Internet, boys mostly prefer to stay true to the self and exaggerate aspects of their own gender in the seemingly liberating and equalizing virtual world.

Further Reading

Ellison, Nicole, Rebecca Heino, and Jennifer Gibbs. "Managing Impressions Online: Self-Presentation Processes in the Online Dating Environment." Journal of Computer-Mediated Communication, 11(2), article 2, 2006. <http://jcmc.indiana.edu/vol11/issue2/ellison.html>.
Huffaker, David A., and Sandra L. Calvert. "Gender, Identity, and Language Use in Teenage Blogs." Journal of Computer-Mediated Communication, 10(2), article 1, 2005. <http://jcmc.indiana.edu/vol10/issue2/huffaker.html>.
Kendall, Lori. *Hanging Out in the Virtual Pub: Masculinities and Relationships Online.* Berkeley, Los Angeles, and London: University of California Press, 2002.
Thomas, Angela. *Youth Online: Identity and Literacy in the Digital Age.* New York and Washington: Peter Lang Publishing, Inc., 2007.

Andra Siibak and Veronika Kalmus

Teen Second Life

Teen Second Life, a multiuser virtual environment (MUVE) for 13- to 17-year-olds, is an offshoot of Second Life, by Linden Lab in San Francisco. The teen site started in 2005 and was intended to offer a 3-D socializing space for teenagers. In its first year it opened from noon to 10 p.m. Pacific time; since then it has been open 24 hours a day. The grid was originally designed entirely as a teen world, but a year later educators and nonprofit organizations requested to join Teen Second Life. Adults undergo a criminal background check before allowed to join and all share the same last name for easy identification. Much like in Second Life, institutions of learning (schools, libraries, community organizations, and universities and colleges) have set up libraries, college fairs, summer camps, and classrooms for teenagers to learn and interact virtually. These spaces or regions (virtual land) are called islands and sell for approximately a little over $1000. More money is spent to furnish these islands. Teen players can own land as well if they upgrade their accounts, which only guarantees them 512 square feet. They can purchase more land and pay additional for monthly land use. Experiential education is thus given an entirely new meaning. Educators are taking advantage of the space's popularity to maximize learning and engage students. As of 2007 there were

40,000 members on Teen Second Life from all over the world, yet most are from the United States and Canada (mainly for logistical reasons in sustaining clearance systems). Basic membership is free and additional or premium memberships are approximately $10. Linden currency (L$, online currency) has an exchange rate of 270 linden dollars to 1 U.S. dollar. Not surprisingly, most members are 16-year-old males. Teen Second Life has explicit community standards against vulgar language, sexual content, harassment, and bullying. The question always looms as to how well these are enforced, particularly how immediate sanctions or consequences are given before a detrimental pattern is established. More and more virtual spaces geared toward children, tweens, and teens are launched from popular TV shows, toys, or companies that have had a long-term interest in children's programming or that are just starting to see potential profits. Among the most popular are Webkinz, from the line of stuffed animals; Nicktropolis, by Nickelodeon; Penguin and Pirates of the Caribbean, from Disney; Gossip Girl, from by the CW Television Network; Gaia Online (a cross between traditional MMORPG and MUVE environments) by Gaia Interactive; and There.com, by Makena Technologies (the last two are for ages 13 and older).

Teen Second Life is a space in which historical, traditional, stereotypical, imagined, and alternative performances of boyhood and masculinity play out. With increased accessibility to cyberspaces, boys and young men are using these as extended realities, spaces to live pieces of who they are, many times as escape or havens from the tangible everyday lived experience. Several questions follow: Do these experiences enhance boys' sense of self? Do these experiences allow for imagined communities that strengthen a deeper gendered consciousness or do they reinforce stereotypical masculinities? Are these experiences just extensions of seeing life as a game? Other necessary questions for this inquiry deal with the anonymity of Teen Second Life. Avatars can be representative or utterly surreal. Many switch genders, personalities, and identifiers in creating alter egos. Regardless of the designed body, the agent of these choices is evident, and in this case it is the young male agent that is the focus.

How avatars are created, what communities they form, and what they do online are the first areas of interest when one enters any online environment, whether it is a multiuser environment, a multiplayer role-playing game, chat rooms, or instant messaging. The possibility to create alter egos without parental monitoring allows boys and young men to craft imagined capacities, sport different physiques without physical exertion, consume food without restriction, and interact with others across social categories otherwise unheard of in their daily material worlds. Teen Second Life can provide the immediate gratification they search for daily but do not achieve. The virtual world offers a different type of immediacy and a multisensory stimulation while only moving a mouse or pressing select keys on their keyboard. Skills unused in the increasing boredom of schools soar in the online environment; therefore, part of developing status in Teen Second Life depends largely on your knowledge, tech savvy, and familiarity with what can be done. Many boys (or any child, regardless of gender) engage in some type of fantasy play, consequently many

childhood studies note the importance of a fantasy life to "normal" development. When does normal cease to be so? When it involves a not so surreal second life, one in which children and teens participate with each other on a
regular basis? And when does this second life shift to first position? Some
adults are fearful of any virtual world's impact (much like fears instilled in the
early part of the twentieth century in regards to comic books), other adults see
the immense potential to engage youth in learning and activism. Teen Second
Life, much like other such sites, appeal to boys' desire for fantasy, competition,
community, belonging, enjoyment, exploration, and challenge. The parameters of their material worlds may be determined by adults in their life, obliga-
tions (school, hobbies, sports, odd jobs or chores, etc.), and needs. Online
environments are largely free of these expectations. Boys design their own
destinies and through what identities they play these out. For some this may
provide a sense of escape from their day-to-day reality. For others, who may
withdraw in the material world, Teen Second Life can provide a means to connect and perhaps excel.

Avatar design and construction is an important entry step to the online
space. What choices boys make about and on their avatars afford certain clues
about their wishes, strengths, and risk-taking behaviors. Switching genders
can be very interesting, although this is extremely popular for all sorts of reasons, but what these are for them and what type of "girl" they become online
still provide a wealth of information on both how they see the other and the
self. To borrow from Roymieco Carter's work on hyperspace heroes in this
encyclopedia, boys develop various identities (ballers, slayers, soldiers, and
healers) through video games. In other types of online spaces outside of pre-
set role characters, boys employ some of the above identity traits as they play
up fragments of their own personalities (real or imagined). These fragments
could be exaggerating some physical feature (larger muscles, larger stature,
great hair, tattoos, piercings, etc.), a wry sense of humor, astute technological
or intellectual skill, music ability, sporting skill or façade, reading preferences
and ways of thinking, ability, or desire. In creating their avatars, boys perform
not only for their peers but for whomever they wish to attract. Teen Second
Life is a fully customizable experience. There are 150 appearance sliders
(choices) for many physical traits. Players can choose different attachments
and accessories, clothing, skin color, tattoos, and even customize gestures,
moods, reactions, and movements.

Boys are growing up amid a tremendous amount of conflict, the United
States is at war, foreign policy is less than ideal, U.S. economy is suffering,
unemployment is rising, schools are ever segregating by cliques and identity
politics, learning is completely zapped of any creativity, often based on rote
memorization and recall, as teachers are pressured to teach to the test, the
hypermasculine heroes of the 1980s are back (Rambo, Die Hard, Indiana
Jones), new techno and anime heroes fill cartoon network, sci-fi network, and
G4 television; yet, many other venues in popular culture offer critical opportunities for learning and self-development. The growing accessibility of gaming through home game consoles, personal/portable game consoles,

computers, and the Web allow for different types of exploration and reification. Some boys are caught in the proverbial tests of masculinity, striving to fit in, to perform the stereotypes of strength, valor, courage, and disinterest, increasingly concerned with body image, superficial humor, or lackluster brain power. Other boys, still caught in the trials of masculinity, rely on their keen humor and intelligence only to meet disdain for their budding critique of the way things are. Many other dispositions are caught between these two brief vignettes and every permutation is played out in Teen Second Life and other gaming experiences. Virtual worlds do not create any immunity or safety from harassment, insults, racism, homophobia, bullying, or any other offenses, despite virtual community standards against it. These community standards do give way to communal policing and evaluation in perhaps less amorphous ways then in boys' material worlds. Teen Second Life can offer a different space to negotiate conflict mediated by an avatar who might resemble the self, but is not the self, therefore providing a necessary distance to work out possibilities (more appropriate to the situation, or less so). These negotiations may indeed spill into the boys' material worlds, increasing the ways they are able to learn about who they are and wish to be. Teen Second Life can afford many ways for boys to socially explore their gender, sexuality, disposition, demeanor, consciousness, and conscience, particularly if they are able to discuss their choices and learn from them.

Many educators have taken advantage of this and created various traditional and nontraditional opportunities through Teen Second Life. I have not discovered any yet specifically dealing with gender, but there are a few projects attempting to expand young people's understanding of the world and what is available. Two such groups are Global Kids, a New York–based nonprofit organization concerned with getting urban youth involved in transnational issues and public policy with the intent of creating community leaders and active global citizens; and Eye4You Alliance, a partnership between the Charlotte-Mecklenburg library system in North Carolina and Alliance library system in Peoria, Illinois, focusing primarily on teen outreach. Global Kids offers a free 4–5 week camp every summer, where participants select an issue, develop an action plan, and implement a project in Teen Second Life. Initially, Global Kids offered a US$100 (not Linden) incentive to participate and Linden money to refer other teen avatars. Teens need to apply (the application involves a short essay) to be part of the camp, which meets for 3 to 4 hours each day. This past summer (2007) 40 teens applied and 15 got in. The first camp dealt with child trafficking; for the second camp Global Kids partnered with UNICEF to launch the Convention on the Rights of the Child. Later in the summer of 2007 Global Kids coordinated the nonprofit and philanthropy thread at the 3rd Annual Second Life Community Convention. In the fall of 2007 Teen Second Life had its first virtual college fair sponsored by Eye4You Alliance. They have also partnered with various community organizations to develop youth mentoring programs, various book discussions, and tech skills workshops. Middle schools and charter schools have also started educational islands featuring literary-based, science, and other projects.

Most posts on blogs about these projects are by male avatars. We cannot assume more boys are involved because they are writing about it, but we can note the fact that boys are engaging in these spaces. Their imagined selves are real agents in Teen Second Life. I am sure educators and community organizers alike hope what boys learn on the teen grid expands into their everyday lives. These spaces open up great possibilities for both the burgeoning boyhood studies and masculinities studies. There is an incredible amount of rich knowledge to follow here and it is no surprise that it is as enticing to boys and youth in general as it is for adults. So will Second Life stay runner-up to First Life, or did it leave it in the wind? Ask any boy with an avatar in Teen Second Life and his answer might engage you to learn more.

Further Reading

Czarnecki, Kelly, and Matt Gullet. 2007. Meet the New You. *School Library Journal*, 53(1): 33–39.
Foster, Andrea L. 2008. Using Second Life as a Platform for Education: Professor Avatar. *The Education Digest*, 73(5): 12–17.

Leila E. Villaverde

Video Game Play

Today's new technologies provide opportunities for youth to enhance the ways in which they engage with the world, including communication (through cell phones, Facebook, and Web sites), entertainment (through iPods, video games, and the Internet), and education (through Google searches, Wikipedia, blogs, and Moodles). These new technologies have greatly impacted the way in which boys learn, interact, and socialize with each other, offering them a much wider range of opportunities to engage with each other and the broader community. This article will explore ways that boys' identities, affinity groups, and knowledge development have been affected by their interest in and interaction with these technologies. In particular, this section will explore the sophisticated ways in which boys engage to inhabit new virtual worlds and to create new, more accessible and inviting worlds for themselves.

Video games are a relatively new phenomenon in the world of technology and entertainment, gaining general popularity in the early 1970s, with arcade and home console versions of games such as Pong. Since then, PC games, console games, and arcade games have reached the interest and attention of millions of people around the world—predominantly males.

Research suggests many reasons why boys engage differently in the world from girls. From a biological perspective, boys will be boys—"That's just the way they are made." From a psychological/cognitive or brain-based perspective, it is said that their brains are hardwired to be that way. And from a socialization perspective, their environment and culture affects how they behave as gendered beings, and we are socialized to have particular gendered expectations, a self-fulfilling prophecy. Regardless of the research paradigm that we draw on, boys and girls grow up differently. They have different experiences, different expectations, and different opportunities. And as a result of these differences, new interactive technologies such as video games have more appeal to boys than to girls, as evidenced by the percentage of male gamers, male computer programmers, and male video game designers.

Why Are Video Games Appealing to Boys but Not to Girls?

Engagement with video games requires a propensity for experimentation in learning and a particular attitude that enables risk taking and play. Boys have been enculturated to believe that it is all right to try things out, to adapt tools and situations to suit their needs, to change the rules, and to challenge authority. Hence their willingness to have a go, to push a button, to find out what will happen, to try out a new controller, to engage in a new environment. Rather than being afraid of the outcome, they find excitement in challenging existing structures. They have been, it seems, socialized to feel comfortable exploring new environments, testing out new situations, and learning from their experiences. They are rewarded for these explorations—their adventurous spirit is acknowledged by parents and teachers, they are noted for their innovative ideas, and they have more fun as they learn. These are not the attributes that girls are rewarded for; rather, they are praised when they are conscientious, when they pay attention to the rules, and when they comply with existing rules. It is little wonder, then, that the challenging, complex, unknown worlds of video games do not hold much appeal for many girls. Rather than being an inviting place to explore, video game technology is unfamiliar, uninviting, and risky. The space of new technologies, then, is left to the boys.

These generalizations are not without substantiation. Repeated visits to video arcades provide evidence that these games are being played almost exclusively by boys. If there are girls in the place, they are standing back from the game, looking over the shoulders of the male players. In school computer labs with 50 stations, only two are occupied by girls, whereas the rest of the stations are occupied by boys. When many females think about playing a video game, they usually choose a puzzle game (Freecell, Tetris, Bejewelled). Meanwhile, males of all ages are engaging in highly sophisticated and complex role-playing games, simulations, and online MMORPGs, trying out complex controllers, finding cheats, interacting online with players around the world, creating their characters or avatars, and engaging in new fantastic worlds.

Impacts on Learning

These electronic play environments have considerable impact on learning for those who engage. Many video games offer opportunities for knowledge development, so that players can access information about historical events (Civilization, Age of Empires, Great Invasions), sports (Madden, Tiger Woods Golf, Need for Speed), language (Guild Wars, City of Heroes), fashion (Grand Theft Auto, Evil Genius), and other aspects of youth culture. Boys tend to use knowledge as social capital that can be traded and shared with their peers as they define and redefine their communities or affinity groups. They choose to read newspaper accounts of sports figures and events, to read statistics on players and teams, to engage with texts that show them how and why things work, and to find Internet and magazine commentary or cheats about better ways to engage with games. Video games fulfill the same function—that is, to provide knowledge and cultural capital that boys use in order to converse and communicate with others.

Video games also offer ways to enhance learning ability; information and ideas are presented in a variety of modes, including visual, oral, and written, which enhances players' ability to be successful and draw on a range of textual cues simultaneously. Rather than being in learning situations that they find difficult or that provide little interest or engagement, video games provide boys with active, immersive worlds that challenge and stimulate their interest. Video games allow players to co-construct their play environments, actively engaging in changing the game to best suit themselves, and to gain immediate feedback about their success. Players can repeat a game sequence or a move over and over until they are satisfied with their own performance. Or they can move on to another sequence if they choose. Choice is an important element of activities that are engaging and meaningful for the learner/player. Choice allows for them to take control of their own learning, recognizing when they need to repeat, change their practice, or move on to more challenging activities.

Active engagement in their own learning enables youth to develop and cultivate positive attitudes about their abilities and interests. Through video game play, boys experience success in a wide range of activities that they have selected as important to them. The successful play, becoming more challenging and complex as boys spend more time engaging, enhances self-esteem and boys' ability to see future potential. As psychologist Lev Vygotsky has described in his zone of proximal development concept, learners will develop if the tasks set are within their range of difficulty, not too easy and not too difficult. Video games are structured to scaffold the players' learning, enabling them to see the time they expend on tasks have immediate and positive payoff by way of successful movement through the game levels. And through all of the energy and time they commit to successful game play, they are enjoying themselves. Whether they are challenging their own previous success, or the success of another player/opponent, the engagement is fun! It keeps them coming back to try again, to strategize differently, to problem solve, to puzzle things out, in other words, to think deeply about problems.

Games allow players to become part of the decision making, and part of the game design. James Gee, a noted video game theorist, suggests that by playing a game, the players are co-creating the game by interacting and making choices about what will happen. Boys who have perhaps not experienced enjoyable engagement in classroom activities, or who have not experienced success, have renewed opportunities to see themselves as successful learners, able to engage with communities of learners. Through engagement with games in which they make personal connections to their avatars or characters, boys are able to see themselves in a positive light, to create an identity (or several identities) in which they are heroic, successful, and intelligent. This might be a new experience for lots of boys who have struggled with societal expectations in formal educational settings, where playing with action figures and collector cards, or enacting heroic deeds is not valued or appreciated.

As boys develop their identities as gamers, and see themselves as successful in gaming environments, they also develop social connections and networks with others. Far from being isolating, anti-social activities, video games create spaces in which boys can come together and communicate with each other through common enterprises. These groups of like-minded individuals, or affinity groups, come together to play a video game, have conversations about a game or a strategy, and connect as fellow human beings. As today's society becomes more frenetic, detached, and virtual, boys particularly are seeking ways to form connections with others. Spaces created by video games, whether real or virtual, transcend age, race, gender, and ability, valuing instead the abilities and insights of players who share and trade their knowledge in order to play a better game and have a more enjoyable interaction. They are able to connect through action rather than conversation, through knowledge rather than status. Technologies such as video games create vehicles through which boys have discussions, show their knowledge, and share new ideas. The affinity groups change or morph depending on the activities that boys engage in, and allow for a wide range of connections among individuals. Through video game play, boys are learning how to live well in an attention economy, both paying and receiving attention from others in their affinity groups, which helps them improve and engage. It is perhaps time for formal education to consider the issue of attention, and to consider ways that digital technologies attract the attention of so many students, boys particularly.

Video games create a synergy with other new technologies that also fascinate many boys. Through engaged play, players want to find out ways to become more successful in their play, and they seek out hints, tips, tricks, secrets, otherwise known as cheats, often located on video game Web sites. Cheats provide ways to continue in the game rather than being stalled because the way forward in the game cannot be discovered. There are also other ways to find out how to progress in the game. Web sites and blogs also provide the latest news about favorite video games, images of games, forums or discussion groups, strategy guides, reviews of games, previews of new games, and technical information.

Chat rooms (synchronous conferencing, sometimes in graphical social environments), YouTube (a video sharing Web site on which users can upload, view, and share video clips), and text messaging provide other ways to gain and share information and ideas. As video games take on a greater range of content, controller, and interactive approach, there is greater use being made of new technologies supporting each other. There are video games that are physically engaging and interactive such as Wii Sports Games, Guitar Hero, Rock Band, and Dance Dance Revolution. Similarly, there are games that are mentally engaging such as Halo 3, World of Warcraft, and also emotionally engaging such as BioShock. For example, gamers are using YouTube to seek out original renditions of 1960s rock songs so that they can better play Rock Band or Guitar Hero; they are creating blogs to share thoughts, reflections, and questions about the games they are playing; they are using virtual spaces to meet each other in combat for MMORPGs such as Guildwars. Gamers also locate code online so that they can reshape some of the games they are playing, replacing pieces of code with other pieces in order to customize the game to their own needs and interests. All of these overlapping uses of technology take considerable time and effort, but boys find the focused and concentrated time spent as worthwhile to create playable and engaging products.

Adult Concerns about Videogame Playing

The way that youth, particularly boys, like to "play" with new technologies, new games and new toys, can be puzzling and even worrying to adults. There are worries about the amount of time spent on video game play, leading to what has been described as addictive behavior. It is difficult for those of us who have not spent time engaged in video game play to understand its immersive qualities and the attraction of using new tools to explore exhilarating story lines, exciting heroic identities, and fantastic new worlds—not unlike reading a really good novel. There are also perceptions about the isolation and antisocial engagement of video games; however, after considerable observation of boys playing video games, the social aspects are evident. Boys play together in their living rooms or bedrooms, at recreation centers, even in school computer labs, wherever there is a space to play. They interact with each other through the games, gesturing, commenting, providing suggestions and strategizing together. They share funny stories and previous successes they have had with friends and family members. Although there are occasions where they play alone, more often they look for friends to share the experiences with and to show off new skills and new uses of the technology.

Another concern expressed by adults about boys playing video games relates to the violent and aggressive behaviors exhibited by the characters in the games—controlled by the players themselves. The overt acts of aggression that create much of the action in video games might, it is feared, cause the boys themselves to act in more aggressive and violent ways in real-life situations. What might be overlooked here is the violence-based games that boys have engaged in throughout time, whether it was cowboys and Indians, war games, or wrestling. A question that we might ask is how we can encourage engagement with more thoughtful types of games, those that require problem solving or strategy, rather than mindless eradication of opponents. We also want to encourage games that do not draw on racist, sexist, or homophobic types of characters and story lines; rather, we should encourage boys to engage in games that challenge hegemonic masculinity in its character development, story line, and situations.

Benefits of Playing Video Games

Rather than feeling anxious about boys' engagement with video games, we as adults should attempt to learn more about boys' experiences, why they enjoy engaging with new technologies such as video games, and how we can capitalize on their attraction to these new technologies. There are many powerful learning principles embedded in video games—reasons why technology is so appealing to many boys. For example, active and critical learning is a key aspect of game play, allowing for fast-paced immersive learning in which plays are repeated over and over until the players can progress in the game. The technology allows for repeated practice in places where practice is not boring, but is in fantasy worlds that are exciting for learners at all stages of expertise and where learners experience ongoing success. The technology allows for feedback to be immediate and specific, so that the play is not slowed down. Collaboration is possible, both face-to-face and in virtual spaces, whether it is a MMORPG, a text-messaging system, or discussion forums. There are many opportunities for multiple uses of technology, and many ways to manipulate existing technologies to serve the purposes of engaged play. And there are also lots of opportunities to "play around," both within the game structures and outside the virtual worlds, where there is room for exploration, active engagement, and enjoyment.

Conclusion

Why are new technologies, particularly video games, so appealing to boys? The opportunities to use the latest technologies in purposeful and exciting ways and to learn more about possible worlds and about themselves are compelling. The encouragement that boys are given to explore the world in active and embodied ways, to try things out, and to take risks, fits well with the new tools and toys that technology affords. Technologies such as those described in this paper, continually changing and evolving, provide ongoing challenges and stimulation for boys' learning—about the ways the world works, about the ways they work in the world, and the ways they are seen and how they see the world around them. It is hardly surprising, then, that the world of video game play is an ongoing source of education and entertainment for many boys in our twenty-first-century world.

Further Reading

Gee, James Paul. *What Video Games Have to Teach Us about Learning and Literacy.* New York: Palgrave Macmillan, 2003.
Johnson, Steven. *Everything Bad Is Good For You: How Today's Popular Culture Is Actually Making Us Smarter.* New York: Penguin Group, 2005.
Prensky, Marc. *Digital Game-Based Learning.* New York: McGraw Hill, 2001.

Kathy Sanford

Video Games and the Battle of the Sexes

Since the video game industry boom of the late 1970s and early 1980s, video games and the consoles they are played on have been subsumed under the category of boy culture in the popular imagination. Studies show that even kindergarten children perceive video games to be boys' toys. From the rather phallic creation of the joystick to Nintendo's Gameboy SP (marketed with the tagline "for men only"), it is not surprising that video games have come to be associated with the male sex, though their age appropriateness has been determined by their status as games or toys. But is this perception that video games belong to boys unquestionably accurate?

Although video games may be considered masculine terrain, a look into their past reveals that they were originally gender-neutral in design; and a glimpse into their present and future suggests that a gender war has been launched since the Girls' Games Movement of the 1990s, with females subsequently gaining a strong foothold in the video game industry. Statistics released by the Entertainment Software Association of Canada in 2007 suggest that females over the age of 18 account for 34 percent of game players. The most recent statistics from the United States, furthermore, demonstrate that women over the age of 18 represent a larger portion of the game-playing population (33%) than boys under the age of 17 (18%) (Entertainment Software Association, 2009). These statistics hardly suggest that video games are strictly a boy culture. So how did this gendered perception of video games begin, and where is it heading?

Let the Games Begin: Early Gender-neutral Video Games

When William Higinbothom, a senior nuclear physicist with the U.S. government, invented a game that could be played on an oscilloscope using an analog computer in 1958, he had no idea he was laying the foundation of the entire video game industry. In fact, Higinbothom's game, which premiered at an Open House for his government office in October of that year, was dismantled shortly after the Open House. Tennis for Two, as guests of the exhibit called it, was an electronic game resembling table tennis in which players controlled the motion of the ball using a box with a knob and a button. Higinbotham never patented the game and never sold a single video game in his life. For him, Tennis for Two was a mere novelty meant to entertain Open House visitors, and nothing more.

By the late 1960s, Higinbotham's gender-neutral game concept would be resurrected as the basis of the first video games. Tennis for Two reappeared with slight variations—mainly because of technological advancements—under a number of different guises. First, in 1968, a military contractor named Ralph Baer invented a tennis game that could be played on a television set. He sold the licensing of the game to Magnavox in 1971, and they used the game to create the first ever video game console: the Magnavox Odyssey. In 1972, another tennis-like game was created by Al Alcorn, an engineer with a then little-known company called Atari. The coin-operated game was called Pong, and by 1975, because of its unprecedented success, the company created a home version sold exclusively by Sears. The home version of Pong was equally successful, and it became Sears' top-selling product in 1976.

As Pong's massive popularity demonstrates, in the early years of video games gender had little to do with game design or sales. The tennis game concept was hardly directed toward a male audience. In fact, psychological studies demonstrate that the sport of tennis is one of the few sports that is equally popular among boys and girls. Likewise, these video game versions of tennis, along with most first-generation video games, were embraced by youth of both genders. The broad popularity of video games, however, did not last for long. It is difficult to pinpoint exactly where and when the mass appeal of video games shifted, giving way to a near complete market penetration on behalf of boys; most video game scholars agree, however, that the appearance of violence in video games marks the beginning of their appropriation by boy culture.

The Gender of Violent Video Games

Video games have become more popular among boys than any other demographic primarily because of game content. Most video games contain some degree of aggression, whether it is fantasy violence or violence directed toward humans. Research shows that boys are more likely to choose to play violent video games than girls, a fact that correlates to the way boys play: traditional boys' games such as cops and robbers and play-fighting, or even some sports such as hockey or football tend to be aggressive in nature. In fact, some of the most popular video game series among boys include Electronic Arts Inc.'s Madden NFL and NHL Hockey, which even allow players to injure characters during a game. Besides its appeal to the lucrative market of young males, there are a number of reasons why violence has become a prominent motif in video games. First, the majority of video game designers are male, and studies show that game designers tend to make assumptions about video game players' likes and dislikes based on their own interests and experience. The violent content of video games is, in part, a reflection of male game designers' own interests. Second, the nature of the video game itself may be a contributing factor to the prominence of its violent content; theorists suggest that one of the main elements of a video game is conflict.

Even though conflict may be fundamental to video games, the first-generation games, including Pong, are characterized as nonaggressive. Violence and aggression found their way into the industry with the second-generation games, such as Gun Fight. A Japanese one- or two-player arcade game released in North America in 1975 by Midway Manufacturing Co., Gun Fight was the first video game to include human-to-human combat. Players maneuvered cowboys using joysticks with a trigger button to shoot their opponent with their pistols. Featuring all-male avatars (the playable characters in a video game), Gun Fight was successful among young boys and eventually made its way into American homes on the Bally Astrocade console.

It was the success of the video game Death Race, however, that truly steered the industry toward violence. Loosely based on the film *Death Race 2000*, Exidy's Death Race was the first video game to instigate a public outcry about its violent content. While driving along a haunted road in the game, players were to hit as many gremlins and skeletons as possible to earn points. When a player hit these targets, the gremlins would scream, and then a tombstone would materialize as they disappeared. Concern about the game arose because the gremlins and skeletons were, essentially, stick people; it was soon revealed that the game's original concept featured human "pedestrians" as targets, not gremlins or skeletons. In an outrage, one woman from New York launched a campaign against the game and video game violence that was highly ineffective: sales of Death Race soared amid controversy. Although it was eventually banned, the game has since been credited with fueling the video game industry boom in the late 1970s, which had seen relatively little growth until that point. Death Race had taught the industry a valuable lesson: violence sells.

Throughout the 1980s and 1990s, human violence in video games increased dramatically, often alienating female gamers. Though research suggests that girls show a considerable interest in fantasy violence games, such as Nintendo's Super Mario Bros. or Sega's Sonic the Hedgehog, they tend to be bored by games that exploit human violence, which are immensely popular among boys. Perhaps the most poignant example of the popularity of human violence in video games among boys is Midway Manufacturing Co.'s Mortal Kombat. Originally an arcade game, Mortal Kombat was released as a console game in 1993. Like Death Race, Mortal Kombat spiked in popularity because of controversy over its violent content: in hand-to-hand combat, human avatars would attack one another often with extremely graphic results. One of the game's most salient features, fatality—in which a player would finish off its opponent using a trademark finishing move, such as ripping the victim's heart out of his or her chest—caused such public concern that senators Joseph Lieberman and Herbert Kohl of the United States launched an investigation into the issue of violent video games' impact on children. Nevertheless, sales of Mortal Kombat soared because of the media attention it garnered. When Nintendo released a censored copy of the game, the more violent version distributed by Sega outsold it by 75 percent (Kent, 1997). Of course, by that point, Sega had already secured a much larger portion of the video game consumer population of teenage boys. The Mortal Kombat story demonstrates that the public obsession with games exploiting human violence has, in part, contributed to the popularity of video games among boys.

Girl Power: Bringing Girls Back into Play

Video games' growing status as boy toys throughout the 1980s and early 1990s was supported by the abundance of male avatars available to them in the games. Meanwhile, girls' estrangement from video games grew because of a paucity of female avatars. Those games that did feature active female characters, furthermore, limited the players' choice. Mortal Kombat, for example, was one of the few games at the time to include a female character, Sonya Blade; however, of the game's nine active characters, she was the only female. Furthermore, Sonya's character was stereotyped as the strawberry-blonde seductress whose self-explanatory finishing move was dubbed "the kiss of death." Similarly, Lara Croft of Core Design's Tomb Raider, although one of the only female characters to be featured as a game's sole avatar, was scantily clad and appealed more to male gamers than any other demographic. The subsequent availability of an unsanctioned patch enabling gamers to play

Tomb Raider with Lara Croft in the nude confirmed her status as a sex symbol, while the casting of Angelina Jolie as Lara Croft in the *Tomb Raider* movie made the character's sexuality iconic. Female characters such as Sonya and Lara provided little room for girls to negotiate their given subject positions within the realm of video game play; nor did they significantly improve video games' appeal to girls.

In 1996, however, a video game emerged that managed to attract a female audience unlike any game before. Mattel Inc.'s Barbie Fashion Designer, released on CD-ROM, sold half a million copies after only two months on the market, outselling immensely popular games such as Quake and Doom during the Christmas rush. Though it was neither the first game developed for girls, nor the first Barbie video game on the market, Barbie Fashion Designer is considered the first of both to include an element of action: the game enables players to design and create clothing for Barbie dolls using printer-compatible fabric. Barbie Fashion Designer challenged assumptions made by video game corporations that girls were not a viable market for their product. The video game not only initiated copious studies about girls' interest in video games but also opened the floodgates to the Girls' Games Movement. The Girls' Games Movement saw a prolificacy of interactive games designed specifically for girls by women, such as Girl Games' Let's Talk About Me—a game that includes a series of magazine-inspired personality quizzes, a hair and clothing design application, and horoscopes—or Purple Moon's popular Rockett's World series.

The battle between boys and girls over video games had begun. Despite Barbie Fashion Designer's success, however, many critics view it as a loss for the girls rather than a win. The strongest criticism leveled at Barbie Fashion Designer is that it does little to challenge the stereotyping of women because it restricts the possibilities of clothing design to gendered apparel: there is no option to create a Barbie football uniform, for example, whereas there is an option to design a cheerleading one. Others argue that Barbie Fashion Designer is not a video game at all. Devoid of any element of conflict, the game has an extremely loose set of rules and lacks a clearly defined goal or purpose. It is perhaps more accurately described as an accessory for playing with Barbie dolls than what purists would call a video game, especially because it was only released in CD-ROM format. Nevertheless, Barbie Fashion Designer broke new ground in the video game industry, paving the way for the many girl-designed and inspired games that followed its success.

Gender and Video Games in the New Millennium

Despite the advent of the Girls' Games Movement and the surge of girl games that followed in its wake, video games continue to fall under the rubric of boy culture in the popular imagination and within the industry itself. Violent content and gender stereotypes persist as dominant features of many video game designs. For example, one of the best-selling games of 2007 is the first person shooter Halo 3, designed by Bungie Studios for the Xbox 360. Part of the Halo trilogy, the game stars the faceless but hypermasculinized protagonist Master

Chief Petty Officer John-117: a cybernetically enhanced soldier who defends humanity from aliens. Including Master Chief, the game has four playable characters—none of which are female. Halo 3's incredible success (arguably one of the most anticipated games in history, it sold more copies in the first 24 hours of its release than any video game before)—along with the success of other boy-oriented video games, such as Madden NFL 07 and Rockstar North Ltd.'s Grand Theft Auto: San Andreas—continues to fuel the belief that girls have little interest in gaming.

A look at recent console sales figures, however, may suggest otherwise. Of all the gaming systems on the market, 2007's best-selling video game console was the Nintendo DS. A handheld system released in 2004, the Nintendo DS managed to outsell the more recent releases of the Xbox 360 and Playstation 3. The system's best-selling video game happens to be a real-time pet simulator called Nintendogs, in which players assume the role of a pet owner and trainer. Lacking any element of conflict or aggression, the game is, not surprisingly, most popular among young girls. In fact, almost all of the Nintendo DS system's best-selling games are either girl-oriented (in that they include some element of caregiving or teaching), as in Nintendo's Animal Crossing: Wild World or Game Freak's Pokémon Diamond and Pearl; or they fall under the girl-friendly category of fantasy violence, as in Nintendo's New Super Mario Bros. or Super Princess Peach (the first game to feature the popular Mario series character as the main protagonist). Nintendo designed its DS handheld console and games if not specifically for girls, then at least with the intention to attract female gamers in a way that other video game companies have yet to attempt.

Nintendo's most recent console, the Nintendo Wii, affirms the company's efforts to make video games more accessible to females. The aesthetics of the console are even suggestive of femininity: with its sleek and crisp-white design that sits vertically in a cradle, the system conjures typically Western symbolism of purity and innocence often associated with women (think of a wedding gown, for instance). Like the Nintendo DS, the Wii also offers a variety of games designed specifically for girls, such as Majesco Entertainment's Cooking Mama: Cook Off and Electronic Arts Inc.'s The Sims 2: Pets. The majority of Wii games, however, are designed to appeal to both genders, as well as all ages and ethnicities, which has become the console's main marketing message. To this end, the Wii includes a feature enabling players to create their own avatars, called Miis, which can be used as active characters in a number of Nintendo games. Among these games is the bundled Wii Sports (sold with the console), a combination game that includes baseball, bowling, boxing, golf, and of course, tennis.

With the Nintendo Wii and *Wii Sports* the video game industry has come full circle, returning to the nonaggressive and gender-neutral game designs that were its foundation. Although the violent motifs—attractive to boys and boring to girls—that emerged with the second-generation video games are still prominent, the Girls' Games Movement sparked a revolution in video game content. There has since been a steady increase in games made to appeal to girls and women that include female avatars and themes such as caregiving, teaching, singing, dancing, and fashion design. Girl gamers and game designers have fought hard to stay in the game (or video game in this case), and although many continue to think of video games as part of boy culture today, they may simply be thought of as popular culture tomorrow.

Further Reading

Cassell, Justine, and Henry Jenkins, eds. *From Barbie to Mortal Kombat: Gender and Computer Games.* Cambridge, MA: MIT Press, 1999.

Entertainment Software Association. "Industry Facts." http://www.theesa.com/facts/index.asp (accessed March 9, 2009).

Entertainment Software Association of Canada Web Site. "Facts and Research: Essential Facts about the Canadian Computer and Videogame Industry." http://www.theesa.ca/pdf/esa_e.pdf (accessed March 2008).

Kent, Steven L. "Super Mario Nation." In *The Medium of the Videogame,* edited by Mark J. P. Wolf, 35–48. Austin, TX: University of Texas Press, 1997.

Kerr, Aphra. *The Business and Culture of Digital Games: Gamework/Gameplay.* London: Sage Publications, Ltd., 2006.

Michèle Rackham

Video Games and Violence

Video games invaded the North American market in the mid-1980s. Very soon, the marketers of these games started including violence in them. Soon after their invention, the U.S. Army started using them to train their young recruits. After using a video game named Doom, the rate of soldiers that could actually kill other human beings went up from 50 percent to 90 percent (Grossman, 1998). Doom proved to be a First Person Shooter (FPS) video game that could be considered a murder simulator. It had the objective of breaking down the inhibitions that soldiers had against killing, and of increasing their "killer-efficiency."

In 2003, the global sales of the industry producing and marketing video games exceeded 18 billion dollars a year, more than television and movies together. It was the fastest-growing sector in the entertainment industry, second only to music in profitability. Violence became so popular that in 2008, across North America, half of 9 to 12-year-old kids could play FPS video games, also called killer games. After playing such games, researchers found measurable decreases in prosocial behaviors, a 43 percent increase in aggressive thoughts, and a 17 percent increase in violent retaliation to provocation. Playing violent video games accounts for 13–22 percent of the variance in teenagers' violent behavior, a higher impact than smoking cigarette, which accounts for 14 percent of the variance in lung cancer. Lt. Col. Dave Grossman, who has been a psychologist for the U.S. Army for 20 years, has described how video games affect brain functioning. His two books show how and why video games actually give players the skill, the will, and the thrill to kill. Apart from the tendency of video games to arouse aggression, these games provide little mental stimulation to the brain's frontal lobe, an area that plays an important role in the repression of antisocial impulses. A lack of stimulation before the age of 20 prevents the neurons from thickening and connecting, thereby impairing the brain's ability to control such impulses as violence and aggression.

In December 2007, the (German) Society for Scientific Discussion of Psychotherapy (GwG) proposed a ban on violent video games. The GwG is the largest organization of its type in Europe. It stated that brutal computer games destroy compassion and asked European parents to avoid killer games as gifts for children. Psychotherapists demanded the prohibition of games in which young people are rewarded for the killing and torture of human beings. They believed that simply labeling videos as shooter games does not make them less damaging. The GwG also mentioned that media literacy frequently functions as a smokescreen for the industry.

For most young players, violence-promoting games are a catastrophe from the standpoint of their psychological development. Many specialized psychotherapists working in counseling centers and schools have witnessed the profound damages to children and teens. They believe these games hurt souls just like landmines hurt bodies. Some believe that child abuse by the media has reached such a scale in recent years that political decision makers must take action without delay. In 2007, the news reported 37 school shootings in the United States alone. Tolerance for the commercialization of killer games allows children and teens to lose contact with reality, to increase their own frustration, and to punish innocent people around them, including members of their own family. German psychotherapists agree with U.S. pediatricians, psychologists, criminologists, and scientists who point at the entertainment industry's responsibility for the increase of youth violence. Many believe that the production, sale, and marketing of killer games should be legally prohibited and become liable to prosecution.

After being immersed for hours and days in a brutal world, after using destruction and killing as amusement and fascination, an increasing number of young children are losing their natural compassion. The younger they are, the more deeply they are affected. They behave more aggressively and find no interest in solidarity. An increasing number of teenagers spend more time with killer games than in school. And more parents become helpless and desperate when trying to compete with the power of the media. Killer games also provide a new device that helps avoid parents' monitoring. When clicking the escape icon, the killer game disappears from the computer screen and is replaced by a game of solitaire.

German psychotherapists note that the concept of media literacy has been manipulated by the media industry for a long time. Big media funds the production of "media literacy" kits for schools. To critics, such educational tools are biased enough that they avoid blaming the industry that makes money by intoxicating kids with violence. In some North American states, the video game industry has firmly opposed any regulation of sales of violent games to minors. Where such regulations have been adopted, the industry's lawyers have challenged them in court, arguing that they deny them freedom of expression, protected by the First Amendment of the U.S. Constitution. Some industry advocates argue that "prohibition increases the appeal." Other advo-cates argue that computer games are "objects of cultural value." Killing and violence can thus be accepted as an "artistic convention." Educators and parents answer that the video game industry, like other members of the global village, has the responsibility of promoting a culture of cooperation, of human rights, and of peace, instead of conditioning youth to find pleasure in killing human beings.

Further Reading

Grossman, Lt-Col Dave. "Trained to Kill." http://www.killology.com/print/print
_trainedtokill.htm (accessed April 3, 2008).
Rich, Michael. "Violent Video Games Testimony." http://www.aap.org/advocacy/
rich-videogameviolence.pdf (accessed April 3, 2008).
Robinson, Thomas N. "Effects of Reducing Children's Television and Video Game
Use on Aggressive Behavior." *Journal of the AMA.* http://www.edupax.org/
Assets/divers/documentation/4_defi/SMARTAggressivity.pdf.

Jacques Brodeur

SECTION 12

Boys and School

African American Male Adolescents and School

By the time African American males reach adolescence, they are aware of the negative messages and images that society has of them. As a result, many of these youth begin to internalize these messages (Duncan and Jackson, 2007). Thus, African American males have become disenfranchised in schools across America for many reasons. However, in order to affirm the positive identities of African American male adolescents, it has been suggested that measures can be taken to incorporate their cultural heritage into the school curriculum by introducing "ethnic studies courses, ethnic celebrations, and inviting guest speakers from the community" (Hipolito-Delgado and Lee, 2007). These activities can assist in instilling a sense of community and pride in these young men, thus aiding in a positive sense of self (Grantham and Ford, 2003). Teaching young African American male adolescents about their ancestors may give them a foundation for understanding their origin and what they must do to continue to succeed in life (Newman, Myers, Newman, Lohman, and Smith, 2000). Whiting (2006) also suggests that incorporating career days and leadership development workshops led primarily by African Americans might be a way to motivate students to succeed. School counselors can also play a vital role in the success of African American male adolescents.

There are countless theories that school counselors can use in their work with African American male adolescents. One such theory is the theory of empowerment, which can be used in small group counseling sessions as well as individual sessions (Hipolito-Delgado and Lee, 2007). This theory allows students to become actively involved in their schooling process, and it can have positive effects on students' overall identity development. Given our experience, this may be the preferred style of delivering messages to adolescents as it fosters school counselors' understanding of students' experiences in a respectful manner. Equally important is the need for role models in the lives of these young men. African American adolescents often lack positive role models in their lives. African American male role models can assist in fostering positive identities in African American male youth. Lee (2003) asserts that competent African American males are the only ones in a position to teach male youth how to be men. Furthermore, being connected to one's community can also be beneficial.

Community service and community leadership is another strategy that can assist African American adolescents. Building strong ties to the community can give adolescent males a sense of pride and responsibility to their community and foster a greater sense of self (Bailey and Paisley, 2004).

There are countless things one can do to assist African American adolescent males in their academic and career success. There are also strategies that young men can take in conjunction with their school counselors to improve academic success. Ideas include:

- Young African American males must be aware of their academic standing in high school. College recruiters look closely at grade-point averages; particularly the grades received in the junior year.
- Students need to stay abreast of programs that are there to assist them. If they are interested in a particular field, students should talk to their school counselor as soon as possible about programs at local universities, community colleges, and in the community that would aid in the development of their *chosen* field.
- Students need to understand that their sophomore year in high school should be spent preparing to take the ACT exam in the junior year of high school. Taking the ACT exam in the junior year is vital because if students do not get the score they desired, they can apply to retake the exam early the senior year.
- Advanced placement (AP) classes are also a good step if students are interested in going to a four-year university. AP classes can really prepare students for the academic coursework that they will face in college.
- Students need to get involved in extracurricular activities and community service activities. This makes them more well-rounded students and college applicants. It's not enough to get good grades; students need to also be flexible enough to balance extracurricular activities.
- Students should complete a career interest inventory. School counselors have access to many different online tests that are designed to find the best matches between students' personal interests and different career options. Once there is an idea of a good match, the school counselor can then give students additional information regarding the career of their choice.
- Students should also develop professional relationships. School counselors are skilled in developing relationships with community members. As such, they may be able to pair students with mentors who may allow students to shadow them at work, which would give them a better idea of what it is like to work in a career similar to their mentor's.
- Students should get to know their school counselor. School counselors often have information about college nights, financial aid, and summer programs that could be vital to academic and career development.

Further Reading

Bailey, Deryl F., and Pamela O. Paisley. 2004. Developing and nurturing excellence in African American male adolescents. *Journal of Counseling and Development*, 82(1): 10–18.

Duncan, Greg A., and R. Jackson. Making a way out of no way: Black male students at City High School. In J. Kincheloe & K. Hayes, eds. *Teaching city kids: Understanding and appreciating them.* New York: Peter Lang, 2007, pp.109–119.

Grantham, Tareck C., and Donna Y. Ford. 2003. Beyond self-concept and self-esteem for African-American students: Improving racial identity improves achievement. *High School Journal*, 87(1): 18–29.

Hipolito-Delgado, Carlos P., and Courtland C. Lee. 2007. Empowerment theory for the professional school counselor: A manifesto for what really matters. *Professional School Counseling*, 10(4): 327–333.

Lee, Courtland C. 2003. Empowering young Black males—III: A systematic modular training program for Black male children and adolescents. Greensboro, NC: ERIC Counseling and Student Services Clearinghouse. (ERIC Document No. ED473749.) Retrieved Feb. 7, 2008, from ERIC database.

Lee, Courtland C. 2005. Urban school counseling: Context, characteristics, and competencies. *Professional School Counseling*, 8(3): 184–189.

Martin, Don, Magy Martin, Suzanne Gibson, and Jonathan Wilkins. 2007. Increasing prosocial behavior and academic achievement among adolescent African American males. *Adolescence*, 42: 689–698.

Milsom, Amy, and Pamela Paisley. 2007. Group work as an essential contribution to transforming school counseling. *Journal for Specialist in Group Work*, 32(1): 9–14.

Newman, Barbara M., Mary C. Myers, Philip R. Newman, Brenda J. Lohman, and Victoria L. Smith. 2000. The transition to high school for academically promising, urban, low-income African American youth. *Adolescence*, 35:45–66.

Perry, Theresa, Claude Steele, and Amy Hilliard. *Young, gifted, and Black: Promoting high achievement of African-American students.* Boston: Beacon Press, 2003.

Polite, Vernon C., and Earl J. Davis, eds. *African-American males in school and society: Practices and policies for effective education.* New York: Teachers College Press, 2001.

White, Nathan J., and Dixon A. Rayle. 2007. Strong teens: A school-based small group experience for African American males. *The Journal for Specialists in Group Work*, 32(2): 178–189.

Whiting, Gilman W. 2006. From at risk to at promise: Developing scholar identities among Black males. *Journal of Secondary Gifted Education*, 17(4): 222–229.

Delila Owens and Malik S. Henfield

African American Boys and Special Education Services

In truth, special education is a service. Its purpose is to provide educational support and services to students (between the ages of 3 and 21) with proven disabilities (as classified by a child study team) and to educate the student according to an individualized education plan (IEP). The goal of special education is to educate such students to enable them to lead successful and productive lives in the future. In practice, many teachers and school administrators think of special education as a place where Black and African American males (in particular) are separated from the typical students and are offered basic skills and remedial instruction from workbooks and dittos. This watered-down approach to teaching is limiting and stigmatizing, often preparing these students to become unskilled laborers who perform menial jobs as adults instead of raising the educational expectations for these young men to become professionals, such as architects, doctors, educators, lawyers, and scientists.

Maybe this image of special education exists because prior to 1975 public schools could legally deny children with special needs. Without access to the public schools, families looked for alternatives. Some families would send their children away to special private schools, place them into state-operated institutions, or restrict their young to stay within the home. Perhaps this explains why people consider special education a place—for nearly 100 years, children with special needs were housed and/or educated separately from the public. In fact, many of those alternative places were substandard classrooms, shoddy schools, or buildings in disrepair.

Fast forward to the twenty-first century and there are still thousands of schoolchildren being educated separately from their general education peers—in a special corner within the classroom, pulled out and taken to the resource room, or within self-contained classes. These figures show an obvious overrepresentation of Black males within the special education system (Sen, 2006). This leads to the question of why there are so many Black and African American males receiving special education services. Before answering that question, a brief history about special education in the United States is in order.

Following the pinnacle of the 1960s Civil Rights Movement, and its demands for fairness and equality, the United States Congress passed a law requiring schools to admit and educate children with disabilities. In 1975, the United States Congress passed Public Law 94-142, The Education for All Handicapped Children's Act (PL 94-142). This law made it illegal for public schools to deny the admittance of children with special needs. PL 94-142 gave thousands of youngsters a chance to enroll in public schools and receive an education at no additional financial cost to them or to their families.

PL 94-142 also mandated that schools provide instruction in the Least Restrictive Environment (LRE). This meant (where possible) educating students with disabilities in the general education classroom—not the resource room—alongside their peers without disabilities. Under LRE, students with disabilities are only separated from their general education peers when their needs cannot be met inside of the classroom with supplemental materials, accommodations and modifications, related services, resources, and teachers. In other words, special education services come to the student in the general education classroom instead of sending the student to a place where the services are delivered. Although LRE has been around since PL-94-142, today this learning arrangement is called *inclusion.*

As the population of students grew and their needs changed, in 1990 and later in 1997, Congress revised, reissued, and renamed the old law to PL 105-17 The Individuals with Disabilities Education Act (IDEA). Despite IDEA, Black and African American males (in particular) continue to receive special education services apart from classmates without disabilities.

Reasons for the Overrepresentation

There are several reasons for the overrepresentation of Black and African American males in special education. One reason is racial bias and misperception of Black culture. Racism has a long, ugly, history in the United States. Many public school teachers and special education professionals—most of whom are White—have little firsthand knowledge of or relating to Black and African American males. Teachers and special education professionals rarely visit or live among the students whom they serve. Due to a lack of shared experiences with Black and African American males, most school professionals are unaware of the realities of where and how Black males live. This leads to mistaking popular media for reality. The misperceptions of Black culture stem from sources such as HBO's *The Wire,* Black Entertainment Television (BET), and the evening news. These instances of popular culture convey incorrect images of deficiency and depravity about Black life. In turn, education professionals may view Black males as intimidating, incapable of high achievement, and in need of special education services due to the misrepresentation and sensationalism of the media. True, some students are poor economically, with countless living in cities, but through the school, students and their families have frequent access to various resources such as civic and social service agencies, libraries, and businesses, which thrive and offer a range of positive opportunities.

A second reason for the overrepresentation is teachers' lack of effective and relevant instruction. The majority of teachers in the United States are White middle-class females unaware of teaching and learning styles preferred by African American males. Several researchers and scholars contend that schooling in the United States favors White middle-class values that align more with teachers' backgrounds than Black male students' experiences. In response to this mismatch, during the 1970s, teacher education programs began adding topics about multiculturalism to the curriculum to help teachers understand diversity. Later in the 1980s, scholars began stressing the existence of learning and teaching styles based upon Black culture. Scholars suggested Black males' preference for lively and active instruction. Jawanza Kunjufu, who has studied and written extensively about African American males, routinely informs teachers, families, and other professionals who work with youngsters about the high energy level of Black males. He emphasizes that teachers who want to be effective with African American male students must modify traditional teaching methods to include movement, group work, music, and drama. Other experts agree, indicating that Black students benefit from learning activities that involve call and response, repetition, change in speech pace, catchy statements, gestures, and symbolism that lets students freely participate. Since many teachers represent mainstream culture and behaviors, and there is a large emphasis on standardized testing, particularly in light of No Child Left Behind, other nontraditional methods are absent from the classroom.

Teachers who remain unaware of such teaching methods or are unwilling to learn relevant strategies are inclined to rely upon their cultural norms to teach and interpret student behavior. Teachers who are unfamiliar with the values that Black males bring to school frequently refer them for special education services due to misperceptions in learning styles, behaviors, and communication.

A third reason for the overrepresentation of Black males receiving special education services is due to unfair evaluation procedures. A trained team of professionals (sometimes called Student Support, Child Study Team, or IEP Team) is responsible for reviewing the teacher referral and administering diagnostic tests to determine eligibility. For both the referral and tests, professionals often rely upon professional judgment. Because such opinions are not based upon verifiable biological data, this allows for personal subjectivities and misperceptions to influence the eligibility process.

Test bias is another factor contributing to unfair evaluations. Depending upon the details of the referral, assessments such as the Rorschach, Stanford-Binet, and Wechsler Intelligence are commonly used. Yet, mainstream values have long served as the basis for test questions and procedures. Reliance upon middle-class values usually contrasts with African American norms, which makes the test unfair to African Americans. There is further test bias when determining results because Black students' performances are compared with that of White students, while White students' results are compared with that of White students. Researchers and psychologists acknowledge that intelligence tests deal unfairly with ethnic and racial groups—and still they are used.

Outcomes from the Overrepresentation

African American male students are overrepresented receiving special education services due in part to cultural bias along with unsuitable teaching and unfair testing methods. Although the original purpose of special education is to help students with proven disabilities receive an education to become productive adults, the outcome of receiving special education services for African American males is frequently negative. The outcome may be negative because it labels students as disabled—a label that is difficult to lose. Much of the eligibility determination occurs when males are in middle school, between the ages of 11 and 14 (Jones and Menchetti, 2001). Once given the special education designation, fewer than 10 percent of students lose such classification (Kunjufu, 2005). This means African American males in particular will maintain their association with being disabled. Peers and adults who are unaware of what it means to have a disability routinely use disability labels, such as *handicapped, special education student,* or *emotionally disturbed person,* which overshadows the student's identity and is stigmatizing.

Black males' participation in special education programs has additional negative outcomes. Approximately 63 percent of male students classified as disabled under IDEA receive their high school diplomas (OCR, 2006), while 27 percent of African American males receiving special services graduate from high school (Kunjufu, 2005). With drugs such as Ritalin and Adderal typically prescribed for behavioral disorders in students, it is no wonder that as children and as adults they are at risk for drug abuse, addiction, and criminal behavior. For many Black males, special education has become a *school-to-prison* pipeline. Upward of 90 percent of adjudicated youth are believed eligible for special education services (Tulman, 2008), and as adults, most Black males will earn a GED while incarcerated (Smith, 2005).

Racial bias, racial profiling by the criminal justice system, and inadequate education can lead to crime later in life for African American males. Further, the consequences of these statistics are devastating to the community in part

---

Actions to Reduce the Number of African American Students in Special Education Courses

Here is some advice that will help African American students cut down on the disproportionate number of them who are placed in special education courses.

Regardless of whether you are receiving special education services or learning from a general education curriculum, you can help alleviate the overrepresentation of Black and African American students in special education programs. Learn about President Clinton's 1997 Race Initiative. This project was designed to urge U.S. citizens to dialogue, research, and act to examine race relations in the country. Ask your teachers and friends to agree to work with you or alone to explore Black culture, race, and bias. The exploration will help everyone involved to begin to understand what life is actually like for people unlike themselves instead of relying upon misinformation.

Be your own advocate. A great way to advocate for yourself begins with discovering your strengths and weaknesses. Make a list of your skills and needs, take a personality test, or complete a learning styles inventory. Then share that information with your instructors when you are struggling, requesting that they use practices and activities that support your strengths. Consider asking for tests and assessments that are unbiased as well. Many schools and universities have centers, programs, and initiatives to assist students who need extra help and academic resources.

Advocate for other people. Identify services in your community or elsewhere, and then work to introduce those programs to people. Whether or not you are receiving special education services, self-advocacy is a useful strategy for every student. If you are unable to find helpful services and programs, talk to your teachers, professors, or school administrators about sponsoring or providing a service. Another idea is to volunteer through a national service program such as AmeriCorps. Many of today's African American students, especially individuals receiving special education services, could benefit greatly from additional positive role models, supportive siblings, encouraging mentors, organized programs, and community services.

Think about becoming a teacher. There is a teacher shortage in the United States, especially among males and men of color, in the primary grades. Investigate programs, such as Call Me MISTER and Teach for America, that are created to increase the pool of available classroom teachers. Not only is it important for Black males to have access to male teachers, but also all students would benefit from a greater diversity of schoolteachers. New generations of men need to step up to the challenge of educating the youth, serve as positive role models, and broaden the spectrum of education professionals.

Black and African American males are overrepresented and are receiving segregated special education services in public K–12 education. Just knowing about the situation is important; however, working to alleviate this overrepresentation may prevent someone from being mislabeled or dropping out of school—your efforts may assist in rebuilding a young man's life.

because these outcomes reduce the number of Black males in families and positive images of Black males.

The Types of Referrals

A student becomes eligible for special education services when it has been determined that he or she has a disability. Although a family member or another concerned person may request special education services for a student, a classroom teacher usually requests the evaluation called a referral. There are 13 categories of disabilities recognized in IDEA. Of the disabilities, African American males are most often identified as having specific learning disability (SLD), mild mental retardation (MMR; also called educable mental retardation or cognitive impairment), and serious emotional disturbance (SED). Depending upon the state, other terms may be used, but collectively they are considered high-incidence disabilities because they rely more upon subjective judgment (e.g., teacher's interpretation of student behaviors) than empirical tests and are the basis for qualifying most of the students for special education. Many times overlooked when determining high-incidence disability are poor or ineffective teaching. As far back as 1968, the U.S. Office of Education reported that upward of 80 percent of the students in MMR classes included African American males. In recent years, it is estimated that close to 20,000 African American male students are inappropriately classified as mentally retarded—suggesting a 300 percent over-classification in U.S. public schools (Holzman, 2006).

Further Reading

Harry, Beth, and Janette K. Klingner. *Why Are So Many Minority Students in Special Education?: Understanding Race & Disability in Schools.* New York; London: Teachers College Press, 2006.

Holzman, Michael. *Public Education and Black Male Students: The 2006 State Report Card.* Cambridge, MA: The Schott Foundation, 2006.

Jones, Lee, and Menchetti. "Identification of Variables Contributing to Definitions of Mild and Moderate Mental Retardation in Florida." *Journal of Black Studies,* 2001; 31(5): 619.

Kunjufu, Jawanza. *Keeping Black Boys Out of Special Education.* Chicago: African American Images, 2005.

Noguera, Pedro Antonio. The Trouble with Black Boys: The Role and Influence of Environmental and Cultural Factors on the Academic Performance of African American Males [Online 2002]. In *Motion Magazine* <http://www.inmotionmagazine.com/er/pntroub1.html>.

Office for Civil Rights. *2006 Civil Rights Data Collection.* U.S. Department of Education, 2006.

Sen, Rinku. *A Positive Future for Black Boys: Building the Movement.* Cambridge, MA: The Schott Foundation for Public Education, 2006.

Smith, Rosa A. "Building a Positive Future for Black Boys." *American School Board Journal,* 2005; 192(9): 26–28.

Tulman, Joseph B. "Time to Reverse the School-to-Prison Pipeline." *Policy & Practice of Public Human Services,* 2008; 66(1): 22–27.

Danné E. Davis and Lauren Smith

Attitudes toward School

Much of the press has lamented the supposed backslide of boys' academic success in the classroom. This concern comes from statistics that indicate girls generally have greater academic success, at least with regard to test scores, grades, and graduation rates. Some researchers, however, argue that boys are not doing worse in school, girls are simply doing better. Regardless, boys still consistently perform better in areas such as math and science. And although the class makeup in undergraduate institutions is evenly split between girls and boys, Ivy League colleges are still disproportionately male. Therefore, while girls are certainly making academic progress in all areas, boys are still largely succeeding as well.

Although there is some debate about the relative decline of boys' academic achievement, it is generally accepted that there are some sizeable differences in how boys and girls view and react to school. Academic success has been feminized among students, in that doing well in school is perceived to be a girl's activity. There is a tendency to view activities related to scholastic success such as making good grades, participating in class, and studying for tests as unmasculine. If a boy does engage in such behavior, he risks being made fun of by his peers and called a *nerd* or a *geek.* As a result, boys who try to perform well in school often want attention diverted from their activities. In one study, the researcher found that two-thirds of boys who participated in school assignments and tried to learn went to great lengths to avoid appearing studious to their peers. In an effort to divert attention from their efforts, they teased other students, downplayed their success, or engaged in disruptive behavior to distract fellow classmates.

Sometimes boys try to offset the perceived femininity of their scholastic efforts by displaying masculinity and toughness through other ways. This can be achieved either legitimately or illegitimately. Legitimate displays of masculinity are usually tied to sports where boys can look athletic, strong, and fast. Other times, however, boys try to look manly to their peers by engaging in illegitimate aggressive behavior. Bullying and fighting are just a few of the unacceptable ways boys try to assert their manliness. In addition to attempting to offset geek status through sports, boys may also form peer groups that support and defend their endeavors, regardless of what they may be. This safety in numbers approach allows boys to pursue academic accomplishments without being ostracized completely.

Interestingly, boys still strive to outdo their female peers in schoolwork. Apparently, claiming to be smarter than girls is not perceived as too feminine. Researchers have found that boys do this by inflating their SAT scores and bragging about their success in relation to their female peers. This paradox is interesting: boys cannot study or excel in school for fear of ridicule by other boys, but boys desire to be more academically successful than girls. In general, boys have a relatively high academic self-esteem even when their grades and/or test scores may not reflect the same view. That is, they believe that they are smart and will succeed in academic pursuits more so than females believe they will achieve success. Ironically, though, boys have less positive attitudes toward school when compared to girls. In contrast, girls are more likely to be doubtful and insecure about their academic potential, even in the face of repeated scholastic success. Additionally, female students are more likely to have positive attitudes toward school and knowledge acquisition.

Two possible motives for boys' rejection of academic work have been pinpointed. First, rejecting schoolwork gives boys an excuse for failure. If a boy puts in the hours studying for a test and fails, it is much harder to deal with than if he fails without putting forth the effort. If a boy never actually tries to succeed, disappointment in failing to meet higher expectations can assumedly be avoided. Second, as is previously mentioned, boys reject academic work because it helps them appear masculine to their friends. This is especially true in situations where sports accomplishments or supportive peer groups are not present. It has been discovered that rural and inner city boys are more at risk than their counterparts for exhibiting poor academic performance. The strong focus on masculinity in these environments is one potential explanation for this discrepancy.

Boys generally are more confident in their academic efforts yet exhibit disinterest in scholastic pursuits. This is largely due to the desire to look tough and is driven by the motivation to not appear feminine to one's friends. Additionally, avoidance of effort provides an excuse for failure. Boys do wish to appear successful, especially to girls, but do not wish to look geeky or nerdy by displaying the studious behavior necessary to succeed. Although research has detected differences in attitudes and academic accomplishments between girls and boys, all students do not, of course, fit this generalization. In the future, continued research will shed light on the subject by tracking the progress of both American girls and boys as compared with one another and in relation to their international peers.

Further Reading

Rivers, Caryl and Rosalind Chait Barnett. "The Myth of 'The Boy Crisis.'" *The Washington Post*, April 9, 2006.
Tyre, Peg. "The Boy Crisis." *Newsweek*, January 30, 2006.

Carly T. McKenzie

Boys and Their Stories

We live stories all the time. We attend to the stories of others. We linger in the stories of dreams, imagination, fantasy, and memory. We read stories in school and at home; we hear stories from friends and strangers; we view stories on television, the Internet and movie screens; we understand the past in terms of stories, just as we seek to understand the future in stories. We explain our actions in stories, and we tell the same stories over and over at family gatherings. Our understanding of identities, our beliefs and values, our accounts of emotional and psychological needs and desires are all woven through and through with stories. But, in spite of the pervasive importance of stories in our lives, most of us have great difficulty telling our own stories. Most of us have little confidence about our abilities as story-makers.

Autobiography means "to write one's own life" (*auto* = self, *bio* = life, and *graphy* = writing). Autobiography is a way of understanding lived and living experiences. To write a life is to open up ways for understanding both our experiences as well as exploring other possibilities for living. We often think that only famous people can write autobiographies, but we all live in the world autobiographically; our writing and speaking are always autobiographical; we are all autobiographers. We need to pay more attention to our own stories because to write our own stories is to explore the experiences and situations that significantly shape us into the kind of people we are and might be.

Boys often do not write about their personal lived experiences. For generations, writing in diaries and journals has generally been connected with girls and women. Now, with personal Web sites and blogs and social networking sites such as Facebook, we have many new and inviting opportunities for writing autobiographically, and boys are beginning to explore possibilities for writing about their lives in more creative ways.

We do not need to imitate the kinds of stories that we read in novels or watch on TV. We can write the stories of our own daily lives. We can write about the events, experiences, and emotions of growing up in our own homes, neighborhoods, schools, and towns. We can write about the stories and people that are personally meaningful to us. By engaging in autobiographical writing, we not only can learn to share our stories with others, but also we can learn from the stories of others.

Boys are often caught up in cultural roles for living. Boys often seek to imitate limited cultural expectations or images of being a boy or a man. We grow up with images of warriors, adventurers, and cowboys; we grow up with images of heterosexual, muscular, square-jawed men who rescue the world with their strength, wily wits, and rugged good looks! We grow up with images of men who do not cry, confess fear, or show weakness. Most boys have great difficulty in navigating these roles that are constructed again and again in the popular culture, but they seldom realize that they do not need to imitate these narrow kinds of roles. Boys can write autobiographically about their own daily lived experiences in the specific locations where they dwell; and from these local locations, they can seek to understand their relationships to others in their locations. In other words, they can simply refuse the authority of stereotypical or popular narratives to write them in given positions. Instead, they can write their stories as diverse narratives full of possibilities.

Autobiographical writing is always both personal and public, and we need to write autobiographically in order to connect with others. The two most frequently used words in the English language are the pronouns *I* and *you*. Often we think that autobiography is all about the *I*, but in fact we are always connected to numerous other people. So when we write from the perspective of *I*, we are really writing about our relationships or connections with many people whom we perceive as *you*. Of course, all those *you's* each individually understand themselves as *I's*. So, in our autobiographies, we are writing ourselves, our sense of identities, and possibilities as creative people among other creative people in the world.

If we do not learn to appreciate the significance of our own lived experiences, then we will always live in the frustrating illusions of fictive creations shaped in the images of popular and dominant cultures. In order to know the possibilities for our unique presence in the world, we need to be connected to words that represent as well as challenge our daily understandings of who we are and who we are becoming. We need to know our stories before we can attend to the stories of others with respect and care. Autobiography is a process of becoming in the world, a process of growing through language and writing.

Autobiography is frequently criticized as too personal and emotional, too self-centered or self-indulgent, too confessional or revealing. Autobiographical writing frequently leaves people feeling that they are being told things they do not want to hear or know, but we need to compose and tell our stories as creative ways of growing in humanness. We need to question our understanding of who we are in the world. We need opportunities to consider other versions of identity. We need to tell our stories more. And we need to tell more stories. In the end, the stories we write and tell about our lived experiences will teach us how to live with more creativity, confidence, imagination, and truthfulness. For example, there is a growing autobiographical literature by men who are remembering their relationships with their fathers, and who often feel wounded by the lack of close, emotional relationship that they had with their fathers. Sons and fathers need to write autobiographically as a way to communicate more truthfully and personally with one another.

We can write about our names, memories, childhood objects, favorite places, dreams, family photographs, and pets. We can write our funniest stories, or the stories about times we were upset, or we learned something, or we did something stupid. We can interview family members and friends. There are endless possibilities for writing our stories, just as there are endless stories. Instead of being caught up in somebody else's cultural preconceptions for whom boys are and can be, we can write autobiographically and, thereby, acknowledge how the cultures and identities of boys are always in process, always being written in new ways, always being created.

Further Reading

Amis, Martin. *Experience*. New York: Hyperion, 2000.
Baldwin, Christina. *Storycatcher: Making Sense of Our Lives through the Power and Practice of Story*. Novato, CA: New World Library, 2005.
Gosse, Douglas. *Jackytar*. St. John's, NL: Jesperson Publishing, 2005.

King, Thomas. *The Truth about Stories: A Native Narrative.* Toronto, ON: House of Anansi Press, 2003.

Shields, David. *Enough about You: Adventures in Autobiography.* New York: Simon & Schuster, 2002.

Carl Leggo

Feminization of Schools

It has almost become a trend in recent years to describe shifts in Western societies in terms of gender differentiation that seems to provide one with a new interpretive tool to look at different social phenomena, but which maintains some bias that one is able to observe in classical binary oppositions of male-female. From the feminization of single parenthood to the feminization of poverty and work, certain social *failings* have thus come to collocate with feminine in a manner that might suggest recapturing of some of the old essentialist determinations that sought explication in organic grounds such as biology. Now the feminization of schools has joined in the discourses of gendered failings, with specific relation to an assumed crisis that affects boys who seem to fall behind their female peers in the area of school performance and achievement. A boy crisis in schools is said to be an effect of educational settings that are becoming more feminized in different ways.

Parallel to the feminization of schools and how boys are falling behind girls discussions, one could also refer to another discourse of crisis, which frames the discussions around how the United States is falling behind other industrial nations in the field of mathematics and the sciences. Two elements are involved here. The first concerns the belief that competitiveness is a male thing, so when the United States seems to lose its competitive edge over other nations, instead of grounding such discussions in analyses of global economic changes and shifting political factors, some may refer to how this external failure is an association of the changing gender scenery within the schools. The other element is traditional projection that boys, because of their inherent dispositions, are more likely to study sciences and mathematics and to excel in them—the classical opposition between mind and soul, abstraction and hands-on practicality. One should investigate the current gender tendencies to study hard sciences, which may lead to a picture that is relatively less straight forward than the image of girls staying home and boys venturing into the world outside.

The issue has also been critiqued in terms of the depiction of boys as homogeneous representation in relation to a crisis in schools. The implications of such crisis differ considerably across ethno-cultural groups. Dropout rates among African American boys are higher than that of White boys. Internal differentiations alike are glossed over to suggest a generalized boy underachievement versus a girl better achievement. Male students are heterogeneous because of obvious attributes such as socioeconomic background, ethno-cultural and linguistic identities, urban upbringing, and so on. Such variety could not be homogenized into a single marker of gender when comparison is made with the population of female students. In this respect homogenization could be seen as defensive response to a growing sense of crisis, a crisis that seems to affect the representation of primarily the White male. In this sense the crisis regains its global meaning of being a crisis of and in American society, some of whose manifestations are the uncertain economy, demographic changes within the United States, the challenge that the rise of other global powers may present, and so forth. In other words, and because of masculinist hegemony (maintaining dominance over women through census around what constitutes male roles and associations socially, economically, discursively, and politically), males could represent more readily the magnitude and extent of the crisis of the nation. However, the argument that we are making here seeks to examine the question at hand in a less straightforward and dichotomic (only two-sided like black and white) fashion to suggest a picture where cultural and political factors interplay in complex and diverse ways.

A New Gender Gap

According to recent surveys the gender gap of the 1960s in high schools has closed and it is now boys who fall far behind girls. According to National Assessment of Educational Progress (NAEP), girls outscored boys in reading and writing tests between the years 2002 and 2007, and there was little difference between the scores of math and science assessments; moreover, more girls participated in school activities such as having memberships in prestigious societies and debate clubs. Recent reports underline that female students have displayed high self-esteem and school enjoyment. On the similar line, Manhattan Institute's nationwide research on high school graduation rates, *Leaving Boys Behind: Public High School Graduation Rates,* displays a big gender gap for the class of 2003. According to report while female students graduated at a rate of about 72 percent, graduation rate was only 65 percent for the male students. The gender gap between male and female graduation rates among African American and Hispanic populations is much higher. While 58 percent of Hispanic and 59 percent of African American females earned high school diplomas, only 49 percent and 48 percent of males in the same categories, respectively, graduated from high schools.

Discussions encompassing the boys' failure or new gender gap in education revolve around three major themes: feminization of school culture, female teacher domination, and gender-biased policies.

Feminization of School Culture

Although the word *female* refers to a biological category, the term *feminine* refers to a cultural construct and many of those traits traditionally attributed to women or girls in a given society. What is usually regarded as feminine in a particular society mainly counts on being different from what is considered as masculine or vice versa. Culturally determined femininity encompasses gender roles and stereotypical generalizations ascribed to the female body such as being submissive, polite, caring, and good-looking. Although gender roles are not innate but learned, within the process of cultural integration, people are taught to believe that these traditionally attributed roles are naturally part of having a male or female body and need to be internalized.

All nerdy types of activities such as carrying heavy books, taking notes, obtaining high grades, doing homework properly, sitting still in front of the class, and answering to the questions are considered as girly and thus associated with femininity these days. All these attributions have become feminine and most boys do not want to fall under the category of feminine. Today, therefore, in high schools the image of the new nerd may be female. Although all culturally paired binary oppositions match masculinity with activity and femininity with passivity, in high schools this key othering principle has been challenged with the newly emerging idea of femininity, which means investment of energy in school. While American girls traditionally get higher grades, go beyond boys on many of the standardized tests, and dig up higher class ranks, in order not to be seen as feminine, boys develop antagonistic positions toward education and educational institutions. Resistance to dominant school culture by associating it being feminine or gay (without any reference to homosexuality) means frequent trips to school psychological counseling rooms for boys more than ever, which could be seen as another widening gap between boys and girls. Often boys are creating more problems and are put on pacifying drugs such as Ritalin. One could look at the overrepresentation of boys in school counseling in two ways: the first one is the pathologization of yet another aspect of underperforming in Western cultures where performance is key both at individual and collective levels. Performance as such is enforced in upbringing as well as in practical life of employment. The overrepresentation of boys in counseling is related to classroom discipline, challenges that teachers could hardly leave unaddressed, especially with over crowdedness as a major feature that goes hand in hand with the prescription of crises in public education. Thus, any disruption of a prescribed classroom discipline gets pathologized as a most practical solution to difficulty at which teachers find themselves having to perform multiple roles that neither their training nor their time seem to be able to accommodate satisfactorily. This is similar to how students with limited English proficiency get referred to special education classrooms for having an almost *de facto* learning impairment not distinguishable from other kinds of learning impairments such as reading. So counseling becomes the depositary that could respond, albeit unsatisfactorily, to classroom control and a crowdedness challenges. In this sense impairment gets expanded to include behavioral deficiencies that affect school performance, and not only inherent deficiencies that are usually thought to undermine learning and achievement.

Educational Policies and Feminist Interventions

Talking about the feminization of schools does not only suggest a shifting gendering of education, but it also emphasizes a causality that blames feminist (in favor of women) interventions in theory and pedagogy for the many failures that are said to have affected male students. According to critiques of feminist interventions, popular victimization of girls in educational policies (and public) created unfriendly school settings for boys. The Women's Educational Equity Act (WEEA), for example, was released in 1965 so as to encourage *equity* in educational policies. The Act was based on the common wisdom that educational activities and initiatives in the United States were unfair to girls (for more information see No Child Left Behind Act, 2001). In 1992 American Association of University Women (AAUW) released its report *How Schools Shortchange Girls* and described America's teenage girls as silenced and victimized in school settings. Women's advocacy groups, newspapers, and television programs wrote stories on the report and carried out an intense campaign to promote the idea that educational system did not provide equal opportunities for the female students. All those campaigns have become successful and the image of teenage girls as victims in need of new policies and extra funding has become the major concern for the government, education establishment, and also for the public. Eventually boys fall behind for the reason that their educational needs have not been addressed in educational policies; rather schools have been transformed to a more girl friendly environment.

On the other side of the spectrum, grounded on the feminist theories, it was claimed that instead of blaming *girl friendly* educational policies, one should look at how hegemonic masculine ideas and associations may have played a role in the conditions of boys in schools so much lamented today. In other words, schools may be seen more feminine not because of more empowered feminist presence, whether at the level of policy and planning or the day to day practice of teaching but because of, on the contrary, feminization stems from a challenged masculinist hegemony that sees in every confrontation to its un-contested domination a threat that is worthy of the name crisis, a concept which is hard to swallow. One effect of this displacement might be substitution of gender association when it comes to school related functions that have historically been identified as a male attribute (e.g., discipline, hard work, time management, etc.). These attributes would conjure up the image of the disciplined (male) soldier which is suggestive of male power and resilience. But this image almost disappears in a school setting where male power and resilience may be represented by a sense of resisting to become a good student and resisting to conform to school rules and generalizations as to what constitutes success. So a successful student, generally called nerd in popular culture and everyday school discourse, could now be called *gay* to suggest a feminine dimension to the hardworking type of students. And this labeling comes from male peers as well, not female teachers or girls. It is no longer the well-known game of labeling in group belongingness alone—hard working vs. lazy. It is also an extra genetic opposition that probably aims at reclaiming some of the comforts of easy explanations that rely on biological differentiations. This could result more from a displaced masculinist hegemony than a real transformation that feminism could have contributed. Gayness, therefore, could bear the mark of displaced masculinist hegemony rather than emulation of female gender roles in areas that have been historically or situationally associated with maleness (e.g., the army). So a nerd male student could be called gay by his male peers for nothing other than what they see in him as shifting from how masculinity, especially in urban settings, is configured today.

Female Teacher Domination

Division of labor in almost every society is highly gendered and political subject matter and cannot be thought independent from existing power relations. Biological traits of the sexes and socially enforced gender roles determine how and by whom the human activities are organized and performed (e.g., women take care of children; men work outside). In other words, translation of this view into labor organizations of societies appropriates gender-specific occupations, which in turn profiles the division of labor in a certain time period and context. Traditionally, teaching has been considered as a female occupation grounded on the assumption that women are inherently predispositioned for teaching profession because of their nurturing and care-giving nature.

Although female teachers have always outnumbered male teachers in schools, particularly in primary education, concerns about the representation of male teachers in school settings have become the center of attention for the last two decades along with the invention of a boys' crisis. According to one point of view, female teachers in school settings are one of the sources for the victimization of female students. The AAUW report advocates this premise by alerting readers to the issue that the majority of America's teachers are female and their patriarchally framed behavioral patterns make them favor boys. Thus, female students need more attention to regain their lost self-esteem.

It has been argued that numerical domination of female teachers also contributes to feminization of schools; therefore, this reinforces mismatch between boys and schooling. This idea is linked to inadequacy observed in emotional and psychological development of boys who lack male role models and thus alienate themselves from schools. According to this camp, particularly during the transition period to manhood, boys need male role models for identification and need confidantes who will show better understanding for their active nature. More often than not, for a female teacher a boy's energy in the classroom setting is a kind of potential obstacle having negative connotations such as creating troubles for the others and disturbing the quiet learning environment; furthermore, a female teacher rarely displays enthusiasm for a naturally energetic and active male student. Female teachers are generally quick to stigmatize such an active student as slow in learning or the one having behavioral problems. On the other hand, girls are seen as more ambitious to get an education, more willing to have responsibility and to participate in class; in essence, they are more academically engaged in school activities. Female students are mostly the ones who are academically inspired and who receive favored treatment from their teachers. Whereas female students' involvement in school activities, their success in group works and verbal skills are praised by their teachers; boys are told to sit still and behave more like these female students. Boys have grown negative attitudes toward schools since they are expected to correct their boyish behavior. They are less likely to take part in classroom activities, join school clubs, do their homework, and attend classes.

A parallel phenomenon could be found in how single parenting has been gradually feminized in the United States, and through it and because of it poverty as a psychological, socioeconomic articulation has also gained a feminized aspect. Both reference to the discourse of crises, which has expanded considerably since the 1980s; in other words the social and economic crises that have marked the U.S. society and culture have eventually been superimposed on gender roles and gender dispositions toward certain social functions. So the lack of a male figure is not only responsible for the disintegration of the social fabric because of the displacement of the traditional family unit, but it also contributes much to the failure in terms of underrepresentation of male teachers and the role model they could project to the benefit of male students.

One final point of critique and the sum of our approach toward boys crisis in education is how the cultural dimension of the question at hand usually gets explored, which mainly focuses on how gender and schooling takes on different manifestations across cultures. So, boys in culture X behave differently in the classroom from their peers in culture Z; or female teachers in culture A teach differently from their counterparts in culture B. What we have here is an understanding of culture as decimation along ethno-culture divide, rather than a formulation of culture as determination of gender (i.e., male vis-à-vis female cultures within a specific situational/functional context). It becomes possible to talk about boy culture in urban schools as an effect of gender rather than homogenization of the different male subcultures that are determined ethno-culturally. In other words it is culture that is informed situationally above and beyond its constituent decimated sources that could very well explain the variations in individual behaviors. It is a global culture, so to speak, rather than a specific culture that could explain how a boy culture at schools could differ from a girl culture.

Further Reading

American Association of University Women. *How Schools Shortchange Girls: A Study of Major Findings on Girls and Education.* Washington, DC: AAUW Educational Foundation, The Wellesley College Center for Research on Women, 1992.

Cleaver, Frances. *Masculinities Matter!: Men, Gender, and Development.* New York: Zed Books, 2002.

Educational Testing Service, *Differences in the Gender Gap: Comparisons across Racial/Ethnic Groups in Education and Work.* Princeton, NJ, 2001.

Francis, Becky, and Christine Skelton. *Reassessing Gender and Achievement: Questioning Contemporary Key Debates.* New York: Routledge, 2005.

Greene, Jay. *High School Graduation Rates in the United States Report.* Manhattan Institute, 2002.

Phillips, Melanie. "The Feminisation of Education." *Daily Mail, August 19, 2002.*

Pollack, William. *Real Boys: Rescuing Our Sons from the Myths of Boyhood*. New York: Owl Books, 1999.

Mustafa Sever and Sule Okuroglu

Getting Young Boys to Read

How can male students become engaged in reading and writing at school? In the last quarter of a century, boys are further behind academically in literacy than girls.

Meaningful Reading

The teaching of literacy involves understanding what topics interest boys and the various ways they learn. Educators need to be aware of the genre preferences of the books that boys choose. Many boys and girls do like reading novels; however, novels are just one type of literacy. Boys tend to enjoy nonfiction books because they engage them in learning about animals, other living things, and how things work. These types of books satisfy boys' curiosities about the world and provide relevant information to them. On the other hand, it is often thought that girls seem to like reading fiction books about relationships.

Many of the fiction books read in school involve more female lead characters than male lead characters. Most boys like reading fiction books with a male lead character. On the 50th anniversary edition (2002) of her classic novel *Henry Huggins,* author Beverly Cleary shared that she wrote the book in answer to her difficulty in finding fascinating books for boys when she was working as a children's librarian. There were very few books on the shelves those boys wanted to read. One day, a boy asked where would he find the books for boys like us? Beverly Cleary realized there were not any.

In the last 20 years, there have been many books published with a male as the lead character. Some of the relevant and enjoyable children's literature for boys with a lead male character include *Bud not Buddy* by Christopher Paul Curtis, *Holes* by Louis Sachar, and *Harry Potter* by J. K. Rowling. Another book series reluctant male readers as well as proficient boys seem to gravitate toward is the Captain Underpants Collection by Dave Pilkey.

Magazines, newspapers, game instructions, comic books, novels, graphic novels, picture books, and Web sites are all forms of literacy and they could fit into the category of school reading. Comics, comic books, and graphic novels are a popular choice of reading material especially for boys who are considered shy, reluctant, or struggling in reading. Some teachers have implemented using comics in the classroom and have had successful outcomes. While reading comic books and graphic novels, boys can visualize and create meaning as a result of the combination of images and words.

If multiple genres of literacy resources such as novels, picture books, magazines, newspapers, comic books, and instructional manuals were provided in the classroom, reading could be considered a pleasurable and engaging activity for many boys.

Boy Writing

It is important to understand the ways boys view writing and the components that can make writing meaningful and engaging for boys. Many boys struggle with writing because they find handwriting, getting their thoughts down on paper, and the mechanics of writing difficult. As a result, they do not enjoy writing. It is not possible for educators to ignore this generation of boy writers. Writing is an important skill that no boy and no human being can do without. It is critically essential to examine the writing process through the lens of a boy focusing on what is engaging them and what is not engaging them.

When writing, many boys like to include violence, risk-taking activities, sports, and humor (including bathroom humor) in their stories. If boys are constantly told by educators and administrators that they cannot include these boy engaging components, they will probably be turned off to writing.

Boys can learn to record their thoughts, stories they heard, or interesting pieces of real life information they observe or learn. Many boys would be encouraged to use it even more so if they could also draw in it (Fletcher, 2006). There are ways to make the writer's notebook boy friendly and therefore it does not need to be problematic for boys.

Struggles with Handwriting

The difficulty of actual handwriting for many boys connects to writing not being an enjoyable part of the school day. Approximately 50 percent of the school day, students are involved in some type of writing task. Meeting standards in handwriting is necessary. For example, students should be able to complete a normal amount of written work in the classroom, therefore meeting the standards of the teacher and the school curriculum. Half of the school day is a long time for a boy to have to be involved in writing, especially for those boys who struggle with it.

Neat handwriting, coming from brain maturation, is an area in which boys struggle. This can make it hard for them to get their thoughts down on paper. The producing of written text requires the connection of several skills, such as the coordination of forming letters, thinking of ideas, and structure in syntax. If the teacher constantly criticizes their handwriting, boys will not want to write at all.

IMs (Instant Messages) Are Writing

Boys might do instant messaging or texting at home or with a group of his friends, which is definitely promoting literacy. The instant messaging helps build stronger friendships between boys. Boys are able to express themselves through written text. It is also a social context for learning. Many boys choose to do instant messaging from home or a friend's home where they feel relaxed, not to be judged by a teacher or parent. Boys find it socially gratifying receiving instant messages. They can use anonymous screen names so the person who receives the instant message does not know who sent it. When boys instant message, their spelling is usually incorrect. They usually abbreviate words. Parents usually get concerned about what content their son is instant messaging, their poor spelling, and lack of punctuation.

With increased books, manga, anime, and graphic novels, as well as the use of text messaging and blogging, young males can increase their literacy abilities.

Further Reading

Booth, David. *Even Hockey Players Read: Boys, Literacy and Learning*. New York: Pembroke Publishers, 2002.

Fletcher, Ralph. *Boy Writers: Reclaiming Their Voices.* Portland, ME: Stenhouse Publishers, 2006.

Gurian, Michael, & Kathy Stevens. *The Minds of Boys: Saving Our Sons from Falling Behind in School and Life.* San Francisco, CA: Jossey-Bass, 2005.

Jon Scieszka [Online, January 2008]. Guys Read Web site <www.guys read.com>.

Mead. Sara. The Evidence Suggests Otherwise: The Truth about Boys and Girls. [Online, June 2006]. < www.educationsector.org>.

Todd Feltman

Gifted Boys

Gifted boys face greater gender issues than non-gifted boys. While all boys and young men have immense pressure to prove their masculinity, gifted boys' pressures to do so are intensified by the need and desire not to appear or be branded as nerds. This pressure comes from within as well as from parents and classmates, and the result is that gifted boys may overextend themselves by trying to do it all; cultivate their intellectual gifts while engaging in *masculine activities* such as competitive sports.

Gifted boys face numerous other issues and pressures that may limit the realization of their potential. While one would expect gifted boys to be more successful in adulthood than non-gifted boys, several studies have shown that this is not the case. Many gifted boys fall into the success trap—putting success before happiness—which in the long run hinders success. The immense pressure to succeed, especially from fathers, can push gifted young men to choose vocations they are not sure of or comfortable in. The desire and/or strain to conform and fit it leads gifted boys to downplay their intelligence (more than gifted girls), especially in high school. Also, trouble fitting in with other boys may lead to an introverted and self-conscious personality, which may hinder success in later life, both socially and professionally. What's more, research shows that the heightened focus on gifted boys' intelligence and the high expectations put on them, often results in a lack of rights, self-identity, and incapacity to express emotions. All of these factors can limit the realization of greater potential.

Parents play a very important role in the well-being of their gifted sons. Parents of gifted adolescents must remember that their sons are prone to all the same tendencies and dispositions as other adolescents. Puberty and *teen angst* can be misread by parents of gifted boys as unwillingness *to shine*. However, the inability or reluctance of parents to see their gifted boys as *normal kids* can be very detrimental to these young men, especially because gifted boys are highly sensitive and contemplative. This situation can lead to decreased achievement in school. Numerous studies have revealed that family support is crucial to the academic accomplishment of gifted boys. Those who view their parents as unconditionally supportive and their families as more closely knit are more likely to achieve success both in and out of school. Gifted boys need emotional, social, and scholastic support from their families, as well as proficiency in self-identity and socialization. At the same time, some studies suggest that too much support and focus on achievement can be detrimental, as mentioned above.

Finding a balance between supporting and pressuring children is especially difficult—yet important—in families with children with larger potential. Parents of gifted boys and girls need to realize that their children are multidimensional. These youth have many talents and interests, and therefore benefit from exploring many activities. Given the social pressure on males to be decision makers and to stick to decisions, gifted boys in particular should be able to try many things without the pressure of having to make a long-term commitment to all of them. Exploring several activities does not make them poor decision makers or dilettantes; rather, it is a healthy expression of their complexity.

Further Reading

Jackson, Susan, and Jean Peterson. Depressive Disorder in Highly Gifted Adolescents [Online]. Davidson Institute for Talent Development. <http://www.geniusdenied.com/articles/ArticlePrintable.aspx?rid=13872>.

Rimm, Sylvia. Social Adjustment and Peer Pressures for Gifted Children [Online]. Davidson Institute's GT-Cybersource. <http://www.gt-cybersource.org/Record.aspx?NavID=2_0&rid=11287>.

Webb, James T., Edward R. Amend, Nadia E. Webb, Jean Goerss, Paul Beljan, and Richard Olenchak. Counseling, Mulitple Exceptionality, and Psychological Issues [Online]. <http://www.sengifted.org/articles_counseling/Webb_MisdiagnosisAndDualDiagnosisOfGiftedChildren.shtml>.

Ghada Chehade

Nerds

The term *nerd* first emerged in the 1950s. From a Dr. Seuss storybook (*If I Ran the Zoo*) to the mainstream media (*Newsweek*), the term *nerd* entered the North American vernacular in the early 1950s. Initially intended to refer to a dull person, the definition and its use gradually expanded. Decades later in the 1970s, nerd entered into common everyday use particularly among teens, with a strong connection to bookishness and social ineptitude. Though nerd applies to both boys and girls, it is often intended for and directed at White, middle-class boys. Largely connected to assumptions intersecting masculinity and computer use, the term is employed differently when referring to girls. *Nerdette,* for example, is one form used to refer to female nerds.

In part, popular culture has revolutionized the nerd identity. A popular 1984 movie, *Revenge of the Nerds*, introduced a White male invested in and obsessed with the technical and, moreover, one who is an outcast because of this obsession and accompanying social ineptitude. In keeping with earlier conceptions of nerd, *Revenge of the Nerds* highlights a general awkwardness linking together a physical appearance and an intellectual sophistication. Add to this concept of nerdiness, the main characters Lewis and Gilbert struggle to get dates, which in turn heterosexualizes the male nerd. And though the movie is about the *revenge* of the nerds, it does little to dislodge stereotypes, but rather it broadens the definition to develop a more encompassing notion of nerd identity for *all* people who are not a part of the popular crowd. The intersection of racialized nerd identities has not been widely popularized in the mainstream media, though a popular television show, *Family Matters* (1989–1997), introduced Steve Urkel, an African American teenager. The binaristic nature of a nerd identity and the contradistinction between nerds and others is the fact that Urkel's surname comes from the Italian meaning Hercules. Urkel is far from being a Herculean figure. The physical appearance of Steve Urkel accentuates the bookishness of the character associated with glasses, suspenders, and mis-matching clothes. He was further made peculiar or odd because of an unusually high-pitched voice, which, though it did not emasculate him (he pursued Laura Winslow), it served to distinguish him differently from other young men.

In addition to the popularized notion of nerd captured by movies, the advent of technology in the mid-1980s brought a resurgence of the term *nerd* and its application in different quarters. The expansion of technology use into the public domain saw nerds and nerd-like behavior legitimated but also diluted. In other words, the power of the term *nerd* lost potency as people were increasingly and more routinely involved in various forms of technology in their everyday lives. The apparent isolation and exclusion associated with being a nerd was blurred when a wider segment of the population began using computers at home and at work. In school settings, nerd remained a largely pejorative term used as a form of verbal alienation and marginalization of particular kinds of boys. And while nerd has gradually become a term applied outside of schools, the characteristics and stereotypes of a nerd still remain fairly consistent. With the marketization of computers and increased commercial use, nerd may no longer apply as widely as before. However, nerd identities remain much a narrowly defined identity particularly within schools where it is both reserved as a verbal taunt and an oppressive identifier among White, middle-class males in particular. As such, *nerd* is one way that those with power and various forms of privilege related to being a boy and exalted forms of masculinity usually name particular boys who demonstrate a lack of sartorial sophistication, a high level of technological sharpness, a lack of physical attraction, and an accompanying social inadequacy among boys as well as girls. This description being a stereotypical construction of a nerd, it is worth noting that there are times when nerds and the term have been applied with a sense of affection for the above-mentioned qualities.

Being a nerd then has remained much the same, but the perspectives from the outside looking in on nerd identities have shifted. That is not to suggest that people strive to be a nerd, but rather that some of the qualities associated with being a nerd have lead to relatively less ostracization and more popularization of a limited number of the qualities of a nerd, namely a competence in computer use.

Further Reading

Hayes, B. (2000). The Nerds Have Won. *American Scientist,* retrieved October 15, 2008. http://www.americanscientist.org/issues/pub/2000/5/the-nerds-have-won.

Kendall, L. (1999) Nerd Nation: Images of Nerds in US Popular Culture. *International Journal of Cultural Studies* 2 (2), 260–283.

Kendall, L. (2000). "Oh No! I'm a Nerd": Hegemonic Masculinity on an Online Forum. *Gender and Society,* 14 (2), 256–274.

Michael Kehler

Reading Problems and Boys

Boys Can't Read!

During the past two decades, girls have consistently performed better than boys on literacy achievement tests. This achievement gap has created a great deal of concern about boys' ability to read and write. Words such as *trouble, risk, failing, worrying, gap, alarmed,* and *mediocrity* have been used in the media to describe boys' failure to achieve, and in Ontario, the Ministry of Education has suggested that educators need to create a more boy-friendly learning environment in schools. This means providing topics and reading materials that would appeal more to boys' interests, such as sports. It has been suggested that more male teachers are also needed to address the problem of boys' failure in schools.

However, it is important to understand that not all boys are doing poorly on literacy tests. Clearly many boys continue to perform well on these tests (80% passed the Ontario Secondary School Literacy Test in 2006–2007) and in the English classroom, so it seems that in addition to asking why boys are failing to achieve on literacy achievement tests we must also ask which boys (EQAO, 2008). To suggest that literacy underachievement is solely a gender issue might be misleading. Other contributing factors such as the way gender is defined in society and our narrow definition of literacy must also be taken into consideration.

Boys—An Amazing Story

Lorne is a seven-year-old boy who lives in a middle-class neighborhood. He is also the sole proprietor of the Grindstone Way Public Library. This library is located in Lorne's bedroom. The entire collection is displayed on four shelves of Lorne's bookcase. The bookcase is divided into two sections: fiction and nonfiction; the books are in alphabetical order. Five of Lorne's friends, all boys between the ages of 7 and 11 who live in the same neighborhood have library cards for Lorne's library. As a group, they made the cards, which include their names, telephone numbers, nicknames, the titles of the books they have checked out, and the due dates. Lorne's grandmother, recognizing the merit in this enterprise, is funding the operation. On a regular basis, she buys more books for Lorne's library, which he proudly displays on a separate shelf as new releases.

Although some may argue that this game of make-believe is typical for boys who may one day be entrepreneurs and that it says more about their business skills than it does about their reading, the fact remains that this enterprise grew out of their love of books, reading, and friendships. It is their book club. They check the books out, read them, discuss them, make recommendations to one another, and spend time together; it provides them with an opportunity to belong to something.

Why is this story amazing? Why do we find stories about boys who enjoy books and reading anomalies? If this story was about a group of girls who started their own library, would it be so amazing? The fact that we find it extraordinary speaks to societal expectations for the way boys behave. Boys are not supposed to enjoy books.

Boys Will Be Boys

Boys will be boys is an expression that is often used to explain or excuse behaviors perceived to be typical of boys, such as loud, aggressive, silly, or immature horseplay. Essentially, the expression says do not make a big deal about the hours boys spend playing violent video games because it is just something boys do; it is just the way they are. It says that a boy's biology determines who he is and how he interacts in the world. This type of thinking suggests that the way boys are is fixed or unchangeable, that their birth predispositions them to like science but hate English; love action films but hate romantic comedies; choose hockey over figure skating or football over gymnastics; and play the guitar instead of the flute.

Many of the strategies currently being proposed and implemented in schools in Ontario (boy-friendly resources and teaching strategies, same-sex schooling, a call for more male teachers) are supported by a *boys will be boys* way of thinking, which suggests that in order to help boys succeed, educators need simply to get to know more about their interests, hobbies, learning styles, and assessment preferences and design their lessons to cater to these needs and preferences. This way of thinking makes solutions simple. Boys, because of their biological makeup, are predisposed to particular learning styles, interests, and environments. Therefore, if schools change to cater to these preferences, boys will succeed in the classroom.

Schools Are for Girls

What proposals that suggest we need to make schools more boy-friendly are suggesting is that schools are for girls, and yet historically educating boys has been a priority. In fact, in some cultures today, girls continue to be discouraged from or forbidden to pursue an education. So how can schools be better suited for girls? Some argue that because schools, particularly elementary schools, are filled with female teachers, schools have become more and more suited to the learning styles and interests of girls. If that is so, we must consider whether or not it is naturally that way or if it has been constructed that way by society.

Usually when we speak of construction, we are speaking of building something physical, something we can touch: a model airplane, a house, a football stadium. However, the term may also refer to the ideas that we form or build with our minds. For example, the sport of figure skating has been constructed as a sport for girls, whereas hockey is a sport for boys. That does not mean that boys do not figure skate and girls do not play hockey, but it does mean that these sports are thought to be more suited for one gender or the other.

The way various sports, films, music, games, school subjects, and so forth are constructed is directly related to boys' and girls' involvements with these activities. For example, a boy who is gifted academically and loves to read might try to conceal his gifts, interests, and the reading that he does because they do not support the image of a boy that has been constructed in his mind. The construction of these ideas is formed in relation with significant others in our lives—family members, friends, teachers, coaches—and also by institutions in our society, in particular, the media, sport organizations, and schools themselves.

Hockey and Literacy

Some argue that the construction of various aspects of society is directly related to biological makeup. Others suggest that the social construction of activities or ideas has nothing to do with innate abilities and interests. For example, it could be argued that boys are naturally more suited to play sports than they are to excel in the English classroom. Others point out that many of the characteristics of an elite hockey player are the same characteristics that are valued in the English classroom and school in general. In addition to physical skills, such as skating and stick handling, an elite hockey player must be confident, disciplined, willing to undertake challenges, motivated to learn, focused, a leader, and committed to improvement. All of these characteristics describe a high academic achiever as well, and yet many boys who possess these qualities eagerly demonstrate them at the hockey arena and conceal them in the classroom. Their reluctance to achieve in the classroom has more to do with the way achievement in the classroom is constructed than it has to do with natural ability. Of course, a hockey player who fails to practice and demonstrate skills may soon be left behind or labeled an underachiever. This phenomenon is no different in the classroom. A failure to practice and demonstrate literacy skills leads to a failure to achieve at or above Provincial standards on literacy achievement tests and in the classroom, and a designation as an underachiever may be acquired.

In society, boys who are talented hockey players receive attention; boys who play library with their friends do not. In fact, there is a good chance that as Lorne and his friends mature, the doors to their library will close. Most boys are very aware of what is deemed acceptable behavior and what is not. The images of boys whom they see in films, video games, and music videos, for example, seldom present positive images of boys who love to read and write. As a result, stories about boys who do read and write are portrayed as amazing or abnormal, while images of successful male hockey players abound. Interest in sports and skills on the ice are rewarded socially; and social acceptance is important, especially for adolescent boys.

Defining Literacy

Troy is a seemingly confident, particularly articulate 16 year old who has already made one unsuccessful attempt at ninth grade English. Despite this failure, Troy is a mature teenage boy who has excellent reading comprehension, critical thinking, and verbal skills for his age. He attributes his failure to laziness, but he also expresses some confusion about the purpose of English class. He believes he can read and write and does so when it is connected to his interests in sports, cars, and music as well as his relationship with his father, who shares Troy's interests. However, in school, he often puts his head on his desk and disengages; and sometimes he does not come to class at all because the learning he does in English is not (in his mind) useful and connected to his life experiences.

Traditionally, literacy has referred to one's ability to read and write print texts, and, of course, literacy skills on standardized tests are assessed in this way. Although print forms of literacy continued to be valued in society, and the school system would be doing its students a disservice by not preparing them for this reality, its refusal to broaden its definition of what it means to be literate in the twenty-first century is equally a disservice and adds to the disengagement and confusion of students such as Troy who struggle to see the connection between what is taught in high school English and their literacy experiences beyond the classroom walls.

Traditional concepts of literacy must be broadened to include a variety of informational and technological texts. Broader definitions of literacy include meaning-making that is interdependent, critical, and functional. We live in a digital, technology-obsessed world, in which blogs, MSN, chat rooms, Web pages, face book, and reality television shows have infiltrated every aspect of our lives. As a result, students such as Troy enter the English classroom with multiple literacies. Troy uses literacy skills to navigate his way through an instructional Web site to help him fix the family car or chat online with his friends about the guitar. Troy's rich and complex literate life outside of school could, if connected and valued, make literacy learning relevant and purposeful in the classroom. The out of school literacy activities of many boys such as Troy are so far disconnected from the reading and writing that they do in school that they do not even consider them literacy activities. To them, chatting on line, searching the Net, creating Web pages, watching a film, and playing video games—although meaning-making experiences—have nothing to do with literacy and school.

Conclusions

Boys' literacy underachievement is a complex issue. Boys' biological makeup and socioeconomic background, as well as society's construction of gender and definition of literacy, and the structure of our schools and literacy education are all important to debates about boys' literacy underachievement.

Further Reading

Booth, David. *Even Hockey Players Read: Boys, Literacy and Learning*. Markham, ON: Pembroke Publishers, 2002.

Education Quality and Accountability Office. (2008). *EQAO's Provincial Report on the Results of the 2007–2008 Ontario Secondary School Literacy Test* [Electronic version]. Toronto: Queen's Printer for Ontario. Retrieved on March 13, 2009, from http://www.eqao.com/pdf_e/08/CPRR_Xe_0608_web.pdf.

Ontario Ministry of Education. *Me Read? No Way!: A Practical Guide to Improving Boys' Literacy Skills*. Toronto, ON: Queen's Printer for Ontario, 2004.

Tyre, Peg. "The Trouble with Boys." *Newsweek,* January 30, 2006.

Anne Watson

Reading Problems and Rural Boys

Boys who live in rural areas have different opportunities for literacy than do boys who live in urban areas. The socioeconomic status of the rural family and the educational attainment level and interests of the parents can determine a boy's access to and use of print and electronic forms of literacy.

Rural boys are particularly motivated by reading when there is a connection between the literary content and their real lives. The social practices of electronic communication and the practical literacy practices of hunter safety classes and driver education serve to engage rural boys in more meaningful reading. Club activities such as Air Cadets and 4-H provide further opportunities to engage in literacy practices. Cooperation, learning together with more knowledgeable others, and sharing of available resources are fundamental basics of these group activities. For these boys, reading charts, maps, graphs, and tables as well as completing learning logs and project books provide authentic connections between literacy and real life.

The boys borrow books through the school library and the public library in town. They buy books at book fairs held in school, at book stores in urban areas, and through Internet bookstore Web sites. School libraries provide books for in-school reading, while the public library and the bookstores provide reading for pursuing personal interests and enjoyment. Often, the mother's frequency of use of the public library and of the urban and electronic bookstores determines a rural boy's access to these sources of literacy.

The boys' out-of-school literacies are motivated by participation, usually with their fathers, in family, and in agricultural activities. They engage in literacy practices for a number of very functional purposes. For a teenage rural farm boy, studying to get a driver's license is a very important time. Rural children learn to drive at an early age to assist the family farm and they learn to become interested in the mechanical aspects of vehicles and machinery. Obtaining a driver's license is a rite of passage for many young men in rural communities, and with it comes more social privileges and responsibilities. While assisting in the day-to-day routine of machinery maintenance, rural boys observe their fathers consulting machinery manuals and machinery service guides. Through an apprenticeship of observation with their fathers, these rural boys learn to navigate the technical writing of texts and diagrams for maintenance procedures, troubleshooting problems, and care and upkeep of the machines. Conversations with family members or neighbors increase their understandings of the features of technical and informational texts. Jeffrey Wilhelm's research indicates that, for boys, reading as a form of inquiry to see details and patterns emerge, make inferences, draw conclusions, and then form larger meanings to connect to their real lives is very meaningful. His research is particularly applicable in the lives of rural farm boys.

Electronic literacy practices are an important part of a rural boy's life. Cell phones, previously used by only the adults for business and travel safety on remote rural roads, have now become part of the everyday lives of rural farm boys. Cell phones are very much a part of their daily lives in school, at after-school activities, and with their friends. In the author's recent study, rural boys preferred texting their friends with their cell phones over actually making the phone calls. They saw the reading and writing of text messages as a more private and more powerful literacy event which provided fewer interruptions than the actual phone calls.

Internet service to rural areas in Canada, for example, is mainly the slower and more economical dialup service of 21 kbps. Some families have access to high-speed service provided by satellites or by wireless cell towers located in rural areas. Most rural families have at least one computer on Internet service with other computers in the home used for word processing and gaming activities. Rural boys with dialup service report spending less time on the Internet than rural boys with high-speed service because of the less efficient transfer of larger files and the need to share the computer with other family members. Chatting on MSN, the use of Facebook, and frequent use of the Google search engine are popular pastimes.

Most rural boys engage in functional writing tasks, such as making lists, sketching, and charting more than expressive writing tasks, such as writing narrative stories. Boys who participate in computer games, both online and offline, report an increase in time spent drawing cartoons based on Pokémon or Manga themes with the accompanying dialogue, which reflects plot lines and adventures of the computer games.

Authenticity and practicality are important for these boys. They often find the fiction that they have to read in school as unconnected to their current or future lives. When they do select fiction for their own enjoyment, it tends to be realistic adventure fiction with strong plot lines. Rural farm boys are given a great deal of adult responsibility around the farm early in their lives, including being entrusted with expensive machinery, doing physical chores, and taking care of animals. Rural boys sometimes find it difficult to become engaged with the Eurocentric narrative fiction that is a traditional part of the school curriculum. Engaging in purposeful and authentic literacy activities to assume responsibilities is a powerful motivating factor in the lives of rural boys.

Further Reading

Kelly, Brenda M. (In progress). Unpublished doctoral dissertation. University of Alberta, Edmonton, Alberta, Canada.

Wilhelm, Jeffrey. *You Gotta Be the Book.* Teachers College Press, New York, 1996.

Brenda Kelly

Space, Place, and Masculinities in Boys' Schools

During the past two decades there has been growing interest and significant research in the schooling of boys and masculinities in schools. Key questions to this growing research include: What masculinities are being produced in schools? In what ways? For what purposes? And how do these constructions of masculinities impact the experiences of boys? There are multiple and diverse masculinities formed, played out, regulated, embedded, and disciplined in school in many ways. The various masculinities do not coexist harmoniously because they compete for control and dominance; some celebrated at any one given time, while others become inferior and marginalized.

The relationship between architecture, power, and education is also important to consider. For example, research has focused on the architectural design and quality of school facilities and their relationship to academic achievement. There is also growing interest in investigating the social dynamics of school place, its relation to physical space, and the interaction between the two. Spatiality is known as the production of place through the interaction of the physical and the social. This research investigates how place contributes to the production of subjectivities and identities. Identities which are performed, contested, negotiated, and produced in practical, material, and affirming ways in place and in relation to place. It builds on the research and work of geographers, sociologists, historians, environmental psychologists, anthropologists, and architects. Place is usually defined as what a space becomes when we get to know it better and invest it with meaning and value, as place can mean different things to different people. It can be understood as a material thing in the world, as well as a way of seeing, knowing, and understanding the world in which we live.

However, there is little research that investigates how the production of place intersects with the production of masculinities in schools. Studies of the construction and regulation of masculinities in schools refer to spatial metaphors. Yet in these inquiries, the actual spaces and places, the material *setting*, where particular forms of masculinities are played out, produced, policed, and regulated have largely gone unexamined and are taken for granted. There are certain ideas about boys, men, and masculinities that inform the design and decoration of particular spaces in schools. These choices may not always appear as conscious or calculated; they do, however, affect and impact the types of masculine performances that are possible. In boys' schools, it is not unusual to find emblems of success and achievement (trophies, medals, certificates, etc.) displayed in the entrance hall, along with class-group photographs of former students, images of the founding fathers, and past principals. It appears normal and given that the entrance hall—the first introduction to what happens within the school—should display photographs of former class groups, artifacts of achievement, and symbolic references to the school's identity.

While this way of setting up the entrance hall of schools is commonly understood to be normal, together with other material artifacts, it is a place that can be perceived, experienced, read, and interpreted. As Brian, an eleven-year old participant in O'Donoghue's 2006 study of space and place in boys' schools, explains, "these are here to show that our school has had so much success, that we have all the trophies, and that they are in the hall as you walk in, and you know that you can kind of show them off. When you are passing all them you'd love to be like, oh wouldn't I love to get one of them for my school now." These visual representations and material objects are symbolic representations which reinforce, in particular, gender stereotypes of a place. As a result, boys and others learn a great deal about adult expectation and power structure. These practices of representation in school spaces impact the formation of boys' sense of self and masculinity Another way to think about this, is to use Ted Killian's idea of the power of access and the power of exclusion. What practices and performances of masculinities are being recognized and acknowledged here? What performances are not? How do place-making practices position, distribute, and rank individuals according to a norm and in relation to each other? What forms of masculinities are dis/qualified and in/validated?

Such space-providing and place-making practices represent specific values, beliefs, and traditions. Certain masculine performances are encouraged, expected, and demanded in particular spaces within the school. At other times, spaces can allow for particular association, alignment, or alienation to masculine identities. Certain places lend themselves to the certain ways of performing particular masculinities. These spaces either enable or close off certain performances of masculinity. However, these spaces can always hold out the possibility of other ways of being masculine. To examine place-making practices in boys' schools is to find another way of coming to know and understand how masculinities are performed, negotiated, and challenged in schools. R. W. Connell describes gender politics within masculinity as the relations between dominant masculinities and subordinated masculinities. This entry expands on the idea that place, like discourse, is an active agent in masculinizing processes in schools. Using one case study, it will focus specifically on how the production of place intersects with the production of masculinities in schools. It focuses on the places where masculinities are produced, played out, regulated, and disciplined obvious and subtle ways, focusing in particular on how place is constructed in accordance with, and used to support further, or disrupt certain types and performances of masculinities.

An 11-year old boy Daniel, who attends a single-sex boys' elementary school in Ireland, made what appears to be an image of the schoolyard—the place where more than 170 boys gather together every day to play. But, as Daniel explains, this image is more than a mere representation of a particular school space. It is a representation of how he experiences, engages with, and identifies with the dominant roles of masculinities in school in and through time and space.

> Well I took it because over there is a happy spot [Daniel points to the space right of the black pole] because I don't mind being over there . . . and I split it in two. Sad spot one side and happy spot the other side: The side with the door is the happy side and the side with the pencil is the sad side . . . well that's because, that side I get teased at a lot of the time, and the other side I don't get teased at . . . its actually I don't like that side because I do get pushed around there still, and the other side I don't get pushed around there. (Daniel, aged 11)

Daniel's statement describes what can and does happen in schoolyards. In his description, Daniel speaks indirectly of how other boys act in this space as he speaks directly of his experience of being on the receiving end of these actions. His statement regarding his image is evidence to how space is always significant in experience. Here is an instance where a school space created for a particular purpose and understood in and through certain expectations of what should happen. For Daniel it takes on a range of additional (and likely unintentional) set of associations that go some way in shaping and defining his and others' construction of his masculine identity. As Daniel's statement suggests, the yard offers different experiences depending on who inhabits it when, where, and for what purpose. Different masculinities are being played out and performed in this place (different ways of doing boy). Hidden and clear messages about how boys ought to act are being communicated in and through this space. This is similar in many respects to Paul Monette's experience of the basement corridor which he recalls in his autobiography *Becoming a Man, Half a Life Story*. Monette tells of how as a sixth grader he learned the importance of *passing for straight* (of not being recognizably *Other*) in the basement corridor just outside the boys' lavatory. It was here away from the gaze of teachers that he witnessed a classmate being beaten senseless by a group of thuggish schoolboys simply because he was suspected as being homosexual. Monette recalls that this came to structure his relationships with others boys during his school days.

As with the text, Daniel's image tells of a divided place, a zoned place, two different places to inhabit: one wide-open, enclosed only by the walls of the school, and visually sparse, a site for bullying, harassment, and exclusion; the other a more familiar place, enclosed by a number of surrounding walls, a site for friendship and belonging. The large expansive open space that the viewer looks into, divided roughly into two equal parts by the black pole, plays a key role in shaping the type of behavior that Daniel reports. Here, each day during break-time, boys come together to play football. The senior and junior students alternate between the upper and lower parts each day, with the junior students having access to the upper space (which is larger in size) during the morning break. Senior students occupy this larger space during lunch break. The management and routinizing of space in this way divides categories of boys not only in terms of age (and class level, junior and senior), but also in several other ways. A designated space is provided for boys who play football. For those who do not, they sit and chat and exchange cards in the shed. They hang out on the steps. They occupy these nondesignated gathering spaces and social places: "I don't play football; I just watch them or go down and sit on the benches or play cards with other boys," Daniel explains. Boys such as him find existing spaces fitting for their recreational use which is not aided by school administration Daniel and his non-football-playing friends do not follow the common sense connection between this place and what is meant to happen here. More precisely, encoded in the designation and provision of space for particular activities and interests is the belief that *real boys* like to do particular things—obviously football in this instance. What does it say about boys who do not do what is expected, such as play/exchange cards and hang around and chat? Daniel is a member of this latter group. The management of space in this instance sustains difference. Moreover certain spaces legitimate certain activities, while the lack of designated spaces for other activities stigmatize and devalue those in turn.

Daniel speaks to the structured, sterile nature of this place—hard edges and right angles. He positions the viewer just inside a place that means something to him, a place that goes some way in shaping, defining, and categorizing his masculine identity. He positions the viewer not in the space that excludes (the school yard). Instead he places the viewer on the edge of that place, on the margins—a similar position to where Daniel is positioned in the hierarchy of masculinities at play in this space. While the eye of the viewer is now in the very same position as Daniel's was when he took this image with the viewer now seeing exactly what Daniel saw, the relationship of the viewer to the image is somewhat different. Daniel is selecting and setting up an image to communicate; the viewer is reading the image. This viewpoint prohibits us from entering the schoolyard and inhabiting it. The emphasis on surface qualities and detail in the foreground of the image (the black pole) and the blurring of the middle ground and background further prohibits easeful entry beyond this point. The clarity of the black painted pole retains the eye and keeps it from wandering into the image. To what extent can these interpretations of the image made by Daniel be understood as an attempt to draw attention to his relationship with the dominant model of masculinity in this place?

Daniel too has framed and emphasized the word *FUCK* in his image. FUCK is scratched out of the paint on the pole, an act of resistance in itself.

The word FUCK was found, framed, and positioned as the main focal point. The very act of scratching FUCK (a provocative word in this space) from a hard surface requires effort and involvement and a desire to change, to subvert, to take control, to resist, to leave one's mark, to re/shape. To record it in a two-dimensional image is another act of appropriation and communication. In one sense it is an example of how students appropriate space to demonstrate their resistance to school and its practices. So to what extent can Daniel's experience and engagement with this space be described as a sense of being out of place, an effort to rebel against the forms of masculinities made visible by the school? Does Daniel's image and text speak to the silence of the difficulty being a boy who does not participate in dominant, expected, and celebrated forms of masculinity? What is made invisible in this image? What is not spoken about in his statement? What might be suggested but not named? On the one hand, both image and text are evocative but deeply disturbing accounts of segregation, exclusion, and displacement. On the other hand, both are a powerful image of resilience, redress, and empowerment.

This image and accompanying text raise questions about how one's actions and behaviors are built into the design, structure, and form of school buildings. What makes certain types of gathering easy, while making other forms more difficult, and even impossible? And what structures work against the creation of egalitarian, inclusive places? In addition, Daniel's image and statement raises important questions about the creation of place in schools and its implication for understanding, performing, and representing masculine identities. Therefore, the following questions should be raised: In schools, what boys produce what places, and for what purpose? What particular forms of place-making provide for the performance of certain forms of masculinities and limit opportunities for other forms of masculinities to be performed? Who gets to define, control, and monitor spaces and places in schools? Who has the power to assign meaning on certain places at certain times? How do boys claim and use space to exercise dominance and control? How do boys use space to make visible or hide their male identities and sense of masculinity? Why do some boys feel out of place in certain school spaces, while others do not? How do boys use space to magnify difference? To what extent is learning masculinities in school place-based? What happens when individuals (be they students, teachers, parents, administrators) defy the supposedly common sense connection between a place and what is meant to happen there? Through this example we can begin to think about what current arrangements of space in boys' schools with their related practices might mean to and for boys who occupy and perform less dominant and more marginalized masculinities. Place-making in schools is both an historical and power-based activity deriving from, and giving cultural and historical meaning to educational practices, schooling, gender, and curriculum among other things. It is built around supposedly common sense understandings of the purpose of schooling, of teaching and learning, and of the positioning of students, teachers, and management within these particular ideas and ways of thinking about education, gender, and sexualities.

Further Reading

Kehler. M. D. (2004). Masculinities and resistance: high school boys (un)doing boy. *Taboo 8*(1), 97–113.

Lesko, N. (2000). *Masculinities at school.* Thousand Oakes, CA: Sage.

O'Donoghue, D. (2006). Situating place and space in the making of masculinities in schools. *Journal of Curriculum and Pedagogy, 3*(1), 15–33.

O'Donoghue, D. (2007a). 'James always hangs out here': Making space for place in studying masculinities at school. *Visual Studies 22*(1), 62–73. (Special Issue, The Visible Curriculum).

O'Donoghue, D. (2007b). Place-making in boys' schools: Researching with and through art practice. *Journal of Artistic and Creative Education, 1*(2), 68–101.

Sanders, Joel. (1996). (Ed.) *Stud: Architectures of Masculinity.* New York: Princeton University School of Architecture.

Donal O'Donoghue

Teaching Boys

In North American culture, many boys perceive success in school as something to be avoided. As a result, some boys may attempt to disguise their intelligence because it can expose them to ridicule from their peers. This may take the form of boys refusing to do homework or putting only minimal effort into assignments. It has been argued that a refusal to put effort into schoolwork prevents boys from being ridiculed for being intelligent. In the event that they fail, their lack of success can be brushed off as unimportant. Boys are often criticized by their peers for participating in behaviors that are seen as being inappropriate. Specifically, intelligence and success in a school setting is seen by boys as feminine and is, therefore, something to resist.

Despite this reluctance to excel in school, boys continue to perform extremely well in math, science, and hands-on activities (e.g., building). Boys seem to be less restricted in performing tasks that require them to build, construct, design, be hands-on, be physically active, calculate, and be competitive. Competition has the advantage of motivating boys to complete tasks but can have the adverse effect of making the learning process self-centered, which can encourage negative behavior (e.g., aggressiveness). One strategy to effectively use competition is to have boys compete in groups. They can be assigned work that relies on communication, understanding, and teambuilding skills while having them compete collaboratively with other groups. That way, the learning activities encourage boys to excel while not making the exercise a negative experience.

It has been argued that boys underperform in school settings because they lack positive male role models. However, recent research has not been able to find reliable evidence to support that theory. Boys taught by female instructors perform as well, if not better, compared to those taught by males. What seems to be more important than the sex of the teacher is the relationship that the teacher creates with the boys. This is especially true since boys are much more likely than girls to challenge authority and the figures representing authority. Therefore, it is important for teachers to implement effective strategies to ensure that their authority is respected while being careful not to appear oppressive (that would only further boys' desire to resist authority). Specifically, it has been shown that boys react more positively to teachers that encourage a student-centered approach to learning.

Boys become excited when participating in decision-making processes; boys generally don't like being told what to do. Offering a limited number of choices of activities is one effective way of encouraging them to actively participate in learning activities. It is also very important that they see a reason for the activities they are participating in. Tasks that are meaningful for boys are most effective as they are motivated to complete tasks that seem immediately valuable to them. Boys are particularly motivated to excel in school when their personal interests are incorporated into the educational exercises. For instance, if a particular boy is interested in football, an essay or project on the subject will be particularly motivating for that student. When boys are allowed to explore and incorporate their excitement for a particular topic in the educational setting, they will put substantially more effort into the task at hand. Therefore, they can be encouraged to enjoy learning and to see the immediate value inherent in the activities they are engaged in.

Boys' interests vary widely but there are some commonly held interests: sports, television shows, movies, and video games. Interests will vary with each individual boy; it is important to purposefully appeal to the needs of each individual student. Furthermore, it is important to not reinforce stereotypes by assuming that boys will be interested in the same activities. Instead, boys should be encouraged to explore avenues of interest to them. They will be more comfortable (and less likely to be ridiculed) with subjects that they are already excited about. Student-centered assignments can encourage all boys, no matter their interests, to complete the tasks at hand.

Further Reading

Gurian, Micheal, Kathy Stevens, and Kelley King. *Strategies for Teaching Boys and Girls—Secondary Level: A Workbook for Educators.* Hoboken, NJ: Jossey-Bass, 2008.

How Should We Teach Boys? [Online, October 2008]. *The Independent* <http://www.independent.co.uk/news/education/education-news/how-should-we-teach-boys-746718.html>.

Younger, Mike. Mind the Gap: Tackling Boys' Underachievement [Online, October 2008]. *Teaching Expertise* <http://www.teachingexpertise.com/articles/boys-underachievement-101>.

David Roemmele

Vocational Schools

As it was stated in the Carl Perkins Vocational and Technical Education Act of 1984 (reauthorized in 1998 and 2006), the major purpose of the vocational education is to accelerate the economic growth while connecting academic content to technical skills in order to address the needs of industry. The primary task of the students attending vocational school was to instill technological developments and their by-products, such as cnc machinery, electronic devices, computer applications, and so forth into work places. By this way, while students are getting opportunities to have occupations, at the same time the industry would be provided with the required educated/skilled staff members without wasting money and extra time on training. Although there is a claim that vocational schools (or career and technical education according to 2006 Perkins Act) do not only serve to prepare students for work right after high school graduation, but also provide them with advanced academic and intellectual tools through rigorous course contents. Yet still there remain controversial questions and political concerns, such as who goes to vocational schools, who takes more technical and vocational credits in high schools, and what they do after graduation.

Students who would potentially attend vocational schools work as middle men—people who work, for example, under engineers but above unqualified workers. In this sense, they are holding the responsibility of bridging two edges of work settings. They are also in between in terms of life opportunities regarding education. Although they are not getting advanced education preparing them for professional positions as their affluent counterparts, they are much luckier than their friends who could not get any more education mainly because of academic reasons, as underachievement is the biggest factor contributing to the decision of attending vocational schools.

While preparing students for the occupational positions that industry requires, vocational education is also deemed to become safe shelters for the boys who otherwise would wander around the city streets aimlessly and prone to be criminals. These schools are promoted as feasible alternatives for the working class kids who were already marginalized from the school system as academic failures or who were considered as hopeless to be able to get a college degree. For this reason, especially the poorer segments of the society showed a great interest in vocational education. Uneven distribution of the wealth leaves no choice but to subscribe to viable alternatives offered to them. They became the school of working class kids (and to some extent they become popular in rural areas as well). Actually, the roots of the vocational schools could be tracked down to the emergence of manufacturing industries both in socialist and capitalist states, which demonstrates their lucid connections with blue collar or working class people.

Effects of globalization informed with neo-liberal ideals created new realities and practices for work settings. Footloose companies moved their manufacturing plants to poorer parts of the world under the political banner of economic liberty seeking for cheaper labor. Shifts in the economy from manufacturing to service and information sectors yielded two major consequences for the vocational education and working class kids, especially in the United States. First, deprived of decent job opportunities, working class people are forced to get higher education degrees (mainly because of increased competition to get a job) for the jobs which were held by them before without a college degree or they are left to the mercy of chain stores in which the employee turnover is extremely high. Secondly, male dominated industrial jobs such as mechanics, transportation, construction, and so forth are replaced by information and service jobs, including health care, nursery, and communication, which traditionally have been considered as ideal female jobs. This has been reflected on vocational schools as an increasing trend in girls' recruitment, although vocational schools were conceived as conventional male dominated spaces. This is partly because of the socially constructed tendencies toward choosing gender typical occupations (e.g., child care for women, machine operating for men). With their thickened masculinities, working class boys who have been already rubbing their identities against feminine constructions of school settings and responding them through underachievement and dropout are now forced to adapt new subjectivities, albeit painfully and confusingly, in order to survive in this new deal. This is because identities are also formed through institutional conventions that operate as public repositories of social and cultural symbols of societies.

Further Reading

Gray, Kenneth, and Edwin L. Herr. *Other Ways to Win: Creating Alternatives for High School Graduates.* Thousand Oaks, CA: Corwin Press, 2006.

Koch, Janice, and Beverly J. Irby. *Defining and Redefining Gender Equity in Education.* Charlotte, NC: Information Age Publishing, 2002.

Lakes, Richard, and Patricia A. Carter. *Globalizing Education for Work: Comparative Perspectives on Gender and the New Economy.* New Jersey: Lawrence Erlbaum, 2004.

de Vires, Marc J., and Ilja Mottier. (Eds.) *International Handbook of Technology Education.* Rotterdam: Sense Publishers, 2006.

Walsh, W. Bruce, and Samuel H. Osipow. *Handbook of Vocational Psychology: Theory, Research, and Practice.* NJ: Lawrence Erlbaum, 1995.

Mustafa Sever

Selected Bibliography

Alloway, Nola, Peter Freebody, Pam Gilbert, & Sandy Muspratt. *Boys, Literacy and Schooling: Expanding the Repertoires of Practice.* Canberra, AU: Department of Education, Science and Training, 2002.

American Men's Studies Association. http://mensstudies.org/.

Beyond Beats and Rhymes. DVD. Directed by Byron Hurt. Northampton, MA: Media Education Foundation, 2006.

Bilz, Rachelle Lasky. *Life Is Tough: Guys Growing Up and Young Adult Literature.* Lanham, MD: The Scarecrow Press, 2004.

Blaise, Mindy. *Playing It Straight: Uncovering Gender Discourses in the Early Childhood Classroom.* New York: Routledge, 2005.

Booth, David. *Even Hockey Players Read: Boys, Literacy and Learning.* Markham, ON: Pembroke Publishers, 2002.

Cassell, Justine, & Henry Jenkins. (Eds.). *From Barbie to Mortal Kombat: Gender and Computer Games.* Cambridge, MA: The MIT Press, 1999.

Cleaver, Frances. *Masculinities Matter! Men, Gender, and Development.* New York: Zed Books, 2002.

Connell, Raewyn W. *The Men and the Boys.* Sydney: Allen & Unwin, 2000.

Epstein, Debbie, & Richard Johnson. *Schooling Sexualities.* Buckingham, UK: Open University Press, 1998.

Francis, Becky, & Christine Skelton. *Reassessing Gender and Achievement: Questioning Contemporary Key Debates.* London: Routledge, 2005.

Frank, Blye, & Kevin Davison. *Masculinities and Schooling: International Practices and Perspectives.* London, ON: The Althouse Press, 2007.

Frosh, Stephen, Ann Phoenix, & Rob Pattman. *Young Masculinities: Understanding Boys in Contemporary Society.* Basingstoke, UK: Palgrave, 2003.

Groth, Miles, & Diederik Janssens (Eds.). *Thymos: Journal of Boyhood Studies.* Men's Studies Press, Fall 2009.

Hammett, Roberta, & Katherine Sanford. *Boys and Girls and the Myths of Literacies and Learning.* Toronto, ON: Canadian Scholars' Press, 2008.

Janssen, Diederik (Ed.). *Culture, Society & Masculinities Journal.* Men's Studies Press.

Kimmel, Michael. *Guyland: The Perilous World Where Boys Become Men.* New York: Harper Collins, 2008.

Kindlon, Dan, & Michael Thompson. *Raising Cain: Protecting the Emotional Life of Boys*. New York: Ballantine Books, 2000.

Lingard, Bob, Wayne Martino, & Martin Mills. *Boys and Schooling: Beyond Structural Reform*. London: Palgrave MacMillan, 2009.

Martino, Wayne, Michael Kehler, & Marcus Weaver-Hightower (Eds.). *The Problem with Boys' Education: Beyond the Backlash*. New York: Routledge, 2009.

Martino, Wayne, & Maria Pallotta-Chiarolli. *Being Normal Is the Only Way to Be: Adolescent Perspectives on Gender and School*. Sydney: University of New South Wales Press, 2005.

The Masculinity Project. http://blackpublicmedia.org/project/masculinity/media.

Men Can Stop Rape. http://www.mencanstoprape.org/.

Messner, Michael. *Power at Play: Sports and the Problem of Masculinity*. Boston: Beacon Press, 1992.

Mills, Martin. *Challenging Violence in Schools: An Issue of Masculinities*. Buckingham, UK: Open University, 2001.

Mullins, Chris. *Holding Your Square: Masculinities, Streetlife and Violence*. Portland, OR: Willan Publishing, 2007.

National Organization for Men against Sexism. http://www.nomas.org/.

Newburger, Eli H. *The Men They Will Become*. Cambridge, MA: Da Capo Press, 2000.

Nikkah, John. *Our Boys Speak: Adolescent Boys Write about Their Inner Lives*. New York: St Martin's Griffin, 2000.

O'Donnell, Mike, & Sue Sharpe. *Uncertain Masculinities: Youth, Ethnicity and Class in Contemporary Britain*. London, UK: Routledge, 2000.

Pascoe, C. J. *Dude, You're a Fag*. Berkeley, CA: University of California Press. 2007.

Pollack, William. *Real Boys: Rescuing Our Sons from the Myths of Boyhood*. New York: Henry Holt and Company, 1998.

Raphael, Ray. *The Men from the Boys: Rites of Passage in Male America*. Lincoln, NE: University of Nebraska Press, 1988.

Renold, Emma. *Girls, Boys, and Junior Sexualities: Exploring Children's Gender and Sexual Relations in the Primary School*. London; New York: RoutledgeFalmer, 2005.

Sax, Leonard. *Boys Adrift: The Five Factors Driving the Growing Epidemic of Unmotivated Boys and Underachieving Young Men*. New York: Basic Books, 2007.

Skelton, Christine. *Schooling the Boys: Masculinities and Primary Education*. Buckingham, UK: Open University Press, 2001.

Stephenson, Bret. *From Boys to Men: Spiritual Rites of Passage in an Indulgent Age*. Rochester, NY: Park Street Press, 2006.

Steinberg, Shirley R. (Ed.) *Kinderculture: The Corporate Construction of Childhood. 2nd Edition*. Boulder, CO: Westview Press, 2010.

Steinberg, Shirley R. and Kincheloe, Joe L. (Eds.) *Kinderculture: The Corporate Construction of Childhood*. Boulder, CO: Westview Press, 1997; 2004.

Think Before You Speak. http://www.thinkb4youspeak.com/. A campaign to promote a culture of awareness against making unthinking, casual slurs against those who are gay, lesbian, bisexual, or transgendered.

Thorne, Barrie. *Gender Play: Girls and Boys in School*. New Brunswick, NJ: Rutgers University Press, 1993.

Way, Niobe, & Judy Y. Chu. (Eds.). *Adolescent Boys: Exploring Diverse Cultures of Boyhood*. New York: New York University Press, 2004.

Wellard, Ian. *Sport, Masculinities and the Body*. New York: Routledge, 2009.

The White Ribbon Campaign. http://www.whiteribbon.ca/. From the Web site: The White Ribbon Campaign is men working to end violence against women. "In over fifty-five countries, campaigns are led by both men and women, even though the focus is on educating men and boys."

World Health Organization. What about Boys? A Literature Review on the Health and Development of Adolescent Boys. [Online 2002]. World Health Organization Web site http://whqlibdoc.who.int/hq/2000/WHO_FCH_CAH_00.7.pdf.

XY Online: Men, Masculinities and Gender Politics. http://www.xyonline.net/.

Index

About the Editors and Contributors

LINDSAY CORNISH is a freelance editor and writer. Along with being the coeditor of *Taboo: Essays on Culture and Education* (with Shirley Steinberg and Peter Lang, 2010), she was the editorial assistant of *Girl Culture: An Encyclopedia* (Greenwood Press, 2008). Her research interests include gender and sexuality studies.

MICHAEL KEHLER is associate professor at the Faculty of Education, the University of Western Ontario, London, Canada. His research addresses masculinities, literacies, and the counter hegemonic practices of adolescent young men. He is published in journals including *Discourse: Studies in the Cultural Politics of Education*, *Canadian Journal of Education*, *McGill Journal of Education*, and *Taboo*. He is coeditor and contributor to *Boys' Bodies: Speaking the Unspoken* and *The Problem with Boys' Education: Beyond the Backlash*. He has also contributed chapters to *Boys, Girls and the Myths of Literacies and Learning* and *Masculinities and Schooling: International Practices and Perspectives*. He is conducting a nationally funded study to examine the intersections of adolescent masculinities, health, and body image in Canada.

SHIRLEY R. STEINBERG is the cofounder and director of The Paulo and Nita Freire International Project for Critical Pedagogy. At present, she teaches at McGill University. She is the author and editor of many books in critical pedagogy, urban and youth culture, and cultural studies. Her most recent books include: *19 Urban Questions: Teaching in the City* (2010); *Christotainment: Selling Jesus Through Popular Culture* (2009); *Diversity and Multiculturalism: A Reader* (2009); *Media Literacy: A Reader* (2007); the award-winning *Contemporary Youth Culture: An International Encyclopedia; Kinderculture: The Corporate Construction of Childhood* (2010, 2004); and *The Miseducation of the West: How Schools and Media Distort Our Understanding of the Islam World* (2004).

She is currently finishing two books: *Writing and Publishing* (Fall 2010) and *The Bricolage and Qualitative Research* (Fall 2010). A regular contributor to CBC Radio One, CTV, the *Toronto Globe and Mail*, the *Montreal Gazette*, and *Canadian Press*, she is an internationally known speaker and teacher. She is also the founding editor of *Taboo: The Journal of Culture and Education*, and the managing editor of the *International Journal of Critical Pedagogy*. The organizer of The

Baeza Congress, she is committed to a global community of transformative educators and community workers engaged in radical love, social justice, and the situating of power within social and cultural contexts.

CAROLYNE ALI KHAN is a teacher at Community Prep High School in Manhattan. She is a recipient of the Chancellor's Fellowship as a doctoral candidate in the Urban Education program at the Graduate Center, City University of New York (CUNY).

CHRISTIAN ALMONTE is a student at Community Prep High School in Manhattan. He has exhibited and received honors for his visual artwork.

JEANNE ANGUS is an assistant professor of education, Brooklyn College, Brooklyn, New York. Her work has focused on children with special needs, particularly Asperger syndrome (AS). She has coauthored a series of books for children with Autistic Spectrum Disorders (ASD), *Everyday Stories,* and continues her research with individuals with ASD and their families.

RAMONA PARKASH ARORA is a high school teacher from Markham, Ontario, Canada, who teaches a variety of courses in geography and the humanities, as well as an introductory course in philosophy for high school juniors. She is completing doctorate at McGill University, examining the career and educational pathways of young islanders and expatriates in the Caribbean.

CHARLES R. BATSON is an associate professor of French and Francophone Studies at Union College, Schenectady, New York. The author of studies on twentieth- and twenty-first-century theater and dance, including *Dance, Desire, and Anxiety in Early Twentieth-Century French Theater* (2005), he recently won Union's Stillman Award for Excellence in Teaching.

HEATHER BLAIR is a professor at the University of Alberta, Canada, specializing in the intersections of gender, ethnicity, and literacy. She has recently completed a six-year longitudinal study of adolescent boys and literacy. Currently she is working with a primary teacher research group examining literacy issues for young boys.

MARCUS BREEN has worked as a journalist, researcher, consultant, and academic in Australia, the United States, Latin America, and the Caribbean. His area of research covers the political economy of the culture industries and new technology, as well as popular music. He teaches in the Department of Communication Studies, Northeastern University, Boston. His most recent book is *Rock Dogs: Politics and the Australian Music Industry* (2006).

JACQUES BRODEUR, formerly a physical education teacher, directed collections of war toys to build Monuments for Peace in 1986. Among actions and campaigns to oppose violent entertainment, he created and experienced the 10-Day Challenge, a successful approach to reducing exposure to television and video games in over 70 schools in Québec and Ontario. The 10-Day Challenge has proven to reduce violence by challenging some negative aspects of the culture of masculinity with children and teenagers.

DAVID CAMPOS is an associate professor of education at the University of the Incarnate Word, San Antonio, Texas. He is author of *Sex, Youth, and Sex Education; Diverse Sexuality in Schools; Understanding Gay and Lesbian Youth;* and *Expanding Waistlines.* He coauthored *Practical Ideas that Really Work for English Language Learners.*

JOSEPH CARROLL-MIRANDA, born and raised in Puerto Rico, obtained his doctoral degree in curriculum and instruction from New Mexico State University. He is currently a Research Fellow at the College of Education at the University of Puerto Rico. Some of his areas of interest are youth culture, the open source community, learning technology, and pedagogies of freedom.

ROYMIECO A. CARTER is an assistant professor of digital media in the Art Department of Wake Forest University, Winston-Salem, North Carolina. He teaches courses on graphic design, digital media, visual literacy and theory, and social criticism. He has written articles on graphic design education, art education, gaming, human computer interaction, and graphics computer animation.

JACQUELINE CELEMENCKI is currently pursuing her doctorate at McGill University, Montréal, Québec. Her recently completed master's degree thesis examined hip-hop culture's impact on the gendered, linguistic, and ethnic identities of her male youth participants. Her current research examines the linguistic integration of Montréal's Haitian youth community and the forms of cultural production that emerge from these experiences.

SANTANU CHAKRABARTI is a doctoral candidate at the Department of Journalism and Media Studies at SCILS, Rutgers University, New Brunswick, New Jersey. His research interests include issues of identity formation in a globalized world, the role of affective media in influencing subjectivities and the political economy of popular film and music.

SANDRA CHANG-KREDL teaches at Concordia University. Her areas of study include cultural constructions of childhood, children's literature, and multimodal texts.

GHADA CHEHADE is completing a doctoral degree. Her research is interdisciplinary, and she has published on numerous issues, including popular culture, alternative media, and U.S. foreign policy. Her most recent publication in the journal *Taboo* (2007) critically examines the pop culture character Borat. She is also a poet/spoken word artist focusing on social justice issues.

EMILY CHIVERS YOCHIM completed her doctorate in Communication Studies at the University of Michigan in 2007. She studies youth subcultures and alternative masculinities. Her dissertation, "'This is how I think': Skate Life, Corresponding Cultures, and Alternative White Masculinities," is an ethnographic account of skateboarding culture. She has also written about vinyl record collectors in *Media, Culture & Society*.

JUDY Y. CHU is a lecturer at Stanford University, California, where she teaches a course on Boys' Psychosocial Development. Her research examines boys' relationships and development during early childhood and adolescence. She is coeditor of *Adolescent Boys: Exploring Diverse Cultures of Boyhood* (2004) and is writing a book on boys' relational capabilities.

BETSY CRANE is a professor and director of Graduate Programs in Human Sexuality, Widener University, Chester, Pennsylvania. She coedited the book, *Sexual Lives: Theories and Realities of Human Sexualities* (2003).

RUSS CRAWFORD is an assistant professor of History at Ohio Northern University in Ada, Ohio. He has presented conference papers on Chip Hilton as a cold warrior, and included a chapter on the fictional star in his dissertation. His dissertation on sports and the Cold War is currently in the process of being published.

GIULIANA CUCINELLI is a faculty lecturer for the Department of Communication Studies at Concordia University. Her doctoral work centered on youth and social media. She works as media producer for the Paulo and Nita Freire International Project for Critical Pedagogy, and has produced many films on critical pedagogy. She also runs the Freire Social Media Project, a media education initiative exploring learning and living in an era of media convergence (www.giulianacucinelli.com).

DANNÉ E. DAVIS is an assistant professor of Elementary Education at Montclair State University, Montclair, New Jersey. Her research interests include race, critical pedagogy, and multicultural education.

ROBERT ANDREW DUNN is a doctoral student in communication and an adjunct instructor of journalism at the University of Alabama, Tuscaloosa, Alabama. He has written for newspapers for seven years in both Alabama and Florida. He has also taught communication courses at Florida Southern College, Lakeland, Florida.

JOAN EVANS is an associate professor and director of the Communication Skills Program in the Division of Medical Education. She also holds a cross-appointment to the School of Nursing, Dalhousie University, Halifax, Nova Scotia, Canada. Her research is in the area of masculinities in relation to men's work in nontraditional occupations and men's health across the life course.

VENUS EVANS-WINTERS is an assistant professor at Illinois State University, where she teaches in the Department of Educational Administration and Foundations. Her research interests are school resilience, urban children and adolescents, and community-based organizations. She is also the author of *Teaching Black Girls: Resiliency in Urban Classrooms* (2005).

TODD FELTMAN is a literacy coach at an elementary school in Washington Heights in New York City. He also is an adjunct lecturer in Hunter College in the Department of Curriculum and Teaching. He is writing his dissertation on the subject of the socioemotional and cognitive needs of fourth and fifth grade boys in elementary school.

NICOLE FIORE is completing her thesis on narrative literature in Iran and Afghanistan and the use of autobiography in predominantly Muslim countries. She is the organizer of the Baeza Conference for Critical Pedagogy.

CURTIS FOGEL is a graduate student in the department of sociology at the University of Calgary, Alberta, Canada. He is currently writing his doctoral dissertation on consensual crime in Canadian sports, looking specifically at violence, hazing, and performance-enhancing drug use.

BLYE FRANK is a professor and Head of the Division of Medical Education and the Head of the Department of Bioethics in the Faculty of Medicine at Dalhousie University in Halifax, Nova Scotia, Canada. Beginning with his doctoral thesis "Everyday Masculinities" (1990), he has researched in the area of masculinities with a particular emphasis on young men.

JULIA GERMAN is an MA graduate from Warsaw University, American Studies Centre, Poland. She has also graduated from Postgraduate Studies of Advocacy and Decision-Making Processes. She has written on women's rights and lobbying. In 2006, she won The Most Meritorious Award of American Studies Centre and spent one semester at the University of Rochester, New York.

MICHELE GILL is a part-time doctoral student at Newcastle University in the UK. Her research examines the representations of boyhood in contemporary young adult fiction written in the UK, the United States, and Australia in relation to social anxieties about boys' lives. She teaches modules in children's literature to undergraduate students at Northumbria University, Newcastle, UK, and previously worked in children's librarianship in London, England.

V. W. GOEBEL is completing his doctorate in education at McGill University. He is works for the Government of Canada by day and is a musician by night.

EHREN GRESEHOVER has worked at an independent record label, been a radio DJ and contributed music and pop culture criticism to a variety of national and local publications. He is currently a columnist for *New York Magazine's* culture blog, The Vulture.

MILES GROTH is a professor of psychology at Wagner College, Staten Island, New York. He is founding editor of *THYMOS: Journal of Boyhood Studies*, the first periodical devoted to the topic. His current scholarly interests include the meaning of boyhood in Western technological societies and the transition from boyhood to full male maturity.

MEGHAN GUIDRY is a writer living in the Boston area who has written for *Some Other Magazine* and *The Ugly Couch*. She has written on the cultural significance of video games, flash animation, and graphic novels. Her work has been published in *The Merrimack Literary Review* and *The Pitkin Review*.

NAOMI HAMER is a doctoral candidate at the Centre for Children, Youth, and Media at the Institute of Education, University of London, UK. Her main research interests are children's literature and media. Her doctoral work explores the reading and digital cultures of preadolescent girls. She also holds an MA from the University of British Columbia in children's literature and a BA from McGill University, Montréal, Québec.

RYDELL HARRISON is Minister of Music and Worship at College Park Church, Greensboro, North Carolina. He has written and presented on the intersections of social homelessness, education, and theology while a graduate student at Duke University, Durham, North Carolinia, and the University of North Carolina–Greensboro. In 2006, he was the recipient of the North Carolina Principal Fellowship.

ROBERT HEASLEY is an associate professor of sociology at Indiana University of Pennsylvania and President of the American Men's Studies Association. He coproduced the photo-narrative exhibit, *Shifting Gears: Finding Intimacy in Men's Friendships* and is coeditor of *Sexual Lives, A Reader on the Theories and Realities of Human Sexualities* (2003).

KAL HEER has worked as a high school English and social studies teacher for the past eight years. He is completing a doctorate in Educational Studies doctoral program at the University of British Columbia. His main research interests are critical pedagogy, cultural studies, and media representations of minority populations.

MALIK S. HENFIELD is an assistant professor in the counselor education program in the College of Education at The University of Iowa. His research agenda is focused on the academic achievement of ethnic minority students. He is particularly interested in the factors that influence the educational experiences of African American students in K–16 educational settings.

SADIE HEWITT is finishing her degree in journalism at the University of South Florida in St. Petersburg.

MICHAEL HOECHSMANN teaches in the Faculty of Education at McGill University, Montréal, Québec. His research interests are in the area of youth, new media and technologies, media education, and cultural studies. He is the author, with Bronwen E. Low, of *Reading Youth Writing: "New" Literacies, Cultural Studies and Education* (2008).

DENISE A. ISOM is an assistant professor of Anthropology of Education at Calvin College, Grand Rapids, Michigan. Her research on racialized gender identity has been presented at numerous conferences. Her latest article on boys, "Performance, Resistance, Caring: Racialized Gender Identity in African American Boys," was published in the *Urban Review* in 2007.

DIEDERIK F. JANSSEN is a Dutch independent researcher. He is co-founding and managing editor of *Thymos: Journal of Boyhood Studies* and publishes on anthropological aspects of masculinity and sexuality over the life course. He also maintains www.boyhoodstudies.com which features a roughly 2,500-entry bibliography on boyhood studies.

VERONIKA KALMUS is an associate professor of media studies in the Institute of Journalism and Communication at the University of Tartu, Estonia. Her current research focuses on socialization in the informatizing society. She has written on young people's values, gender roles in school textbooks, and gender differences in Internet use. Her research is supported by Estonian Science Foundation, grant No. 6968.

BRENDA KELLY is a Doctoral Candidate at the University of Alberta, Edmonton, Alberta. She has taught classes at the middle school level and at the university level in literacy and language arts. Her present research examines the literacy practices of rural, farm male adolescents.

MYUNGHEE KIM is completing her doctorate at McGill University, Montréal, Québec. Her research involves creating a culturally critical approach to teaching English to Koreans. Her research interests include media literacy, curriculum development, and critical language education.

SINA-MAREEN KOEHLER is a researcher associate at the Centre of Schools and Education Research of the Martin-Luther-University Halle-Wittenberg in Germany. She writes about childhood, youth culture, and peer groups in Germany.

KYLE KUSZ is an associate professor of Cultural Studies of Sport and Physical Culture at the University of Rhode Island, Kingston, Rhode Island. His book, *Revolt of the White Athlete: Race, Media, and the Emergence of Extreme Athletes in America* (2007), critically examines the meanings articulated with white masculinity in new millennium American sport media.

JOANNE LARSON is the Michael W. Scandling Professor of Education at the University of Rochester's Warner Graduate School of Education and Human Development, Rochester, New York. She researches how language and literacy practices mediate social and power relations in schools and communities.

MELISSA F. LAVIN is a doctoral candidate in The Department of Sociology at the University of Connecticut–Storrs. Her areas of interest include deviance and medicalization, social theory, gender and the body, and medical culture. Her current research includes the examination of neonatal circumcision and the social organization of strip clubs.

CHRISTOPHER LEACH teaches European and military history at the University of the Fraser Valley, Abbotsford, BC, Canada. He is currently researching the way in which warfare was represented in British mass culture prior to World War I and after World War II, including through the media of toys and games.

DEREK LEDUC is a master's student in the School of Health and Human Performance at Dalhousie University, Halifax, Nova Scotia, Canada. He completed a BSc (Health Promotion) in May 2007 and has received student research awards from both CIHR and NSHRF. His research focuses on young men's health, masculinities, help-seeking behavior, and health promotion.

CARL LEGGO is a poet and professor at the University of British Columbia, Vancouver. He is the author of three collections of autobiographical poems: *Growing Up Perpendicular on the Side of a Hill, View from My Mother's House,* and *Come-By-Chance,* which all focus on growing up in Newfoundland.

GLYNN A. LEYSHON is a professor emeritus from the University of Western Ontario, London, Ontario, and has authored or coauthored 17 books, including a history of high school wrestling in Ontario, a history of Judo in Canada, a history of wrestling in Canada, and coauthored two books on the Olympics.

MIA LONG is a doctoral student in the College of Communication and Information Science at the University of Alabama, Tuscaloosa, Alabama. Her research interests include the role and representation of minorities in mass media. Her recent studies have included the implied effects of celebrity-endorsed advertising on African American youth.

CURRY STEPHENSON MALOTT works and lives in New York. He has published in many areas such as cultural studies, critical pedagogy, philosophy, and global capitalism and education. Most recently, he is the author of *Teaching Native America Across the Curriculum: A Critical Inquiry* (2009) and *A Call to Action: An Introduction to Education, Philosophy, and Native North America* (2008).

RUTHANN MAYES-ELMA completed her doctorate in educational leadership at Miami University of Ohio, Oxford, Ohio. She is currently a classroom teacher and researcher. Her areas of research include gender studies, children's literature, and urban education. She is the author of *Females and Harry Potter: Not All that Empowering* (2006) and *Harry Potter: Feminist Friend or Foe?* (2007). She also has chapters in various other books and is on the editorial board of two research journals.

CARLY T. MCKENZIE is currently a doctoral candidate at the University of Alabama in Tuscaloosa, Alabama. She worked for an advertising agency in media planning prior to beginning her postgraduate work. Her research interests include political communication, media effects, voter behavior, and public opinion.

CYNTHIA S. MEE is a professor of middle level education at National Louis University, Skokie, Illinois. She is committed to sharing young adolescents' voices and their culture to enhance classroom practices. Her book, *2000 VOICES: Young Adolescent Perceptions and Curriculum Implications,* in its fourth edition (1997), introduced her gender identification and media literacy research.

ANITA MENON is a teacher in Toronto and has completed her Master's thesis on the influence of Western media and Bollywood on identity development for South Asian adolescents living in the Canadian diaspora.

CLAUDIA MITCHELL is a James McGill professor in the Faculty of Education, McGill University, Montréal, Québec. Her research interests include work on the visual and material culture of childhood, teacher identities, visual participatory methodologies, and gender and sexuality in the age of AIDS. Her most recent coedited book is *Girl Culture: An Encyclopedia* (2008) and she is a cofounder editor of a new journal called *Girlhood Studies: An Interdisciplinary Journal.*

TONY MONCHINSKI is a special education teacher at Fox Lane High School in Bedford, New York. He completed his doctorate at the CUNY Graduate Center on Political Theory, and he is the author of *Critical Pedagogy and the Everyday Classroom* (2008) and the novel *Eden by Tommy Arlin* (2008), as well as a columnist/photographer for *MuscleMag International.*

CRESHEMA MURRAY is a doctoral student in the College of Communication and Information Sciences at The University of Alabama, Tuscaloosa, Alabama. Her research interests include minority representation and presentation in the media, cultural rhetorical studies, and intercultural organizational communication. Recent studies have included the use of hip-hop music as an educational tool to toddlers and workplace rhetoric.

DONAL O'DONOGHUE is an assistant professor and chair of Art Education at The University of British Columbia, Vancouver, Canada. His research addresses issues of masculinities and schooling. As a multimedia artist he is particularly interested in exploring what research practices located in the visual arts can offer in conceptualizing, doing, and representing educational research.

SULE OKUROGLU is a research assistant and doctoral candidate of English literature at Middle East Technical University (METU), Ankara, Turkey. In

2007, she won a grant from the Turkish government and spent a year as a visiting scholar at State University of New York (SUNY)–Buffalo, New York.

TAMMY OLER is a writer and pop culture critic whose articles and essays have been featured in *Bitch Magazine,* as well as several online publications, including Vulture, New York Magazine's culture and entertainment blog, and the Feminist Review. She is also a contributor to *Girl Culture: An Encyclopedia.*

DELILA OWENS is a former school counselor. She received her doctorate in counselor education from Michigan State University, East Lansing, Michigan, in 2002. Her research interest include factors that affect school counseling outcomes for inner city African American children and factors that affect the career aspirations of inner city children.

PRIYA PARMAR teaches adolescence education with an emphasis on language and literacy education at Brooklyn College—The City University of New York (CUNY). She writes and conducts research on critical literacies and popular culture within a cultural studies framework. Her most recent book is *Knowledge Reigns Supreme: The Critical Pedagogy of Hip Hop Artist, KRS-One* (1009). She edited *Contemporary Youth Culture: An International Encyclopedia, Volumes I & II* (2006) with Shirley Steinberg and Birgit Richard.

JOHN PASCARELLA teaches in Newark, New Jersey. His doctoral research examined teacher identity development, curriculum studies, literacy, and new media through blogging.

C. J. PASCOE is an assistant professor of sociology at The Colorado College in Colorado Springs, Colorado. She has written extensively about issues of sexuality, youth, and new media. Her recent book *Dude, You're a Fag: Masculinity and Sexuality in High School* won the 2008 Outstanding Book Award from the American Educational Research Association.

KARLEEN PENDLETON JIMÉNEZ is a writer and assistant professor of education at Trent University, Peterborough, Ontario. Her most recent work can be found in the animated film *Tomboy* and in her coedited anthology *"Unleashing the Unpopular": Talking about Sexual Orientation and Gender Diversity in Education.*

K. L. PEREIRA is a writer, teacher, activist, and feminist. A graduate of the Gender/Cultural Studies Program at Simmons College, Boston, Massachusetts, and the M.F.A. Program in Creative Writing at Goddard College, Plainfield, Vermont, she writes extensively on popular culture, gender, and sexuality.

BRIAN M. PETERS holds a doctorate from the Universite de Montréal in Québec and teaches in the English Department at Champlain College, St. Lambert, Québec. He teaches courses in cultural studies, comparative gothic, modernism, and gender. He has published in the *Tennessee Williams Annual Review,* the *Comparative Literature Culture WWWeb Journal,* and the *Journal of*

Homosexuality. His recent publication submissions include essays on *Buffy the Vampire Slayer,* and Emo Boys.

JAY POOLE is a visiting assistant professor of social work at the University of North Carolina at Greensboro. His recent essay, "Good 'Ol Boy: A Tale of Transformation from the Rural South," was published in *Men Speak Out,* Shira Tarrant (Ed.). He received the Mary Francis Stone award for outstanding teaching in 2007.

BRAD J. PORFILIO is an assistant professor of education in the Department of Educational Studies at Saint Louis University, St. Louis, Missouri. He has published numerous articles and book chapters on neoliberalism and schooling, gender and technology, urban education, critical pedagogy, and action research.

CHRISTINE QUAIL is an assistant professor at McMaster University in Hamilton, Ontario. Her research interests include reality TV, global television formatting, Canadian television, and youth and media. She is the coauthor, with Kathalene A. Razzano and Loubna H. Skalli, of *Vulture Culture: The Politics and Pedagogy of Daytime Television Talk Shows* (2005).

ANDREA QUINLAN is a graduate student in the Department of Sociology at the University of Calgary in Alberta, Canada. She is currently researching the use of sexual assault evidence kits within the legal processing of sexual violence cases in Canada.

MICHÈLE RACKHAM is a doctoral student in English literature at McGill University, Montréal, Québec. Her research focuses on the interartistic relationships between Canadian poets and visual artists during the twentieth century. She presently holds a CGS doctoral scholarship from the Social Sciences and Humanities Research Council of Canada.

JACQUELINE REID-WALSH is an associate professor at The State University of Pennsylvania (Dept. of Curriculum and Instruction and Women's Studies) in Philadelphia, Pennsylvania. Her research interests include historical children's literature and culture, children's and youth popular culture, comparative media literacy, and gender studies. Her most recent book is *Girl Culture: An Encyclopedia* (2008) and she is a founding editor of a new journal called *Girlhood Studies: An Interdisciplinary Journal.*

ERNESTO RENTAS-ROBLES, born and raised in Puerto Rico, obtained his doctoral degree in social psychology from the University of Puerto Rico. He is currently a professor at the Department of Psychology at the University of Puerto Rico. He has a vivid passion for philosophy, literature, and music.

DANIEL RHODES is a doctoral candidate in cultural studies at the University of North Carolina–Greensboro where he just completed a graduate certificate in women and gender studies. He received his masters in social work at the UNC–Chapel Hill and has worked as a psychotherapist for the past 12 years.

TERESA RISHEL is an assistant professor of middle childhood education at Kent State University, Kent, Ohio. Her writing focuses on adolescent suicide and the school lives of students, which include *Raging against the Machine: The Internet and Teen Suicide* (2007) and *Suicide, Schools and the Young Adolescent* (2007). She received the *Outstanding Dissertation Award* in 2004 at Purdue University.

DAMIEN W. RIGGS is an Australian research council postdoctoral fellow in the School of Psychology at the University of Adelaide. His current research examines issues pertaining to foster care in Australia, and he is the author of the book *Becoming Parent: Lesbians, Gay Men, and Family.*

NELSON M. RODRIGUEZ is an assistant professor of women's and gender studies and critical theory in education at The College of New Jersey in Ewing, New Jersey. His research and teaching interests include critical masculinity studies, queer theory, gender and sexuality studies in education, and popular culture. His most recent publication (with William F. Pinar) is *Queering Straight Teachers: Discourse and Identity in Education.* His forthcoming book is *Queer Masculinities: A Critical Reader in Education.*

DAVID ROEMMELE is a course lecturer at McGill University. His main areas of research are masculinity and alternative forms of education.

KATHY SANFORD is an associate professor of education at the University of Victoria, British Columbia, Canada. She has written a number of publications about videogame play as it relates to boys' learning, development of identity, and their reasons for choosing to play videogames.

RAJ SANGHERA is an inner city public school teacher as well as a graduate student at Simon Fraser University, British Columbia, Canada. She has been a presenter at the Popular Culture Association conference where she presented a paper on adolescent tough masculinity. Her interests lie in critical media literacy.

LAUREN SARDI ROSS is a doctoral student in the Sociology Department at the University of Connecticut, Storrs, Connecticut. Her research interests include sex and gender, masculinities, body image, and social psychology.

MUSTAFA SEVER is a research assistant in Ankara University, Turkey. He is currently a doctoral candidate in Department of Educational Leadership and Policy, University at Buffalo in New York. His main research focuses on critical ethnography and social transformation.

ANDRA SIIBAK is Extraordinary Research Fellow in the Institute of Journalism and Communication at the University of Tartu, Estonia. Her main research interests are concerned with the construction of young people's gender identities in the online context. Her research is supported by Estonian Science Foundation, grant No. 6968.

ROBERT SIMMONS is an assistant professor of teacher education at Eastern Michigan University in Ypsilanti, Michigan. His research interests and publications include topics on cultural diversity, African American male student achievement, and social justice.

CHRISTINA SIRY completed her doctorate in urban education at the Graduate Center of the City University of New York, and she is an instructor at Manhattanville College, Purchase, New York. She is presently living and writing in Luxemburg.

LAWRENCE SIRY is a public defender in New York City. He has worked in both family and criminal court in rural and urban settings. He is now working in Luxemburg.

LIAM SIRY is a ten-year-old boy who is a brother to one boy and two girls. He enjoys playing Legos and sports with his brother. He is an expert secret-keeper and expert sword player. He hopes one day to change the world through his discoveries in nature and science.

JUMANNE SLEDGE is founder and president of World Class Leadership Academy LLC, an academic educational consulting firm focused on leadership development. His research interests and publications include topics on social justice, teacher leadership, minority student achievement, cultural competence, and curriculum development. He is a former teacher, principal, and professor.

LAUREN SMITH is a graduate student at Montclair State University, Montclair, New Jersey. She is pursuing a master's degree in elementary and special education.

LOURDES DIAZ SOTO is the Goizueta Foundation Endowed Chair and Professor of Education at Dalton State University. Her recent publications include *The Praeger Handbook of Latino Education in the U.S.* Her recent research focuses on how issues of social justice and equity impact Latina and Latino learners in the United States.

CHRISTOPHER DARIUS STONEBANKS is an associate professor of education at Bishop's University, Québec. Stemming from his half-Iranian, half-European heritage and immigrant experience in Canadian schools, he has written extensively on how formal and nonformal curriculum shapes the voice and identity of Middle Eastern students. He is the coeditor of *Teaching Against Islamophobia* (2010) and *Muslim Voices in School* (2009).

ABOUBACAR SYLLA is an immigrant boy and a student at Community Prep High School, Manhattan, New York. He is originally from Guinea, West Africa.

ELOISE TAN taught part-time at the Ontario Institute of Studies in Education and her research interests include how to teach multicultural education and how diverse student populations grow and learn through hip-hop culture. She will be doing post-doctoral research in Ireland.

P. L. THOMAS grew up collecting, reading, and drawing from comic books in the 1970s; today he is a writer, teacher, and scholar. He taught high school English for 18 years and currently is a teacher educator at Furman University, Greenville, South Carolina, where he writes widely about teaching, literacy, and poverty.

GEORGE H. THOMPSON is the humanities librarian at California State University, Chico, California. He is engaged in research on libraries and popular culture, popular magazines, and book history.

ERIC D. TORRES is a Peruvian educator residing in Southern Pines, North Carolina. He currently teaches at Pinecrest High, Moore County Schools. He is a Franklin/Houston Scholar and a doctoral candidate in the School of Education of the University of North Carolina at Greensboro.

PETER PERICLES TRIFONAS teaches at the Ontario Institute for Studies in Education/University of Toronto. He has taught at schools and universities in North America and Europe. His books include *The Ethics of Writing: Derrida, Deconstruction, and Pedagogy; Revolutionary Pedagogies; Pedagogies of Difference; Ethics, Institutions, and the Right to Philosophy with Jacques Derrida; Communities of Difference;* and *CounterTexts: Reading Culture.*

KIMBERLY A. TRUONG is a doctoral student in the higher education program at the University of Pennsylvania in Philadelphia. She earned a Bachelor of Arts in Fine Arts and Politics from Brandeis University in Waltham, Massachusetts, and a Master of Education in Higher Education from the Harvard Graduate School of Education in Boston, Massachusetts.

TOMOYA TSUTSUMI is a master's student in culture and values in education at McGill University, Montréal, Québec. His master's thesis examines current inclusive education and diverse student populations in the Canadian educational context. His other research interests include critical pedagogy, curriculum studies, and primary education.

LUIS URRIETA, JR. is an assistant professor of cultural studies in education and Mexican American studies, and a fellow in the Lee Hage Jamail Regents Chair in Education at the University of Texas at Austin. His general research interests are on issues of identity, agency, and social movements in education.

HEATHER M. VELTMAN teaches art and art education in different universities in Montréal, Québec. Her research focuses on children's gender issues in the intersection between art, psychological development, and identities.

LEILA E. VILLAVERDE is an associate professor of educational leadership and cultural foundations, and the graduate studies director in the Women's & Gender Studies Program at the University of North Carolina–Greensboro. She has taught courses on curriculum studies, history, gender studies, and visual literacy. She has published on white privilege, secondary education, feminist theories, art education, aesthetics, and critical pedagogy.

GERALD WALTON completed his doctorate at Queen's University in Canada in 2006 on bullying and is on the Faculty of Education at Lakehead University in Thunder Bay, Ontario. He teaches and conducts research in the areas of diversity, difference, sociology of education, power and privilege, social justice in education, and educational policy and leadership.

ANNE WATSON is a secondary school English teacher in London, Ontario. She has recently completed her MEd and currently a doctoral student in education at the University of Western Ontario. While completing her MEd, she won The W. A. Townshend Gold Medal for excellence in academic achievement.

LISA S. WAUKAU is a Native American, who was born and raised on the Menominee Indian Reservation. She has worked as a high school social studies teacher for the past 27 years. Currently, she is on leave from her job to serve as chairwoman of the Menominee Tribe.

LAUREN "CANDY" WAUKAU-VILLAGOMEZ is an assistant professor of education at D'Youville College in Buffalo, New York. She was born and raised on the Menominee Indian Reservation. She has worked in various educational positions on the Menominee, Pine Ridge and Lac du Flambeau Indian Reservations during her career.

MARCUS B. WEAVER-HIGHTOWER is an assistant professor of Educational Foundations and Research at the University of North Dakota. He has written extensively on boys' education and male learning across the lifespan. He is author of *The Politics of Policy in Boys' Education* (2008) and coeditor of *The Problem with Boys' Education: Beyond the Backlash* (2009).

MAYA A. YAMPOLSKY is a graduate student in the Experimental Psychology Program at the Université du Québec à Montréal, where her focus of study is identity and cultural psychology. Her research interests include multiculturalism and acculturation, cross-cultural and subcultural studies, and yogic studies.

MAREN ZSCHACH is research associate at the Centre of School and Education Research of the Martin-Luther-University Halle-Wittenberg in Germany. She writes about childhood, youth culture, and peer groups in Germany.